John James Audubon

The Watercolors for

THE BIRDS OF AMERICA

John James Audubon

The Watercolors for
THE BIRDS OF AMERICA

Annette Blaugrund and Theodore E. Stebbins, Jr., Editors

Catalog entries by Carole Anne Slatkin

Essays by Theodore E. Stebbins, Jr., Annette Blaugrund,
Amy R. W. Meyers, and Reba Fishman Snyder
Executive editor Holly Hotchner

BARNES
&NOBLE
BOOKS
NEW YORK

PAGE i, detail from *Golden Eagle, Aquila chrysaetos* (Linnaeus). Watercolor, pastel, graphite, and selective glazing; 38 × 25½ in. (96.6 × 64.7 cm.). The New-York Historical Society. See page 233 for full illustration.

FRONTISPIECE: *Wild Turkey, Meleagris gallopavo* Linnaeus. Watercolor, pastel, graphite, gouache, metallic paints, and selective glazing; 39¼ × 26¼ in. (99.7 × 67 cm.). The New-York Historical Society.

PAGE x: *Greater Flamingo, Phoenicopterus ruber* Linnaeus. Watercolor, graphite, gouache, and selective glazing; 33³⁄₁₆ × 24⅛ in. (84.1 × 61.3 cm.). The New-York Historical Society.

1997 Barnes & Noble Books

ISBN 0-76070-666-2

Printed and bound in Spain by Artes Graficas Toledo
D.L.: TO-685-1997

97 98 99 00 M 9 8 7 6 5 4 3 2 1

AGT

Contents

Preface and Acknowledgments

In 1863, The New-York Historical Society purchased 464 original drawings, 430 of which were for *The Birds of America*, from John James Audubon's destitute widow, Lucy Audubon. These drawings were recognized even in 1863 as one of the finest accomplishments in American art and one of the most important documents of natural history in the world. The four volumes of prints completed in 1838 were the largest and most expensive set of volumes published in their day. The collection of watercolors from which the prints were made bear witness to the great visionary achievement, the prodigious energy, and the indefatigable determination of John James Audubon.

This book accompanies a major traveling exhibition that represents the first opportunity for the public to view a large group of these remarkable works outside the Historical Society since their acquisition in 1863. The book itself is meant to allow an even greater number of people to appreciate these watercolors as works of art and to study Audubon's development as an artist.

Audubon has received more attention than almost any other American artist: more than twelve biographies document his life and career. Yet these efforts have been eclipsed by Audubon's own inventive reminiscences and have focused on the prints and not the watercolors. This book provides a long-overdue visual and written documentation of Audubon's watercolors, which gives great insight into his astonishing technical innovations and esthetic sensibility.

From 1820 on Audubon transported the drawings on many excursions in the United States and abroad and periodically exhibited them. They were used as working drawings by Robert Havell, Jr., in translating the watercolors into engravings and then as marketing tools to sell subscriptions. Audubon was concerned with the safety of the watercolors throughout his lifetime; indeed, the works suffered various mishaps early on, including consumption by rats and misplacement. As early as 1835, Audubon considered giving the drawings to the U.S. Congress to ensure their future longevity. Philip Hone, former mayor of New York, described them as "the most significant collection on the subject in the world and ought to be purchased by our government to form the nucleus of a great national museum."

It is ironic that despite Audubon's great renown and standing as one of the most gifted American artists of his time, his wife would become destitute shortly following her husband's death. In 1861, Lucy Audubon put the drawings up for sale, urging The New-York Historical Society's librarian George Henry Moore to purchase them to keep them from ending up at the British Museum. She wrote, "It was always the wish of Mr. Audubon that his forty years of labour should remain in his country."

The Historical Society most definitely did not want the watercolors to end up in an institution outside the United States but decided it could not immediately afford to purchase the drawings. Instead it formed a special committee to raise the required four thousand dollars by subscription, a technique that Audubon himself had used quite successfully in marketing his prints. In a circular sent to potential subscribers, the institution issued a plea to keep the watercolors in the United States. "As a work of our national art and our natural history, this opportunity should not be lost, to deposit near the home of the distinguished artist, these memorials of his genius, according to his wish, in a secure place like that of the Art Gallery of this Incorporation."

In March 1862, Frederic De Peyster, president of The New-York Historical Society, reported to the special committee Lucy Audubon's devotion to her husband's legacy and her concern for securing an appropriate home for his work. "Mrs. Audubon stood beside the committee hour after hour . . . and carried out the task of examining each of the large sheets, on which the drawings were made; she quietly aided in turning every one of them in order that she might explain the circumstances connected with them; in relation to the toil, and privations incident to their preparation and completion." Upon learning that the Historical Society could not yet buy the drawings in April 1863, Lucy Audubon wrote to De Peyster, "It is somewhat singular that my enthusiastic husband struggled to have his labours published in his Country and could not; and I have struggled to sell his forty years of labour and cannot." In the same year, Lucy Audubon again wrote to De Peyster in an effort to sell her copy of Audubon's five-volume *Ornithological Biography*, the text that accompanied the prints. She wrote, "Will not your Society give me something for all I have, say even a dollar a volume rather than have them destroyed?" She additionally entreated the Historical Society to buy the copperplates from which the engravings were made, and although not purchased at the time, the Historical Society today retains four of these plates and several copies of the *Ornithological Biography*. She was forced to sell most of the remaining plates for scrap copper.

By June 1863, the committee had managed to collect 4,230 dollars toward the purchase, a remarkable feat considering the difficulties of fund-raising in the midst of the Civil War. With this money, the Historical Society purchased 464 drawings—including those of *The Birds of America* (acquired for about nine dollars per watercolor) and several unpublished ones. The acquisition occurred during a pivotal period when the institution was evolving from a traditional nineteenth-century museum that documented the natural and social history of the United States to a more modern institution concerned with fine arts. At the time, the Audubon collection established the core of the Historical Society's fine-arts holdings, along with two other great American and European art collections of the period—the Luman Reed collection, which came to the Historical Society in 1858, and the Bryan collection, acquired in 1867.

The Historical Society today is the largest single repository for Audubon watercolors, prints, and Auduboniana. Holdings include 431 original watercolor drawings, 68 unpublished drawings of birds, bats, and mammals, four copperplates, and one complete set of *The Birds of America* engravings in four volumes known as "the Duke of Newcastle Elephant Folio." Over the years the collection has grown significantly with the addition of several oil paintings, Audubon's life mask, his folding lap desk, photographs, miniatures, several octavo editions of both birds and quadrupeds, and a significant group of manuscripts and books.

Two years after their purchase, Maria Audubon (John James's granddaughter) came to the Historical Society to see the drawings exhibited. She reported that they were "in a dull, dingy room, part chapel, part lecture hall where some 25 or 30 of the drawings were very cheaply framed and hung on the empty walls." When the Historical Society moved to its present building in 1908, the works still had a low exhibition pro-file. A reporter from *The New York Times* in 1917 found "30 hanging on the dingy walls of the basement . . . near the coal-bunkers and the engine room."

Until 1978 the Audubons were treated primarily as natural history documents as American art did not begin to receive extensive appreciation and study until the decades after World War II. Originally stored in the library book stacks the works finally received their own small, permanent gallery space in 1946. However, it was not until 1985, on the occasion of the two hundredth anniversary of Audubon's birth, that all 431 *Birds of America* were exhibited for the first time. (The *California Condor* was donated in 1966 by Mrs. Gratia R. Waters.) This was the first large-scale public exhibition of the originals in more than a century. Today, thanks to the foresight of the Historical Society's 1860's board, the Audubon watercolors remain the institution's most widely visited and highly appreciated collection.

Audubon has been hailed as a nineteenth-century romantic figure, creator of his own myth. He was known as a naturalist, an explorer, a publisher, an entrepreneur, a writer, and an environmentalist. Yet what ultimately survives are the intense studies and beautiful watercolors that make Audubon an artist, one of America's most creative and innovative. It is hoped that both the Historical Society and Audubon will receive their appropriate due, the Historical Society as the great institution whose founders had the vision to preserve this American treasure in the United States, and John James Audubon as a rightfully prominent figure in the history of American art and culture.

A number of individuals dedicated to Audubon's unique genius as an artist have been of invaluable assistance to the organization of the exhibition and the book.

The decision to allow a large group from the original *Birds of America* to travel for the first time outside The New-York Historical Society and to be published in their newly restored glory was fully supported by Barbara K. Debs, former president of the Society, and Norman Pearlstine, former chairman of the Board of Trustees.

It has been my great good fortune to have seen the entire project through from its inception to its completion. I initiated this project in 1989 because I believed that these watercolors, one of the Historical Society's most important collections, deserved to be seen by a wider public. I would like to acknowledge the contributions of the team of scholars and conservators who joined me in this ambitious endeavor, especially the cocurators of the exhibition, Annette Blaugrund and Theodore Stebbins, who have selected a group of ninety-five watercolors that represent Audubon's development as an artist and show the range and virtuosity of his work.

Dr. Stebbins set out to place Audubon as one of America's great and unique artists. He has done this with eloquence and insight. At the Museum of Fine Arts, Boston, those to be acknowledged with thanks include Désirée Caldwell, Judith Downes, Patricia Loiko, Sue Reed, Alan Shestack, and Janice Sorkow. We are also grateful to Leslie Morris at the Houghton Library, Harvard University, for her superb cooperation with Dr. Stebbins's project.

Annette Blaugrund is to be thanked for her editorial work on the book and for skillful management and coordination of the material for this publication. Her essay adds significant new research and material to our understanding of Audubon as entrepreneur and artist, publisher and salesman. For help with Dr. Blaugrund's essay we thank Ruth Eisenstein, Mary Le Croy, Douglas Lewis, Susanne M. Low, Charlotte Rubin, Wendy J. Shadwell, Susan Sivard, and Ann Weissmann.

Much gratitude and admiration are extended to Carole Slatkin, who has devoted many years of her life as an ornithologist and art historian in the interpretation and understanding of Audubon's watercolors and prints of *The Birds of America*. She has been active as the previous director of the public programs department and former curator of the Audubon collection at The New-York Historical Society. Her catalog entries and chronology in this volume greatly increase our understanding of Audubon's work. For reviewing the scientific information in Ms. Slatkin's entries, we thank Noble Proctor and Gerald Rosenband. For their research assistance, we thank Catherine Keen, Margaret Meyers, Margie Schiller, Gil Taylor, and Judith Throm.

Sincere thanks go to Amy Meyers, whose essay contributes new understanding and scholarship in the area of Audubon's relationship to the naturalist painting tradition. For their assistance in researching Dr. Meyers's essay we thank Rex Banks, Malcolm Beasley, David Brigham, Thomas V. Lange, and Carol Spawn.

The overall project has included the first comprehensive survey and conservation examination, treatment, and rehousing of the collection, further ensuring their future. Reba Fishman Snyder has dedicated several years in leading a team of paper conservators through the first systematic examination and analysis of Audubon's technique. Her essay contributes to the understanding of Audubon's work and adds to the literature on American watercolor technique. Mary Cropley assisted in the conservation of the watercolors, along with Mindy Horn, Beryl Fishbein, and Michelle Gewirtz. Bryn Jayes was responsible for all of the rehousing, rematting, and reframing of the watercolors.

Allison Whiting was invaluable in the coordination of the project at large. Jean Breskind assisted in many details of the catalog.

Albina De Meio and Jack Rutland worked tirelessly in the coordination of the exhibition.

For their efforts on the publication of this elegant volume, thanks go to R. Andrew Boose and David Resnicow, and to Tony Holmes for his beautiful transparencies of the entire collection.

It has been a great pleasure to work with the dedicated staff at Villard Books, Random House, in the production of this book. Our sincere thanks go to Harry Evans, Diane Reverand, and Doug Stumpf for taking a chance on publishing an art book on this scale. The efforts of Leslie Chang for her editorial work, copy editor Anne Cherry, production editor Martha Schwartz, and Kathy Rosenbloom and Bruce Campbell for the superb design and execution of the book are deeply appreciated.

HOLLY HOTCHNER
Director of the Museum

Essays

PLATE 1. *Wood Thrush*, August 14, 1806. Watercolor and graphite on paper; 15¾ × 9¾ in. Houghton Library, Harvard University.

Audubon's Drawings of American Birds, 1805–38

THEODORE E. STEBBINS, JR.

John James Audubon was born Jean Rabine in April 1785 in the town of Les Cayes on the southern coast of Saint-Dominque, present-day Haiti. He was the illegitimate son of Captain Jean Audubon, a sailor, adventurer, merchant, slaver, and sometime official, and of Jeanne Rabine, a chambermaid who died a few months after the birth of her son.[1] The young Audubon grew up around Nantes, a coastal city in Brittany, in the home of his father and his father's wealthy wife, Anne Moynet. At age eleven he went for four years of naval training to Rochefort-sur-Mer. In the summer of 1803, when he was eighteen, the young Frenchman was sent to the United States by his father, who aimed to have him learn English, look after his property at Mill Grove, near Philadelphia, and avoid Napoleon's far-reaching conscription. He went back to France in March 1805 before returning for good to the United States fourteen months later, in May 1806.

Although Audubon was primarily occupied with trying to sell his father's land at Mill Grove, exploring his new country, courting his young neighbor Lucy Bakewell, and forming a mercantile partnership in Kentucky, he still found time to draw. Shortly after his arrival in 1803, he was an accomplished enough artist to give drawing lessons in exchange for being tutored in English; in the end he would become an eloquent writer in the English language. He had learned the rudiments of his drawing style in France, but the questions remain: where and from whom? Audubon wrote that he had loved to draw birds and flowers since childhood, producing (and later destroying) "hundreds of these rude sketches annually."[2] In his own account of his technique, Audubon says that he studied briefly "in my youth under good masters,"[3] and in the *Ornithological Biography* the artist reported that as a student in France "David had guided my hand in tracing objects of large size"[4]—suggesting that he, like many others, had learned to draw by copying casts of ancient sculptures. For Audubon's statement to be true, he would have had to have gone to Paris in 1801 or 1802 as a teenager to work with Jacques-Louis David (1748–

1825), and there is no record of this; it seems more likely that the boy worked briefly with a student or admirer of the master, perhaps at the Free Academy of Drawing in Nantes. That city had boomed as a cultural center under Louis XVI and during Audubon's youth it was the home of such local masters as René Chancourtois (1757–1817), a landscapist, and André Claude Boissier (1760–1833), professor of drawing and history painter who was himself a slavish follower of David's. Moreover, Nantes benefited significantly under Napoleon, its museum being founded in 1801, and in 1804 and 1809 receiving from Paris a portion of the Napoleonic redistribution of master paintings. It was also the home of the great collector François Cacault (1743–1805), French ambassador to Rome; during the years 1799–1804 his art museum and school were built in nearby Clisson. Growing up, Audubon would have had every opportunity to learn of the major traditions of European art.[5]

Audubon probably exaggerated the extent of his connection to David; indeed, for all his life, in both his art and his writing, he demonstrated a penchant—born of insecurity—for youthful overstatement, for allowing wishful thinking to become stated fact. His exuberance, his ambition, and his single-minded determination won him many admirers and made possible his great achievements, but they also made him the frequent object of ridicule and envy. Perhaps Audubon had worked briefly with David, or had met him, or only admired him from a distance; the important thing is that he saw himself as David's follower, as carrying on his teachings—drawing always what one saw, copying nature assiduously, practicing draftsmanship always as a means to an end—in the New World.

In his 1828 article Audubon wrote, "I may thus date the *real* beginning of my *present collection . . .* as far back as 1805."[6] The artist's memory in this instance seems to have been accurate; while he apparently destroyed his earliest drawings, he began to preserve many of his efforts in 1805 when he was twenty. Harvard University owns by far the most extensive collection of

PLATE 2. *Belted Kingfisher*, July 15, 1808.
Pastel and graphite on paper; 16 × 8½ in.
Houghton Library, Harvard University.

PLATE 3. *Carolina Parrot*, June 9, 1811.
Pastel, watercolor, and graphite on paper; 17 × 11 in.
Houghton Library, Harvard University.

these early works, having about 109, which date primarily from 1805 to 1812. The earliest surviving work, and the only one from Audubon's first visit to America, is a profile drawing of a bird on a branch titled the *Long-tailed Mountain Tit-mouse* (fig. 1) that already contains hints of the verve and the touch typical of his mature style. The aspiring artist drew his subject only with pastels and dated his work "le 22 janvier 1805."

Returning to France in March, Audubon spent much of his time in the fields and forests around Couëron, a village a few miles west of Nantes where his father and stepmother lived. The drawings he made that June with pastel, chalk, and wash still have a very tentative look; the birds seem to be smaller than life. One of them, dated 7 June 1805, and inscribed "Near Nantes" in English, bears a telling bilingual double title: *The Creeper of Willughby/Le Grimperan de M. de Buffon.* Even at this early date, Audubon was thinking of himself as an ornithologist, for he identifies his subject first according to the pioneering English systematist, Francis Willughby (1635–72), and second as it was called by the important French writer, publisher, and naturalist Georges Louis Leclerc, the comte de Buffon (1707–88), creator of a ninety-volume encyclopedia including everything known about nature. He had been introduced to the work of Buffon and other ornithologists by the talented local naturalist, Dr. Charles d'Orbigny. From the start Audubon was keenly aware of the work of his predecessors in France and England, and he looked to them for guidance both for nomenclature and in the rendering of various species. The picture of the little creeper, a member of the nuthatch family, is also worth noting because it shows the bird hunting for its dinner, an early example of Audubon's interest in the feeding habits of birds.

The *Redstart* (called by Audubon *le rossignol de murailles de Buffon* and dated August 1805), like his other early drawings, shows the bird in profile in the traditional manner of eighteenth-century naturalists. The subject is drawn somewhat awkwardly in pencil and pastel, but Audubon was more successful in rendering the red and black berries and the leaves, marking the first of many occasions when he would include the fruit or flowers that typically attracted a given species. By the end of the same year, the young artist had improved markedly. *Le Verdier* (fig. 2), dated December 22, 1805, and inscribed "Near Nantz," portrays a green-headed finch that is subtly colored, with a far more sophisticated use of the pastel medium in the blending of the grays and yellows of the bird's body. During these months in France, Audubon was already drawing his birds roughly to scale. For *La Corbine ou Corneille Noire de Buffon,* which he subtitled *English Crow* (fig. 3), he used a large sheet of paper, about

Fig. 1. *Long-tailed Mountain Tit-mouse,* January 22, 1805. Pastel and graphite on paper; 12 × 9⅜ in. Houghton Library, Harvard University.

Fig. 2. *Le Verdier (The Green Finch),* December 22, 1805. Pastel and graphite on paper; 11 × 8 in. Houghton Library, Harvard University.

Fig. 3. *La Corbine ou Corneille Noire de Buffon (English Crow)*, c. 1805–6.
Pastel and graphite on paper; 26 × 20 in.
Houghton Library, Harvard University.

26 × 20 inches. Using pure pastels, mixing blacks with dark blues to suggest the sheen and texture of the feathers, and then adding an extra study of the beak, the artist gives an indication of accomplishments to come.

Audubon later wrote that "immediately upon my landing" back in America, "prompted by an innate desire to acquire a thorough knowledge of the birds of this happy country," he resolved to spend all his leisure time drawing each American bird in "its natural size and colouring."[7] How could a twenty-one-year-old Frenchman, little trained in art, unstudied in science, struggling with the English language, and facing a career in storekeeping and trade, have formed such an outlandish ambition? And why would he then decide within a year to set off for the westernmost part of the young nation?

One longs to know what Audubon as a boy in France had heard and read of America. Almost immediately after he arrived, he identified seemingly instinctively with its wildlife and wilderness. He became a citizen in 1812, but even before that he was a champion of the country, and not only of its birds and beasts but of its national character as well. During the first and second decades of the nineteenth century, when American landscape painters were busy painting prospects of cultivated land and views of country seats of the wealthy, before the Hudson River School existed, Audubon plunged into the wilderness to paint the beauty and richness of America through its birds. He explored the whole of the young nation, from Key West to the northern tip of Maine and beyond, from New York, Philadelphia, and Charleston to the wilds of Pennsyl-

vania, Kentucky, and Louisiana, traveling as no American artist had before him. He would awake, as he said, "on the alder-fringed brook of some northern valley, or in the midst of some yet unexplored forest of the west, or perhaps on the soft and warm sands of the Florida shores, listening to the pleasing melodies of songsters innumerable."[8] Before long he would unembarrassedly style himself "The American Woodsman."

The American wilderness and its flora and fauna had long been of interest to French writers and travelers, who debated their merits. The comte de Buffon, for example, whose works on European birds were well known to Audubon (for he frequently cited them), thought all of the species of the New World to be punier, uglier, and scarcer than in the Old. Buffon opined that the human species as well was on the decline in America, due to the cold, damp climate of the continent.[9] Audubon believed differently, and it is almost as if he devoted his life, especially his art and his writings, to proving Buffon wrong on every count.

There was a more substantial body of French opinion, which Audubon may well have known, that held a positive and increasingly romantic view of the American wilderness. Seventeenth-century writers such as Marc Lescarbot had identified the North American Indians with the Greeks and the Romans, and in the next century Jean-Jacques Rousseau—who idealized the noble savage while demonstrating the corrupting influences of civilization—found the Indian's natural state to be healthy and admirable.[10] St. John de Crèvecoeur, who had lived in Pennsylvania and New York for more than a decade, published his *Letters from an American Farmer* in 1782, celebrating the American landscape and its inhabitants. In answering the question "What is an American?" he spoke in panegyric terms much like those Audubon would use in his own writings.

Finally, one inevitably thinks of François-August-René Chateaubriand (1768–1848), a disciple of Rousseau who traveled in 1791 to the American wilderness, preparing to write tales that Hugh Honour would describe as "the most beautiful and vivid that had yet been inspired by America."[11] Chateaubriand let his hair and beard grow, "bought a complete outfit from the Indians," went up the Hudson, then to Niagara, Pittsburgh, and the Ohio River. His two great romantic tales, *Atala* and *René*, were published in 1801 and 1802, and both became highly popular; *Atala*, for example, was reprinted twelve times between 1801 and 1805 and would have been easily available to the teen-age Audubon on the verge of his own voyages to America.[12] In *René*, the romantic, melancholy hero retreats to the Kentucky wilderness, as Audubon would do shortly afterwards, while its pendant *Atala* is set on the Mississippi River in Louisiana, which the author describes as a primitive, pristine "New Eden." Chateaubriand admired the broad vistas with the eye of a landscape painter, and he wrote of the natural scenery in a way that recalls Audubon's own later descriptions:

> Caribou bathe in the lake; black squirrels frolic in the thick foliage; mocking birds and Virginia doves . . . fly down to grass patches red with strawberries; green parrots with yellow heads, crimson-tinged woodpeckers and fire-bright cardinals spiral up to the tops of the cypresses; hummingbirds sparkle on the jasmine of the Floridas, and bird-catching serpents hiss as they swing, like lianas, from the forest domes.[13]

Perhaps inspired by these tales, Audubon arrived back in the United States in late May 1806, and spent the next months working with his partner, Ferdinand Rozier, on the sale of the property at Mill Grove and making steady progress in his drawing. His beautiful rendition of a Wood Thrush (plate 1) which he inscribed "Mill Grove 14 août 1806," was his most accomplished work to date. One feels the artist working less laboriously than before and taking pleasure in the abstract, decorative qualities of the pastel medium, particularly in the subject's black breast spots and the nicely varied red berries above and below it. The single bird is still seen in profile, but there is increased attention to its surroundings, in the berries and green leaves as well as the branch on which it rests.

Working in New York during the early months of 1807, Audubon continued to draw, with varying results. For the *Spring-tailed Duck* (actually a Northern Pintail) in February he used a large sheet of paper about 19 × 27 inches, enabling him to depict this large duck in its actual size. In late summer he and Rozier set off to open a general store in Louisville, Kentucky, a burgeoning trading town on the Ohio River with a population of little more than a thousand. Audubon brought his bride, Lucy Bakewell, to Louisville in April 1808, and in 1810 they moved downriver to Henderson, Kentucky, a village of no more than two hundred, where they raised their two sons, Victor Gifford (b. 1809) and John Woodhouse (b. 1812). Audubon lived in the state for some twelve years, longer than he stayed anywhere else. Although his commercial career foundered there during the financial panic of 1819, Audubon would ever after think of himself as a Kentuckian.

On June 29, 1808, Audubon drew a bird that he inscribed "*Le Ministre à Buffon*/Indigo Bunting—A. Wilson." Although he was still relying to an extent on Buffon for his identifications, as

he had in Nantes, that French naturalist dealt only with European birds, and Audubon was now also aware of the work and nomenclature of the Scotsman Alexander Wilson (1766–1813). Wilson had been in the United States since 1794 and was well established in Philadelphia scientific circles as a friend of Charles Willson Peale, the naturalist William Bartram, and others. In 1805 Wilson had begun his own project of drawing and studying all of the birds of America; his small folio *American Ornithology* in nine volumes had begun to be published in 1808. As Annette Blaugrund describes in her essay in this volume, Wilson would play an important role for Audubon, first as inspiration, then as the primary rival whose work Audubon aimed to surpass. The *Indigo Bunting* is also noteworthy because Audubon for the first time includes both the male and female of the species; the blue male sits below, facing left, while the brown female is placed above it, facing to the right—thus the couple lacks the sense of domestic harmony that one finds suggested in many of his later works.

Audubon's *Belted Kingfisher* (plate 2), dated July 15, 1808, like the *Indigo Bunting*, is inscribed "Chute de l'Ohio," or "Falls of the Ohio," as Louisville was called. This is a tour de force of pastel handling, advancing even over the *Wood Thrush* of two years before. The single bird is seen in profile, as before, but is now more strongly modeled. At the same time, it has—even more than the artist's later birds—a human look in its smart, jaunty expression, its large head and sharp eye. Audubon would always tend to anthropomorphize his subjects, portraying them as having human feelings and attributes. Finally, one of the last of the Louisville drawings, made in December 1809, depicts the famous Passenger Pigeon (fig. 4). This work shows a single, rather flat bird in profile, and it offers an interesting compari-

Fig. 4. *Passenger Pigeon*, December 11, 1809.
Pastel and graphite on paper; 17½ × 11¼ in.
Houghton Library, Harvard University.

Fig. 5. *Red Owl*, c. 1810.
Pastel and graphite on paper;
16½ × 8½ in. Houghton
Library, Harvard University.

Fig. 6. *Flicker*, c. 1810.
Pastel and graphite on paper;
14¾ × 8½ in. Houghton
Library, Harvard University.

Fig. 7. *Scarlet Tanager*, August 1810. Pastel, watercolor,
and graphite on paper; 15¾ × 8½ in.
Houghton Library, Harvard University.

son to the wonderfully graceful composition showing a male
and female of the same species, each on a different branch, one
feeding the other in a moment of seeming intimacy, which
Audubon made fifteen years later and used for his *Birds of America* (page 138). Though highly accomplished, clearly he still had
a distance to go before reaching his artistic maturity.

The years 1810–12 saw Audubon, now in Henderson, working in pastel with ever greater dexterity while experimenting
with increasingly varied and inventive uses of graphite for certain details and textures. In his *Red Owl* (fig. 5) of 1810 (now
called the Eastern Screech Owl), one finds extensive, lyrical use
of pencil lines, especially around the beak. In the colorful *Flicker*
(fig. 6), the artist similarly employed pencil extensively; one sees
graphite rubbed on the wings and head to suggest iridescence,
while pastel is brilliantly used for the body. (See page 138 for his
1836–37 drawing of the same species.) The hawk that Audubon
called the Frog Eater, with its beautifully drawn claws, the su-

Fig. 8. *Le Pic Noir à Bec Blanc (Ivory-billed Woodpecker)*, July 30, 1810. Pastel and graphite on paper; 19 × 13½ in. Houghton Library, Harvard University.

perbly handled pair of Hooded Mergansers, drawn entirely in pastels, and the Scarlet Tanager (fig. 7) all date from 1810 and demonstrate the high level Audubon had now reached. The tanager in particular foreshadows the future in various ways: the technique is more varied, with the leaves executed in watercolor, and the sheet is filled out decoratively with branch, leaves, and berries, as would become Audubon's habit when depicting the smaller species. Still thinking partly in French, Audubon in 1810 called his drawing of the Ivory-billed Woodpecker *Le Pic Noir à Bec Blanc* (fig. 8); it was made at Red Banks (as Henderson was called early on), and with its strongly drawn black subject on the white sheet, it has graphic, abstract qualities more frequently found in the following decade. A related drawing, also in the Harvard collection, made two years later depicts a pair of Ivory-billed Woodpeckers on opposite sides of a tree; executed primarily in pastel with pencil touches, rather than the more varied technique of the twenties, this

drawing nevertheless has all the confidence of the mature work.

Although Audubon was still some years away from deciding to undertake his great *Birds of America* project, he apparently saved the most successful of his drawings from these early years, and though they were all profile depictions of static subjects, some of them satisfied him enough to be used years later when Robert Havell produced the engravings for Audubon's magnificent book. Thus, for example, in about 1829 while preparing a composition of the *Northern Goshawk and Cooper's Hawk* (page 80) for Havell to engrave, he reached back some twenty years and carefully cut out a Cooper's Hawk he had drawn in pastel around 1809, then pasted it at the lower right of a new sheet. The artist then added a second collaged pastel at lower left, one of an adult goshawk dating from about 1810–12, and pasted on a third and final cutout, an immature goshawk drawn with watercolor around 1829. Departing from his usual practice, Audubon left the birds without any indication of a background; the engraver then added a marsh and mountain scene to the composition (fig. 9).

Audubon continued to combine his drawing of birds with establishing a business and frequent travel during 1811 and 1812, and the quality of his art varied as a result. His *Bank Swallow* of April 1811 is an awkward fellow, while the *Killdeer Plover* of the same year—though wearing a slightly humorous expression—is elegantly modeled in pastel with touches of graphite. The *Male Yellow-billed Rail* (now known as the Virginia Rail) of October represents an early attempt to show a bird in motion walking with one foot raised, seen against a complex marshy background. Noteworthy also is Audubon's *Carolina Parrot* (plate 3), which he drew in Henderson on June 9, 1811. This handsome composition includes a single bird of an inexplicable medium blue (in life, the bird is green), with a yellow head and a red patch around its eyes. It is pictured in profile against a complex background of branches and leaves, eating a nut. Audubon, as a busy amateur, had by this time reached Wilson's level. If he wasn't yet the elegant pencil draftsman that Wilson was, he was his superior in terms of composition and color, in drawing birds to scale, and in depicting their natural habitats. Yet Audubon still had not reached the height of his powers, as one can see in comparing the *Carolina Parrot* with the drawing of the same species that he made about 1825, which Havell engraved for *The Birds of America*. The later work (page 154) shows the artist more than a decade later, at full strength; in it Audubon celebrates the liveliness, beauty, and abundance of these spectacular creatures as he depicts seven of them crowded together in a way that allows the viewer to examine them from every angle. The earlier bird is a specimen, albeit a handsome one; the later ones are noisy, living, real creatures. Audubon noted that these birds were themselves destroyers and were thus being rapidly and easily exterminated by farmers and hunters: the species became extinct in 1914. Today, there is a prophetic and bittersweet tone in the artist's comment that "the woods are the habitation best fitted for them, and there the richness of their plumage, their beautiful mode of flight, and even their screams afford welcome intimation that our darkest forests and most sequestered swamps are not destitute of charms."[14]

During the following year, 1812, Audubon worked with increasing facility; spending the first half of the year in Pennsylvania, he made his finest drawings to date. In the *White-throated Sparrow* in April he used pastel and pencil for the richly colored bird, pencil and watercolor for the branch and berries beneath

Fig. 10. *Whippoorwill*, May 7, 1812. Pastel, watercolor, and graphite on paper; 17 × 10⅞ in. Houghton Library, Harvard University.

Fig. 9. Robert Havell, Jr. (1793–1878), after John James Audubon. *Northern Goshawk and the Cooper's Hawk* (Havell XLI). Hand-colored etching and aquatint; 38 × 25¼ in. Museum of Fine Arts, Boston, Gift of William Hooper, 1921.

it. Then on two consecutive days in May he took another step forward: drawing *Whippoorwill* on May 7 (fig. 10), then on May 8 the related *Nighthawk.* Both birds are shown in flight, marking the first time Audubon had done this successfully; both are marvels of an increasingly rich pastel technique. In the *Whippoorwill* particularly, there is an indication of light and shadow; and the warm reddish tones on the wings exactly suggest the texture of its feathers. The nocturnal hunter's mouth is open, as if it were about to capture one of the insects that constitute its diet. One feels both the artist's precision and enjoyment, as he adds a detailed study of the bird's foot at the right, in pastel, then sketches its beak in pencil at the left. As with the *Carolina Parrot,* one can compare this work to a final version that was engraved by Havell (page 182). The later picture is another compositional tour de force: it includes three birds, two on a branch and one in flight, seen from underneath, along with two marvelous moths, a caterpillar, and a complex arrangement of branches and leaves. The later birds are executed in watercolor rather than the earlier pastel since Audubon came to realize that the latter medium alone did not allow the level of detail he desired. A comparison between the two drawings suggests that by 1812 Audubon had taught himself to render a bird with an extraordinary technique, while at the same time his own special vision, particularly the way in which he saw and composed his subjects, was still being formed.

Only a handful of drawings survive from the years 1813 to 1820; we can surmise that Audubon was much less active as an artist during these years, due to the press of his business and personal affairs. He purchased property in Henderson, then with several partners built a timber mill in 1816. The Audubons' two-year-old daughter, Lucy, died in 1817; Captain Audubon, the artist's father, died in Nantes during 1818, which set off years of litigation over the estate; and during the financial panic of 1819 Audubon's fortunes hit their nadir, with the collapse of his enterprises and his personal bankruptcy. Looking back, Audubon was inclined to blame himself for his failure, recalling: "For a period of nearly twenty years, my life was a succession of vicissitudes. I tried various branches of commerce, but they all proved unprofitable, doubtless because my whole mind was ever filled with my passion for rambling and admiring those objects of nature from which alone I received the purest gratification."[15]

Virtually penniless, with a wife and two young sons, Audubon turned back to his artistic talents to support himself. In the fall of 1819, at Shippingport, Kentucky, he attempted a portrait drawing of his late friend Nicholas Berthoud (fig. 11). The evocative profile likeness in black chalk was a success, leading to a portrait of Mrs. Berthoud, then to other sittings. By November, in Louisville, he was able to make a strong likeness of Henri de Gallon, showing this small birdlike man in profile, with light shining on his face and cap, his form silhouetted against a dark background. Early in 1820 he moved a hundred miles up the Ohio River to Cincinnati, a larger city that provided increased patronage for his portraits, where he worked for a time as a taxidermist and habitat painter for the new Western Museum. Audubon's rapid progress in delineating people doubtless relied on his parallel improvement in rendering birds; his portraits show him learning to depict light and shade and to model human features convincingly in both pencil and charcoal. In July 1820 he made a largely successful attempt to depict Thomas Best frontally and by October was able to make convincing portraits of the Rev. Allan D. Campbell and of Gen. and Mrs. William Lytle, all with their heads turned at a three-quarters angle. As Edward H. Dwight points out, at this difficult period of Audubon's life, when he was living by his wits, he won his first success as an artist in Cincinnati.[16] Not only was he steadily employed in his museum job and in making portraits at twenty-five dollars apiece but he "established a large drawing-school" there with twenty-five students and enjoyed favorable notices for a small exhibition of his bird drawings (one critic noting, "there have been no exhibitions west of the mountains which can compare with them.").[17]

It was at this point, during 1820, that Audubon's life changed. He would leave both his beloved Kentucky and his unlamented mercantile career behind in order to find and draw all the birds of America, from the Atlantic to the Mississippi, from New England to Florida, realizing the dream he had nur-

Fig. 11. *Nicholas Berthoud*, 1819. Black chalk on paper; 10 × 8 in. J. B. Speed Art Museum, Louisville, Kentucky.

tured since 1806. As he wrote Henry Clay in 1820, "After having spent the greater part of fifteen years in procuring and drawing the birds of the United States with a view of publishing them . . . having a desire to complete the collection before I present it to my country in perfect order, I intend to explore the territories southwest of the Mississippi."[18] Audubon's interest in birds, which in the beginning had been a leisure-time avocation, now became his obsession and the guiding force of his existence.

At the beginning of a new journal, Audubon wrote: "Thursday—Ohio River Oct 12th 1820. I left Cincinnati this afternoon at half past 4 o'clock, on board of Mr. Jacob Aumack's flat boat—bound to New Orleans."[19] Having primarily drawn the birds of Pennsylvania and Kentucky, he was anxious now to study the species resident on the Mississippi River, particularly those of Louisiana. He took as his companion and helper a boy of thirteen, Joseph Mason (1808–42), who was the first in a series of talented assistants who aided Audubon in the making of the drawings. On November 17 the flatboat had left "the beautiful and transparent water of the Ohio," as Audubon said, and had entered "the Muddy Current" of the Mississippi. The pace was slow, allowing plenty of time for Audubon and Mason to go hunting ashore or to take skiffs ahead of the boat; even after entering the Mississippi, with its four-knot current, the flatboat would make only twenty-five miles on a good day, and much less on a poor one. Audubon hunted for birds for the whole of the three-month trip, measuring and weighing them, studying their exteriors to know more about their size and appearance, examining the contents of their stomachs to learn about their diets, and drawing them. Shooting was clearly both his work and his pleasure; he was surely describing himself when he wrote of the Kentucky woodsman, "nature and industry bountifully supply all his wants; the woods and rivers produce his chief dainties, and his toils are his pleasures."[20] On one occasion, on November 23, he shot what he called a "Beautiful white headed Eagle" (i.e., a Bald Eagle), which he immediately began to draw. He continued work on this drawing on the flatboat for the next two days—longer than he usually devoted to a drawing, in this case doubtless necessitated by the size of his subject; usually he would finish a drawing in about a day's time. A few weeks later, on a typical day, he recorded killing "a Crow, a Great Horned Owl, and a Winter Falcon." On the following day he wrote: "Killed a Carrion Crow, a Winter Wren, and 16 Parokeets. I heard and saw once a thrush unknown to me but could not get a shot at it—Immense flocks of Parokeets and Swamp Blackbirds."[21]

In his river journal, Audubon commented on the birds and all the other living beings that he observed along the way, including the people. He admired the Native Americans he saw, writing that "they looked so independent, free & unconcerned with the world that I gazed on them, admired their spirits, & wished for their condition," but he had only disgust for poor whites he saw living at the edge of the river, eating racoons—"a worst part of the worst without doubt."[22] Knowing as he was about the ways of the river and forest, Audubon proved naive when it came to city life. Arriving in New Orleans, he promptly had his pocket picked and concluded to "try to grow wiser if possible."[23] He had surely become a man of the wilderness and of the frontier, an American: at a New Orleans dinner, this former Frenchman reported, "We had . . . a great deal of mirth that I call *french Gaiety* that really sickened me. I thought myself in Bedlam."[24]

Audubon enjoyed a productive eighteen months in Louisiana and Mississippi supporting himself through teaching, executing portrait drawings, and making watercolor copies of such paintings as Vanderlyn's *Ariadne* and Trumbull's *Death of General Montgomery in the Attack on Quebec,* while working on a

number of new bird drawings. His portraits, such as *Jean Baptiste Bossier* (fig. 12) were increasingly sophisticated, with the subjects now seen from varied angles. But most importantly, Audubon was focused on his goal of drawing and then publishing all the birds of the United States, and during 1821 and 1822 he made a sudden breakthrough in his work. He literally started over, developing a new technique and a new compositional format for the birds; though he already had drawings of as many as two hundred species in his portfolio, with very few exceptions none of these earlier works met his new standard, and they were replaced by new drawings over the next seventeen years as he worked feverishly and obsessively on his great project. He felt relieved now to bend every effort toward achieving his ambition; as he wrote Lucy, "During all my life I have felt a great propensity toward following what I am now at." At the same time, he wasn't at all certain that he would ever succeed, and he often doubted the quality of his drawings; in May 1821 he wrote, "That they will pay my time, I cannot know. Sometimes I think well of them; at other moments, [I] look at them as daubs and wish they had never existed."[25]

During 1821 and 1822 Audubon, goaded by a determination to depict birds more beautifully and more accurately than anyone had before him, learned a full range of techniques for drawing with color. He already knew the traditional French medium of pastel very well; he had been perfecting it since he was a young man. Now he added to his repertoire a crystal-clear watercolor technique, the ability to use gouache effectively, and an extraordinary varied use of the pencil, together with the talent for combining all these graphic means to render a single bird. No one in America equaled him for graphic inventiveness until Winslow Homer some sixty years later; as for European parallels, one can only think of the great English watercolorists, both contemporaries of Audubon: J. M. W. Turner and Samuel Palmer.

Audubon at this time developed two quite different compositional formats—one for the small songbirds, another for the larger species, the hawks, owls, and shorebirds. The small species—the warblers, finches, sparrows, swallows, and the like—were drawn to scale on small to medium-sized sheets of paper, always in vertical compositions. The birds—usually at least a male and female pair, and sometimes three or more in number—were typically portrayed on branches of their natural habitat, and the compositions were frequently enhanced by the inclusion of the appropriate flowers, berries, fruit, and insects. These backgrounds are not presented as landscape habitats but rather as decorative vignettes. The birds are positioned so that

Fig. 12. *Jean Baptiste Bossier*, 1821. Crayon and ink over graphite on paper; 12¾ × 9½ in. Nelson-Atkins Museum of Art, Kansas City, Missouri.

the viewer can learn as much as possible about their appearance. Thus if one bird is seen from the side or top, its mate will be viewed from underneath; one bird's wings will be closed, another's spread. For the large species, a much larger sheet was employed, up to 26 × 38 inches; the composition might be either horizontal or vertical. With ducks and other water birds, Audubon continued to depict a male and female pair, but for the largest species generally only one bird could be included. Rather than the elegant patterns of leaves and fruit that Audubon invented for the smaller subjects, he was inclined to include—or at least to outline in pencil—a landscape setting behind the large birds.

It is clear that Audubon had a dual purpose in his drawings, aiming on one hand to give accurate, informative portraits of each species, and on the other to make works of art that were inventive, varied, and beautiful. The drawings were made primarily as guides to a future engraver, still unidentified; and while Audubon always kept the "collection" intact for this purpose, he also relied on his work's quality and effectiveness for a variety of purposes, including attracting the paying public to exhibitions of the drawings, inspiring the engraver, gaining subscribers for the book, and impressing and winning the support of societies of artists and scientists.

Within a few weeks of arriving in New Orleans, Audubon in late January 1821 took on the challenge of drawing an immature Brown Pelican (page 83). He boldly filled a large sheet with his very large subject, making a grand S-curve of it from upper left to lower right, showing it with its bill open, standing on one foot. A landscape background in oil was added later. Audubon relied on pastel for much of this drawing, as he would continue to do for several more years, but he used it now with extraordinary dexterity. The bird's lower mandible is made with watercolor and pastel, its unfeathered throat pouch with thin strokes of pure pastel, and pure strokes of dry brush below. For the feathers on its body, the artist turned to pencil hatching combined with pastel, a technique he would greatly refine during the following years. Interestingly, Audubon drew an effective but very different adult Brown Pelican a decade later (page 218), showing this bird standing on a branch; Havell engraved the 1832 drawing as plate CCLI of the *Birds of America*, but Audubon later had him engrave the 1821 drawing as well, and it became plate CCCCXXI. This is one of several instances where a single species became the subject of two different prints in Audubon's book.

Later in the same year, Audubon took on the challenge of fitting the tallest of American birds, the Whooping Crane, a species now rebounding from the brink of extinction (page 86), onto a sheet of paper measuring some 37 × 26 inches. He succeeded admirably by showing the bird doubled over, feeding on baby alligators. Here he uses practically no pastel at all but instead a mixture of graphite, watercolor, and gouache, again with an oil background added later.

During the same period, Audubon developed his highly original vision of hawks and their relatives in action. He drew the *American Swallow-tailed Kite* during the summer of 1821 (page 99), an extraordinary composition, perhaps the first where he filled his sheet with the powerful form of a large bird in flight. He used pastel sparingly, primarily employing watercolor, even for the fine hatched strokes denoting the feathers of the wings. Audubon left the dramatic, silhouetted form alone on the white paper and did not add any suggestion of sky or earth when the print was made. A presentation of the life-and-death struggle that goes on without pause in the natural world, the drawing is a celebration of the beauty of American birds. Audubon treasured these creatures, writing again and again of their melodious songs, their grace and courage, wishing even to speak with them ("How often have I longed to converse with the feathered inhabitants of the forest").[26] He tells us that the harshness of nature, the cruelty and killing, were inevitable. On one occasion he describes with great feeling the persevering, courageous character of a giant black bear, the shooting of the bear's cubs, and finally a bloody battle to the death—which he encouraged—between the bear and a pack of hunting dogs. Another time, having felt the frightening, destructive power of a tornado, he wrote, "Having witnessed one of these awful phenomena, in all its grandeur, I will attempt to describe it."[27]

An even more powerfully romantic image than the *Swallowtailed Kite* is that of the *Red-tailed Hawks* (page 102), a pair shown in midair, fighting over a hare. Audubon reports witnessing such a battle in his entry on this species in the *Ornithological Biography*. This drawing, which may have been reworked later, shows an amazing range of technique, including pastel over watercolor for the male's tail-feathers, white outlines of feathers on its body created by use of "reserves" (areas where he left the white of the paper untouched), extensive mixture of pastel, watercolor, and graphite, along with black ink lines over watercolor to denote the hare's fur. Equally dramatic though quite different is the *Bald Eagle* (page 108), which shows the bird sitting calmly for its stately portrait befitting what Audubon mistakenly believed to be a new species, in his opinion "the noblest bird of its . . . genus."[28] He proudly named it "The Bird of Washington" after the nation's founder. Here again he employed little pastel: from now on he would use it selectively and sparingly. When Audubon did employ pastel in years following, it was most often to exploit the subtle blending of colors it allowed and to suggest the texture of birds' feathered bodies. Even then, pastel would rarely be employed alone but combined with graphite and watercolor.

Audubon's treatment of small songbirds changed equally dramatically in 1821 and 1822. He turned almost exclusively to watercolor, which proved a far more effective medium than pastel for depicting the diminutive forms and sharp colors of the birds and their environments. The songbird compositions are more complex than those of the bigger subjects; the hawks, owls, and later on the waterbirds were normally pictured in simple landscape settings, which they dominate, but for the little birds Audubon developed a more decorative scheme and became remarkably inventive. In these works, birds and plant life are depicted on the white paper without any indication of earth or sky; these are images remarkable for their color and liveliness, for their variety, and for their success in conveying ornithological information. Audubon became a master of composition in his drawings: in the large ones, large shapes and graceful curves dominate, while for the small ones he relied on his elegant, restrained sense of pattern and color.

Joseph Mason's role in these breakthrough works is difficult to determine, but it was surely an important one. At a very young age, Mason was already a botanist and a fine watercolorist; as Audubon himself wrote his wife, Lucy, on May 23, 1821, "he now draws *flowers* better than any man probably in America."[29] Mason later said that he had made between 150 and 200 plant and flower drawings for Audubon, but there are only two surviving works that bear definite attributions to him. One is the *Northern Parula* (page 88) which Audubon inscribed "Plant by Joseph Mason"; the other is the *Pine Warbler* (1863.17.140). Mason's case was later taken up by the critic John Neal, who accused Audubon of "foul play" in not giving him due credit. Mason exhibited a portrait at the Pennsylvania Academy in 1823 and was sporadically active after that, but unfortunately did not leave behind any later watercolors, so we have no evidence as to what he might have accomplished in that medium independently from Audubon.

In the *Northern Parula*, which is dated March 27, 1821, one sees a flowering red or copper iris, which Mason drew before Audubon added the birds. The flowers are delicately rendered in watercolor with extensive and subtle graphite shading; Mason displays a touch both delicate and certain, particularly in his handling of a very fine brush in drawing the blossoms' red and yellow membranes. The thick green stems below are quickly and confidently rendered in watercolor with a little gouache added. Mason had an ability to suggest both light and shade and the three-dimensionality of objects, and it seems possible that Audubon may have learned some of his own watercolor technique from his assistant.

In some of the presumed collaborative works of 1821–22, Mason's contributions actually overpower Audubon's birds. In the *Cerulean Warbler* (page 90), for example, the mottled leaves have a range of subtle colors from yellow-brown to sharp green, but the bird seems awkward as it looks up at a tiny spider. Havell's print (XLVIII) includes a second bird at the lower right, and a careful look at the drawing reveals that Audubon sketched this bird faintly in pencil on his drawing, suggesting that Havell—as usual—was following Audubon exactly. Similarly, the static profiles in Audubon's *Summer Tanagers* (page 92) are still reminiscent of his earlier work, while the muscadine grapes and leaves beside them are richly and convincingly depicted. Mason drew branches and stems smoothly and realistically, using watercolor mixed with gouache so that it looks rather like pastel: thus the honey locust branch and leaves in the *Red-eyed Vireo* (page 112) and the details of the cotton gum tree in *Dark-eyed Junco* (page 114) both seem safely attributable to the young artist. The juncos themselves are beautifully delineated: Audubon relied on pastel to suggest the warm, dark grays of their heads and bodies, watercolor for the wings of the male, minute pencil work for its breast, and fine watercolor strokes for the female's breast.

Two of the richest songbird compositions of this period are the *White-breasted Nuthatch* (page 110) and the *Tufted Titmouse* (page 116). Mason may have drawn the superbly varied pine cones and needles in the former but probably played no role in the latter picture. In the masterful *Nuthatch*, Audubon included four of the acrobatic birds: one seen from below, another from the side, and two from above. The birds all face left, as if aware of an approaching predator. The lichen-encrusted tree trunk is pure Audubon, drawn in his typical manner with watercolor washes and minute watercolor lines.

Thus it is possible on stylistic and, occasionally, documentary grounds to attribute some but not all of the foliage and flowers in the watercolors of 1821–22 to Mason. At the same time, Audubon was clearly the primary draftsman and always the designer. Throughout his career he made excellent use of assistants in his work, including Mason, George Lehman, Maria Martin, and his two sons; he had the ability to make the most of their strengths while he himself supplied the overall guidance and energy for the great project he had undertaken.

During the same two-year period in Louisiana and Mississippi, Audubon also developed several compositional schemes for birds of medium size, drawing from the solutions he had reached for the songbirds and the eagles. Woodland species were shown in male and female pairs, as one sees in the highly effective *Chuck-will's-widow*, a watercolor with touches of gouache and graphite, dated May 7, 1822 (page 106), in which the two birds react violently to a coral snake in their tree. Rarely did the artist surpass his performance here either in the composition or rendering of the birds. Interestingly, Audubon (or perhaps Havell) added branches and berries to the engraving, which detract from the original composition.

Shorebirds were also treated in pairs and were usually depicted within a believable shore scene or landscape. The *Blue-winged Teal* (page 118) of February 1822 includes a pair of the birds in flight, the female slightly behind the male; in Havell's later print the female is placed directly over its mate, making a more static, less energized composition than in the drawing. The Red Knot (page 121), a member of the sandpiper family, is

Fig. 13. Emperor Hui-Tsung (reigned 1101–25). *The Five-colored Parakeet.* Hanging scroll, ink and colors on silk; 21⅜ × 45 in. Museum of Fine Arts, Boston, Marie Antoinette Evans Fund.

again seen in a male and female pair, each posed characteristically, with an unusual romantic marine view—including a ship under full sail—behind them. In the print this was replaced by a less effective flat sea. Finally, mention should be made of another New Orleans drawing of 1822, the *Anhinga* (page 124). Audubon pictures two of these cormorantlike birds seated on a single branch, with the male's body mostly blocking one's view of the female behind it. Though he drew the male's extraordinary black-and-white plumage brilliantly, using watercolor and pencil, when it came time to make a print of this species in 1836 (Havell cccxvi), he made another drawing, this time separating the two birds so that each can be seen clearly.

Audubon's mature works, beginning in 1821–22, are reminiscent of Chinese and Japanese paintings and prints. We are inclined to think of the Western connection with Asian art—*japonisme*—as primarily stemming from the 1860s and later, when Whistler, Tissot, Monet, Degas, and others were influenced by Japanese prints and porcelain. However, it is difficult to believe that Audubon was unacquainted with Asian art, as his drawings evoke a wide variety of parallels with it. A painting by the Emperor Hui-tsung (reigned 1101–25), *The Five-colored Parakeet* (fig. 13), can be compared to any number of Audubon's depictions of songbirds, including the *Red-eyed Vireo* (page 112). Like the Chinese master, Audubon places his subject near the center of his composition, seats it on a graceful branch cut off from the rest of the world, and organizes his uncluttered space with great restraint. Even more relevant are the works of Japanese printmakers of the eighteenth and nineteenth centuries. The *Book of Birds*, a series of colored woodblock prints by

合衆國有名の禽學者縣度楼を時
放行す々々多年思愚かに摸冩して
粉本を箱へ置とて数月にして
家へ帰り箱を開て見れ其内へ乘
らひ画圖の巻ゝ器を噛て碎ける
郷度挽ハ是を見う大いに心を傷
既さ又舊の如く小鋭と手ふ
擧林ハ八ゝ禽鳥を捕へ其形狀を
手々次ゝ々々画又箱に満ち摸冩を前

Fig. 14. Meiji Period (1868–1912). *Audubon Discovering that Rats Had Eaten His Drawings.* Japanese woodblock print, ink and color on paper; 14¼ × 9⁷⁄₁₆ in. Daval Foundation, from the collection of Ambassador and Mrs. William Leonhart of Washington, D.C.

Fig. 15. Ando Hiroshige (1797–1858). *Three Geese Flying Under Full Moon.* Japanese woodblock print; 15 × 10¼ in. Museum of Fine Arts, Boston, Gift of Denman Waldo Ross.

Utamaro (1753–1806), includes several illustrations of male and female pairs depicted from differing angles, as Audubon often did. Moreover, Utamaro's *Goshawk* and *Rooster* both illustrate single, large birds whose body and stretched-out wings nearly fill the whole sheet, recalling Audubon's treatment of eagles and hawks. Interestingly, Audubon was known and appreciated in Japan and was the subject of at least one nineteenth-century print (fig. 14), which tells the story—recounted by Audubon himself—of how he returned from a long trip to find that rats had destroyed many of his drawings. His work, in fact, prefigures certain prints by Hiroshige and the Utagawa School; the literally bird's-eye view that one finds in Hiroshige's print of *Three Geese Flying Under Full Moon* (fig. 15) recalls a device frequently employed by Audubon—in his *Common Tern* (page 254), among others—of silhouetting his subjects against the sky, with only a hint of the earth below. The relationship between Audubon's work and Asian art has been little studied but is certainly worthy of further investigation.

During the fall of 1823 Audubon left Mississippi with his son Victor, first going back to Kentucky, then traveling in 1824 to Philadelphia to seek an engraver for his drawings. Though he won a friend and admirer in Thomas Sully, most of the artistic and scientific establishment of that city were predisposed against Audubon and his art; they found him to be boastful and flamboyant, and his work was seen as romantic, unrealistic, and not in the scientific tradition they admired. He went on to New York City, again failing to find a publisher, then to Albany, Rochester, and Niagara Falls, and by the fall of 1824 was in Pittsburgh. He and Lucy were finally reunited in Louisiana in November of that year, when he began planning a trip to Europe to find the engraver and the patronage he so desperately needed; he would finally sail for England in June 1826.

During this busy four-year period, from the summer of 1822, when Mason left him, up to his departure in 1826, Audubon continued to draw. Though his artistic production slowed, his compositional style became denser and richer, his treatment of the birds themselves more effective. His *American Goldfinch* (page 130) proved that he could execute superb foliage without Mason's help, and the *House Wren* (page 132), with its memorable felt hat, makes one wish that he had undertaken some pure still lifes. Several pictures of medium-sized birds can be rated as among the most complex and successful of any of his work, including the *Wood Duck* (page 152), the *Carolina Parakeet* (page 154), and the *Blue Jay* (page 156). Each of these good-sized species is presented in multiple examples, seen from every side, drawn with believable three-dimensionality in vertical compo-

16

sitions filled with such an organized welter of branches, fruit, and blossoms that the whole seems about to burst from its confines. During the same period Audubon worked out a new horizontal format for showing large birds of prey attacking their quarries on the ground. In *Peregrine Falcon* (page 145), the artist has cut out and collaged onto a new sheet the female bird on the right, executed in 1820 mostly in pastels; it is shown in profile atop its victim, a bloody Green-winged Teal. The left-hand bird, the male, was drawn at Niagara in August 1824; its wings are spread, its claws stretched out, its head turned toward both its prey and, beyond that, the viewer. Executed largely in watercolor, it is considerably more lifelike than its companion of just four years before. In a related work (page 149), Audubon depicted the "terror and confusion"—as he put it—that prevailed when a Red-shouldered Hawk attacked a large covey of Northern Bobwhites. In both cases, Audubon's compositions recall the bloody animal battles painted by Peter Paul Rubens, Frans Snyders, and other Flemish artists of the seventeenth century. The only painter that Audubon refered to in his writing with any regularity was David, but he must have been aware of major currents in European art. In making his watercolors, he went far beyond the confines of traditional ornithological illustration; he appears to have drawn on a wide variety of artists and artistic traditions in an instinctive rather than slavish way.

Both in chronological terms and in the fact that he turned to Europe for the bulk of his patronage, Audubon might be classed with such contemporaries as Allston, Vanderlyn (whom he met in New Orleans), and Morse—the early-nineteenth-century painters who had failed in their ambition to create an American art in the grand European tradition. Though Audubon was their age, we must remember that he practiced only as an amateur, part-time, artist between about 1801 and 1820. His mature style developed in the early 1820s through his supreme dedication, his keen observation of nature, his long travels, and his keen sense of himself as an American artist painting uniquely American subjects. In this respect his career parallels that of another immigrant painter, Thomas Cole, who had arrived in this country in 1819, at the age of eighteen. Cole, like Audubon, found his true subject matter in the American wilderness they both loved. Both artists were realists, and both were Romantics; both observed very carefully but then perfected or exaggerated reality in their work. The two revered nature as had no Americans before them, and they were ambivalent about the expansion of the young nation over the continent. In his poem "The Lament of the Forest," Cole

speaks of the onrushing "human hurricane" that has "marked . . . our sanctuary, this secluded spot."[30] Audubon foresaw the coming scarcity of deer because of overhunting, despite their present "incredible abundance," and elsewhere he warned that a "war of extermination" carried on by the eggers of Labrador had nearly wiped out some species of ducks, gulls, and guillemots.[31] Audubon's writings, like Cole's, are too little read, yet both painters were important nature writers. In his essay "The Ohio," Audubon writes of his first days in Kentucky in terms reminiscent of those of the Hudson River School painter:

> When I think of these times, and call back to my mind the grandeur and beauty of these almost uninhabited shores; when I picture to myself the dense and lofty summits of the forest . . . unmolested by the axe of the settler; when I see that no longer any Aborigines are to be found there, and that the vast herds of elks, deer, and buffaloes . . . have ceased to exist; when I reflect . . . that the woods are fast disappearing under the axe by day, and the fire by night, . . . I pause, wonder. . . .[32]

Audubon envied no one; as he said, "The rich may produce a better, or a more sumptuous meal; but his feelings can never be like those of the poor woodsman."[33] He proclaimed himself the kind of unfettered, self-reliant American that Emerson and Thoreau would idealize; in "The Prairie" he wrote, "My knapsack, my gun, and my dog, were all I had for baggage and company."[34]

In his writings, as in his drawings of birds, Audubon of course was at the same time both influenced by myth and a maker of myth. Just as Thomas Cole went to Italy to paint *The Dream of Arcadia*, then returned to America to paint its own golden age, so Audubon carried on the same tradition. He painted fragments of the wilderness, numerous healthy, beautiful, perfectly formed birds that existed in countless numbers in this new Eden. In his pictures, both the ones in watercolor and pastel and the written ones, Audubon follows Cole's practice of heightening reality; whereas Cole preferred to "wait for time to draw a veil over the common details," Audubon spent years searching for the best possible example of each species, which he then presented as typical. Like Cole, he identified with the Native Americans, but he went further; Cole included Indian settlements in his views of the Catskills, suggesting their natural harmony with nature, while Audubon admired the Indians to such an extent that he took from them many of his attributes of dress and his persona as a lonely hunter completely at home in the trackless forests.

Both Cole and Audubon were also keenly aware of the myth of Daniel Boone (1734–1820), the settler of Kentucky. Boone was the archetypal "solitary, Indian-like hunter of the deep woods" who—as Richard Slotkin tells us in his important study—"became the most significant, most emotionally compelling myth-hero of the early republic."[35] One of Cole's early paintings (Amherst College collection) depicts Boone in the wilderness, sitting outside his simple cabin. As Slotkin points out, the myth of Boone on the frontier had wide currency in France; Audubon propagates it further in his essays in the *Ornithological Biography*, drawing a picture of Kentucky settlers as hospitable and generous hosts of joyful dances without "pomp or affectation," and of their state as a place where fish and game and every natural resource existed in plenitude. Audubon himself symbolized a new intersection, one where the noblest traditions of European art and European ornithology met with wilderness America. Audubon made this link explicit in his writings about Kentucky and especially his meeting with "Colonel Boon" himself. According to the painter, he and Boone went on a hunting expedition together; the artist described him as having, even in old age, "gigantic" physical stature and superb skill as a hunter.[36] Most of Audubon's essay is devoted to Boone's purported retelling of some legends of his heyday in Kentucky, when he escaped from Indian captors—tales that had been widely circulated by this time. Boone would have been seventy-six in 1810, the year when he returned to Kentucky from Missouri, which makes Audubon's tale unlikely. Yet as with Audubon's link to David, the connection between Audubon and Boone is no less important for being, most probably, imagined rather than experienced. In spite of all the real and terrible difficulties he had experienced, Audubon recalled his years in Kentucky as "the golden age, which I here found realized."[37]

Audubon remained in Great Britain, including a side trip to Paris from July 1826 to the late spring of 1829—a crucially important time for the artist. He won widespread artistic and scientific acclaim for his drawings, found the London firm of R. Havell & Son to engrave them, published several learned papers, gained election to a number of prominent learned societies, and, not least, found enough subscribers to make it possible to proceed with publication. The success that Audubon had craved in Philadelphia and New York had been won in Liverpool, Edinburgh, and London; the artist had been raised and trained in France and had adopted America without qualification but, as he said, "to Britain I owe nearly all my success."[38]

To earn money during these years Audubon turned to making copies of his bird drawings both in oil and watercolor.

Fig. 16. Robert Havell, Jr. (1793–1878), after John James Audubon. *Yellow-breasted Chat* (Havell cxxxvii). Hand-colored etching and aquatint; 25 × 37½ in. Museum of Fine Arts, Boston, Gift of William Hooper, 1921.

Though he had little time or opportunity to add to his "collection" of American birds, in London he did execute an excellent watercolor copy of the *Bald Eagle*, which he had originally drawn largely in pastels in November 1820 while on the Mississippi. As the national symbol this was an important subject to him. Moreover, his composition directly and obviously challenged Alexander Wilson, for it was clearly based on Wilson's picture of the same species. The new London version (page 161), engraved by Havell as plate xxxi, is more convincing than the earlier one (page 160) in its realism and especially in such details as the eagle's head and claws. Here Audubon substitutes for the bloody goose—the eagle's prey in the first work—a well-drawn, bloated catfish.

Audubon returned to the United States in May 1829, and for eleven months he feverishly sought both American subscribers and American birds, traveling to New York, New Jersey, Maine, Pennsylvania, Ohio, and Kentucky, to Louisiana to pick up Lucy, and finally to Washington and Baltimore before they both sailed back to London on April 1, 1830. Despite his incredible pace, the artist continued to work at the height of his powers. His *Snowy Owl* (page 184), for example, pictures a pair of the large predators seated on a dead tree, their white bodies posed dramatically against a dark, blue-gray, stormy sky. Both birds are well modeled in pure watercolor and pencil. His *Osprey* (page 166) probably executed at Great Egg Harbor, New Jersey, is also a superb composition, with one wing—remarkably—seen from underneath, the other from the top, and dramatic placement on the sheet, combining a plethora of accurate ornithological detail with supremely confident pure watercolor and graphite technique. The raptor is seen in flight, straining to carry aloft a large weakfish into which it has sunk its bloody talons. Audubon's drawings are frequently more effective than the prints Havell made from them. In this case the engraver (or perhaps Audubon himself) lessened the powerful abstract design of the drawing by adding a conventional view of sea and mountains at the bottom of the print. However, there are cases where the opposite is true, and where elements found in Audubon's original drawing were omitted—beneficially—from the engraving; one example of this occurs with the *Yellow-breasted Chat* (page 174), where the awkward bird at the upper left of his drawing was left out of the print (fig. 16).

Leaving the static, flat works of earlier years far behind, Audubon worked with increasing confidence, showing birds of all sizes in action—feeding, fighting, or flying. Living, believable beings, they live in small, isolated worlds of great beauty. To judge from the drawings, one would think Audubon had all the time in the world during these months; the chat's nest, for example, is modeled with great accuracy, and the leaves and flowers surrounding it form a superb still life. During the same month, June 1829, he drew the *Marsh Wren* (page 170) and, as with the *Yellow-breasted Chat*, the *Sharp-tailed Sparrow* (page 172), and a few others, he used pure watercolor combined with dexterous pencil hatching and shading to depict birds and nest in a highly detailed manner. Audubon's style in depicting lush green vines and grasses in these New Jersey works makes one wonder whether he could possibly have known Albrecht Dürer's magnificent watercolors; it also prefigures, in a way, the exacting approach popularized by the English critic and watercolorist John Ruskin a quarter-century later. As Audubon's birds become more lively, they increasingly take on human qualities. In the *Brown Thrasher* (page 180) Audubon pictured three male birds fighting off a black snake near their nest, while the female seems to swoon below. In the *Ornithological Biography* Audubon spoke of witnessing such a battle, writing of "the courageous spirit which the male bird shows, as he defends his nest, and exerts all his powers to extricate his beloved mate

from the coils of the vile snake." He notes that two other thrashers had come to the couple's aid, and asks—doubtless thinking of his own trials—"should this alliance of noble spirits prove victorious, will it not remind you that innocence, although beset with difficulties, may, with the aid of friendship, extricate herself with honour?"[39]

The Audubons returned to England together in April 1830 to oversee Havell's printing of the plates and to begin work on the five-volume *Ornithological Biography*. This would contain a natural history of each of the 435 species he illustrated, interspersed with five introductory pieces and some sixty other essays dealing mostly with Audubon's America. Bearing such titles as "A Racoon Hunt in Kentucky," "The Wreckers of Florida," and "The Bay of Fundy," these writings comprise a self-portrait of the artist that is eloquently informative on many levels.

Audubon landed back in New York in early September 1831 and promptly set off with his new assistant George Lehman (c. 1800–70) on a trip to draw the birds of the southern states. Lehman, unlike Mason before him, was already an established artist; in 1829 he had painted and then engraved a series of views of Pennsylvania towns, and in the same year, he exhibited a landscape oil at the Pennsylvania Academy. His hand is distinguishable in many of Audubon's drawings of shorebirds from 1831–32. For example, the *Long-billed Curlew* (page 189) of 1831, made near Charleston, includes Lehman's detailed, distant view of that South Carolina city that is unlike any background Audubon had attempted on his own. Lehman also apparently made the lush grassy background for the *Black-crowned Night-Heron* (page 192) and the excellent, topographically exact views of South Carolina farmhouses that appear in the backgrounds of the *Common Snipe* (page 198) and the *Snowy Egret* (page 208). Lehman traveled with Audubon on a cruise up the St. John's River in Florida, and then on to the Florida Keys in April and May 1832; it was doubtless he who painted the view of Key West seen in the distance in the *Great Blue Heron* (page 205), which Audubon dated May 26, 1832. Despite his contributions to these and other drawings, he was rarely credited by Audubon. However, after his long discussion of the *White-crowned Pigeon* (page 220) in the *Ornithological Biography*, Audubon appended a note on the rough-leaved cordia plant, whose leaves and flowers play an important role in his composition; it concludes, "I procured a large bough, from which the drawing was made, with the assistance of Mr. Lehman."[40]

Audubon took special interest in the various herons he found in South Carolina and Florida, calling these elegant wading birds "the most difficult to imitate of any . . . I have yet undertaken."[41] The subtle coloring in the *Little Blue Heron* (page 195), ranging from grayish browns on the head to slate blue on the back and wings, was rendered with a combination of pastel, watercolor, and graphite; here Audubon used pencil extensively for the fine feathers on the bird's back. Audubon found the Great Egret especially frustrating, and he drew it three times. One version (page 210) shows the white bird against a dark gray background, as he had done with the *Snowy Owl*; the preening bird is drawn in a vertical composition, with the artist using strokes of gouache for the long, thin plumage at its tail. Despite its elegance, the painter inexplicably found it unsatisfactory and drew the same species again in June 1832, in Charleston (page 213), adding a new, collaged head to a well-executed body. He took great pains to render the bird's breeding plumage in great detail, and this was the version that Havell would engrave (Havell ccclxxxvi).

Audubon and his family traveled north to Philadelphia, New York, and then Boston, where they spent the winter of 1832–33. The summer of 1833 saw one of the artist's last major trips to find birds that had not yet been drawn, as he mounted a sailing expedition with his son John to Labrador. He had been well received in Boston, winning subscriptions from Harvard College, the Boston Athenaeum, the merchant Thomas Handasyd Perkins, and a number of others; for his cruise he was able to recruit four "young gentlemen," as he described them, from prominent local families, including Joseph Coolidge, George Shattuck, Jr., William Ingalls, and Thomas Lincoln. They sailed on the *Ripley* to Eastport, Maine, then east across the Bay of Fundy, to Halifax, Nova Scotia, and finally north through the Canso Straits to Newfoundland.

In Boston, Audubon purchased a live Golden Eagle, which he spent some two weeks drawing. The result (page 232) was one of his most highly Romantic images, the huge bird straining to stay aloft while carrying a rabbit it has just killed. Below it lies a mountainous landscape, empty except for the tiny figure of a hunter making his way across a chasm on a fallen tree. Man is dwarfed by desolate grandeur, and one cannot help reading the figure as a miniature self-portrait. It suggests something of Audubon's continuing struggles to keep his project going in the face of constant difficulties in finding enough backers and in tracking down missing birds. Interestingly, in the Havell print the great bird and its prey are raised to allow a fuller view of the wintry landscape, and the small human figure has been omitted. Audubon's composition—with the huge bird pushed to the front plane, the small figure seen in the distance, and the Alpine setting—all recall Jacques Louis David's Romantic

masterwork of 1801, *Bonaparte Crossing the Great St. Bernard* (Musée National du Chateau, Malmaison, France), which Audubon—David's admirer—might have known.

The trip to Labrador in a sense completed Audubon's explorations. His experiences in the north gave him knowledge of the whole of America, and his essays on the area ("Cod-fishing in Labrador," "The Eggers of Labrador," "The Bay of Fundy," and so on) provide telling counterpoint to his writings about Kentucky, Louisiana, and Florida. He records his horror at the "cruelties" of the poachers "destructive pirates," as he calls them, writing that "the eggers themselves will be the first to repent the entire disappearance of the myriads of birds."[42] Under often difficult circumstances he made a number of highly successful drawings on board his chartered schooner, the *Ripley*. On June 22, for example, in the midst of squalls and while fighting seasickness, he drew the immature and adult Northern Gannet (page 239), and on the following day added in watercolor—with effective scraping—a dark, stormy sky. He continued to use graphite together with watercolor in extraordinarily inventive ways, on the back of the male Puffin (page 236), for example, creating a fine hatching that suggests the texture of its wings. The birds take on a comfortable, familial look: the Puffins seem very content and domestic, while the Cormorants, the Black Guillemots (page 246), and the Arctic Loons (page 251) are all pictured with their young. Audubon demonstrates his confident touch and his love of abstract detail in the elegantly varied black-and-white pattern on the back of the male loon at the left of that composition. Finally, mention should be made of the magnificent terns that he drew around this time. Compositionally, they are descendants of the great *Swallow-tailed Kite* of 1821 (page 99), but the format has become even simpler and more elegant. In these pictures, one sees the white tern diving straight down, as if toward some prey, silhouetted against a blue or gray sky. In the *Common Tern* (page 254) the bird nearly fills Audubon's sheet, a study of whites against darker grays, the red foot and the red beak balancing each other and providing color notes, the whole a nearly perfect image of the grace and beauty of nature.

In Charleston during the autumn of 1831, Audubon met a gifted naturalist, the Rev. John Bachman, who became a close friend and collaborator; later Audubon's two sons would marry Bachman's daughters, thus connecting the families closely. Maria Martin (1796–1863), the sister of Mrs. Bachman, was already a talented amateur watercolorist with an interest in floral subjects when Audubon met her; under his guidance, she assisted in making the floral backgrounds for two dozen or

Fig. 17. Robert Havell, Jr. (1793–1878), after John James Audubon. *Black-throated Green Warbler* (Havell CCCXCIX). Hand-colored etching and aquatint; 25 × 37½ in. Museum of Fine Arts, Boston, Gift of William Hooper, 1921.

Fig. 18. Robert Havell, Jr. (1793–1878), after John James Audubon. *Golden-winged Warbler* (Havell CCCCXIV). Hand-colored etching and aquatint; 25 × 37½ in. Museum of Fine Arts, Boston, Gift of William Hooper, 1921.

more of his drawings.[43] She went on in later years to make both copies of Audubon's drawings and floral studies of her own. Audubon credited her for contributing to several of his works, including *Bachman's Warbler* (page 230), made in Charleston during the fall of 1833. Bachman had first seen this hitherto-unknown bird (now probably extinct) earlier that year. Audubon never saw a living member of this species but made his drawing from skins Bachman had collected—which may account for their rather stiff appearance in the drawing. In the *Ornithological Biography*, Audubon writes that these warblers are accompanied by "one of the most beautiful of our southern flowers, originally drawn by my friend's sister, Miss Martin."[44] Even at her ablest, as here, Martin lacked the confident touch of Mason or Lehman; her watercolor technique is less firm than

theirs and is distinguished from theirs in its purity, as she rarely employed gouache.

In March 1834 Audubon went back to Great Britain for a third time, returning to the United States in the summer of 1836. Early in 1837 he undertook a final trip in search of more species, which was unproductive artistically. July of that year saw a final return to England, where he completed the last of his drawings for *The Birds of America* during early 1838. By late June 1838 all of the drawings had been engraved, and all that remained was completion of the *Ornithological Biography* during the following year.

Despite intense pressure to finish the project, and despite his new willingness—born of that pressure—to draw birds from skins purchased or borrowed from other naturalists, Audubon continued to make some drawings of the highest quality, along with other, more hurried, efforts. For the first time he became willing to put more than one species into a single drawing, and he ransacked earlier drawings for birds that could be put to use. For *Winter Wren, Rock Wren* (page 276), he had drawn in watercolor a pair of the diminutive Winter Wrens (the birds at the lower left and upper right of his drawing) in Maine during 1833; on this sheet he added as a collaged cutout another of the same species, a pastel drawn on the Mississippi in 1820; he then pasted on the larger Rock Wren at the center, having in 1836–37 drawn this bird—which he never saw—on the basis of a skin procured from Thomas Nuttall. A similar process took place with the *Hairy Woodpecker* (page 288): here the pairs of Hairy Woodpeckers and Red-bellied Woodpeckers at the top of the composition were drawn about 1822, while the composition was finished with Martin's help in 1836–37, when three more species were added—the large pair of flickers at the center, the pair of Lewis's Woodpeckers on the tree trunk, and the pair of Yellow-bellied Sapsuckers on the branches at the bottom. In the print, Havell altered the position of several of the birds, which brought some improvement to a somewhat chaotic composition. To give a final example, in *Black-throated Green Warbler* (page 281) he included nine birds of five different species; some of these subjects he had observed, but for others he had only the observations and skins supplied by Nuttall or Edward Harris. In Audubon's watercolor the crowded birds are seen largely in profile, in a way reminiscent of his style of twenty years earlier. Havell, doubtless with Audubon's advice, found a solution to

the confusion by making two separate prints from the original, using the five birds at upper right for one engraving (fig. 17), and the other four for another (fig. 18). Havell reproduced most of Audubon's earlier drawings exactly, or with minor additions; however, during the second half of the project, and particularly near its hurried end, one finds increased numbers of cases where Audubon's work needed to be amended in the final print. Thus he drew the Sabine's Gull (page 270), an arctic species that he did not know well, in a flat profiled pose. When Havell came to engrave it, Audubon discovered that they had neglected to include a drawing of a sanderling in the engraving of that species (Havell ccxxx), and so they added the sanderling and a somewhat conventional seashore to the print of *Sabine's Gull* (fig. 19).

On the other hand, during these same years, and especially while in London, Audubon made some of the most powerful of all of his drawings. The Great Gray Owl, for example, had long eluded him; he went to Salem, Massachusetts, to see one in February 1831, but it disappeared before he got there. During the following winter he observed one flying about Boston Harbor but couldn't get close to it. Finally he settled on making his drawing "from a remarkably fine specimen in the collection of the Zoological Society of London," as he forthrightly reported.[45] The work that resulted (page 258) was another high point of his watercolor and graphite technique: the artist's painstaking attention to the symmetry and rhythm of brown and yellow shapes leads to a magical portrait of this huge bird. Audubon drew the owl's compelling face in slightly sharper focus than the rest of its body, and placed the main part of its

Fig. 19. Robert Havell, Jr. (1793–1878), after John James Audubon. *Sabine's Gull* (Havell CCLXXXV). Hand-colored etching and aquatint; 25 × 37½ in. Museum of Fine Arts, Boston, Gift of William Hooper, 1921.

body in shade, so that the viewer returns again and again to its quizzical expression. On his drawing, Audubon instructed Havell to "rise the bird about 4 inches on the copper higher than in this drawing and put a landscape below of wild mountains." Havell followed the first part of these instructions, raising the bird and extending the vertical branch, but did not put in a landscape below. As a result, the print (fig. 20) lacks the compelling immediacy of Audubon's original.

In London, Audubon also made his superb drawing *Anna's Hummingbird* (page 290). As with many of his late subjects, Audubon had never seen living members of this western American species but nonetheless drew the four males along with the female on her nest as graceful, lively beings. He then added a faint pencil sketch that indicated an alternative, lower, position for the male flying upside-down, at the upper right. Havell (see fig. 21) reproduced Audubon's five original birds while altering their relative positions slightly and added a decorative flowering pink hibiscus by Maria Martin. Similarly, Audubon knew the California Condor (page 296) only from the reports of Dr. John Townsend and from specimens in London, but his watercolor rendering of the huge, brooding bird (another of Audubon's subjects that is now extinct in the wild) is superb.

Finally, mention should be made of the *Gyrfalcon*, made in London about 1837, which some observers have considered the most beautiful of all of Audubon's works. Audubon's son John and two companions had shot a pair of these gray-phase arctic breeders on the coast of Labrador in 1833; calling them Labrador Falcons, he drew the male and female perched on branches, one above the other, a composition Havell engraved as plate CXCVI. Four years later in London he saw a living white-phase female of the species; after the bird died, he studied it carefully and then used it as the model for both birds in a new drawing (page 292), which was engraved as plate CCCLXVI. Audubon used every technique at his disposal—pastel, watercolor, gouache, delicate washes, and extensive pencil drawing—to render them both as living creatures and as abstract black-and-white forms of great graphic power. He seemed to take special pleasure in painting the black spotting and barring on the back and wings of the bird in flight and in the spectacular presentation of both birds against a dense blue sky.

Even while Audubon's book was being produced in London, debates began about its merits. One of the earliest English reviews was by the naturalist William Swainson, who in April 1828 published his laudatory comments on the first thirty plates of Audubon's "magnificent undertaking."[46] He found it a work

Fig. 20. Robert Havell, Jr. (1793–1878), after John James Audubon. *Great Gray Owl* (Havell CCCLI). Hand-colored etching and aquatint; 25 × 37½ in. Museum of Fine Arts, Boston, Gift of William Hooper, 1921.

of genius: "Devotedly attached to the study of nature, no less than to painting, [Audubon] seems to have pursued both with a genius and an ardor, of which, in their united effects, there is no parallel." Swainson had also read two of Audubon's ornithological pieces, and found in them a special "freshness and originality." Similarly, the *American Journal of Science and Arts* a year later considered the first forty-nine plates and concluded that the book "forms the most magnificent work of its kind ever executed in any country."[47]

However, controversies of various kinds arose soon after, and during the 1830s Audubon came under attack both in England and America. In London, Charles Waterton accused him of not having actually written the *Ornithological Biography*, on the basis of his having hired the Scottish naturalist William MacGillivray to help. In America, the chief attacker was Wilson's friend George Ord, and the debate centered on Audubon's ac-

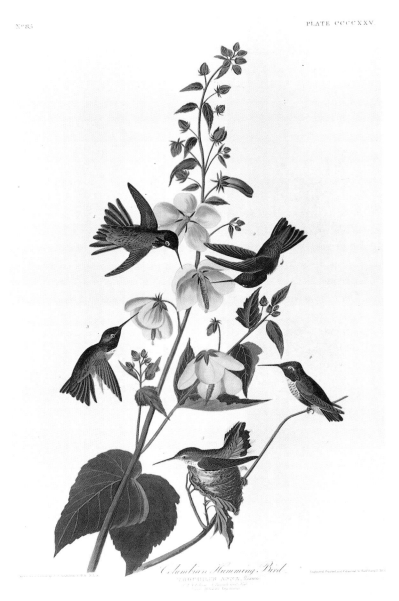

Columbian Humming Bird.
TROCHILUS ANNA, *Lesson.*

Fig. 21. Robert Havell, Jr. (1793–1878), after John James Audubon. *Anna's Hummingbird* (Havell ccccxxv). Hand-colored etching and aquatint; 25 × 37½ in. Museum of Fine Arts, Boston, Gift of William Hooper, 1921.

curacy in depicting a rattlesnake climbing a tree, the habits of vultures, and the like. William Dunlap, the pioneer art historian, was inclined to take the side of Audubon's critics, and gave him a generally critical review in his 1834 survey of American art.[48] For nineteenth-century critics, an artist's personality counted significantly in judging the art. Dunlap, like a number of his contemporaries, found Audubon to be unreliable, overbearing, and a braggart, and held this against his art. At the same time, there were many others who liked and admired Audubon. The prominent New Yorker Philip Hone, for example, met him in April 1833 and described him in his diary as "an interesting man of about 55 years of age, modest in his deportment, possessing general intelligence, an acute mind, and great enthusiasm."[49]

By the 1860s, a pattern was established, which lasted for a

century or more: Audubon was written about a great deal, but was rarely given serious consideration by historians of American art and culture. There were, for example, three separate biographies published in England and America before 1870, more than for any other American artist up to this time; yet C. E. Lester, Henry Tuckerman, and James Jackson Jarvis, the major critics of midcentury, paid his work little heed. Late-nineteenth-century historians such as George W. Sheldon and Samuel G. W. Benjamin fail to mention Audubon, and the same is true of Sadakichi Hartmann, Samuel Isham, and Charles Caffin, early in this century.[50]

Museum exhibitions played a role in beginning a modern reconsideration of Audubon's work, which was well represented in two landmark shows in New York; the Metropolitan Museum's *Life in America*, mounted during the World's Fair of 1939, and *Romantic Painting in America*, organized by James T. Soby and Dorothy Miller of the Museum of Modern Art during 1943. In the following year, E. P. Richardson, one of the outstanding historians of the period, took up Audubon's cause in his pioneering study *Romantic Painting in America*. By the time of Richardson's important survey *Painting in America* (1956), he had expanded on his treatment of the artist, now describing the whole process of publishing *The Birds of America* as "one of the most fantastic instances of talent and energy in the history of American art." Richardson treated Audubon, for the first time, as a major artist, concluding, "Birds, one might say, are his subjects: but his theme is Nature—wild, grand, multiplex, and infinitely beautiful."[51]

Subsequent scholars, however, did not always follow Richardson's lead. Audubon's oeuvre consisted largely of drawings and watercolors, and it has been difficult for art historians to accept works on paper as having equal importance to oil paintings. Another practical problem has been that so much of Audubon's mature work is found in just one collection. Moreover, his achievement was unique, and thus resistant to the kind of classification that historians like. It is difficult to know whether he belongs to Allston's generation or to Cole's; he has been considered both a neoclassic artist and a Romantic one. Some have grouped him with Catlin and other artist-explorers of the West, which has some justification. For a few writers he was the end of a tradition of natural-history illustrators that began with Mark Catesby (c. 1679–1749), while for others he represents an early instance of "the artist as scientist."[52] The fact that Audubon's subjects were mostly living birds and mammals prevented our leading scholars of American still life, such as William H. Gerdts, from considering his work in their studies, though—anomalously—similar pictures by Martin J. Heade (1819–1904) of living hummingbirds shown with various tropical flowers are included in those volumes.

Audubon's life and, especially, the *Birds of America* project, have been the subject of extensively researched, valuable studies in recent years. Alice Ford examined the artist's life and career in depth in a series of articles and books, culminating in her biography of 1988.[53] The New-York Historical Society's 431 watercolors for *The Birds of America* were reproduced in a handsome manner in 1966, with insightful commentaries by Marshall Davidson.[54] Another longtime student of Audubon, Waldemar H. Fries, published in 1973 his extraordinary research on the making of Audubon's great book, with special attention to identifying each of the subscribers and to tracing each set of engravings that was published.[55] Finally, the prints themselves and the species they depict were the subject of Susanne M. Low's useful *Index and Guide* to Audubon's book, published in 1988.[56]

The prints by Lizars and Havell and the long and complicated process through which they came about have been the subject of far more attention than either Audubon's place in the history of American culture or the original watercolors themselves. Scholars of American literature and students of the American wilderness, from Perry Miller to Richard Slotkin, have inexplicably ignored this highly important figure. On the other hand, historians of American art in recent decades have begun to give Audubon his due. Perhaps the most distinguished modern scholar of his work was Edward H. Dwight, whose articles and whose exhibition catalogue of 1965 present a serious reconsideration of Audubon's work.[57] Although Dwight died before writing the book that he was planning on the artist, work on Audubon has been carried on by investigators of certain specialized fields, including the history of American draftsmanship, ornithological illustration, wildlife painting, and floral painting.[58]

Audubon succeeded in ways that surpassed his greatest ambitions. He had hoped to draw the birds of America for a book of great size, beauty, and scientific importance, and this project was wholly realized. But he accomplished much more. His name has become synonymous with love of birds and with preservation of the environment, in ways that would have astonished and pleased him. Equally important, we no longer hold his personal flaws, the fact that he worked mostly on paper, or his subject matter against him. Rather, he is now recognized as one of the most gifted and original artists of his time in America.

NOTES

For their research assistance I am indebted to David Brody, Janet Comey, Vivian Ladd, Harriet Rome Pemstein, Susan C. Ricci, and Katherine Rothkopf at the Museum of Fine Arts, and Wendy Jane Holohan in Nantes.

1. Alice Ford, *John James Audubon* (New York: Abbeville Press, 1988), pp. 13ff. Jeanne Rabine was French, a native of Nantes, and was not of Creole blood as is often said. See also Jacqueline Baudouin-Bodin, *Sur les traces de Jean-Jacques Audubon* (Nantes, France: Imprimerie Chiffolean, 1989).

2. John James Audubon, *Ornithological Biography, or an Account of the Habits of the Birds of the United States of America; Accompanied by Descriptions of the Objects Represented in the Work Entitled* The Birds of America, *and Interspersed with Delineations of American Scenery and Manners*, vol. I (Edinburgh: Adam Black, 1831), p. viii.

3. John James Audubon, "Account of the Method of Drawing Birds," *The Edinburgh Journal of Science*, vol. 8 (1828), pp. 48ff.

4. Audubon, *Ornithological Biography*, vol. I, p. viii.

5. See Musée des Beaux Arts, Nantes, *Le pays nantois en peinture, 1590–1958* (Nantes, Mai, 1958). The Free Academy of Drawing (l'Ecole Publique et Gratuite de Dessin), founded in 1757, taught figurative, architectural, and perspective drawing, ornamentation, and wash drawing. M. Hussard was director from 1787 to 1825. (Information from the Nantes Municipal Archives, courtesy of Wendy Jane Holohan.) See also Henri-Claude Cousseau, *The Museum of Fine Arts, Nantes* (Nantes: Musées et Monuments de France, 1991); Claude Cosneau, "La Collection Cacault ou du Musée-Ecole au Musée des Beaux Arts," *303, La Revue des Pays de la Loire*, VII (1985), pp. 7–31; also Ville de Nantes, Musée Municipale des Beaux Arts, *Catelogue des Peintures, Sculptures, etc.* (Paris: Braun, Clement, 1903).

6. Audubon, "Account of the Method of Drawing Birds," p. 50.

7. Ibid., p. 48.

8. Audubon, *Ornithological Biography*, vol. IV, p. vi.

9. See Hugh Honour, *The New Golden Land: European Images of America from the Discovery to the Present Time* (New York: Pantheon Books, 1975), pp. 51, 131. The philosopher Abbé Raynal agreed with Buffon's theory, especially as it applied to the Native Americans. See also Gilbert Chinard, "Eighteenth Century Theories on America as a Human Habitat," pp. 25–27. Thomas Jefferson energetically and systematically challenged Buffon's theories in his *Notes on the State of Virginia* of 1787 (William Peden, ed., [New York: W. W. Norton & Co., 1972]).

10. Honour, *The New Golden Land*, pp. 119–20.

11. Ibid. p. 222. Honour goes on to say that *Atala* was "printed and reprinted, adapted for the stage, set to music, imitated, parodied, and of course illustrated." As early as 1802, Claude Gautherot, a student of David, exhibited at the Paris Salon a painting of Chactas carrying the dead Atala to her grave.

12. See Christian Bazin, *Chateaubriand en Amérique* (Paris: La Table Ronde, 1969).

13. François-August-René Chateaubriand, *Atala; René*, trans. by Irving Putter (Berkeley: University of California Press, 1952), p. 19.

14. Audubon, *Ornithological Biography*, vol. I, p. 138.

15. Ibid., p. x.

16. See Edward H. Dwight, "Audubon in Kentucky," *Antiques* (April 1974), p. 850ff.

17. Benjamin Powers, "Drawing," *Cincinnati Inquisitor Advertiser*, about March 1, 1820, as quoted in Edward H. Dwight, "Old and Modern Drawings:

The Metamorphosis of John James Audubon," *The Art Quarterly*, vol. 26, no. 4 (1963), p. 465.

18. Letter, J. J. Audubon to Henry Clay, Speaker of the House of Representatives, August 12, 1820, as quoted in Dwight, ibid., p. 479.

19. Howard Corning, ed., *Journal of John James Audubon, Made During His Trip to New Orleans in 1820–21* (Boston: The Club of Odd Volumes, 1929), p. 3.

20. John James Audubon, "A Racoon Hunt in Kentucky," in *Ornithological Biography*, vol. III, pp. 235–36.

21. Audubon, *New Orleans Journal*, pp. 80–81.

22. Ibid., pp. 31, 39.

23. Ibid., p. 113.

24. Ibid., p. 112.

25. Letter, J. J. Audubon to Lucy Audubon, May 24, 1821, as quoted in Ford, *John James Audubon*, p. 126.

26. Audubon, "The Bay of Fundy," *Ornithological Biography*, vol. II, p. 487.

27. Audubon, "The Hurricane," ibid., vol. I, p. 262.

28. Ibid., vol. I, p. 61.

29. Letter, J. J. Audubon to Lucy Audubon, May 23, 1821, as quoted in Irving T. Richards, "Audubon, Joseph R. Mason and John Neal," *American Literature*, vol. 6 (1934), p. 122.

30. Marshall B. Tymn, *Thomas Cole's Poetry* (York, Penn.: Shumway, 1972), pp. 111–12.

31. Audubon, "Deer Hunting," *Ornithological Biography*, vol. I, p. 335; "The Eggers of Labrador," vol. III, p. 85.

32. Audubon, "The Ohio," ibid., vol. I, pp. 31–32.

33. Audubon, "A Racoon Hunt in Kentucky," ibid., vol. III, p. 235.

34. Audubon, "The Prairie," ibid., vol. I, p. 81.

35. Richard Slotkin, *Regeneration Through Violence: The Mythology of the American Frontier, 1600–1860* (Middletown, Conn.: Wesleyan University Press, 1973), p. 21.

36. Audubon, "Colonel Boon," *Ornithological Biography*, vol. I, p. 503.

37. Audubon, "The Great Pine Swamp," ibid., vol. I, p. 54.

38. Audubon, "Introductory Address," ibid., vol. I, p. xvi.

39. Ibid., vol. II, p. 102.

40. Ibid., vol. II, p. 448.

41. Audubon, *New Orleans Journal*, p. 141.

42. Audubon, *Ornithological Biography*, vol. III, pp. 82–85.

43. See Annie Roulhac Coffin, "Maria Martin (1796–1863)," *The Art Quarterly* (Autumn 1960), pp. 281–99; also Coffin, "Audubon's Friend—Maria Martin," *The New-York Historical Society Quarterly*, vol. XLIX, no. 1 (Jan. 1965), pp. 29–51.

44. Audubon, *Ornithological Biography*, vol. II, p. 483.

45. Ibid., vol. IV, p. 364.

46. William Swainson, "Some Account of the Work now Publishing by M. Audubon Entitled The Birds of America," *Loudon's Magazine of Natural History*, vol. I (1828–29), pp. 43–52.

47. "Report of a Committee Appointed by the Lyceum of Natural History in New York to Examine the Splendid Work of Mr. Audubon upon the Birds of America," *The American Journal of Science and Arts*, vol. 16 (1829), pp. 353–54.

48. William Dunlap, *History of the Rise and Progress of the Arts of Design in the United States* (New York: Dover Publications, 1969), vol. II, p. 402. Dunlap in his *Diary* (New York: Benjamin Blom, 1969), p. 706, writes: "Lawson says that Audubon is a liar impostor."

49. Allan Nevins, ed., *The Diary of Philip Hone, 1828–51*, vol. I, (New York: Dodd, Mead & Co., 1927), p. 91.

50. It should be noted, however, that during this period specialized publications on Audubon continued to appear, including Maria R. Audubon, *Audubon and His Journals* (New York: Scribner's Sons, 1897); Francis H. Herrick, *Audubon the Naturalist: A History of His Life and Time* (New York: D. Appleton & Co., 1917); Howard Corning, *New Orleans Journal* (Boston: Club of Odd Volumes, 1929); Howard Corning, ed., *Letters of John James Audubon, 1826–1840* (Boston: Club of Odd Volumes, 1930), among others.

51. E. P. Richardson, *Painting in America* (New York: Thomas Y. Crowell, 1956), pp. 159, 160. Note also that Perry T. Rathbone included significant consideration of Audubon as a frontier artist in *Westward the Way* (St. Louis: City Art Museum of St. Louis, 1954).

52. See, for example, John Wilmerding, *American Art* (New York: Penguin Books, 1976), pp. 123–25.

53. See Alice Ford, *John James Audubon* (Norman: University of Oklahoma Press, 1964; expanded second edition, New York: Abbeville Press, 1988).

54. *The Original Water-color Drawings by John James Audubon for "The Birds of America,"* introduction by Marshall B. Davidson (New York: American Heritage Publishing Co., 1966).

55. Waldemar H. Fries, *The Double Elephant Folio: The Story of Audubon's "Birds of America"* (Chicago: American Library Assoc., 1973).

56. Susanne M. Low, *An Index and Guide to Audubon's* Birds of America (New York: Abbeville Press, 1988).

57. For Dwight's articles, see notes 16, 17, 18. See also Edward H. Dwight, *Audubon Watercolors and Drawings* (Utica, N.Y.: Munson-Williams-Proctor Institute, and New York, N.Y.: Pierpont Morgan Library, 1965).

58. See, for example, Martina R. Norelli, *American Wildlife Painting* (New York: Watson-Guptill Publications, 1975); Theodore E. Stebbins, Jr., *American Master Drawings and Watercolors: A History of Works on Paper From Colonial Times to the Present* (New York: Harper & Row, 1976).

The Artist as Entrepreneur

ANNETTE BLAUGRUND

It is not the naturalist that I wish to please altogether I assure thee[,]
it is the wealthy part of the community[;] the first can only speak well
or ill of me but the latter will fill my pockets.[1]

John James Audubon (fig. 22), as revealed by his own words, was an entrepreneur as well as an artist and naturalist, and the abiding interest in his life and work is both esthetic and economic. Modern collectors, like those in Audubon's day, are still willing to pay substantial amounts of money to obtain his life-size etched and hand-colored images of birds, and periodicals continually feature articles about the value and popularity of *The Birds of America.*

Audubon would likely be astonished by the many mass-produced items that bear his name or replicate his pictures. Generations of Americans recognize him as an artist and naturalist—an early-nineteenth-century romantic figure who continues to inspire countless books and articles. Yet for many years before beginning the *Birds of America* project he struggled with business projects that repeatedly failed. His enduring fame rests as much on the success of his Herculean struggle to produce, publish, and market *The Birds of America* as on his exceptional artistic and ornithological legacy. Energetic, engaging, ingenuous, irritating, and persistent, this complex genius eventually achieved his goal through hard work and perseverance, despite many difficulties. Ultimately Audubon's extraordinary talent combined with his singleness of purpose and compulsive dedication served him well.

The dramatic change from an inept businessman to a highly motivated artist and entrepreneur and the context of Audubon's commercial activities are the focus of this essay. Born illegitimate, he apparently felt shame and as a result drove himself not only to succeed at all costs but also to self-promotion and manipulation of his autobiography. "The cloud that still hangs over my birth requires silence," he confided to his journal in 1828.[2] To hide the truth he created a grandiose past for himself, one that connected him with French royalty and with the renowned French artist Jacques-Louis David.[3] His granddaughter Maria continued this tradition of misrepresentation by bowdlerizing his journals before publishing them in 1897. More than two hundred years after his birth, scholars—academic and amateur alike—still search for the real Audubon.

EARLY ENTERPRISES

From the time of his arrival in the United States in 1803 until 1820, when he began to devote himself solely to artistic and ornithological activities, Audubon embarked on various business ventures, none of which succeeded. His difficulties resulted in part from inexperience and naïveté as well as from the fact that his mind was on other things, but circumstances beyond his control—embargoes, war, naval blockades, national economic policies, and bank failures—were also contributing factors.

Audubon's first business assignment was to manage his father's modest estate, Mill Grove, outside Philadelphia, where he had been sent by his father in 1803 to avoid conscription into Napoleon's army. In America Audubon lived the life of a country gentleman, drawing birds for his own enjoyment, a favorite pastime since childhood. Although he began to act like a frontiersman, he had been educated as a gentleman in France and could play the violin, dance, fence, and draw. He visited his family in France in 1805 and returned to the United States the following year with a business partner, Ferdinand Rozier. The two mismanaged the Audubon landholdings, and the property was sold by 1807. During that time the partners apprenticed in an importing firm, and they decided to open a retail store and import business in booming Louisville, Kentucky (fig. 23). With his business established, Audubon married Lucy Bakewell in 1808. Unfortunately, the Embargo Act, passed by Congress in 1807 in reaction to the Napoleonic Wars, cut off overseas trade, curtailing Audubon's business.

In 1810 Audubon moved to Henderson, Kentucky. With

Fig. 22. John Woodhouse Audubon (1812–62). *Portrait of John James Audubon*, c. 1840. Oil on canvas, 44¼ × 33 inches. The New-York Historical Society.

Rozier, he set up a trading business in Sainte Geneviève, Missouri, a village not far from St. Louis. Again, the Embargo Act, coupled with the excessive amount of time Audubon spent hunting and drawing birds, eventually led to the demise of the business and ultimately of the partnership. While the French-speaking population of Sainte Geneviève attracted Rozier, Audubon preferred Henderson and reopened his general store there. In Henderson he was successful for a while; he bought land and built a house.

Soon after, he and his brother-in-law Thomas Bakewell established a firm in New Orleans, becoming middlemen in the trade of pork, lard, and flour. Within a year, that venture became a casualty of the War of 1812, when the British blockaded New Orleans and other ports. Undaunted, Audubon set up another business partnership with Bakewell in 1813. They built and operated a steam-powered mill to grind grain and saw wood in Henderson. By 1816 the partnership had dissolved, but Audubon remained in business.

Eventually, the continual progression of enterprises and financial setbacks caused Audubon's fiscal affairs to deteriorate to such a degree that he was remanded to debtors' prison in

1819. He and Lucy had to sell most of their possessions, and he declared bankruptcy in order to be released. Stripped of his assets, Audubon went through a period of depression from which he recovered with a new resolve: "Without any Money My Talents are to be My Support and My enthusiasm my Guide in My Dificulties [sic], the whole of which I am ready to exert to [meet] keep, and to surmount."[4]

Turning to his art Audubon, at the age of thirty-four, with a wife and two children to support, scraped together a meager income by drawing profile portraits in chalk. By the end of 1820, he was charging five dollars for a portrait. Encouraged by Dr. Daniel Drake, secretary of the Board of Managers of the Western Museum, the family moved to Cincinnati, where Audubon worked part-time as a taxidermist and painter of backgrounds for the newly opened museum. He opened a drawing school, which attracted about twenty-five pupils.[5] While living in Cincinnati, he apparently made the decision to transform his avocation into his vocation: the creation and publication of a work that would include life-size illustrations of all the birds of America in their natural habitat.

Returning to New Orleans, Audubon dedicated himself to the project, and his bird drawings took on a new seriousness. He introduced himself to other artists working in New Orleans, from whom he solicited both work and advice. In order to improve his skills, he took lessons in oil painting, and although he never brought his technique in that medium up to the level of that of his watercolors, he eventually was able to paint well enough to sell his oil paintings.

Audubon continued to support himself by portraiture and teaching, charging up to twenty-five dollars for a portrait (see fig. 12). For several months he tutored the daughter of a plantation owner and received a steady income of sixty dollars a month, plus lodging. These earnings freed him to concentrate on gathering more material for his bird project. When the tutoring job ended, his financial situation deteriorated. He resorted to painting signs and steamship murals and teaching drawing, fencing, and dancing—anything to bring in some money. Lucy Audubon also worked—as a governess and teacher—to augment their income. As a result, the poor and peripatetic Audubon family was frequently separated until the completion of *The Birds of America*.

GENESIS OF AN IDEA

Most certainly Audubon was influenced by the ornithological publications of the comte de Buffon (Georges Louis LeClerc, 1707–88) and Alexander Wilson (1766–1813) in his decision to publish a comprehensive illustrated book of North American birds. His great project utilized his innate artistic talent for depicting birds and also reinforced his obsession with these feathered creatures. In March 1810 Audubon and Alexander Wilson met in Louisville, Kentucky; Audubon was working in a store there, and Wilson came in to sell subscriptions for his *American Ornithology* (1808–14), the most complete illustrated survey of American birds yet attempted. During that meeting Audubon displayed his drawings and told Wilson that he had not "the least idea of presenting the fruits of my labour to the world."[6] Nevertheless, the encounter planted the seed of the idea of publishing his own drawings, which his friends claimed were better than Wilson's. According to his journal, it was not until 1824, when he met the twenty-one-year-old naturalist Charles Lucien Bonaparte, Napoleon's nephew and prince of Canino and Musignano, in Philadelphia, that Audubon says the idea took form. But given the compulsivity with which Audubon pursued his interest in drawing and identifying birds, as evidenced by statements in his journal, it is likely that he had decided at least by 1820, at the age of thirty-five, to pursue his passion.

SEARCH FOR AN ENGRAVER

The first step was to find an engraver, and this quest drew Audubon in 1824 to Philadelphia, where he arrived with a portfolio full of drawings. In the late eighteenth and early nineteenth century, Philadelphia was the intellectual and scientific hub of the United States as well as the center of publishing activity. Several English engravers had settled there and were practicing their art, bringing it up to a standard comparable to that found in Britain. But Audubon did not succeed in his mission. Like many insecure people, he was full of bravado, claiming that his drawings were superior to those of others, particularly Wilson's. This was an unfortunate tactic considering that many of the people he approached were friends of Wilson's. Others, like the artist Titian Peale—who was working on Charles Bonaparte's four-volume *American Ornithology: of the Natural History of Birds Inhabiting the United States, Not Given by Wilson* (1825–33)—feared competition. The painter and editor George Ord, who completed Wilson's work with a ninth posthumous volume, and Alexander Lawson, engraver of the seventy-six plates in Wilson's books, set other engravers and publishers against Audubon, having a vested interest in denigrating him.[7] It was not only the competition that defeated Audubon in Philadelphia, and in New York as well, but his own larger-than-life personality. He was regarded as a tactless and abrasive backwoodsman, and his long hair and unfashionable clothes were thought inappropriate.

Despite the negative reception, Audubon managed to publish several natural history papers while in Philadelphia in order to begin establishing scientific credentials. In the process he gained recognition. In fact, he had several admirers. Charles Bonaparte, who was then updating Wilson's book, the painter Thomas Sully, and the artist-naturalist Charles Alexandre Lesueur all tried to help Audubon find engravers, but there were

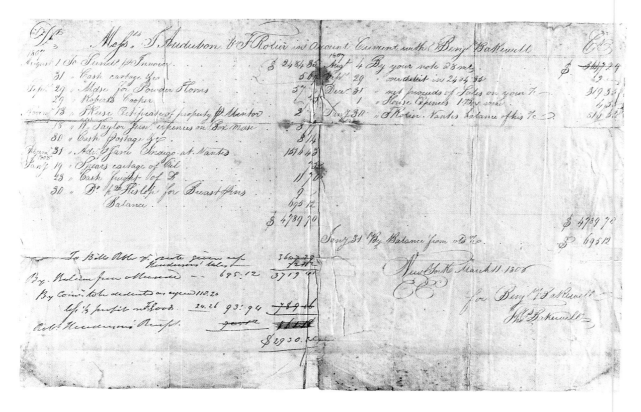

Fig. 23. John J. Audubon and Ferdinand Rozier Expense Account. August 1807–January 1808. The New-York Historical Society.

few engravers in either Philadelphia or New York equipped to handle so large a project. Gideon Fairman, an American engraver who had just returned from England, advised Audubon to seek an engraver there. His admirers recognized that in contrast to other scientists, whose knowledge was often gained exclusively by studying bird skins, Audubon depicted birds with great accuracy, a talent facilitated by his amazing powers of observation. Yet, despite the preeminence of Audubon's ornithological illustrations, his supporters could do little more than recommend that he go abroad. Henry T. Tuckerman, one of America's first art historians, made the point in his 1867 book that "a characteristic fact in the brief history of American art is, that among its earliest products which attracted notice abroad, were illustrations of natural history."[8]

Armed with letters of recommendation and introduction, Audubon arrived in Liverpool on July 21, 1826. Like the American artist Benjamin West (1738–1820) in the 1760s, Audubon was considered a novelty and the egocentric behavior that worked against him in Philadelphia brought him success in England. Eleven days after his arrival in Liverpool, his drawings were exhibited to great acclaim. Based on the advice of English friends and his own knowledge of other illustrated scientific books, Audubon developed a plan to have his work engraved and published.

SERIAL PRINTMAKING

Seriality had been a basic practice since the beginning of printmaking in the fifteenth century. During the eighteenth century the production of serial prints was firmly established and was commonly financed in all subjects—fine art as well as natural history—by subscribers. The eighteenth-century English artist William Hogarth (1697–1764) financed many of his works by subscription. His popularly priced prints after his own paintings reached audiences that could not afford oil paintings, and this practice augmented his income. (In order to stop piracies he persuaded Parliament to enact the first copyright for engravers by 1735 as protection against unauthorized copies.) Subscription financing continued in the nineteenth century despite the fact that some publishing houses began to pay for production and distribution.[9]

A prototype for Audubon's work was the comte de Buffon's comprehensive *Histoire naturelle, générale et particulière*, published in forty-four quarto volumes (1749–1804) and prized for its beautiful illustrations. A number of the bird illustrations that Audubon had produced on his visit to Nantes in 1805 made use of these ornithological illustrations for identification as Audubon noted in his handwritten captions (see fig. 3).[10] But this publication served as a visual model rather than a methodological source.

Audubon was also probably influenced by such pioneering works of scientific illustration as *The Natural History of Carolina, Florida, and the Bahama Islands*, (1731–43), two volumes published by the English naturalist Mark Catesby (1682–1749).[11] Until Wilson's and Audubon's work appeared, Catesby's publication, which contained 220 etchings, had been the best treatment of the flora and fauna of North America. Like Audubon, Catesby had had difficulty procuring funding. In order to produce his book as inexpensively as possible he did his own engraving and most of the coloring of the first volume. It took Catesby approximately twenty years to complete two volumes, issued in eleven installments of twenty plates each, which sold at two guineas (2 pounds, 2 shillings) for each part.[12]

One of the earliest serial publications in this country was a collection of mezzotint prints of various leaders of the War of Independence produced in 1787 by Charles Willson Peale (1741–1827), artist, naturalist, and scientist. The prints, based on Peale's oil paintings, were sold by subscription and were intended to ensure a steady income to supplement the artist's oil painting. In a letter of February 2, 1787, the artist wrote: "My first intention was to have taken subscriptions for a Doz prints which I had selected out of the whole collection of Heads, but on second thought I have judged it best to propose only one at a time which I expect I shall be able to deliver in 6 weeks after I begin work. . . . By this business of Prints I hope I shall get something in return for my great Expense of time and labour in making my Collection of Portraits."[13] Although Audubon may not have been aware of Peale's print series, he surely knew of and visited Peale's Museum in Philadelphia, the first in America, which contained in addition to works of art more than a thousand stuffed birds, often displayed with backdrops showing their natural habitats.[14]

While Audubon did not model his production and marketing techniques directly after those used by Alexander Wilson, they were comparable. Wilson contracted the firm of Bradford and Inskeep of Philadelphia to manage the printing and the payment of employees, while he himself was responsible for obtaining the subscription orders and payments and for supervising the engraver, Alexander Lawson. Half of the money raised was used to cover production expenses, and any profit was split between the firm and the artist. Each of his proposed ten volumes, bound in half-morocco, was priced at twelve dollars; the total came to one hundred and twenty dollars. Wilson sent out more than 2,500 prospectuses and advertised in the cities he visited, but his greatest success came through personal contacts.[15] Working with Peale, whom he had met in 1802, Wilson succeeded in Philadelphia because, unlike Audubon, who later failed there, he became part of the establishment.[16] It was Peale, in fact, who had converted Wilson from botany to ornithology and many of his specimens came from the stuffed birds and animals in Peale's Museum. Yet Wilson never achieved financial success because of the high fees charged by the publishing firm and his agents.[17]

Another pioneering print series was *Picturesque Views of American Scenery* (1819–21) by Joshua Shaw (1776/7–1860), a contemporary of Audubon. This series, engraved by John Hill (1770–1850), introduced American audiences to the coloristic possibilities of aquatint engraving. Although never completed because of a lack of audience and Shaw's inability to cover expenses, the unfinished *Picturesque Views* was reprinted in 1835. By that time the market had improved due to economic expansion and a growing leisure class, which created a demand for images of American scenery.

In 1821 the engraver John Hill was called upon again, this time to participate in the publication of the largest colored landscape prints (14 × 21 inches) to be engraved in the United States at that time: *Hudson River Portfolio* (1820–25), by the young Irish artist William Guy Wall (1792–after 1864). The project consisted of twenty-four hand-colored aquatints issued in six numbers of four views, each number to sell for sixteen dollars, an increase in price over Shaw's *Picturesque Views*.[18] Hill was responsible for engraving, printing, and coloring. Twenty of the twenty-four plates were issued over a twelve-year period, and the number of impressions per plate varied.[19] Despite the fact that the *Hudson River Portfolio* was never completed, Hill profited from these projects, as did the artists and the publishers.

Long-term print projects were frequently never completed. They tended to be excessively expensive and sometimes met with public indifference; moreover, publishing firms often failed or merged. As a result, the artist had to take an active role in financing and promoting a publication, but the work often paid off: during the first half of the nineteenth century many artists expanded both their reputations and their incomes by having their paintings reproduced as prints.

In 1826, the year Audubon left for England in search of an engraver, Wall's much-admired *Hudson River Portfolio* was advertised on August 12 and 14 in the *New-York Daily Advertiser* as a prize for a lottery.[20] It was reissued in 1828 and 1834, testimony to its persistent popularity. In contrast to Audubon, who was not recognized in America until he achieved success abroad, artists like Wall, many of them immigrants from England, found both publishers and patrons in New York and Philadelphia.

Without wealthy patrons or direct government backing to underwrite their projects, artists, writers, and scientists were forced to search for subscribers. The most effective support was endorsement by well-known public figures, especially kings and queens. European royalty and American entrepreneurs alike subscribed to *The Birds of America*, but no government or private subsidy for the entire project was ever obtained. Audubon, like his predecessors and contemporaries, followed the conventional methods of publication, looking to private institutions as well as rich clients to buy individual sets of his book.

MARKETING *THE BIRDS OF AMERICA*

In accordance with contemporary custom, Audubon's marketing plans made use of the following techniques: letters of introduction, exploitation of personal contacts, membership in scientific and social organizations, publication in scientific journals, exhibitions, celebrity endorsements through word of mouth and subscription lists, and newspaper and magazine reviews. Audubon's singular marketing tool, however, was his flamboyant public image which he used to great advantage.

While Americans regarded Audubon's long flowing hair preened with bear grease, his provincial pantaloons, and his foreign-looking black frock coat,—which he alternated with animal hide—as gauche, the English were charmed and fascinated by his frontier apparel and crusty manners. However, when it served him, he would change his appearance from that of an explorer to that of a publisher. In 1827, the Countess of Morton advised him that he could increase his sales if he cut his hair and replaced his wolfskin coat with an English greatcoat. Even though he had ignored previous requests, Audubon followed her suggestion.[21]

The Franco-American woodsman satisfied the English curiosity about the New World with his stories about discovering and observing birds in the American wilderness. He embodied the image of Natty Bumppo, the noble frontiersman who appeared in James Fenimore Cooper's 1823 novel *The Pioneers*, three years before Audubon's arrival in England, playing up the romantic notions that many Europeans held about the American

Fig. 24. Robert Havell Jr. (1793–1878), after John James Audubon. *Bald Eagle* (Havell XXXI). Hand-colored etching and aquatint; 25 × 37½ inches. The New-York Historical Society.

wilderness. For only among the wealthy and cultured circles of Great Britain and Europe could this impoverished artist hope to find the number of subscribers necessary for him to succeed.

Letters of introduction from friends and acquaintances were Audubon's greatest resource. Probably the most valuable was the one to Richard Rathbone, Esquire, of Liverpool given to him by Vincent Nolte, a New Orleans merchant whom he had met in 1811. Rathbone, a man of wealth and influence, and his family, became Audubon's steadfast benefactors and champions, introducing him to other Liverpool families, who both bought and publicized his work. They enabled him to meet many other influential people: scientists, patrons of the arts, and printers—all of whom agreed, after seeing Audubon's drawings, that the work should be reproduced full-size by a master engraver (fig. 24). They also presented him to future subscribers such as Lord Stanley, the fourteenth earl of Derby, and William Roscoe, the eminent historian and botanist. Audubon also received help from his brother-in-law Alexander Gordon, husband of Lucy's sister Anne. Gordon was initially unwelcoming because of family gossip about Audubon's many unsuccessful ventures, but before long he was won over by the artist's affability and began to advise him on business matters.

Audubon also carried letters from Henry Clay, DeWitt Clinton, and Andrew Jackson. Clay's letter dated July 16, 1832, explained: "The Messrs Audubon, father and son, are engaged in the preparation and publication of a work on The Birds of the U. States. . . . The resources of no private individual are competent to the completion of such a work without public aid. These gentlemen need the patronage of the community, from their character, diligence, and the manner in which they have so far executed their design—they want especially the countenance of the opulent, on account of the particularly heavy expense of the work."[22] Clay then went on to recommend Audubon to "all good men wherever they may go." Not surprisingly, Audubon made it a point to obtain letters of introduction wherever he went.

Important personal contacts were often the result of these letters. In England, people like the Rathbones were intent on aiding Audubon and helping him devise a business plan. Rathbone also introduced Audubon to the well-known author Dr. Stewart Traill, coeditor of the *Encyclopaedia Britannica,* and to Henry J. Bohn, London's leading bookseller and a naturalist. Consequently, Audubon's reputation spread, and opportunities for exhibitions and sales proliferated, although ultimately, it was his flamboyant personality and abiding dedication to his project that made him a successful and persuasive salesman.

Exhibitions were an important form of advertising, and, happily, just eleven days after Audubon's arrival in England, William Roscoe arranged to exhibit his drawings at the Liverpool Royal Institution.[23] Audubon, who had arrived with several hundred drawings, exhibited 225 of them. In a letter of August 7, 1826, to his brother-in-law Nicholas Berthoud,

Audubon described the crowds who attended the first three days of the exhibition. The exhibition opened on July 31, 1826, and on the following day 413 people came to see his work. It ran for four weeks without any expense to Audubon, and the admission fees earned him one hundred pounds.[24] This was the first of many exhibitions that introduced audiences to his work. Later he would exhibit completed prints as well as his original paintings as a way of obtaining subscriptions.

Audubon also displayed his work at his lodgings. In Newcastle-upon-Tyne he had so many visitors that he became "tired out holding up drawings . . . all day," but he was "rewarded by an addition of five subscribers."[25] In Edinburgh in 1826, he exhibited his work at Christmastime, and then in London in 1827 at the Linnaean Society, where for the first time he showed a group of prints.[26] Audubon continued to exhibit his work both privately and publicly, whenever the opportunity arose. In Paris, in 1828, Baron Cuvier, one of the greatest naturalists and authors of the period, who also served as zoologist for the duke of Orleans's Museum of Natural History, arranged for him to show the prints at the Royal Academy of Sciences.

Exhibiting the original watercolors remained an important part of Audubon's marketing. On May 28, 1830, he wrote that he had been advised "to exhibit my New Drawings here Next Week when much of the nobility and Gentry it is expected will crowd Manchester. It affords me the opportunity of procuring a few names and of perhaps recalling those who have abandoned the Work."[27] Audubon did indeed capture one new subscriber, and he reclaimed three who had dropped their subscriptions. During his 1831 trip to the United States he continued to exhibit. In the spring of that year he showed some of the prints at the Boston Athenaeum as a way of introducing Bostonians to his work.

Newspapers and magazines provided publicity by carrying advertisements (fig. 25) and by reviewing his exhibitions, for the most part favorably. *The New-York Mirror* on April 20, 1833, for example, praised Audubon in the following manner:

This distinguished ornithologist has been the object of a general interest among the most intelligent classes of

society, during his visit to this city. His pictures of the different kinds of wild-fowl are greatly admired. They are full of spirit and animation, and seem startling with the sudden alarms and impulses of actual life. Mr. Audubon well merits the respectful attention which every where welcomes his approach, for his eager devotion to the branch of natural history which he had so ably and beautifully illustrated. His exhibitions of paintings have been thronged with beauty and fashion, and we learn that in the extension of his subscription list he has received several tokens of regard. Every public institution should possess itself of his costly and superb work, with a view to testify their interest in the subject of ornithology, and their admiration of the art, as well as their admiration of the man.[28]

If Mr. Audubon had composed this encomium himself, he could not have written a better endorsement.

Articles about Audubon and his work were augmented by articles written by him in prestigious journals such as the *Edinburgh Journal of Sciences* and *Blackwood's Magazine*.[29] In France, Baron Cuvier not only helped him exhibit his work but also lauded his drawings in a review presented at the Royal Academy of Sciences. This review was reprinted in *Loudon's Magazine of Natural History* in May 1828, and Audubon included it in all future printings of his prospectus and in his *Ornithological Biography*, the text that accompanied *The Birds of America*. Audubon was his own best public relations agent, providing newspapers with interesting letters and stories about himself. Excerpts from his writings were published serially. His bravery and endurance in search of new species of birds and his progress in producing the prints made good copy. Editors and reporters expanded, dramatized, and glorified the reputation of this appealing, romantic figure.

Scientific organizations also provided contacts, exhibition space, and prospective clients for Audubon. As early as 1826 he was made a member of the Wernerian Society, a learned group from the University of Edinburgh; in 1828 he was elected to the Zoological Society of London and made a Fellow of the Linnaean Society. Many societies in England, France, Canada, and

AUDUBON'S ORIGINAL DRAWINGS—— This beautiful collection of Drawings, representing all the "Birds of North America," is now open for public inspection at the Lyceum of Natural History, No. 563 Broadway. Hours from 9 A. M. till dusk. Admission 25 cents.
oct 1-1w*

Fig. 25. Advertisement. *New-York Commercial Advertiser*, October 8, 1839. The New-York Historical Society.

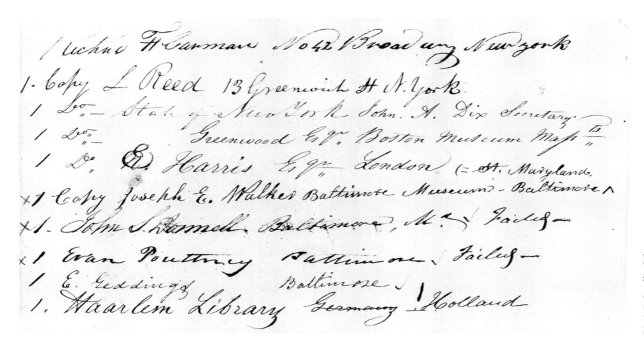

Fig. 26. Page from Audubon's subscription list for *The Birds of America*. The New-York Historical Society, Gift of Samuel P. Reed.

America made Audubon an honorary member.[30] As soon as a society honored him, Audubon added the title to his prospectus as further endorsement.

In addition to institutional endorsements, Audubon collected the names of important and famous people to list in his prospectus. Joshua S. Brookes, American consul in Manchester, England, met Audubon at the exhibition in Manchester in 1826 and suggested that Audubon issue his work serially and finance it by subscription. As early as September 23, 1826, Audubon wrote in his journal, "I have concluded to have a Book of Subscription," indicating that prior to that time he had not yet formulated an exact business plan for his project. William Roscoe sanctioned the subscription plan and convinced Audubon that this was proper operating procedure. Audubon wrote to Charles Lucien Bonaparte, DeWitt Clinton, Henry Clay, General Andrew Jackson, and General William Clark asking them to "honor my list of subscribers with your name."[31]

First and foremost on Audubon's mind was securing the patronage of the English royal family, other members of the nobility, and people of renown. During his visit to London in 1827 he tried to get an audience with George IV, but to no avail. With the help of friends, however, he eventually obtained a subscription from the king and permission to claim royal patronage. The duchess of Clarence, later Queen Adelaide, also subscribed, as did Lord Stanley, then president of the Zoological Society, and Charles Bonaparte. In France, Audubon obtained a subscription from King Charles X of France and the duke of Orleans, later King Louis Philippe. Among Audubon's American subscribers (fig. 26.) were businessmen and art collectors such as Luman Reed of New York and Robert Gilmore of Baltimore, statesmen such as Daniel Webster and Henry Clay, and many major institutions. Although some were endorsers rather than subscribers, and some never completed their subscriptions, the list of dignitaries is as impressive today as it must have been in Audubon's day.

Audubon followed an exhausting schedule. He usually rose before dawn and often traveled great distances to meet new people and visit various cities. In each place he set up exhibitions or showed his work privately to prospective clients he had met through letters of introduction. Much of his time was spent extolling the importance of the project at dinners and at meetings of scientific societies. "The great round of Company I am thrown in has become fatiguing to me in the extreme and does not agree with my early habits. I go to dine out at 6, 7, or 8 o'clock in the evening and it is one or two in the morning when the party breaks up[,] then painting all day with my Correspondence that increases daily[;] my Head is like a Hornets nest and my body wearied beyond calculation—yet it has to be done. I cannot refuse a single invitation."[32] While Audubon complained about dining out frequently, the invitations he received, catapulting him into association with upper-class society and providing prospective subscribers, must have been flattering and, to some degree, enjoyable.

Spare moments were spent recording his adventures in letters to his wife and friends, writing articles, and composing the descriptive text to accompany his engravings. He was, in fact, a prodigious and tireless writer. On November 2, 1828, he wrote to Lucy, "I work I fear rather more now than my constitution will well bear and when I am absent from London I am in a constant state of fear that something wrong should take place."[33] With all that, he found time to produce oil paintings for sale to raise immediate capital for his expenses. "I wish I had eight pairs of hands," he wrote in 1829.[34] Audubon's strenuous routine never abated. Between 1826 and 1838 (with the help of assistants), he produced half of the watercolors, wrote and published the *Ornithological Biography*, crossed the ocean four times, and traveled from the Florida Keys (where in 1832 he painted one of the most popular images, *American Flamingo*, see page x) to Labrador in search of new birds. It is no wonder that on June 2, 1839, he complained to Mrs. Benjamin Phillips, the wife of a friend, "When my labours will all end, God only knows, but it seems, as if as long as I live, I must labour as if at the tread-mill."[35] But personal, if not financial, success was already at hand: Audubon had become famous.

At first Audubon was not only artist and publisher but also salesman and collection agent. He soon found that he had to delegate tasks, and he hired booksellers and agents in various cities to disperse the finished parts and collect payments. This meant that he had to pay commissions of 5 to 10 percent, but he wrote of "having established agents at each place, without whom I could not do without incurring greater expense than the premiums I pay them."[36] His prospectus of May 1828 requested subscribers to apply to him first, then to his engraver, Robert Havell, Jr., and then listed booksellers in Liverpool, Manchester, York, Leeds, Newcastle-upon-Tyne, and London. When possible, Audubon relied on his own family to collect money and sell subscriptions so that he would not have to pay a third party. In this way, unlike Wilson, he controlled his incoming revenue and kept more of it.

One of the first agents that Audubon appointed was Daniel Lizars, the brother of William Home Lizars (1788–1859), his first engraver. In France he appointed M. Pitois of the firm of F. G. Levault. Sometimes Havell was called upon to act on Audubon's behalf.

The expenses Audubon incurred for this project are in some respects immeasurable. His travel expenses and the cost of his forays into the wilderness cannot be adequately assessed, but wherever he went he noted expenditures in detail in his journal and letters. As publisher he had to pay for materials: the paper, the colorists' materials, the copperplates for engraving. He also had to pay the engraver and the colorists. And there were of course the needs of his wife and family. When all was accounted for, his profit was reasonable but not extraordinary.

Audubon also employed various assistants, in addition to his family, to help him meet his continual deadlines: the artists

Joseph R. Mason (1808–42), George Lehman (c. 1800–70), Joseph Bartholomew Kidd (1808–89), and Maria Martin (1796–1863), the taxidermist Henry Ward, and Robert Havell, Jr. (1783–1878), all helped him at one time or another. Havell must be counted as one of Audubon's most important collaborators, for he sometimes completed Audubon's drawings. Some, like George Lehman, who was a professional artist rather than an apprentice like Mason or an amateur like Martin, probably demanded reasonably high compensation, especially since Audubon almost never credited his collaborators.

Audubon's immediate daily expenses were met by copies he made in oil of his drawings as well as by oil paintings of other subjects. While he gave some of these as gifts, he chiefly sold them to picture dealers and to private individuals. In one of Audubon's periods of financial need, the English artist Sir Thomas Lawrence (1769–1830) saved him from destitution by arranging to have friends purchase his paintings for cash. In this way, through careful reckoning of expenses and constant production of paintings, Audubon barely kept ahead of his creditors, the printer being the main one among them. From an 1827 Liverpool exhibition he reported selling "The Otter for twelve Guineas. The ducks for twenty Guineas and The Hawk and Partridge for fifteen Guineas"—goodly sums, totaling about 230 dollars, enough to keep him working.[37]

In 1827, William Lizars, his first engraver, introduced him to a Scottish artist, and Audubon gave the nineteen-year-old three guineas to copy one of his bird paintings. Pleased with Joseph Kidd's work, he then offered Kidd one hundred pounds for copying one hundred works. Such studio copies were commonplace. He hoped to organize a traveling exhibition of these copies, which would not only advertise *The Birds of America* but also provide an added income from admission fees, but Kidd never completed the project.

ENGRAVERS

Through a letter of introduction, in 1826 Audubon had met the printer and zoologist Patrick Neill, who recommended William Home Lizars as the best engraver in Edinburgh. Although Lizars was occupied with *The Birds of England* by Prideaux John Selby (1788–1867) and an edition of Wilson's *American Ornithology*, he was so impressed by Audubon's work that he decided to take it on. He and Audubon reached an agreement by mid-November, and Audubon wrote soon after: "It is now a month since my work was begun by Mr. Lizars; the paper is of unusual size, called 'double elephant' and the plates are to be finished in such superb style as to eclipse all of the same kind in existence. The price of each number, which will contain five prints, is to be two guineas, and all individuals have the privilege of subscribing for the whole, or any portion of it."[38]

Lizars schooled Audubon in the careful management of production and finances and convinced him that they could balance the expenses and risks by producing only fifty copies of the first number and the rest on demand. Payment on delivery gave Audubon the money to finance the succeeding portions. At two guineas per number Audubon's expenses for the etching and aquatinting of the copperplates, paper, printing, and coloring were paid, and he figured a profit of forty-two pounds, nine shillings, and four pence sterling for the hundred. After the publication of the first one hundred copies the cost of the plates would have been amortized, and he would have only the expense of the paper, printing, and colorists.[39]

Audubon had hoped to issue an edition of five hundred but probably completed fewer than two hundred full sets of prints. The exact number is not known, for many early numbers were issued for subscriptions that were never completed. Only ten

plates were completed in Lizars's shop because of a strike by his colorists. Audubon wrote in his journal on June 18, 1827, "This was quite a shock to my nerves."[40] Not only was Lizars unable to continue but Audubon found that the prints he had completed were not delivered on time.

Eventually Audubon changed from the Edinburgh engraver to one in London. Initially, he arranged for Robert Havell, the new engraver, simply to color Lizars's prints, but he soon decided to have the entire process transferred to the London shop. It was not only more expedient but better and cheaper to have the work done there. His profit increased because the paper, which was made in London, did not have to be shipped. More important, Havell charged less than Lizars. At two guineas each, one hundred sets of the first five numbers (twenty-five plates) that actually cost 114 pounds, 16 shillings to produce, brought 210 pounds, yielding a profit of nearly 106 pounds, the equivalent of 530 dollars. The price to the buyer included the cost of the copperplates, the engraving and lettering, the paper and printing, the coloring and the tin cases in which the prints were shipped.[41]

Fig. 27. Robert Havell, Jr. (1793–1878), after John James Audubon. *Burrowing Owl, Little Owl, Northern Pygmy Owl, and Short-eared Owl* (Havell CCCCXXXII). Detail of steel-plated engraved copperplate; 22⅛ × 26½ in. The New-York Historical Society.

The terms Havell offered Audubon, slightly under 115 pounds for five numbers of five plates each, were one-quarter lower than what Lizars had asked. Havell's work was also far superior to that of Lizars. Audubon wrote: "Mr. Lizars himself is struck with the superior beauty of the work done in London, as much as with the cheapness of it. He promised to me that if I would give him a small part of the work to execute, that he would do it at the same price, and on the same style as my London Engraver."[42]

When he and Audubon met, the senior Havell was fifty-eight years old—too old for a long-term project—and he deferred to his son, Robert Junior, who was an artist as well as an engraver. Nevertheless, the elder Havell supervised the printing and coloring of a number of Audubon's watercolors before his death in 1832. Audubon, who was then forty-two, and young Havell, then thirty-four, became lifelong friends.[43]

Audubon monitored the engraving and supervised the coloring, spending a good deal of time in Havell's shop, especially at the beginning. A project of this complexity and magnitude required special skill and artistry, and Havell combined the techniques of etching, aquatint, and line engraving to produce the effects Audubon required (fig. 27). Etching is one of several intaglio printmaking processes, in which the image is either cut or bitten by acid into a metal plate. A needle is used to scratch the image through an acid-resistant ground applied to a plate. The aquatint process consists of treating a copperplate with a porous resin ground that is then heated, cooled, and etched. It achieves a distribution and range of tones where the acid has bitten between the resin grains. Where the acid bites briefly, it prints lightly, while a deeper bite catches more ink and prints a darker tone. Aquatint produces an approximation of the continuous tone of watercolor washes. Havell probably used engraving, a process that entails incising lines with a graver or burin into an untreated plate, for certain effects not attainable by etching.[44] Audubon was pleased with the quality of work but was not always satisfied with the color, especially when it was done under the supervision of the elder Havell. As a result, he constantly monitored the coloring (which was done by hand by as many as fifty people) for consistency and accuracy.

As for the business side of their relationship, Havell not only delivered his work more punctually than his predecessor, Lizars, but often handled billing, shipping, and other matters for Audubon. Havell proudly listed *The Birds of America* as one of his ongoing projects on his letterhead. And as the work progressed, Audubon relied more and more on the engraver's discretion in matters of color and even of composition. Nevertheless, throughout the production, either Audubon or one of his sons, if Audubon himself was busy, would maintain constant supervision.

THE PROSPECTUS

Shortly after arriving in England in 1826, Audubon contemplated the preparation of a prospectus outlining the rationale for his work. Rathbone, Roscoe, and Bohn all recommended publishing one as soon as he had worked out the details of production, and after contracting with Lizars for the publication of the first number of five plates, Audubon issued his first prospectus in March 1827. The prospectus (fig. 28) was frequently revised over the years to include the latest favorable reviews and the names of new subscribers.[45] In this way, it served to advertise and endorse the project as well as to provide sales and publication information.

According to the first prospectus, Audubon initially planned to publish four hundred life-size images of the birds of North America. Differences in plumage between males and females and young and adult birds, the food they commonly ate, and their natural habitats were to be depicted. The images were to be engraved in aquatint on sheets of paper measuring 29½ × 39½ inches, "the paper being of the finest quality."[46] These double elephant folio sheets, the largest available at that time, were chosen to accommodate the biggest birds.

THE BIRDS OF AMERICA

At first there were to be eighty numbers, each containing five prints—one of a large bird, one of a medium-sized bird, and three of small birds—all printed on paper of the same size. The small birds were to be centered on the sheet, with wide margins around them; the large birds were to fill almost the entire page. Because of ongoing discoveries of new species, Audubon added seven numbers at the end, making a total of eighty-seven numbers containing 435 plates; he wanted to add still others, but most subscribers, particularly during the 1837 depression, were not interested in increasing the size of the sets and thereby incurring greater expense. Instead, Audubon made several composite arrangements in the last volume, with many birds on one page. This was one time when Audubon, who rarely seemed to compromise his standards because of cost or complexity, did yield to market limitations.

Five numbers were to be published annually at a cost of two guineas (about ten dollars) each; each number consisted of five

UNDER THE SPECIAL PATRONAGE

OF

Her Most Excellent Majesty,

QUEEN ADELAIDE.

THE

BIRDS OF AMERICA,

ENGRAVED FROM

DRAWINGS

MADE IN

THE UNITED STATES AND THEIR TERRITORIES.

BY JOHN JAMES AUDUBON,

F. R. SS. L & E.

FELLOW OF THE LINNEAN AND ZOOLOGICAL SOCIETIES OF LONDON; MEMBER OF THE LYCEUM OF NEW YORK, THE NATURAL HISTORY SOCIETY OF PARIS, THE WERNERIAN NATURAL HISTORY SOCIETY OF EDINBURGH; HONORARY MEMBER OF THE SCOTTISH ACADEMY OF PAINTING, SCULPTURE AND ARCHITECTURE, &c.

PUBLISHED BY THE AUTHOR;

AND TO BE SEEN AT

MR R. HAVELL'S JUN. THE ENGRAVER,

77. OXFORD STREET, LONDON.

MDCCCXXXI.

Fig. 28. Prospectus for *The Birds of America,* 1831. The New-York Historical Society.

plates. The numbers were delivered in tin cases, but subscribers were advised to purchase portfolios or to have the volumes bound for an extra charge. Subscribers were to pay in installments, upon the delivery of each number. When completed, in 1838, a full set sold for one thousand dollars in the United States, more if it was bound into four volumes. The first three volumes comprised one hundred prints each, and the last volume 135. The fourth volume usually sold for sixty-five pounds, five shillings ($295.50). Ultimately, each of Audubon's subscribers paid approximately $1,050 for 435 hand-colored aquatint engravings issued in eighty-seven parts of five prints each.[47]

THE SEARCH FOR SUBSCRIBERS

Subscriptions served the dual purpose of providing advance financing for the publication and allowing subscribers to pay in installments. Lucy Audubon wrote to Amelia Jane Havell, "In my last [letter] I mentioned that you had better not deviate from the rule in disposing of 'Birds of America' to anyone unless they pay you at once . . . nor does Mr. Audubon like your selling numbers singly."[48] The Audubons tried to maintain economic as well as esthetic control.

By 1827 Audubon had ninety-four subscriptions and was confident that he would obtain two hundred, the number deemed necessary to receive an adequate return on his investment. It was assumed that people would subscribe for the whole series, but a number of the early subscribers never completed their sets. Some lost interest; some died during the twelve-year period it took to complete the project; some had financial reverses. By 1835 so many had dropped out that Audubon wrote to William Horton Bentley, a taxidermist and dealer in rare skins in Manchester, "My opinion is now made up, that not more than 50 or 60 copies complete will exist in *Europe* when I close the concern in about three years from this day, and the

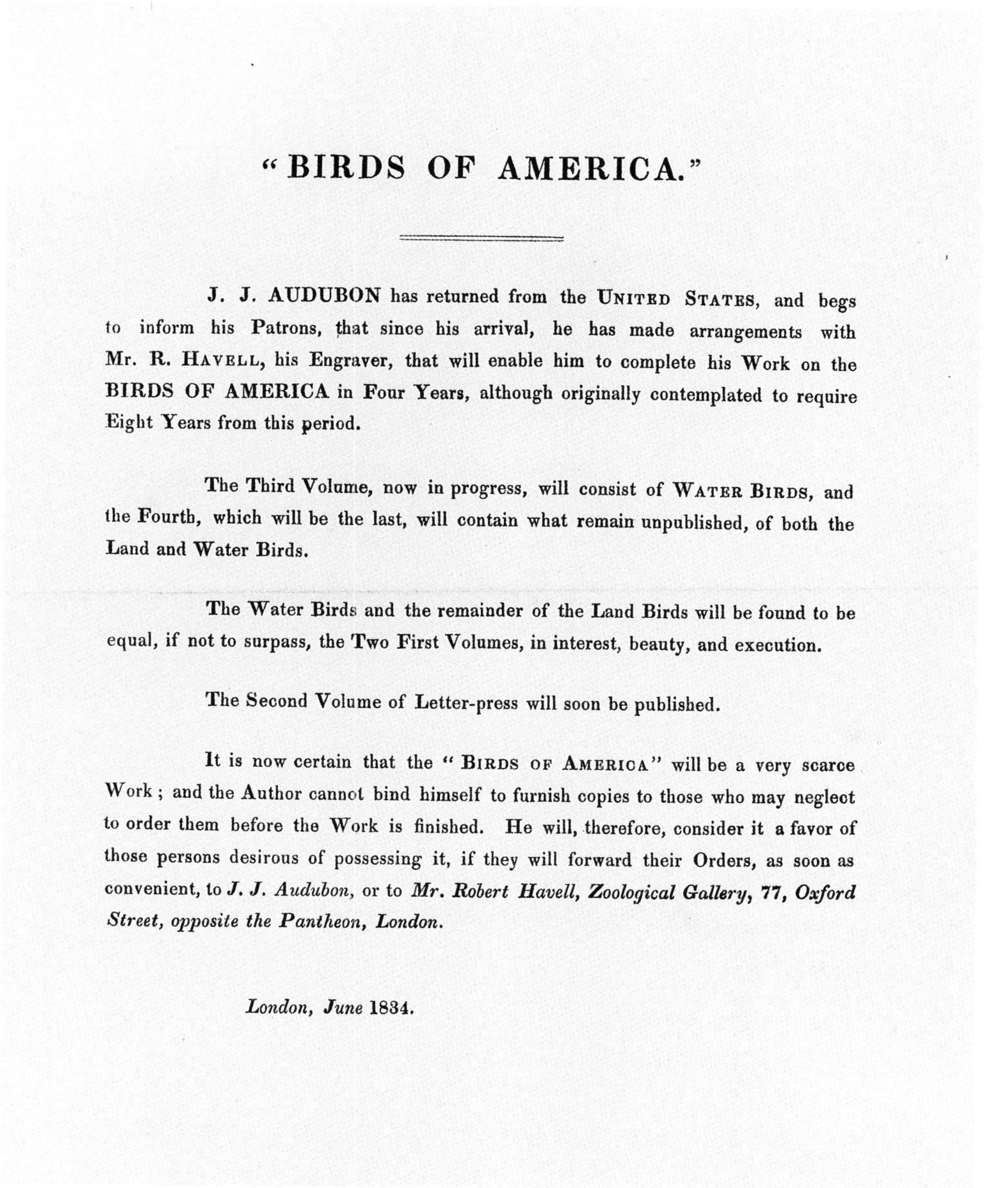

"BIRDS OF AMERICA."

J. J. AUDUBON has returned from the UNITED STATES, and begs to inform his Patrons, that since his arrival, he has made arrangements with Mr. R. HAVELL, his Engraver, that will enable him to complete his Work on the BIRDS OF AMERICA in Four Years, although originally contemplated to require Eight Years from this period.

The Third Volume, now in progress, will consist of WATER BIRDS, and the Fourth, which will be the last, will contain what remain unpublished, of both the Land and Water Birds.

The Water Birds and the remainder of the Land Birds will be found to be equal, if not to surpass, the Two First Volumes, in interest, beauty, and execution.

The Second Volume of Letter-press will soon be published.

It is now certain that the " BIRDS OF AMERICA" will be a very scarce Work ; and the Author cannot bind himself to furnish copies to those who may neglect to order them before the Work is finished. He will, therefore, consider it a favor of those persons desirous of possessing it, if they will forward their Orders, as soon as convenient, to *J. J. Audubon*, or to *Mr. Robert Havell, Zoological Gallery, 77, Oxford Street, opposite the Pantheon, London.*

London, June 1834.

Fig. 29. Broadside, June 1834, London.
The New-York Historical Society.

Birds of America will then raise in value as much as they are now deprecated by certain Fools and envious persons."[49]

More than one-half of the English subscribers never completed their subscriptions, partly owing to the depression of 1836–37.[50] At one thousand dollars a set the price was high, even for people of means. Baron Nathan M. Rothschild was among those who balked at the cost, and Daniel Webster paid reluctantly only after years of being badgered by Audubon. Dropouts had to be replaced because a certain number of subscribers were needed in order to make the project profitable.

After obtaining many important subscriptions in Europe (fig. 29), Audubon returned to America in 1839, not only to find and draw new images for future publications but also to acquire new subscribers for *The Birds of America*. His reputation was secure in England, and his fame had spread to his adopted homeland. Here, where "every industrious man makes and saves money," Audubon found eighty-seven new subscribers.[51]

Nearly all the American patrons subscribed after the first hundred plates had been completed, and Audubon had sent the first bound volumes back to the States in 1831.[52] In 1830, President Andrew Jackson received Audubon "with great kindness," and the Library of Congress as well as the State Department subscribed to his publication.[53] Although Audubon aimed at two hundred, he hoped eventually to reach five hundred. Because of the incomplete subscriptions it is not known exactly how many sets were actually completed, but the estimate of close to two hundred is probably accurate.

As time went on, Audubon's financial problems abated, but his work remained labor-intensive. He reworked and improved earlier drawings and added new ones. He went on expeditions to Florida, Labrador, and Texas in search of new birds. He supervised the engraver's work, collected payments, continually sought new subscribers, and wrote the *Ornithological Biography.* The five volumes, which Audubon began writing in November

Fig. 30. Abraham Bogardus (1822–1908). *Lucy Bakewell Audubon. Carte de visite,* albumen print. The New-York Historical Society.

Fig. 31. Major & Knapp, lithographers. *The Audubon Estate on the Banks of the Hudson* (Minnie's Land). *Valentine's Manual,* 1865. The New-York Historical Society.

1826, were published in Edinburgh between 1831 and 1839. Folio subscribers also received his *Synopsis of the Birds of America* (1839), an index to the elephant folio and the *Ornithological Biography.* These volumes were edited by the young Scottish scientist William MacGillivray.

A FAMILY BUSINESS

Evidently *The Birds of America* was a family business from the beginning. Without Lucy's encouragement and support, Audubon probably would not have succeeded (fig. 30). She relieved him of his familial responsibilities, working to support herself and their sons as well as her husband, and enabled him to concentrate single-mindedly on his project. As his partner, she took care of many chores for him while he was overseas. In a letter of June 10, 1831, she told her rich Derby cousin, Euphemia Gifford: "At present I am obliged to assist as much as is in my power Mr. A. in his letter writing." Lucy added to her husband's letter of July 19, 1831, to Miss Gifford, "our *great* Book demands all our funds, time, and attention, and since I came to England we have not indulged in anything that did not appertain to the advancement and publication of the 'Birds of America'. . . . It is possible that our eldest will return with us to England, for we almost require a person to manage the travelling and writing of the work while Mr. A. is engaged at home superintending the Colouring, printing, pressing, etc."[54] Lucy apparently shared her husband's ambition and kept the same

long hours, even helping him collect specimens of birds and plants on trips. Victor Gifford and John Woodhouse, Audubon's sons, were trained practically from birth to work on *The Birds of America,* and when they were old enough, they assisted their father in all aspects of the project.

SUBSEQUENT PROJECTS

On his return to America in 1839, Audubon immediately began working on two other projects: a smaller version of *The Birds of America,* in royal octavo size (6½ × 10 inches), and *The Viviparous Quadrupeds of North America* in imperial folio size (22 × 28 inches), a work that documented the mammals of North America.

The octavo edition of the *Birds,* one-eighth the size of the double elephant folio, was published in Philadelphia and New York (1840–44). It contained five hundred plates lithographed by John T. Bowen and issued in one hundred parts of five plates each, bound into seven volumes. The parts sold for one dollar each, for a total of one hundred dollars for the entire series. John Woodhouse copied the original watercolors with the aid of a camera lucida, a device that projected the image in a reduced size onto the lithograph stone. He also added new birds. For these projects, Audubon continued as salesman for the next decade in the same effective manner he had perfected in England—an experience he once described as "a begging Journey after Subscribers."[55] His job was aided by the fact that the octavo edition was sold for one hundred dollars, a price that made it accessible to a larger audience. Between 1840 and 1870 about seven editions were printed; the exact number of complete sets published is not known.

The octavo *Birds* helped to finance *The Viviparous Quadrupeds*, which was, in large part, produced by Audubon's sons and John Bachman, who wrote the accompanying text. Because Audubon's health was deteriorating, John Woodhouse drew more than half of the animals, and Victor Gifford did most of the backgrounds. Bowen was again responsible for the lithography of the 150 plates issued in Philadelphia in thirty parts of five each (1845–48). Audubon's early enthusiasm for the *Quadrupeds* was revealed in a letter to his friend Benjamin Phillips of June 23, 1839: "Will you not be surprised to hear that I contemplate publishing the Quadrupeds of America[,] Aye in one Vol. Folio, rather less than half the Size of the Birds of America, in about one hundred Plates, giving all that can be given in such fauna of the Size of Life, accompanied by one Vol. of Letter press."[56]

After Audubon's death, John Woodhouse Audubon attempted to reissue *The Birds of America* in its original size in chromolithography. Of the 450 plates planned, Julius Bien, a New York lithographer, completed only 105 plates by 1860. The price of each number was eleven dollars, for a total cost of 498 dollars—half the price of the original double elephant folio prints. Chromolithography, a process in which a drawing is made receptive to colored inks with greasy materials applied to a smooth stone or metal plate and put through a lithographic press, was new to America in the 1840s. Bien's attempt to reproduce the original copperplates was a major accomplishment that unfortunately was interrupted by the Civil War.[57]

CONCLUSION

Audubon never became wealthy through his publications, but he was at last able to live comfortably. In 1841 he bought a thirty-five-acre tract of land on the Hudson, which he called Minnie's Land (fig. 31), in what is today the Washington Heights section of Manhattan. There in 1842 he built a house large enough for himself and his sons' families. In 1843 he wrote to his friend and collaborator John Bachman that he was "in the lap of comfort and without the hard and continued exercises so lately my lot."[58]

In the late 1840s, however, Audubon began to suffer mental deterioration—probably the onset of early senility or perhaps Alzheimer's disease—and he died in 1851, at the age of sixty-six. His sons, who also built houses on Minnie's land, died several

years later: Victor became an invalid in 1856 and died at the age of fifty-one, in 1860; John died at the age of fifty, in 1862. Lucy was now called upon to support the extended family.

Fate was unkind to Lucy Bakewell Audubon. After years of struggle the quick succession of deaths in the family forced her to rent her house on Minnie's Land and live with Victor's family. Destitute, she put the watercolors for *The Birds of America* up for sale in November 1861. Initially no one was interested, and it was not until 1863 that she was able to sell them to The New-York Historical Society for a mere four thousand dollars, a sum one writer equated with the Dutch payment of twenty-four dollars for the island of Manhattan.[59] Lucy also tried to sell the copperplates but was unsuccessful. Eventually, in 1871, she sold the remaining plates (a number of them had been destroyed) for the value of the metal. About seventy-five of them were saved from the furnace, but the rest were melted down. Minnie's Land was sold in the early 1860s, and Lucy moved to Kentucky, where she died in 1874, at the age of eighty-seven. (The houses on the property were destroyed in 1932 to make way for the West Side Highway.)

Despite the demise of the family, their great project, the conception of a remarkable man, endures. It is the accomplishment of an extraordinary artist whose personality, persistence, and passion made him an equally masterful entrepreneur. John James Audubon's "magnificent obsession" has left a lasting legacy to the world.

NOTES

I am grateful to Holly Hotchner, Director of the Museum, for giving me the opportunity to edit and contribute to this book. My sincere appreciation goes to my coeditor Theodore Stebbins, Jr. and coauthors Reba Fishman Snyder, Carole Slatkin, and Amy Meyers for their enthusiastic collaboration.

1. Letter, J. J. Audubon to Lucy Audubon, December 21, 1826, Edinburgh, in Howard Corning, ed., *Letters of John James Audubon 1826–1840* (Boston: The Club of Odd Volumes, 1930; New York: Kraus Reprint Co., 1969), p. 9.
2. Quoted from Audubon's 1828 diary in Alice Ford, *John James Audubon, A Biography* (New York: Abbeville Press, 1988), p. 247.
3. Audubon was recorded variously as the son of a wealthy Louisiana plantation owner or a deposed French noble, perhaps the lost dauphin, second son of Louis XVI and Marie Antoinette. David (1748–1825) was court painter to Louis XVI and Napoleon. In his biography, edited by his wife, Audubon asserts, "David had guided my hand," but there is no evidence to substantiate this claim.
4. Entry for October 12, 1820, in Howard Corning, ed., *Journal of John James Audubon Made During His Trip to New Orleans in 1820–21* (Boston: The Club of Odd Volumes, 1929), p. 3.
5. Emmet Field Horine, *Daniel Drake (1785–1852): Pioneer Physician of the Midwest* (Philadelphia: University of Pennsylvania Press, 1961), p. 137; Ed-

ward H. Dwight, "Old and Modern Drawings: The Metamorphosis of John James Audubon," *The Art Quarterly*, vol. 26, no. 4 (1963), p. 466. One of Audubon's students in Cincinnati, Joseph Mason, later became his assistant.

6. As quoted from Audubon's *Episode* of "Louisville in Kentucky" in Francis Hobart Herrick, *Audubon the Naturalist* (New York: D. Appleton and Company, 1917), p. 221.

7. They charged Audubon with plagiarism. Joseph Mason, finding that Audubon did not give him credit for his botanical backgrounds, also disparaged him. See Clark Hunter, *The Life and Letters of Alexander Wilson* (Philadelphia: American Philosophical Society, 1983), p. 96.

8. Henry T. Tuckerman, *Book of the Artist* (1867; reprint, New York: James F. Carr, 1967), p. 494.

9. It was, in fact, the method that The New-York Historical Society used to buy the watercolors of *The Birds of America* from Lucy Audubon in 1863. For details, see Preface.

10. These early works, in the John James Audubon Letters and Drawings at the Houghton Library, Harvard University (Pfms, Am 25, 1–9a), were from the collection of Audubon's friend, the ornithologist and naturalist Edward Harris, who accompanied Audubon on some of his expeditions.

11. According to Amy Meyers, the individual sections, called parts or numbers, actually appeared between 1729 and 1747 even though his book records the dates as 1731–43.

12. Alan Feduccia, *Catesby's Birds of Colonial America* (Chapel Hill and London: The University of North Carolina Press, 1985), p. 5. The work contained a total of 220 plates illustrating 109 birds, 33 amphibians and reptiles, 46 fishes, 31 insects, 9 quadrupeds, and 171 plants.

13. Letter to Dr. David Ramsay as quoted in Wendy J. Shadwell, "The Portrait Engravings of Charles Willson Peale," in Joan D. Dolmetsch, ed., *Eighteenth-Century Prints in Colonial America* (Williamsburg, Va.: The Colonial Williamsburg Foundation, 1979), p. 133.

14. Audubon mentions the Peale Museum and its natural-history specimens in his chapter "Great Pine Swamp," *Ornithological Biography*, vol. I (Edinburgh: Adam Black, 1831–39), p. 54. He was acquainted with Peale's sons Rembrandt and Titian.

15. Margaret Welch, "John James Audubon and His American Audience: Art, Science, and Nature, 1830–1860," University of Pennsylvania: Ph.D. dissertation, 1988, p. 106.

16. Edgar P. Richardson, Brooke Hindle, and Lillian B. Miller, *Charles Willson Peale and His World* (New York: Harry N. Abrams, Inc., 1983), p. 126.

17. Welch, *John James Audubon and His American Audience*, p. 109.

18. Richard J. Koke, "John Hill, Master of Aquatint," *The New-York Historical Society Quarterly*, vol. XLIII, no. 1 (January 1959), p. 87.

19. Ibid., p. 89.

20. Ibid., p. 99.

21. Ford, *John James Audubon*, p. 221.

22. Letter of July 16, 1832, from Henry Clay (Secretary of State 1825–29), John James Audubon Papers (bMSAm1482, John James Audubon Papers, Houghton Library, Harvard University). All subsequent citations to Houghton Library are from this collection.

23. Audubon repaid his kindness with a drawing of a robin. Waldemar H. Fries, *The Double Elephant Folio: The Story of Audubon's "Birds of America"* (Chicago: American Library Association, 1973), p. 5.

24. Ibid, pp. 5–6.

25. As quoted in ibid, p. 14.

26. Ibid, p. 17.

27. Letter, J. J. Audubon to Robert Havell, Jr., Manchester (bMSAm1482, #15, Houghton Library, Harvard University).

28. "Mr. Audubon," *The New-York Mirror* (Saturday, April 20, 1833), p. 335.

29. Fries *The Double Elephant Folio*, p. 14.

30. For a listing of Audubon's honorary memberships see Alice Ford, *John James Audubon*, p. 486.

31. Fries, *The Double Elephant Folio*, p. 7.

32. Letter, J.J. Audubon to Lucy Audubon December 21, 1826, Edinburgh, in Corning, *Letters*, p. 11.

33. Letter, J. J. Audubon to Lucy Audubon, November 2, 1828 (Box 2, #53, John James Audubon Collection [C0006], Manuscript Division, Department of Rare Books and Special Collections, Princeton University Library). All subsequent citations to manuscripts from the Princeton Library are from this collection.

34. Maria R. Audubon, ed., *Audubon and His Journals* (New York: Charles Scribner's Sons, 1897), p. 61.

35. Letter, J. J. Audubon to the wife of Dr. Benjamin Phillips, Audubon's close friend and family physician (Audubon Collection, Box 2, #12 and #19, Princeton University Library).

36. Letter, J. J. Audubon to Lucy Audubon, November 25, 1827, Liverpool, in Corning, *Letters*, p. 45.

37. Letter, J. J. Audubon to Lucy Audubon, December 21, 1827, Audubon Collection box 2, #52, Princeton University Library.

38. Audubon's journal, December 10, 1826, as quoted in Fries, *The Double Elephant Folio*, p. 11.

39. Ibid., p. 16.

40. As quoted in ibid., p. 23.

41. Ibid., p. 26.

42. Letter, J. J. Audubon to Lucy Audubon, November 25, 1827, in Corning, *Letters*, p. 44.

43. After his father's death, Havell dropped "Jr." from his name on the plates.

44. The technical definitions of print processes have been taken from the glossary in Barry Walker, *The American Artist as Printmaker* (New York: The Brooklyn Museum, 1983) and A. Hyatt Mayor, *Prints & People* (New York: The Metropolitan Museum of Art, 1971). If Havell used drypoint, it was only occasionally. Drypoint, which gives a velvety line, is suitable only for small editions because of the fragility of the raised burr.

45. Fries, *The Double Elephant Folio*, pp. 385–89.

46. As quoted in ibid., p. 386.

47. The rate of exchange of pound to dollar fluctuated somewhat between 1828 and 1838, and some sets were sold loose while others were bound, which explains the price variations quoted in various publications and manuscripts.

48. Letter, Lucy Audubon to Amelia Jane Havell, December 12, 1839 (#195, bMSAm1482, Houghton Library, Harvard University).

49. Letter, J. J. Audubon to William Horton Bentley; London, March 17, 1835 (Box 2, #72, Audubon Collection, Princeton University Library).

50. Welch *John James Audubon and His American Audience*, p. 110.

51. As quoted in ibid., p. 110.

52. Fries, *The Double Elephant Folio*, p. 197.

53. In a letter of December 21, 1827 (box 2, #52, Audubon Collection, Princeton University Library), Audubon writes to his wife that Gordon advised him to give a promotional copy to the House of Representatives.

54. Letter, J. J. Audubon to Euphemia Gifford, July 19, 1831, transcript of letter in collection of H. J. Lutcher Stark, Orange, Texas, (Box 2, Princeton University Library).

55. Letter, J. J. Audubon to Benjamin Phillips, December 28, 1839, ibid.

56. Letter, J. J. Audubon to Benjamin Phillips, June 23, 1839, ibid.

57. For further details see Fries, *The Double Elephant Folio*, p. 355.

58. Audubon-Bachman Correspondence, November 12, 1843, Minnie's Land (bMSAm1482, Houghton Library, Harvard University).

59. Jerry Patterson, "The Birds to Watch," *Town & Country* (November 1992), p. 190.

Observations of an American Woodsman: John James Audubon as Field Naturalist

AMY R. W. MEYERS

In March of 1828, John James Audubon departed from London, where he was overseeing the production of *The Birds of America*, for a brief visit to Cambridge University. Through letters of introduction supplied by eminent members of London's scientific community, Audubon hoped to make contact with scientists at the university who might wish to subscribe to his "Great Work." He was greeted with warmth and, to his satisfaction, obtained a number of important subscriptions, including that of the Cambridge University Library, the Philosophical Society, and the young Lord Fitzwilliam. He was flattered by the many invitations he received to dine, and, as he reported to his wife, Lucy, he particularly enjoyed an evening of conversation in the rooms of Professor William Whewell, where the geologist Adam Sedgwick impressed him with his lively intellect:

> Professor Whewell took me to his own rooms with some eight or ten others. My book was inspected as a matter of courtesy. Professor Sedgwick was gay, full of wit and cleverness; the conversation was very animated, and I enjoyed it much.[1]

Audubon continued, however, to lament his own lack of formal training and the passive role he was forced to assume when topics beyond the range of his knowledge were being discussed: "Oh! my Lucy, that I also had received a University education! I listened and admired for a long time."[2] It was not until the conversation turned to "the woods, the birds, the Aborigines of America" that Audubon felt comfortable in talking; indeed, he gained the floor as the sole proprietor of knowledge in the field.

Inclusion in the arena of scholarly discourse greatly pleased Audubon, who was quickly gaining stature among British scientific circles through the exhibition of his drawings and the publication of the first numbers of his plates. Audubon's increasing immersion in the world of academic science, however,

caused him to reflect on the deficiencies in his own training—deficiencies that would mark both the persona he would seek to project and the very nature of his contributions to nineteenth-century science.

Audubon's ascendancy as a respected ornithologist had been long in coming. In 1824, when he appeared in Philadelphia after years on the western frontier, he was virtually unknown to the naturalists who formed the largest and most active scientific community in the United States.[3] As an outsider, he was quickly placed in the uncomfortable position of having to defend his drawings against the powerful attacks of George Ord, a wealthy and influential member of the Academy of Natural Sciences. Ord was then reissuing Alexander Wilson's *American Ornithology*, the first illustrated study of American birds to be published in this country, and he was not eager to see another ornithological illustrator rise to prominence. Despite Ord's criticism, Audubon developed collegial relationships with a number of important naturalists, including Charles Lucien Bonaparte, Titian Ramsay Peale, Charles Alexandre Lesueur, and Richard Harlan.[4] These associations would continue for the rest of Audubon's career and would ultimately link him closely to Philadelphia's scientific circle. In 1824, however, Ord's attacks impeded Audubon from accomplishing his major objective—the securing of a publisher for his work—and he was compelled to sail for Great Britain to achieve his goal.

Audubon's identity as an outsider from the frontier may have damaged him in Philadelphia, but it worked famously to his advantage in Britain. By the time he arrived in the cosmopolitan port of Liverpool, the romantic myth of the American trapper-scout, skirting the edge of civilization and living according to natural law, had been popularized across Europe through tales of Daniel Boone and the first of James Fenimore Cooper's Leatherstocking novels.[5] Audubon, with his fine physique, flowing locks tamed with bear grease, buckskin jacket, and exotic accent, must have seemed the very embodiment of this heroic type, and he quickly realized how to exploit the image to his own advantage. His manipulation of his persona to meet European expectations of an American backwoodsman had special ramifications for his entry into the sophisticated world of European science. Audubon came increasingly to realize, sometimes through painful embarrassment, that the contributions he could offer to contemporary ornithology would not be of the same character as those made by naturalists with university training in systematic science and anatomy.[6] As opposed to knowledge gained through the laboratory, lecture room, and library, he would have to offer knowledge gained through his immediate experience with live birds in their natural habitats. The identity that Audubon assumed for himself as a man of the woods would lend veracity to both his drawings and his prose as direct transcriptions of the observations that he had made in the American wilds. It is, indeed, as an "American Woodsman" that Audubon first presents himself in his *Ornithological Biography*—the five-volume text that he wrote to accompany *The Birds of America*.[7] Since the text is as much an autobiography as it is an observation on birds, it seeks constantly to convince the reader that its author was always on the scene, observing his subjects in the field. Ultimately, Audubon came to portray himself as the personification of nature, and to characterize his life as the purest source for empirically derived information concerning the birds he described and depicted.

Even in Audubon's earliest journal entries from his first months in Britain, he expressed slight disdain for naturalists who possessed more sophisticated educations than his own but who lacked his direct experience with the natural world. In October of 1826, for example, when his friend from Liverpool, Edward Roscoe, suggested that Audubon might consider collaborating with the distinguished naturalists Prideaux John Selby and Robert Jameson, who were planning a major ornithological publication with several colleagues, Audubon reflected:

> I think if my work deserves the attention of the public, it must stand on its own legs, not on the reputation of men superior in education and literary acquirements, but possibly not so in the actual observations of Nature at her best, in the wilds, as I certainly have seen her.[8]

Audubon subsequently befriended Selby and Jameson and tutored them both in his method of drawing birds, but he continued to believe his own knowledge of the avian world to be superior. Although Audubon came to respect Selby's *Illustrations of British Ornithology* (1819–34) as the most important work of its kind yet published in England, he was convinced that his own work had a distinct advantage. In February of 1828, when Selby's drawings were compared unfavorably to Audubon's at a meeting of the Linnean Society, in London, Audubon remarked in his journal: "I am quite sure that had [Selby] had the same opportunities that my curious life has granted me, his work would have been far superior to mine; I supported him to the best of my power."[9] The generosity of this statement is undercut by condescension, based entirely on Audubon's conviction that even the most renowned British naturalist could not match his own experience in the field.

Nonetheless, Audubon recognized that he was not sufficiently trained to classify and describe anatomically many of the species he had portrayed, and he solicited his better-educated colleagues for their help in the field of taxonomy. In June 1827, his Philadelphia friend Charles Lucien Bonaparte arrived in London, and in one evening he helped Audubon to assign scientific names to almost fifty new species of birds depicted in his drawings.[10] Audubon also sought assistance with the identifications and anatomical descriptions included in his *Ornithological Biography*. Although initially he wished the English naturalist William Swainson to collaborate with him, Swainson disagreed vehemently with Audubon's terms, insisting particularly on coauthorship. Audubon, who clearly did not conceive of scientific description as the central feature of his publication, did not wish to share credit for his work. Instead, he hired the young Scottish zoologist William MacGillivray, who did not demand equal recognition for his help.[11] While MacGillivray is not named as a contributor on the title page of Audubon's publication, in the Introductory Address he receives Audubon's thanks for "completing the scientific details, and smoothing down the asperities of my *Ornithological Biography*."[12]

If Audubon did not think of scientific description as the major focus of his work, then the question is raised as to what the American Woodsman actually sought to contribute to contemporary science through his firsthand observations. The answer to this query, which is implicit in Audubon's drawings and prints for *The Birds of America* and articulated throughout the *Ornithological Biography* and his journal entries, helps to illuminate both the new directions in which the life sciences would move over the course of the nineteenth century and the critical role that field naturalists would play in initiating the exploration of these new avenues of thought.

STUDIES OF HABIT AND
ENVIRONMENTAL INTERACTION

In October of 1830, as Audubon began his work on the *Ornithological Biography*, he summarized what he hoped to accomplish through the textual accompaniments to his pictures:

> I know I am not a scholar, but meantime I am aware that no man living knows better than I do the habits of our birds; no man living has studied them as much as I have done, and with the assistance of my old journals and memorandum-books which were written on the spot, I can at least put down plain truths which might be useful and perhaps interesting. . . .[13]

Audubon asserts that, through his years of studying birds in the wild, he alone has come to understand their habits, and that he wishes to present these habits in his *Ornithological Biography*.[14] He makes a similar but slightly more elaborate claim in the prospectus for *The Birds of America*, in which he distinguishes his ornithological illustrations from all that have come before by stating that his are the first to portray the characteristic behavior of birds in their native habitats:

> The Author has not contented himself, as others have done, with single profile views, but in very many instances has grouped his figures, so as to represent the originals at their avocations, and has placed them on branches of trees, decorated with foliage, blossoms and fruits, or amidst plants of numerous species. Some are seen pursuing their prey through the air, searching for food

De Aquilaanataria.Lib.III.

198

Fig. 32. *Eagle.* In Konrad Gesner, *Historiae Animalium,* vol. III (Zurich: 1551–58), p. 198 [actually 197].
The Henry E. Huntington Library, Art Collections, and Botanical Gardens.

Fig. 33. Alexander Lawson (1772–1846), after Alexander Wilson (1766–1813). *1. Mississippi Kite 2. Tennessee Warbler 3. Kentucky W. 4. Prairie W.* Hand-colored engraving; 37 × 27 cm. The Academy of Natural Sciences of Philadelphia.

amongst the leaves and herbage, sitting on their nests, or feeding their young; whilst others, of a different nature, swim, wade, or glide in or over their allotted element.[15]

Through *The Birds of America*, Audubon sought to challenge the traditional format for natural history illustration by portraying birds engaged in characteristic activities in their native environments.

The single-profile view against which Audubon contrasted his own work derived from a long tradition of plant and animal illustration originally established by medieval pattern books, herbals, and bestiaries, and carried forward in printed botanical and zoological tracts from the Renaissance. As part of the developing science of systematics, this tradition dictated a compositional approach in which an individual organism was shown apart from its surroundings and isolated against a blank page (fig. 32). Removed from the complex environment in which it was enmeshed in life, the specimen could then be typed according to its physical attributes and placed in a metaphysical chain of being which began with the simplest forms of life and ended with humankind.[16] As taxonomic systems evolved over the seventeenth and eighteenth centuries, the links in this chain increased and its pattern shifted, but the form of the specimen drawing remained relatively constant, so much so that even Alexander Wilson adhered to it in creating his pictures for the *American Ornithology* (fig. 33). Always sensitive to the rival whose supporters criticized his own more innovative style, Audubon probably had Wilson's prints in mind when he remarked that unlike "others," he would move beyond the single-profile view.

Audubon expressly shunned the notion that *The Birds of America* should reflect the structure of an abstract chain of being, arguing that living organisms never actually disperse themselves this way:

> I do not present to you the objects of which my work consists in the order adopted by systematic writers . . . for although you and I, and all the world besides, are well aware that a grand connected chain does exist in the Creator's sublime system, the subjects of it have been left at liberty to disperse in quest of the food best adapted for them, or the comforts that have been so abundantly scattered for each of them over the globe, and are not in the habit of following each other, as if marching in regular procession to a funeral or merrymaking.[17]

Audubon actually went on to outline his plans to publish a systematically ordered *Synopsis of the Birds of the United States,* and he had his copy of *The Birds of America* bound in this order as well.[18] At heart, however, he set as the main objective for his publication the reconstruction of the complex matrix of intra- and interspecial relationships from which birds, along with all other life-forms, had traditionally been removed in scientific illustrations and texts.

Although Audubon considered his studies of environmental interaction to be highly individualistic, based on decades of observation in the wild, his pictures, in fact, reflect an antisystematic trend in thought that had begun to emerge in the eighteenth century and continued to gain force in the nineteenth. In North America, one of the earliest expressions of interest in environmental relationships was voiced by the naturalist John Bartram, who began a botanic garden outside Philadelphia in the 1730s. There he attempted to recreate the habitats from which he had extracted hundreds of exotic specimens collected on his ventures through the northern and southern colonies. For Bartram, this was more than an intellectual exercise. As the greatest supplier of North American seeds and botanical specimens to British aristocrats and wealthy merchants eager to enrich their gardens and natural-history cabinets, Bartram was constantly trying new ways to ensure the survival of his plants.

His son, William, was deeply influenced by these early environmental experiments, and from the 1750s through the 1770s, he executed for his father's British patrons a series of drawings that depict the natural world as a complex matrix of interdependent forms (fig. 34). These vignettes of organic interplay undermined the taxonomic project and posited a new vision of the cosmos as an intricate web of environmental relationships.[19] While Audubon would not have had the opportunity to examine Bartram's drawings during his own formative years, he is known to have read Bartram's *Travels,* a romantic travelogue of far-reaching influence, which, though more conservative than Bartram's drawings, also stresses the interconnected nature of organic creation.[20]

Although the philosophical basis of Audubon's work was part of a clear tradition of antisystematic thought, *The Birds of America* and the accompanying *Ornithological Biography* were unequaled in scale and scope. The motivations that caused Audubon to undertake a project of such magnitude, crystallizing so perfectly the environmental interests of an increasing number of naturalists, can begin to be understood only through an examination of his pictures and texts.

OF BIRDS AND MEN

The drawing that Audubon published as plate LXXI in *The Birds of America* depicts a bird that he named the Winter Hawk, flying low among the grasses of a marsh toward the open water (fig. 35). The hawk has grasped in its talons a large bullfrog, which

Fig. 34. William Bartram (1739–1823). *Tab. II. The Sarasena with a large Yellow Flower,* c. 1767. Black ink; 23.7 × 29.8 cm. The Natural History Museum, London.

Fig. 35. *Winter Hawk* (Havell LXXI). Red-shouldered Hawk, *Buteo lineatus.* Watercolor; 25 × 38 ½ in. The New-York Historical Society.

it clutches firmly by the head. The bleeding amphibian, its back legs outstretched, holds its body taut and straight against the underside of the bird. Although still alive, it can only reach up feebly with its front leg in an attempt to extract the claws of its captor. Thick-bodied and soft, with feet webbed to move through water, the frog appears awkward and defenseless out of its aquatic milieu. As death comes on, its eye is half-closed in pain, and a blood-streaked bubble of saliva exudes from its mouth.

By contrast, the streamlined body of the hawk arches and pumps in flight, with wings cutting the air sharply. The bird's beak is open as if emitting a shattering cry, and the grasses appear bent in submission, pointing the way for the hawk as it carries its prey out of the marsh, into its own realm.

On eye level with the bird, as if belly-deep in the marsh, we are the only viewers of the scene. The immediacy of the encounter is dramatized by the hawk's sharp look, which warns us not to approach any closer. Audubon has created an image that lifts us out of the comfort of our armchairs and places us directly in the midst of a violent interchange between predator and prey. The picture is structured to convince us that we are vicariously experiencing an event that the naturalist has observed during

one of his many forays into the marshlands. Far more than a simple profile view that defines the hawk anatomically, the image is both an examination of the bird's behavior within a specific environment and an argument for Audubon's unparalleled ability as a field naturalist to share this behavior with us.

The description that accompanies the print reiterates Audubon's belief that basic anatomical description cannot convey enough information to define a species adequately. The bird's habits and cry, as well as its peculiar "cast of countenance," are all required to distinguish it as a distinct life-form. Audubon maintains that only the "student of Nature, who examines her productions in the haunts which she has allotted to them" is qualified to make such a discrimination.[21] While defining species was important to Audubon, the only definitions he considered valid were those based on the deepest knowledge of that species' behavior within its own habitat, and such knowledge, he believed, could be gained only through many years of study in the wild.[22]

A sense of immediacy and direct experience is conveyed through virtually all of Audubon's depictions of birds, even those portrayed in the most remote habitats and the most inaccessible environments. His drawing of the Fish Hawk, for ex-

Fig. 36. *Fish Hawk or Osprey* (Havell LXXXI).
Osprey, *Pandian haliaetus*. Watercolor; 37½ × 25⅛ in.
The New-York Historical Society.

Fig. 37. *Golden Eagle* (Havell CLXXXI). Golden Eagle, *Aquila chrysaetos*.
Watercolor; 38½ × 25½ in. The New-York Historical Society.

ample, is structured quite similarly to his drawing of the Winter Hawk, but in this case, we, as viewers, float high in the open air directly beside the bird and the weakfish held in its talons (fig. 36, page 166).[23] Both predator and prey appear startled by our presence, the hawk glaring at us with an aggressive eye and the fish staring at us plaintively. As we examine the scene of predation before us, we become more than passive voyeurs; we are active participants evoking distinctly different responses from the two animals.

In another drawing, illustrating the predatory habits of the Golden Eagle, our sense of being privy to Audubon's unmediated observations is heightened by the inclusion of the naturalist's own figure in the scene (fig. 37, page 232). Audubon not only includes himself in the landscape, reminding us of the direct experience that he is attempting to impart to us as observers; he also draws a clear equation between himself and the subject of his work. Like the eagle grasping its prey, the hunter

carries a large dead bird—perhaps a Golden Eagle—strapped to his back, presumably secured on his quest to obtain specimens for his publication. Though less elegant than the eagle, which he describes as "the king of birds" in his biography of the species, Audubon portrays himself as being equally tenacious and daring, braving all danger to possess his quarry.[24] His presence in the piece also suggests that he is equally ruthless—a thought that often runs through his writings.

In both his journal entries and his *Ornithological Biography*, Audubon relates many instances when he put his feelings of compassion aside in order to secure a specimen for study. A particularly affecting description of such an occasion appears in the entry for July 18, 1833, in his Labrador journal, where he reflects:

On leaving the wood we shot a Spruce Partridge leading her young. On seeing us she ruffled her feathers like a barnyard hen, and rounded within a few feet of us to defend her brood; her very looks claimed forbearance and clemency, but the enthusiastic desire to study nature prompted us to destroy her, and she was shot, and her brood secured in a few moments.[25]

Here Audubon describes his wish to engage in scientific study as an emotional—almost instinctive—urge that leads him to commit an act of cruel but, to his mind, necessary destruction.

The animalistic side of the hunt—even when pursued in the name of science—is clearly explicated in another account, in which Audubon directly associates the satisfaction he felt in securing a specimen of "The Bird of Washington," with the pleasure felt by the bird, itself, in securing its prey:

> With what delight did I survey the magnificent bird! Had the finest salmon ever pleased him as he did me?—Never. I ran and presented him to my friend, with a pride which they alone feel, who, like me, have devoted themselves from their earliest childhood to such pursuits, and who have derived from them their first pleasures.[26]

In this case the behavioral and emotional correspondence Audubon perceived between his own activity as a naturalist in search of specimens and that of a bird in search of prey greatly pleased him; but in the case of the Spruce Partridge he found the correspondence somewhat disturbing. A similar sense of discomfort may account for the fact that he dropped the figure of the hunter with his quarry from his final print of the Golden Eagle. Relating his own activities to the particularly gruesome image of the eagle, with its talon piercing the eye of the hare, may simply have struck Audubon—or his printmaker, Havell—as too brutal an association to commit to print.

And yet the drawing still stands as a testament to Audubon's belief that the behavior of birds and men is, in the end, essentially alike. His studies of habit, encompassing courting and mating rituals, procedures for the care of young, feeding practices, communal interplay, and territorial defense, all reflect human preoccupations and are all discussed in terms of human interests.[27] In an essay on his method of drawing birds, published in the *Edinburgh Journal of Science* in 1828, Audubon wrote:

> . . . I am persuaded that alone in the woods, or at my work, I can make better use of the whole of myself than in any other situation, and that thereby I have lost nothing in exchanging the pleasure of studying *men* for that of admiring the feathered race.[28]

When examining his pictures and reading his prose, one is led to wonder, however, whether it was not precisely through Audubon's thoroughgoing examination of birds that he was also able to pursue an incisive study of human behavior.

THE MORAL TALE AS NARRATIVE CONSTRUCT

In the drawing Audubon executed for plate CII of *The Birds of America*, he portrays three Blue Jays perched in the decaying branches of a dead tree (fig. 38, page 156). A female holds a stolen egg from another bird's nest in the crook of the upper-most branch and hammers it open, allowing the contents to flow lasciviously into the open mouth of the larger male below. As he tips his head back to receive the golden liquid that splashes over his white breast, he spreads his feathers in a showy display. To the left, another jay gluttonously sucks an egg, while glancing at us as if caught in the act. Sharp-eyed and quick, this jaunty group of crested culprits brazenly enjoys its booty without the slightest look of remorse. Like the gaudy trumpet vine, sketched in around the tree and developed more fully in the associated print, these creatures beguile us with their beauty while stealing life from those around them.

Fig. 38. *Blue Jay* (Havell CII). Blue Jay, *Cyanocitta cristata.* Watercolor; 23½ × 18¾ in. The New-York Historical Society.

This wittily anthropomorphized image of Blue Jays as mischievous bandits is matched by Audubon's text from the *Ornithological Biography*, in which he characterizes the species as deceitful and larcenous:

Reader, look at the plate in which are represented three individuals of this beautiful species,—rogues though they be, and thieves, as I would call them, were it fit for me to pass judgment on their actions. See how each is enjoying the fruits of his knavery, sucking the eggs which he has pilfered from the nest of some innocent dove or harmless partridge! Who could imagine that a form so graceful, arrayed by nature in a garb so resplendent, should harbour so much mischief;—that selfishness, duplicity, and malice should form the moral accompaniments of so much physical perfection! Yet so it is, and how like beings of a much higher order, are these gay deceivers! Aye, I could write you a whole chapter on this subject, were not my task of a different nature.[29]

After describing the "selfishness, duplicity, and malice" that define the moral character of the Blue Jay as a species, Audubon goes on to liken "these gay deceivers" to "beings of a much higher order." And while he insists that it is not his objective to pursue the parallels that he has observed between Blue Jays and human beings, he continues to describe the birds' behavior in human terms:

The Blue Jay . . . is more tyrannical than brave, and like most boasters, domineers over the feeble, dreads the strong, and flies even from his equals. In many cases, in fact, he is a downright coward. . . . The Red Thrush, the Mocking Bird, and many others, although inferior in strength, never allow him to approach their nest with impunity; and the Jay to be even with them, creeps silently to it in their absence, and devours their eggs and young whenever he finds an opportunity. I have seen one go its round from one nest to another every day, and suck the newly laid eggs of different birds in the neighborhood, with as much regularity and composure as a physician would call on his patients. I have also witnessed the sad disappointment it experienced, when, on returning to its home, it found its mate in the jaws of a snake, the nest upset, and the eggs all gone. I have thought more than once on such occasions that like all great culprits, when brought to a sense of their enormities, it evidenced a strong feeling of remorse.[30]

In this passage Audubon explicates the full range of ways in which the jay characteristically interacts with other species in its environment, but the bird's interactions are described as if they were those of a human rogue. The inclination to see and examine the moral disposition of an individual human type through the habits of a particular species of bird is evident in many of Audubon's portrayals and descriptions. The cad, the ardent lover, the bully, the faithful spouse, the good parent, the buffoon, and even the gout-ridden old gentleman are all depicted in his work. These "family pictures," as he called them, with their accompanying biographies, serve simultaneously as portraits of birds and human beings.[31]

Although Audubon may protest that it is not "fit" for him "to pass judgment on their actions," he often constructs his pictures and his text as moral tales in the tradition of the fable. Indeed in his essay "My Style of Drawing Birds," he explicitly refers to his enduring love for the "delightful moral fables of Lafontaine."[32] While his depiction of the Blue Jay might be interpreted as a somewhat humorous injunction against the debased character of the cowardly thief, his portrayal of the Carolina Turtle Dove can be seen as a celebration of the devoted lover (fig. 39).[33] In this drawing Audubon juxtaposes a courting couple and a mated pair in a *Stewartia* bush, suggesting the conflation of two different time periods within a single historical sequence, as one might find in a medieval manuscript illumination or early Renaissance painting. The male above appeals to the female, who looks out at the viewer with an undecided eye while spreading her wings and tail feathers as if ready to take flight. Emblematic of the start of this romance, the limb on which this couple sits bears no leaves or flowers and is surrounded only by buds and half-opened blossoms, while the branches that form the rich bower for the nesting pair are loaded with fully opened blooms. Having succeeded in his suit, the male member of the mated couple now reaches down to caress his love, and she readily receives his advances as she warms their eggs.[34]

In the description that accompanies the print made after this drawing, Audubon recasts this simple visual narrative of amorous devotion in the following words:

I have tried, kind reader, to give you a faithful representation of two gentle pairs of Turtles as ever cooed their loves in the green woods. I have placed them on a branch of Stuartia, which you see ornamented with a profusion of white blossoms, emblematic of purity and chastity.

Fig. 39. *Carolina Turtle Dove* (Havell XVII). Mourning Dove, *Zenaidura macroura.* Watercolor; 25⅝ × 19 in. The New-York Historical Society.

Fig. 40. *Great Crested Flycatcher* (Havell CXXIX). Great Crested Flycatcher, *Myiarchus crinitus.* Watercolor; 18⁹⁄16 × 11⁷⁄16 in. The New-York Historical Society.

. . . Nothing is wanting to render the moment as happy as could be desired by any couple on a similar occasion.

On the branch above, a love scene is just commencing. The female, still coy and undetermined, seems doubtful of the truth of her lover, and virgin-like resolves to put his sincerity to the test, by delaying the gratification of his wishes. She has reached the extremity of the branch, her wings and tail are already opening, and she will fly off to some more sequestered spot, where, if her lover should follow her with the same assiduous devotion, they will doubtless become as blessed as the pair beneath.[35]

In both image and text, Audubon relates the progression of what he considers to be the ideal courtship, where the sincerity of the male pursuer is tested by the virtuous female and found to be true. This story is as human as it is turtle-dovish, imparting the lesson that persistent devotion will be rewarded with adoration.[36]

Audubon found the fable, or moral tale, an effective vehicle by which to explore the many ways in which birds—and by extension human beings—interact with members of their own species and with the larger habitats in which they live. Although this narrative form is an ancient one, Audubon utilized it to examine an extensive array of environmental relationships, many of which had never before been recognized. In numerous pictures and descriptions, for example, Audubon explored the tendency of certain birds to compete with members of their own species over food and territory.[37] This intraspecial struggle is delineated with particular clarity in his portrayal of the Great Crested Flycatcher (fig. 40), in which he depicts a victorious male plucking the tail feathers of his defeated foe. In the biography that accompanies the print of this image, Audubon describes the characteristically aggressive behavior of the bird when its domain is invaded:

Tyrannical perhaps in a degree surpassing the King Bird itself, it yet seldom chases the larger birds of prey, but, unlike the Bee Martin, prefers attacking those smaller

Fig. 41. *Shoveler Duck* (Havell cccxxvii). Northern Shoveler, *Anas clypeata* Linnaeus. Watercolor; 20¹³⁄₁₆ × 27⁵⁄₁₆ in. The New-York Historical Society.

ones which inadvertently approach its nest or its station. Among themselves these birds have frequent encounters, on which occasions they shew an unrelenting fierceness almost amounting to barbarity. The *plucking* of a conquered rival is sometimes witnessed.[38]

In this passage the language of combat is still couched in moral terms; indeed, it is the language of disapprobation, warning us against proper instincts gone awry. While Audubon clearly respects the inclination of the flycatcher to defend its home, he suggests that the bird often overreacts, pursuing small birds that wander mistakenly into its territory rather than truly dangerous birds of prey. The special fury with which the flycatcher attacks members of its own species Audubon finds almost barbarous, and he singles out the act of plucking a vanquished opponent's feathers as an example of the bird's savage behavior. It is this act of cruelty and humiliation that Audubon illustrates to characterize the flycatcher in *The Birds of America*—an act he clearly considers essential to a full understanding of this "tyrannical" bird.

The most extreme cases of intraspecial competition explored by Audubon occur in his depictions of mated birds fighting over food. While his image of a male and female Shoveler pursuing the same insect depicts what, on the surface, appears to be a relatively benign encounter (fig. 41), his portrayal of two Red-tailed Hawks locked in aerial combat over a hare fully exposes the violence inherent in such an interaction, fig. 42 (page 102). The biography of the Red-tailed Hawk that accompanies the print made after this drawing elaborates on this combative behavior, explaining that after breeding males and females of this species generally become strangers to one another, fighting over prey. In this passage, Audubon relates the circumstances that led him to portray the hostile engagement illustrated in his picture:

It was after witnessing such an encounter between two of these powerful marauders, fighting hard for a young Hare, that I made the drawing, in which you perceive the male to have greatly the advantage over the female, although she still holds the prey firmly in one of her talons, even while she is driven towards the earth, with her breast upwards.[39]

Here Audubon utilizes the drama of the image and its accompanying text to drive home the most disturbing consequences of estrangement. And yet this story of violent competition between mates constitutes far more than a moral tale. In this portrayal, a sense of nature's cruel power, divested of moral meaning or purpose, is brought to the fore. Even the language of Audubon's account is less judgmental than it is in many of his texts, describing the event in a more straightforward style. In this picture and its accompanying biography, the traditional concept of the natural world as an arena for the teaching of moral lessons slips away and a new and unsettling vision of an amoral cosmos begins to emerge.

The stark picture of creation suggested by this portrayal of the Red-tailed Hawk is, however, relatively anomalous to Audubon's work. He was rarely able to move beyond the structure of the moral tale to examine intraspecial competition as evidence of a struggle for survival basic to the very pattern of life itself. This would be left to the British naturalist Charles Darwin, who, in the next generation, would draw conclusions from observations similar to those of Audubon that would revolutionize Western cosmology. Based on his own work as a field naturalist, Darwin would posit an unstable world, devoid of moral law, where competition functions as the ruling mechanism by which species change. While the constraints of Audu-

bon's world view and the very language by which he constructed his images and his texts would keep him from reaching such conclusions, his creative use of the moral tale allowed him to communicate an important new set of observations regarding the habits of birds—and by extension those of men. Indeed, his suggestion that human beings, like birds, are enmeshed in the larger web of creation through their behavioral responses would have disturbing consequences for the traditional understanding of man's place in the cosmos. Over the course of the nineteenth century, this notion of humankind as an interactive being would subvert the age-old conception of the human species as set apart from the rest of the natural world, in a position of privilege at the head of the Great Chain of Being.

Standing slightly outside the community of organized science, Audubon, as a self-proclaimed American Woodsman, was able to pursue an original examination of inter- and intraspecial interaction and to claim that area of exploration as his own. Through his investigation of behavioral interrelationships, Audubon helped to lead naturalists away from a purely systematic study of the natural world to the more environmental study that prevails today.

Fig. 42. *Red-tailed Hawk* (Havell LI). Red-tailed Hawk, *Buteo jamaicensis*. Watercolor; 37⅜ × 25¼ in. The New-York Historical Society.

NOTES

1. John James Audubon, entry for Thursday, March 6, "The European Journals," in Maria R. Audubon, ed., *Audubon and His Journals*, vol 1, (1897; reprinted Magnolia, Mass.: Peter Smith, 1972), pp. 288–89.
2. Entry for Thursday, March 6, "The European Journals," p. 289.
3. From approximately 1803 to 1807, Audubon had lived at Mill Grove, a property owned by his father outside Philadelphia. At that time, however, he was just beginning his study of American birds, and he did not seek the acquaintance of members of the city's scientific community.
4. Charles Lucien Bonaparte (1803–57) was a nephew of Napoleon whose distinguished scientific career was disrupted by political events in France. From 1823 to 1828 he resided in Philadelphia, where he pursued the study of birds, producing a four-volume continuation to Alexander Wilson's *American Ornithology* (1825–33), in which Audubon's first published drawing of a pair of Boat-tailed Grackles appeared. Many of the illustrations for Bonaparte's publication were executed by Titian Ramsay Peale (1799–1885), the naturalist son of the artist and museum director, Charles Willson Peale. Titian Peale and Audubon corresponded over the years and exchanged specimens. Audubon also came to know Peale's friend and colleague, Charles Alexandre Lesueur (1778–1846), a French artist-naturalist who spent a significant portion of his career in Philadelphia and the utopian community of New Harmony, Indiana, before returning to France to direct the Natural History Museum at Le Havre. Audubon's closest Philadelphia colleague was Richard Harlan (1796–1843), an important early vertebrate paleontologist and comparative anatomist who lectured at the Peale Museum. Audubon and Harlan corresponded actively, exchanged specimens, and coauthored several scientific papers.
5. Audubon's own writings indicate that he was highly conscious of the central role played by Cooper and Boone in promoting a romantic conception of the American wilderness. See especially John James Audubon,

"The Ohio," in *Ornithological Biography*, vol I (Edinburgh: Adam Black, 1831–1839), pp. 31–32; and "Colonel Boone," ibid., vol. I, p. 503ff.

6. While in Edinburgh in 1827, Audubon had delivered five scientific papers on North American subjects that were subsequently released in various journals. Reaching Philadelphia in their published form, these papers came under severe attack. On the advice of John Children, Secretary of the Royal Society of London, Audubon largely limited his future scientific publication to the text accompanying *The Birds of America*. For further discussion of this subject, see Alexander Adams, *John James Audubon* (New York: G. P. Putnam's Sons, 1966), pp. 333–39; and entries for December 6, 1827, and January 9, 1828, in "The European Journals," Maria R. Audubon, ed., *Audubon and His Journals*, pp. 271 and 276.

7. Audubon introduces himself in this way on the first page of his Introductory Address in the *Ornithological Biography*, vol. I, p. v.

8. Entry for October 28, 1826 in "The European Journals," pp. 150–51.

9. Entry for February 24, 1828, ibid., p. 283. For an extensive discussion of Audubon's interactions with Selby, see Christine E. Jackson, "The Changing Relationship between J. J. Audubon and his friends P. J. Selby, Sir William Jardine and W. H. Lizars," *Archives of Natural History*, 18 (3) (1991), pp. 289–307.

10. Entry for June 22, 1827, in "The European Journals," p. 257.

11. For a discussion of Audubon's overture to Swainson and his ultimate invitation to MacGillivray, see Alice Ford, *John James Audubon* (Norman: University of Oklahoma Press, 1964), pp. 270–73.

12. John James Audubon, Introductory Address, *Ornithological Biography*, vol. I, pp. xviii–xix.

13. Quoted in "Audubon," in Maria R. Audubon, ed., *Audubon and His Journals*, vol. I, pp. 63–64.

14. Audubon's intention to describe habits is expressly indicated in the full title of his work: *Ornithological Biography, or an Account of the Habits of the Birds of the United States of America*.

15. John James Audubon, "Prospectus," reprinted in *Ornithological Biography*, vol. I, n. p.

16. For a classic discussion of the Great Chain of Being as a concept developed in antiquity and carried forward into the modern period, see Arthur O. Lovejoy, *The Great Chain of Being* (Cambridge, Mass.: Harvard University Press, 1964).

17. John James Audubon, Introductory Address, *Ornithological Biography*, vol. I, p. xix.

18. The proposed *Synopsis of the Birds of the United States* was published as *A Synopsis of the Birds of North America*, 8 vols. (Edinburgh: Adam & Charles Black, 1839). The publication served as a systematic index to the folio edition of *The Birds of America*. For further discussion of scientific arrangement and Audubon's publications see Ron Tyler, *Nature's Classics: John James Audubon's Birds and Animals* (Orange, Texas: The Stark Museum of Art, 1992), p. 29.

19. For a detailed discussion of Bartram's revolutionary view of the natural world, see Amy R. W. Meyers, "Sketches from the Wilderness: Changing Conceptions of Nature in American Natural History Illustration, 1680–1880," Yale University: Ph.D. dissertation, 1985, pp. 113–193.

20. The full title of Bartram's work is *Travels through North and South Carolina, Georgia, East and West Florida, the Cherokee Country, the Extensive Territories of the Muscogulges, or Creek Confederacy, and the Country of the Chactaws; Containing an Account of the Soil and Natural Productions of those Regions, together with Observations of the Manners of the Indians* (Philadelphia: James & Johnson, 1791). For a brief discussion of Audubon's critique of Bartram's presentation of Florida in his *Travels*, see Ford, *John James Audubon*, p. 290.

21. Audubon, *Ornithological Biography*, vol. I, p. 364.

22. It is ironic that Audubon used this argument in his *Ornithological Biography* to refute Alexander Wilson's claim that the Winter Hawk is simply an immature Red-shouldered Hawk. Audubon asserted that Wilson—and by extension Charles Bonaparte—had not spent enough time in the field to understand the differences between the two species. In fact, it was Audubon who was mistaken, and his portrait of the Winter Hawk is now known to portray a young Red-shouldered Hawk.

23. Audubon also called this bird by the common name of Osprey, the name by which it is known today.

24. Audubon, *Ornithological Biography*, vol. II, p. 466.

25. Audubon, entry for July 18, 1833, "The Labrador Journal," in Maria R. Audubon, ed., *Audubon and His Journals*, vol. I, p. 401.

26. Audubon, *Ornithological Biography*, vol. I, p. 60. The bird portrayed in the picture is now known to be an immature Bald Eagle. Audubon believed it to be a distinct species and called it the "Bird of Washington."

27. In an article entitled "Audubon's Passion," Adam Gopnik introduced one of the first serious discussions of the parallels Audubon drew between the behavior of birds and human beings. See Adam Gopnik, "A Critic at Large (Audubon's Passion)," *The New Yorker* (February 25, 1991), pp. 96–104.

28. John James Audubon, "Method of Drawing Birds," reprinted in *My Style of Drawing Birds*, introduction by Michael Zinman (Ardsley, N.Y.: The Overland Press, 1979), p. 22.

29. Audubon, *Ornithological Biography*, vol. II, p. 11.

30. Ibid. p. 14.

31. Audubon, "Method of Drawing Birds," in *My Style of Drawing Birds*, p. 22.

32. Audubon, "My Style of Drawing Birds," ms. composed in 1831 and reprinted in *My Style of Drawing Birds*, p. 17.

33. The Carolina Turtle Dove is now known as the Mourning Dove.

34. As Audubon points out in his biography of the Passenger Pigeon, this kind of caress is known as "billing," an action in which "the bill of one [bird] is introduced transversely into that of the other, and both parties alternately disgorge the contents of their crop by repeated effort." See Audubon, *Ornithological Biography*, vol. I, p. 325.

35. Audubon, *Ornithological Biography*, vol. I, p. 91.

36. This story is one that Audubon illustrated many times. See, for example, *Passenger Pigeon* (page 138), *Wood Duck* (page 152), and *White-crowned Pigeon* (page 220).

37. In a paper entitled "Domestic Violence: Scientific Themes and Audubon's *Rattlesnake Attacked by Mockingbirds*," delivered at the American Studies Association's Annual Meeting in November 1992, Linda Dugan Partridge offered an insightful discussion of Audubon's portrayals of intraspecial strife. This subject will be explored further in a book she is presently writing, based on her dissertation, "From Nature: John James Audubon's Drawings and Watercolors, 1805–1826," University of Delaware: Ph.D. dissertation, 1992.

38. Audubon, *Ornithological Biography*, vol. II, pp. 177–78.

39. Ibid., vol. I, pp. 268–69.

Complexity in Creation:
A Detailed Look at the Watercolors for
The Birds of America

In 1990, the conservation staff of The New-York Historical Society began an ongoing study of its Audubon collection, which consists of nearly 500 individual works on paper, of which 431 are the drawings used in producing *The Birds of America*. Most of the work for *The Birds of America* was done between 1820 and 1838. This is the first time they had been thoroughly examined by conservators. Each piece was carefully examined, conservation assessments were made, and, when necessary, treatments were planned and executed. As a result, a significant amount of technical information was accumulated, yet there is still much to be learned. Even so, one thing is clear: Audubon, with the help of his assistants, succeeded in creating one of the most beautiful series of artworks in the history of nineteenth-century American art.

More than 300 drawings for *The Birds of America* have been examined as consistently as possible, using a Nikon stereobinocular microscope, ultraviolet illumination, and raking light sources. Few if any chemical analyses were performed since these processes were not critical to the current conservation treatments. Future analysis will be done as required.

Conservation of Audubon's works is difficult because they are not merely watercolors in the traditional sense but complex pieces in a wide variety of media, glazes, papers, and adhesives. In addition, over the course of thirty years Audubon and his assistants made and reworked the drawings, which were then handled by countless people over subsequent generations. The drawings were also used extensively and in many different ways: as promotional material, as preliminary working drawings for the prints, as studies for oil paintings, and for the smaller octavo edition. In the nineteenth century they were sent across America and then to England and Scotland and back again. They were then kept by the Audubon family before ultimately being purchased by The New-York Historical Society. The long history of Audubon's watercolors has, not surprisingly, left physical evidence, which is fascinating not only for what it tells us about the structure of the works themselves but also about what the future holds for them.

PAPERS USED BY AUDUBON

All of the drawings in the Audubon collection are on hard-sized, wove papers which were made on a paper "mold" of woven wire screening. Wove papers have very little "tooth" or surface texture and few irregularities, so they reflect light uniformly. They were designed to accept inks and watercolor evenly but are not especially receptive to friable media such as chalks, charcoal, or pastels, which require more texture to hold the loose pigment particles. They do show subtle variations, however, because one side of the sheet is made against the wire mold while the other, the felt side (often called the top side), can pick up the texture of the paper-making felt. Some artists consistently choose one side or the other on which to draw, but Audubon appeared not to have a preference, a fact demonstrated by the recorded watermarks that are sometimes reversed on the recto of the drawings.

These watermarks indicate that Audubon used the best-quality papers available. They were composed of linen and cotton fibers and manufactured by several different paper mills. The most common watermarks recorded are variations of both J WHATMAN and J WHATMAN/TURKEY MILLS, with and without dates. These papers were produced by two distinct English paper mills; J Whatman belonged to the Balston Mill, and J Whatman/Turkey Mills belonged to the Hollingsworth Mill.[1] The watermark TG & C°, which is the mark for the American papermaking mill (1787–1837) of Joshua and Thomas Gilpin, appears only three times in this collection on drawings that date from 1820 to 1821.[2]

Although the watermarks show a wide range of production dates,[3] these dates do not always directly correspond to the attribution date of the drawing, which can be up to fifteen years later than the watermark date. The collection also includes many unmarked sheets and many with incomplete or indecipherable watermarks belonging to the Whatman family. Because Audubon's papers are typical of high-quality, wove watercolor papers, it is extremely difficult to distinguish one paper from another without the watermarks.

The papers fall into three categories, which correspond to the Whatman production sizes. The Whatman papers used for *The Birds of America* print folio are double elephant size (39½ × 29½ inches), which was also the size used for the largest drawings. The medium-size drawings appear to be on Whatman elephant size (23 × 28 inches), and the smallest drawings correspond to Whatman medium size (17½ × 22 inches). Many of the drawings have been trimmed to smaller dimensions, probably by another hand, in the nineteenth century when they were mounted. In some cases, sheets have been abutted to make pages of unusual dimension as in the *Loggerhead Shrike* (page 158).

It should be noted that Audubon's collage cutouts came from the same type paper as his complete drawings. Audubon often mined his earlier drawings for birds of different plumage, sex, or age to complete later works.

AUDUBON'S GENERAL WORKING METHODS

All of Audubon's drawings were executed in several media. The simplest pieces are pastel and graphite or watercolor and graphite. The others contain any combination of watercolor, graphite, pastel, oil paint, gouache, chalk, ink, overglazing, and collage. Common techniques used by Audubon and his several assistants included the consistent use of a graphite underdrawing as the basis for the composition; scraping back watercolor to make white lines or highlights; the application of a thin layer of a natural gum or gelatin over selected watercolor areas to increase gloss and color saturation; and the combination of white gouache with watercolor for details or more texture. Mostly self-taught, Audubon developed a broad range of drawing techniques and used a wide variety of media to achieve his ends. While many of the techniques used in making his pieces were not unusual for nineteenth-century watercolorists, there are some that are unique to Audubon.

It seems clear that Audubon simply used whatever means and techniques were at his disposal to draw the birds as true to life as possible. Thus, he used mixtures of the media available to him, incorporated earlier elements, and relied on the help of assistants to produce the birds he had studied for so many years, an approach that makes it difficult to be dogmatic in detailing his working methods.

It has been written that Audubon drew the birds first, and the backgrounds were filled in later, either by himself or by his assistants. This is true of many pieces, including the illustration of the white-throated sparrow (fig. 43), in which a central flower is painted over a sparrow, using lead white gouache to cover the opaque bird. However, there are also several clear examples of birds being added after the completion of the background, as in the *Northern Parula* (page 88). Here the upper bird is drawn over the vertical flower stem, and the stem is visible through the transparent watercolor. The addition of cutout birds after the flowers or foliage were painted is another example of background before bird. There are also many examples of birds and backgrounds so completely integrated that it is impossible to say which came first, even when it is known that a collaborative effort occurred. This is true of the *Summer Tanager* (page 92) and the *Tufted Titmouse* (page 116) done with Joseph Mason. Many of Audubon's compositions are so com-

Fig. 43. *White-throated Sparrow* (Havell VIII). Watercolor, graphite, pastel, gouache; 18¼ × 11⅛ in. The New-York Historical Society. This detail of the central flower shows opaque lead white gouache over a previously painted watercolor bird and partial reconversion of darkened lead white.

Fig. 44. *Spotted Sandpiper* (Havell cccx). Watercolor, graphite, selective glazing, black chalk (?); 16⅜ × 22⅝ in. The New-York Historical Society. Detail of graphite landscape, uncolored, in upper left of background.

Fig. 45. *Magnolia Warbler* (Havell L). Watercolor, graphite, pastel, selective glazing, brown ink inscriptions; 18¾ × 11½ in. The New-York Historical Society. Detail of the central bird illustrating the graphite over pastel, which has abraded the pastel on back of the bird of 1812.

plex that careful planning and underdrawing were critical. Different approaches were possible, and it might be that, as Mason's teacher, Audubon drew the entire underdrawing and had Mason complete the flowers once Audubon had done the birds. It is also possible that Audubon drew the outline of the birds and the two or three main branches, then let Mason work freely, and returned to complete the birds. In his later collaboration with George Lehman, however, it seems clear that Lehman painted many of the elaborate backgrounds around Audubon's outlined birds, after which the birds and some of the foreground landscapes were finished by Audubon.[4]

GRAPHITE

One area in which Audubon was consistent was his use of a graphite underdrawing. He wrote in his letters that the most time-consuming part of his drawings was making the "outlines" of the birds.[5] This must refer to the underdrawing, which is usually precise. In his work, the underdrawing is normally overpainted with watercolor, oil paint, or pastel, but under the thin watercolor washes, such as in the *Red Knot* (page 121) and the *Foot of the Great Black-backed Gull* (page 268), there is always some area of it clearly visible. The graphite underdrawing is used to outline the birds, flowers, and foliage, often describing the pattern of the bird's feathers and the reticulation in its feet. In a few pieces, the outline was not precisely followed, and the

graphite lines show minor alterations in the execution of the design. Uncolored areas of underdrawing are seen in the tree branch in the *Summer Tanager* (page 92) and in *Anna's Hummingbird* (page 290). A loose but detailed landscape in graphite is seen in the background of the *Roseate Spoonbill* (page 215) and the *Spotted Sandpiper* (fig. 44). These areas were probably left uncolored because Audubon trusted his engraver, Robert Havell, to adequately complete his work on the copperplates.

Graphite was also used to indicate to the engraver the position of landscape details or design alterations. In the *Sharp-tailed Grouse* (page 278) graphite lines over the oil paint show the position of the mountains on the right, and a small graphite mark on the left bird shows the new position of the right bird in the print. Sometimes delicate graphite elements were even drawn as part of the composition. This technique is seen in the faint spider web above the Red-eyed Vireo (page 112). Occasionally small ornithological details were made in graphite in the drawings' margins.[6]

Audubon also used graphite over pastel in some of his early works in an attempt to shade the forms, as in the feet of the Brown Pelican (page 83) and the top wing of the central yellow bird in the *Summer Tanager* (page 92). This technique is unusual and only moderately successful, since the graphite both compresses and covers most of the pastel pigment. Graphite can also abrade pastel, as seen in back of the Magnolia Warbler of 1812 (fig. 45). Nevertheless, the metallic, slightly iridescent quality of graphite's surface sheen, which is different from that of black or gray pastel, became extremely important in Audubon's later pieces.

Graphite lines were also used to reinforce and clarify details over both pastel and watercolor. Heavier lines are overdrawn, often in those areas that help define a bird's particular characteristics. Note the dark graphite lines around the eyes and claws in the *Dickcissel* (page 78) of 1811 and the pattern on the legs of the left Black-crowned Night Heron (page 192).

Sometimes graphite was used over watercolor or pastel areas in a more delicate way with small curving lines, which could make soft downy feathers on the chest or head of a bird and give greater definition to each form. This technique can be seen in the soft gray shading of the feathers in *Common Tern* (page 254), the neck and tail feathers in *Gyrfalcon* (page 292) and the Osprey's body (page 166).

Audubon's most characteristic use of graphite was the drawing of hundreds of short, repetitive lines over the dried watercolor form of each bird. These lines were used to define the shape and direction of the feathers and were most often drawn on a diagonal, so that each set of lines would catch the light from a different angle. The metallic sheen of graphite was used to great effect in these instances. The fact that the watercolor was first allowed to dry made for clear, sharp lines of graphite that do not deform or tear the paper. One of the best examples is the *Magnificent Frigatebird* of 1832 (page 222), in which the many layers of watercolor have resulted in an iridescent green-black form further defined and enhanced by hundreds of graphite lines. Other, more delicately drawn examples are seen in the wings in the *Barn Swallow* (page 226), the brilliantly colored *Carolina Parakeet* (page 154), and the face in *Great Gray Owl* (page 258).

PASTEL TECHNIQUES

Audubon's earliest works are simply pastel over graphite underdrawing. These include the *Sylvia Trochitus Delicata* (1863.18.005) of 1808 and *Dickcissel* of 1811. Audubon applied each color using individual sticks of pastel to create a sense of volume over the graphite underdrawing. The pastel appears "flat," like a dry pigment on the paper surface. Despite the smooth paper surface, a significant amount of pastel is held by the paper and is deeply embedded in it. It is not clear if this compression was the result of Audubon's heavy application of pastel and some preparation of the sheet or the result of storing the drawings in great stacks. Audubon may have treated or prepared the

Fig. 46. *Black Vulture.* Pastel, watercolor, graphite, gouache, brown ink inscriptions; 28 ⅛ × 20 ¾ in. The New-York Historical Society. This detail shows the entire bird, which is made of many layers of black pastel. Note the lack of modeling and definition of the form.

paper to increase its receptivity to pastel by roughing up the paper surface or coating it with a layer of size, which would act as an adhesive or binder, but there is no remaining visual evidence of this.

Eventually Audubon began to layer different colors of pastel. He created shadows, using darker colors over lighter ones and, at times, would build up extremely dense layers of pastel both black and colors. This is the case with *Black Vulture* (fig. 46) of 1820. Despite this remarkable example of thickly applied pastel, Audubon could not completely modulate the forms using only pastel.

PASTEL AND WATERCOLOR

The combination of watercolor with pastel and graphite underdrawing is a slightly unusual technique. After 1820, Audubon began to use watercolor and more graphite to supplement the pastel. The earliest example in the Society's collection is the

Cooper's Hawk in the lower right of the *Northern Goshawk and Cooper's Hawk*, c. 1809, (page 80). The hawk is pastel with graphite underdrawing, but the landscape is a muddy mixture of watercolor and glazing.[7]

Watercolor washes were used to define with more delicacy features such as eyes, beaks, claws and feathers on individual birds. For example, in the *Bald Eagle* of 1820 (page 160), the landscape and most of the bird are pastel, but the head and claws of the eagle as well as the head of the dead goose are watercolor. Similarly, watercolor is used for the feet and head of the young *Turkey Vulture* (page 294) while the orange body of the bird is pastel.

Another of Audubon's innovations was the use of pastel over a layer of thin watercolor wash in the same color. Examples of this can be seen in the tails in the two Red-tailed Hawks (page 102) and in the birds in the upper left and lower right side of the *Rock Wren, Winter Wren* of c. 1820 (page 276). In these drawings, it appears that the watercolor wash was applied and allowed to dry before the application of the pastel. This allowed the pastel particles to remain loosely bound. They maintain an intensity and reflective quality, which is enhanced by the underlying watercolor layer. The watercolor itself is very difficult to see without high magnification, but a slight line of dispersed watercolor liquid is usually visible at the edges of the forms.

Eventually, Audubon began using a more complex combination of pastel and watercolor, which involved applying pastel—possibly with wet pastel sticks—over wet watercolor. The moisture compressed the pastel and changed its reflectivity, making the effect more like that of thick watercolor or synthetic chalk. This was not a new technique: both natural chalks and pastels had been soaked in oil or water to achieve similar effects long before the nineteenth century. The earliest example in this collection, however, dates from 1815. In the *Blue-winged and Golden-winged Warblers* (fig. 47), black pastel or chalk was applied over wet watercolor in the chest of the left bird while pure watercolor was used for the eye, feet, and some of the wing. In many places it is difficult to distinguish the transition between the watercolor and the pastel, which may be the result of applying additional water over the pastel to blend it. This smooth transition of media is also seen in the chests of the Long-billed Curlews (page 189) and the head of the Blue Jay (page 156) on the left side of the composition.

Sometimes the pastel was applied in a few delicate strokes to add color to a very dark area. The blue pastel over the black body in *Atlantic Puffin* (page 236) is one such example as is *Magnificent Frigatebird* (page 222). Frequently black pastel or chalk was applied over layers of glazed and unglazed black watercolor, creating a subtle range of matte and shiny black surfaces that defined the bird. This is illustrated in the back and wing of the Great Cormorant (page 243) in which black pastel strokes provide a dense matte black in comparison to the unglazed watercolor areas, which, in turn, are matte when compared to the shiny glazed watercolor. Even though Audubon was eventually capable of reproducing virtually any texture or surface in watercolor, he never completely abandoned pastel for its softness and texture, and pastel touches were, in fact, used throughout the production of *The Birds of America*.

WATERCOLOR

Watercolor was a natural choice for depicting birds and foliage because it allowed for the quick rendering of color and detail. Audubon probably used dry cake watercolor for most of his career but may have used moist colors in pans in the 1830s, since they were readily available in England at that time.[8]

Audubon usually applied watercolor in a traditional man-

Fig. 47. *Blue-winged and Golden-winged Warblers.* Watercolor, graphite, pastel, collage, brown ink and graphite inscriptions; 16¾ × 10⅝ in. The New-York Historical Society. This detail of the birds shows the earliest example of wet pastel over watercolor, and the use of pure watercolor and pure pastel.

ner, laying in two or three thin washes of color to make a form. Under magnification, overlapping tidal edges created by water carrying the pigment are visible, but without magnification, the color often appears to be a single, controlled wash. Although this technique was used for most of the birds, flowers, and foliage, in a few of his works Audubon applied innumerable washes of transparent watercolor, building up the layers to make a dense, opaque color. This is most clearly seen in the bright red in the *Scarlet Tanager* of 1836 (page 286), the dark colored blacks in the *Magnificent Frigatebird* (page 222), and the purple-blues in the *Eastern Bluebird*, 1820 (page 96). These intensely colored birds seem to be painted with a single layer of gouache or tempera, but careful examination reveals the many layers of watercolor that were applied. In some of the black birds, the layers can be extremely complex. Black, blue, green, purple, and brown were all used to capture the density and true colors present in a "black" bird. Once the color was built up, smaller strokes were used to make surface texture or to help define the bird's form. Often the paint was scratched to make white lines. In the *American Flamingo* (fig. 48) a brilliant pink pigment has been applied in so many layers and with so much media or excess glazing that the paint film has moved and cracked, a phenomenon more common to oil paint than watercolor. In spite of the damage caused by aging, these watercolors remain remarkably effective in capturing indescribable colors. Note the multicolor effects in the *Passenger Pigeon* of 1824 (page 138) and the brilliantly colored *Carolina Parakeet* of 1825 (page 154).

Fig. 48. *American Flamingo* (Havell ccccxxxi). Watercolor, selective glazing, graphite, gouache; 33³⁄₁₆ × 24¹⁄₈ in. The New-York Historical Society. Raking light detail illustrating the thick and severely cracked paint and glaze layers (full painting appears on page x).

In fact, one benefit of this heavy application of paint is that the finely ground watercolor pigments, which are usually prone to fading, have survived intact. This is probably the result of the presence of large amounts of closely packed pigment. As a result, even if some pigment particles have faded due to exposure to light, the color intensity has changed very little, if at all.

USE OF WHITES

There are three ways of creating whites in watercolor compositions: using the white reserve of the paper; using opaque white pigment (gouache); and scraping away wet watercolor to reveal the paper below. Although Audubon used all three techniques, he preferred using the white reserves. The white areas in the body of the Pacific Loon (page 251) is one good example. The white page reserves were usually given details by delicate overdrawing in graphite or watercolor. Sometimes Audubon used an extremely light wash of black or blue watercolor, which is visible under magnification, allowing the white paper to show through, thus creating the illusion of being white. This is seen in the Crested Caracara (page 224), whose beak is made of a blue watercolor wash.

Audubon also used white paint or pastel to enhance some flat areas of white paper. He generally used such a thin wash of white pigment that it is nearly invisible even under magnification. Its presence can best be seen in the very subtle contrast between the slightly yellowed unpainted paper and the brighter, whiter painted areas. It is likely that these white pigments had some calcium carbonate, an alkaline material that can help protect paper fibers from discoloring. The clearest example may be seen in the delicate, almost invisible feather in the right side of the Tree Swallow (page 134), which is partially defined by thin watercolor lines.

Audubon and his assistants also used white gouache with watercolor for details and highlights. In the nests in *Barn Swallow* (page 226) and *Yellow-breasted Chat* (page 174), the more opaque fibers and the straw in the nest are thin lines of gouache. This kind of delicate white line over darker watercolor is also seen in *Black-billed Magpie* (page 260) and in the upper bird in the *Tree Swallow* (page 134).

Some of Audubon's egrets and herons[9] provide examples of whites that have been thickly applied. In these birds the white is applied in narrow but dense lines, giving a three-dimensional quality to some of the feathers. Heavy impasto whites are also seen in the bumps on the beak in *Great Cormorant* (page 243). This use of thick paint is an unusual technique for Audubon

Fig. 49. *Black-throated Magpie-Jay* (Havell xcvi). Watercolor, gouache, graphite, collage, selective glazing and scraping; 37 ¼ × 24 ⅛ in. The New-York Historical Society. Detail of the bird's head, showing the edge of a collage piece and the lead white used to cover an error and its present conversion to lead sulfide.

but one that clearly captures the effect of the large and delicate feathers of some birds and the texture of the cormorant's beak.

Thickly applied whites were also used to cover mistakes in a few drawings. This is an old technique and is seen around the head of the Magpie Jay (fig. 49). The white used in most areas of heavier impasto appears to be lead white or a mixture of lead with other whites. When used as a watercolor, lead white is susceptible to conversion to a dark gray or black form of lead.[10] This has occurred in a number of pieces in this collection, most obviously in the correction in the *Magpie Jay,* but also in many more subtle areas. Some high impasto parts of the white tails of the herons and egrets have darkened.[11] The same conversion, which has been partially reversed through conservation efforts, is seen in the central flower of the *White-throated Sparrow* (see fig. 43). The visual effects of white becoming dark can be quite disturbing, but the conversion of nearly all of these whites is so complete that reversion to white is not possible.

White lines and highlights were also produced by scraping away watercolor. A sharp tool called a scraper was often used to make a detail, emphasize a form, or add texture as exemplified by the wing in *Trumpeter Swan* (page 299) and the head, bodies, and foliage in *Carolina Parakeet* (page 154). Scraping was used in a broader way to give an uneven, textured look to the nest in *Barn Swallow* (page 226).

GLAZING

The use of a thin layer of a natural gum or gelatin as a glaze over watercolor is often seen in nineteenth-century prints and watercolors. Audubon and his assistants used glazes to intensify colors and alter the surface gloss of certain areas of the landscape and foliage. Glazes were also used to emphasize details, to create more animated surfaces, and to enhance the subtle gloss and matte contrast of birds' feathers.[12] This contrast is often seen in paintings of darker birds like *Great Cormorant* (page 243) and *Double-crested Cormorant* (page 234). The thickest glaze layer in the collection is, however, in the *Blue Jay* (page 156), where the dripping egg yolk is made of a very heavy layer of slightly yellow glaze over darker yellow and brown watercolor.

The glazes are all transparent with a range of yellow tones. Usually, the heavier the glaze, the darker the yellow, although thickness is not the only factor. Both gum and gelatin were probably used by Audubon with slightly different results. The protein-based gelatin is a much stronger adhesive and tends to respond more dramatically to changes in humidity, swelling and shrinking with moisture absorption. These changes can cause cracking and cupping of the underlying paint films, but similar results can occur with thick layers of gum. This is probably the case in the egg in *Blue Jay.* The thinnest glazes show a

Fig. 50. *Great Blue Heron* (Havell CCXI). Pastel, watercolor, graphite, oil paint, gouache, collage; 36 × 25⅜ in. The New-York Historical Society. Detail of the bird's tail where three small pieces of paper have been used to cover a single feather, correcting the design.

smooth surface, while some of the thicker ones exhibit cracking or fracturing of the glaze and the paint below. In some instances, as in a number of the leaves painted by Joseph Mason, the glazes are so thin that it is impossible to say whether they are a separate layer of glaze or simply a watercolor extra rich in gum media. In most cases, even when cracked, the glaze and underlying paint are stable and well adhered to the paper.

No chemical analysis was done of the glazes, but solubility testing demonstrates that all the glossy surface coatings are water-soluble. This means that they are not egg white or egg yolk, which rapidly become insoluble in water. Although the use of egg proteins has often been attributed to Audubon,[13] no evidence of egg white or yolk used as a glaze has ever been proven.

METALLIC PAINTS

One component seen in only three of the collection's drawings is gold-colored metallic paint. It is present in the *Wild Turkey* (1863.17.001), the *Mallard* (1863.17.221), and the *Ruby-throated Hummingbird* (1863.17.047), all of 1825. The paint was applied and then partially covered by watercolor in each case. The overlying watercolor was probably used to alter the color of the metal and resulted in a shiny color-washed gold. In the hummingbird and the mallard paintings, the metallic paint was exposed to the environment and has discolored, probably through oxidation. Since gold does not oxidize, the metal Audubon used was probably brass or bronze. In the *Wild Turkey*, the metal paint still shows some of the reflective sparkle of gold in areas where it has been almost entirely covered by other layers of watercolor. This is visible only under magnification,

however, and only as a result of the partial loss of the overpaint through abrasion and poor adhesion.

The use of a metallic paint is another example of Audubon's interest in experimenting with varied materials to get different effects. Here he may have wanted a reflective, golden shine different from the metallic gray shine of graphite, but his limited use of the paint suggests that he was not particularly pleased with the result.

COLLAGE

Rarely seen in other works of this period, Audubon's use of collage appears to have been related to the production pressures of *The Birds of America*. Although he went to England in 1826 with more than 250 drawings, many more were needed to complete the project. Over the next ten years, in order to save time, he used pieces from earlier drawings as collage elements in later pictures. Most frequently, he would place the older figure among the new birds, then add all or part of the background. One example is the addition of the central bird, c. 1821, to the later birds and foliage in *Wood Duck* (page 152). Sometimes Audubon placed a collage bird on a completely new watercolor background,[14] or on a blank sheet of paper, as in the *Bald Eagle* (page 108), in which the bird of 1822 was completely cut out and repositioned on paper watermarked after 1830. The same technique is seen in the *Northern Goshawk and Cooper's Hawk* (page 80). There is also an unusual example of Audubon applying complex cutout flowers and foliage by George Lehman around his own birds in the *White-crowned Pigeon* (page 220). In a few drawings, tiny pieces of collage have been added to increase the complexity of the landscape.[15]

Collage was also used to make occasional corrections. This is seen in the head in *Great Egret* (page 213), in which a piece of paper was placed over the original, possibly damaged, head of the bird and completely repainted. The watercolor landscape was then painted, integrating the new head of the bird with the background. In *Great Blue Heron* (fig. 50), three small pieces of white paper were applied over a blue tail feather at the upper left. These corrections appear to be a labor-saving device, clearly indicating any changes or corrections to Havell.

The slight angularity on the edge of the cuts and the overlapping cuts at some corners suggest that the collage pieces were cut from a larger sheet with a sharp knife or scalpel-like blade. The poor condition of some of the early pastel collage pieces suggests that these birds were cut out and left unmounted for some period, treatment that resulted in the small tears, creases, and holes we now see.

The collage pieces were applied with a water-soluble adhesive, probably a high-quality gelatin, small amounts of which can occasionally be seen at the edge of a collage piece, as in the *Common Snipe* (page 198), where a smear of slightly yellow adhesive remains in the lower right corner.

In order to position the cutout on the background, Audubon drew light graphite lines or made white scratches over the

Fig. 51. *Arctic Tern* (Havell ccl). Watercolor, graphite, collage, graphite inscription. The New-York Historical Society. Detail of the sky and tail of the collaged bird, showing the thin, scraped white lines, which indicate an alternate position of the collage.

watercolor as guides for placement of the collage piece. The white lines near the tail of the *Arctic Tern* (fig. 51) is one such example. The alteration in placement of the collage, as indicated by these lines, appears to be a conscious choice, not an accidental movement of the collage. There is, however, a rare example of Audubon's placing two collage pieces and then moving them while the adhesive was still wet. In *Townsend's Bunting* (page 228), done with Maria Martin, one can see the adhesive over the watercolor foliage forming the outlined shape of each of the collaged birds. The upper bird now rests securely, slightly higher and to the left of its original position, and the lower bird is now lower and to the left. Within the collection there are also several examples of collage pieces that have shifted from their original positions. It is not clear whether this was a result of the mounting process, later handling, pieces coming off during Audubon's time and being readhered, or if they shifted while the backgrounds were originally painted.[16]

Although the collage pieces are securely attached to the backing paper, many show air bubbles, which are areas of separation on the verso of the collage with little or no adhesive, or where the adhesive may have dried too rapidly to adhere to the paper. Over time, these unrestrained areas of paper have expanded through the absorption of environmental moisture, and they now show the effects of long-term surface abrasion. Other areas appear as deep creases, suggesting that air bubbles were present when the drawings were mounted to card stock. Some of the bubbles were probably crushed under the great weight used to mount the drawings.

OIL PAINT

Areas of oil paint were added to a small number of drawings, often over previously painted watercolor backgrounds. There is no evidence that oil paint was mixed with either watercolor or pastel to make a true "mixed-media" layer and no evidence that oil paint was used in any of the birds. There are, however, several clear examples of oil paint covering an earlier watercolor background.[17] It is not always possible to know what lies beneath these additions. In the *Trumpeter Swan* (page 299) a narrow, unpainted white paper rim around the edge of the bird is visible and shows no trace of a watercolor background. This work also demonstrates how carefully the oil paint was applied around but not over the completed bird.

The oil-paint films are usually thin and often very simple, as in the water and sky of the *Trumpeter Swan*, where two areas of flat color were applied. However, there are a few works in which the oil paint is handled in a more complex and fluid manner, where colors are blended and details are drawn, although the paint is still relatively thinly applied. The best example of this is the background sky of the *Brown Pelican* (page 83).

The use of oil paint with watercolor on paper was quite uncommon in the nineteenth century. The two are distinct materials, and they respond very differently to environmental changes. Oil paint is naturally acidic and can damage the paper support. There is some evidence of oil media leaching into the paper and creating brown stains or haloes. In these drawings the oil halo is small, possibly proving that Audubon used oil paints almost dry—with a minimal amount of oil. Often staining is most obvious on the verso of the paper. Staining behind the oil paint branch in the *Chuck-will's-widow* (page 106) was revealed during conservation treatment, but no oil halo was visible on the recto. In some instances, brown stains appear on top of the oil paint layer. This surface staining may be related to previous handling and is possibly the result of oxidation of finger oils and grime. Such stains appear on the left side of the *Brown Pelican* of 1821 and the upper corners of the *Tundra Swan* (1863.17.411).

Paper expands and contracts rapidly according to changes in environmental humidity. Oil paint film, unlike watercolor wash, however, is relatively inflexible and does not move easily with changes in the paper. It is remarkable then that so few of these works show problems with cracking paint. This might be the result of the mounting of the works onto card stock, which is relatively stable dimensionally. In the nineteenth century oil paintings on canvas were commonly varnished with a natural resin to enhance the colors and protect the painting surface. Works on paper were rarely varnished, however, since it was known that the varnish would discolor and alter the paper and the media and examination of Audubon's oil-painted areas have not shown a complete, intact layer of varnish.[18]

PHYSICAL HISTORY OF THE PIECES

The history of the drawings reveals the rigors to which many of the pieces were exposed and helps explain their current condition. As noted in Audubon's journals and letters, during the production of *The Birds of America*, the drawings were handled by many people and were moved about extensively. Many were used as working drawings for the production of oil paintings as well as the prints, and often such pieces were treated with less than scrupulous care.

Nearly all of the drawings were produced by Audubon and his assistants in various locations between 1812 and 1836. The earliest pieces were produced in Henderson, Kentucky (1809–19), with a few made in Cincinnati around 1819. From 1820–21, a large group of drawings were made while Audubon traveled down the Ohio River with Joseph Mason, who drew the flowers and foliage.

While traveling and after arriving in New Orleans, Audubon showed his drawings to many people at various dinner parties. He describes showing the drawings to the painter John Wesley Jarvis, who "overlooked them, said nothing, then leaned down and examined them minutely but never said they were good or bad."[19] Audubon wrote that after Jarvis completed his inspection, "Joseph rolled up [their] papers,"[20] and they left. Audubon also showed his drawings to John Vanderlyn, who had him lay them on the floor for inspection.[21] In 1824, after months of teaching and drawing, Audubon shipped all his drawings to Philadelphia and followed them. After many more disappointing meetings concerning his proposal for a publication, Audubon left for England in 1826 with his portfolio of more than 250 drawings.

Over the next two years Audubon arranged for several short public exhibitions in Scotland and England, at which more than 200 drawings would be exhibited at each public space. Audubon noted with great emotion that on December 7, 1826, a drawing was stolen from his exhibition in Edinburgh.[22] The drawing was soon returned, but it is important to note the ease with which he imagined the piece was taken. The theft implies that the drawings were merely pinned to the wall, or loosely held, and that it was quick work to remove one. These mounting techniques may also explain the pinholes found in the corners of many of the drawings.

Shipping and traveling also caused unintentional abuse. Audubon carried many works on his trips, each of which could last several months. Once he sent a group of twenty drawings to his wife in Shippingport, Kentucky, via a friend traveling on the river packet.[23] It was not noted how these particular drawings were packed, but letters and journal entries indicate that other drawings might have been rolled and sealed in a tin case. It is also likely that drawings were sometimes shipped flat in a portfolio. Audubon left drawings with friends such as Dr. Bachman and Maria Martin in Charleston in 1832 while he continued his travels. He would recover these works at various times, requesting that the drawings be sent to him, wherever his new location was. In the 1820s, Audubon regularly sent small groups of drawings to Havell in England to maintain the production schedule of the prints. He organized the drawings in groups of five that included one large drawing, one medium, and three small. Drawings coming from America would be aboard ship two to three months before they reached Havell's studio. Audubon was often concerned about their loss or damage during shipping and warned his son Victor to be extremely careful with the "pasted" pieces.[24] Apparently, he was just as concerned with their treatment in London. In 1835 Audubon warned Havell to tell his colorers to "take better care of the Originals than they generally [do]."[25]

Havell held on to some of the drawings for a long time as reference material for himself as the engraver and for the colorists. Audubon wrote about having larger numbers of drawings ready for Havell to copy, saying he had left "enough drawings to keep Havell busy for one year plus part of the next."[26] Between 1827 and 1833, small groups of drawings, totaling at least one hundred and including the *Red-shouldered Hawk, House Wren, Ivory-billed Woodpecker,* and *Carolina Parakeet,* were given to Joseph Kidd to copy as oil paintings. Some of the drawings came directly from Audubon, while others were sent by Havell and Victor from London to Edinburgh, where Kidd had contracted to copy the birds precisely and add more elaborate landscapes. When he completed the oils, he would send small groups of drawings to London for Havell to use.

Once the plates for *The Birds of America* were completed, Audubon brought the drawings back to New York in 1839. They were publicly exhibited by Audubon for the last time at the Lyceum of Natural History. At the time of Audubon's death in 1851, the drawings used to make the plates were in the possession of his family. These works, along with other early drawings not used for *The Birds of America,* were purchased by The New-York Historical Society from Lucy Audubon in 1863. The drawing of the *California Condor* (1966.042) came to the Society at a later date.

As is typical of nineteenth-century collections, there is little written evidence of the early history of the Audubon drawings at The New-York Historical Society. At the time of their purchase, the drawings would have been stored and exhibited in the Society's Second Avenue home. This building, which was extremely crowded, had limited exhibition space, but approximately twenty pieces were framed and exhibited in January of 1864. Subsequent small installations were also held in that year.[27] Along with all the other collections, the drawings were moved to the present home of the Society on Central Park West in 1908. They were then held in the library of the institution, suggesting that they were handled by very few people, most of whom were scholars who came to do research.

Correspondence indicates that the drawings were mounted on cardboard when they were initially offered to the Society in 1862.[28] Today they are still mounted on a green-gray card stock with a layer of water-soluble adhesive, probably an animal glue. The great pressure used in mounting is evidenced by the impression of collage pieces on the versos of the mounts. This occurred because the extra layer of paper, the cutout, received more pressure than the remainder of the piece, and was pushed into the original paper backing and into the mount. Some early, unrelated drawings were paired on single sheets of card stock,[29] causing later confusion regarding the exact number of pieces acquired by The New-York Historical Society.

It is not known if Audubon was responsible for mounting the drawings or if his family had them mounted after his death. The mounts now range in color from gray-green to brown-green and are all decorated with a black ink line around the perimeter of each drawing. Although there is no direct evidence, it is unlikely that they were mounted before 1839, as shipping and transporting mounted works from England would have been difficult.

There is evidence that many of the drawings were trimmed slightly, probably before they were mounted. It is impossible to know if all of them were trimmed to remove small edge damages, or merely those with the worst damages, and the irregular sizes of the papers indicate that many of the papers may have been trimmed only a fraction of an inch. Evidence of trimming can best be seen in drawings where ink inscriptions have been partially and inexplicably cut away, as in the bottom of the large ink inscription of the *Great Egret* (page 213) and the long graphite inscription in the upper-right sky of the *Little Blue Heron* (page 195). There are also pieces in which compositional elements are missing from the drawing yet are present in the print, as in the right side of the *Red-eyed Vireo* (page 112) and the cut-off beak of the upper bird in the *Turkey Vulture* (1863.17.151).

In spite of the mounting, clues to the history of the drawings continue to emerge. Hints of inscriptions in brown ink are now visible as faint strike-through images on the recto of some sheets,[30] and graphite inscriptions in Audubon's own hand were rediscovered on the verso of several drawings during conservation treatment. These inscriptions detail the vital statistics of the specimen on each recto. New information on the date of the *Roseate Spoonbill* was also revealed.[31] These recently uncovered inscriptions suggest that much more information remains hidden behind the mounts.

Throughout a large part of the nineteenth and twentieth

centuries the drawings were stored stacked and flat in drawers at the Society, evidently without any interleaving. The result was direct, long-term contact of the rectos of drawings with the verso of mounts. The damage caused by this storage method is seen in the clear offset patterns of unrelated birds on the versos of some mounts and in the pastel that has offset onto other mounts.

Physical deterioration of some mounts and papers suggests that the largest drawings were frequently exhibited. Uneven, streaky discoloration on the versos of many mounts is visible and can also be seen on the rectos of a few drawings. *The New-York Historical Society Quarterly* of 1946 indicates that a group of 150 drawings was exhibited for six months. This was the first time such a large group had been shown. The drawings were framed without mats, directly against glass, and from 1947 through 1970 a small selection of the drawings, framed in the same manner, remained on display in an "Audubon Gallery." Only after 1970 was the collection archivally matted and framed, and it is now stored permanently framed to protect the fragile surfaces of the drawings and to buffer them from the environment.

The physical evidence of the collection's long history is clearly seen in the numerous tears, punctures and pinholes, dirt, fingerprints, and stray marks as well as embedded grime on some papers. This is visible in the *Wild Turkey* (frontispiece), a piece that both Audubon and Kidd copied in oil and which, as the first drawing to be made into a print, must have been frequently exhibited. It has many old tears, flaking paint, and surface abrasions. Much of this damage occurred long before the piece was mounted to card stock, probably when it was in Audubon's hands. Audubon himself referred to the drawing as "my old soiled one"[32] in 1835 when he considered having the copperplate reengraved. The few pieces in the collection that have been removed from their mounts show additional damage, including layers of accrued grime and watercolor streaks on the versos.

All of the drawings show a characteristic surface burnishing of the paper and media, which is seen as a kind of slight surface crust. Its presence supports the theory that the drawings were stored stacked and flat. Polishing would occur when one sheet was dragged across the underlying piece. This would also account for some smearing of the friable, dry pastel and for some media abrasion and loss, seen in the high impasto tails in the *Snowy Egret* (page 208) and *Little Blue Heron* (page 195).

Other damages are not related to the physical storage and movement of the pieces but to the inherent instability of the various media used for the drawings. The transition of lead white watercolor to a dark gray-black lead sulfide is but one example. Audubon appeared to have been aware that some of the whites he used were "bad,"[33] and wrote to Victor to have Havell correct them in the prints.

It has never been clear exactly how these drawings were copied by Havell and transferred to the copperplates. Each piece was probably copied by tracing and then reversing the trace onto the copperplate. Tracing with a stylus or pencil would leave some evidence of inscribed lines on the rectos of the originals, over the watercolor or oil paints, but this is seen in only a very few cases, most of them made around 1820.[34] The prints made from these drawings appear in the first volume of the folio. The great pressure used in the mounting process may have eliminated evidence on the rectos of the drawings, and there is no evidence visible on the versos because of the cardstock mounts. Thus, the precise method of transfer cannot yet be determined.

CONCLUSION

Technical examination of the Audubon collection has revealed the extraordinary complexity as well as the inconsistencies of Audubon's techniques. Audubon used and combined many traditional techniques (scraping, glazing and layering watercolor, overdrawing, and adding gouache) within individual drawings. He also used these techniques as a starting point to develop his own original methods. His combined use of less common materials (metallic paint, oil paint, collage) with traditional ones has resulted in mixed-media works that are fascinating but whose methodology is often difficult to comprehend. One thing that is clear, however, is that Audubon's overall intent was to create on paper, then translate into print, a comprehensive series of birds rendered as naturally as possible.

The use of early collage works in some drawings and the addition of later oil-paint backgrounds appear to be the result of time limitations. At the same time he was traveling with both drawings and prints to sell subscriptions, Audubon had to maintain a production schedule. His innovative solutions to these pressures were usually remarkably successful and produced more interesting drawings as a result.

Audubon's commitment to quality, as evidenced by his use of fine papers and materials, along with his concern for the production and maintenance of his works, probably ensured their survival in the first half of the nineteenth century, despite the drawings' long history of travel and use. Their acquisition by The New-York Historical Society has further protected them for future generations.

NOTES

I would like to thank the people who have generously contributed their expertise, insight, and time in discussing the Audubon drawings, conserving them, and supporting this project. My heartfelt gratitude goes to conservators Mary Cropley, Mindy Horn, Richard Gallerani, Michelle Gewirtz, Harriet Irgang, Karl Buchberg, and Richard Kowall, and technical assistants Beryl Fishbein and Bryn Jayes. For their advice and patient support I thank Annette Blaugrund, Holly Hotchner, and Michael Snyder.

1. The following watermark variations have been recorded by viewing the papers in strong raking light: TURKEY MILLS/J WHATMAN, with and without dates following, and J WHATMAN/date/TURKEY MILLS, J WHATMAN/TURKEY MILL, with and without date following.

2. The drawings with the Gilpin watermark are the *Cedar Waxwing* (1863.17.043), *Savannah Sparrow* (1863.17.109), and *Bonaparte's Gull* (1863.18.026).

3. These dates have been recorded on the watermarked papers: Following the J WHATMAN watermark: 1808, 1810, 1816, 1817, 1821, 1826, 1827, 1830, 1831, 1834, 1836, 1837. Following the TURKEY MILLS family of watermarks: 1810, 1811, 1817, 1818, 1827.

4. For examples of Lehman backgrounds see the *Long-billed Curlew* (page 189) with Charleston, N.C., in the distance, the *Common Snipe* (page 198), and the *Snowy Egret* (page 208).

5. Howard Corning, ed., *Journal of John James Audubon Made During His Trip to New Orleans in 1820–21* (Boston: The Club of Odd Volumes, 1929), p. 209. February 5, 1827, entry notes that after hearing of a camera lucida he "would like such an instrument if merely to save time in hot weather, when outlining correctly is more than half the work."

6. Ornithological details in pure graphite are seen in the drawing of the beak in the lower left of the *Eastern Wood Pewee* (1863.17.115) and the foot in *Great Crested Grebe* (1863.17.292).

7. A slightly more sophisticated example of mixing pastel with watercolor is the *Eastern Wood Pewee* (1863.18.008) of 1812, where the twig and foliage are watercolor with some opaque gouache. In *Cuvier's Kinglet* (1863.17.055), also of 1812, a fairly elaborate composition in watercolor surrounds the pastel and graphite bird.

8. Prepared, dry-cake watercolors were widely available after about 1780. Moist colors, which usually contained gum arabic, glycerine, and sugars, were stickier than dry cakes but not really wet. Watercolors in tubes were marketed in 1846 by Winsor & Newton. See Marjorie B. Cohn, *Wash and Gouache* (Boston: The Center for Conservation and Technical Studies, Fogg Art Museum and the Foundation of the American Institute for Conservation of Historic and Artistic Works, Inc., 1977), p. 54

9. Some of the birds showing high impasto white gouache are *Louisiana Heron* (1863.17.217), *Great Egret* (1863.18.29), *Snowy Egret* (page 208), *Great White Heron* (page 205), *Great Egret* (page 210), and *Great Cormorant* (page 243).

10. See R. D. Harley, *Artist's Pigments 1600–1835* (New York: American Elsevier Publishing Co., 1970), pp. 156–61 for a discussion of the history, uses, and problems of lead white paint.

11. Some conversion of lead white to lead sulfide is seen in *Great Egret* (1863.18.029), *Great Egret* (page 210), *Tri-colored Heron* (1863.17.217), *Great White Heron* (page 205), and *Double-crested Cormorant* (1863.17.252).

12. Glazes were applied to emphasize such details as the eye and beak in the *Atlantic Puffin* (page 236), the red in the heads in *Anna's Hummingbird* (page 290), and the blood of the dead goose in the *Peregrine Falcon* (page 145). A thin overall glaze was often applied to an entire leaf or wing, as in the large green leaf at lower left in the *Snowy Egret* (page 208).

13. Egg mixed with a finely ground pigment becomes an egg tempera paint, which tends to have a matte surface and to repel water. There is no evidence of large areas of egg tempera paint in this collection, but there are a few small examples of an opaque, viscous-looking yellow material that was applied over other areas of watercolor, which could be pure egg yolk. This yellow material is seen in the yellow shading in the earth clump of the *Water Pipet* (1863.17.080) of 1815 and the yellow smear in the lower left rocks of the *Grasshopper Sparrow* (1863.17.130). Without chemical analysis, it is impossible to say if these are egg or merely an opaque gouache. Any sampling would be invasive and is not necessary for conservation treatment. These areas are completely stable.

14. The *Roseate Tern* (1863.17.240) was placed on an abstract sky of blue watercolor, as were the *Common Tern* (1863.18.033) and *Arctic Tern* (1863.17.250). The *Chimney Swifts* (page 136) are placed on a white sheet with previously drawn nests.

15. The grasses in the foreground landscapes of the *Wild Turkey* (1863.17.001) and *Northern Bob-white and Red-shouldered Hawk* (page 147), and the frog added to the *Black-crowned Night Heron* (page 192) are all small collage elements applied over complex oil and watercolor layers.

16. The bird at left in the *Virginia Rail* (1863.17.205) shows movement of the collage and an uncolored paper halo with adhesive residues is visible below this bird. Similarly, see *Marbled Godwit* (1863.17.238) and *American Woodcock* (1863.17.268).

17. In the *Red-shouldered Hawk*, (1863.17.071), the oil landscape covers part of the collaged frog held by the hawk and also completely surrounds the bird. The earlier watercolor landscape can be seen in the small area where the bird's claw grips the frog. A section of landscape in oil paint on the right side of the *Ruffled Grouse* of 1824 (1863.17.041) is another example of oil paint over a completed watercolor. The strike-through image of grasses from an original background may be seen under a blue oil-paint sky in the *Yellow Rail* (1863.17.329).

18. There are noncontiguous areas of a soft, brown resinous film over the oil landscape of the *Red-shouldered Hawk* (1863.17.071). It is possible that a layer of natural resin or oil was selectively applied and then incompletely removed from this piece. This may have been a later application of a varnish or oil that was applied in an attempt to remove white blanching in the oil paint film, but there is not yet conclusive evidence as to the nature of this film.

19. Entry for January 13, 1821, in Howard Corning, ed., *Journal of John James Audubon Made During His Trip to New Orleans, 1820–21*, p. 116.

20. Entry for March 31, 1821, ibid., p. 143.

21. Ibid., p. 144.

22. Entry for December 7, 1826, in Maria R. Audubon, ed., *Audubon and His Journals* (New York: Charles Scribner's Sons, 1897), p. 178.

23. Howard Corning, ed., *Journal of John James Audubon Made During His Trip to New Orleans, 1820–21*, p. 124. In the entry of February 15, 1821, Audubon listed the twenty drawings he was sending to Lucy via Nicholas Berthoud. He also noted the loss of a portfolio of fifteen drawings, missing from December 31, 1820, to April 5, 1821.

24. Howard Corning, ed., *The Letters of John James Audubon 1826–1940*, vol. I (Boston: The Club of Odd Volumes, 1930, p. 139. Reprinted by Kraus Reprint Co., 1969). Audubon, concerned about losing the drawings during shipping, wrote to Victor on February 13, 1837, "I had forwarded nine drawings by this ship . . . and . . . I have insured the nine drawings for 2,000 dollars," and on January 14, 1834, he warns Victor to be extremely careful of the shipment of drawings he has sent: "As many birds have

been pasted, take great care of those drawings and shew them to a very few of your Friends" (p. 6).

25. Letter, J. J. Audubon to Robert Havell, Jr., September 5, 1835, ibid., vol. I, pp. 82–83.

26. Letter, J. J. Audubon to Lucy Audubon, February 1, 1829, ibid., vol. I, p. 79.

27. The New-York Historical Society archives holds a bill from Searles & Williams, framers, of West 13th Street, dated Jan. 4, 1864, for twenty Audubon frames, and two bills of October 6 and 13, 1864, for sixteen walnut frames for the Audubons from E. H. Purdy & Co., successors to Searles & Williams. A receipt for installation fees on September 13 and 14, 1864, also support the idea of a series of small Audubon installations.

28. In a letter to George Moore of November 24, 1862, in The New-York Historical Society, T. M. Peters (librarian of the Society) describes the drawings as follows: "There are about 460, every one drawn and colored by Mr. Audubon himself. They are mounted on cardboard and are in good order, carefully kept in Portfolios." This and other early documents were brought to my attention by Stephen Edidin, curatorial research associate, and confirmed by Margaret Heilbrun, curator of manuscripts. I thank them for their help.

29. The drawings that have been paired on a single sheet of card stock are: *Orchard Oriole* (page 76) and *Dickcissel* (page 78) formerly U-1; *Vesper Sparrow* (1863.18.003) and *Black-throated Green Warbler* (1863.18.004) formerly U-2; *Marsh Wren* (1863.18.007) and *Eastern Wood-Pewee* (1863.18.008) formerly U-5.

30. Strike-through images of brown ink inscriptions from verso to recto may be seen on the *Black-billed Magpie* (page 260), *Tricolored Heron* (1863.17.217), *Sooty Tern* (1863.17.235), *Sabine's Gull* (page 270), *Red-necked Phalarope* (1863.17.215), and *Winter Wren and Rock Wren* (page 276). All of the inscriptions are indecipherable on the recto.

31. As a result of removing the mounts, inscriptions have been revealed on the verso of the *Whooping Crane* (page 86) and the *Roseate Spoonbill* (page 215). This inscription reads in part: "Florida Keys, May 23 d 1832./J.J.A./ drawn at London 1836."

32. Letter, J. J. Audubon to Robert Havell, September 15, 1835, in Howard Corning, ed., *The Letters of John James Audubon 1826–40*, vol. II, pp. 90–91.

33. Letter, J. J. Audubon to Victor Audubon, September 20, 1833, ibid., p. 252.

34. Incised lines around the edges of each form may be seen in *Louisiana Waterthrush* (1863.17.019), done in September 1821, *Cliff Swallow* (1863.17.068) of c. 1820, *Henslow's Sparrow* (1863.17.070) of 1820, and *Black-throated Magpie-Jay* (1863.17.096).

*Chronology**

*The authors are indebted to Alice Ford for her detailed chronology and to Shirley Streshinsky for her editorial comments.

YEAR	AGE	ACTIVITY
1785 April 26	Birth	Born in Les Cayes, Saint-Dominque (now Haiti) to Capt. Jean Audubon, and his mistress, Jeanne Rabine. Named Jean Rabine.
November 10	6 mos.	Jeanne Rabine dies in Les Cayes.
1788 August 26	3 yrs.	Brought by his father to Nantes, France.
1789 March 7	4 yrs.	Jean Rabine adopted by his father, Jean Audubon, and his legal wife, Anne Moynet, and given name Jean-Jacques Fougère.
March 28		Capt. Audubon buys Mill Grove farm near Norristown, Pennsylvania.
July 14		The French Revolution begins.
1796	11 yrs.	Receives naval training at Rochefort-sur-Mer.
1803	18 yrs.	Arrives in New York. Travels to Mill Grove.
		Louisiana Purchase from Napoleon doubling the size of the United States and essentially eliminating the French presence in North America.
1805	20 yrs.	Makes a year-long visit to his family in France. Draws birds in pastel.
1806 May 28	21 yrs.	Returns to New York with Ferdinand Rozier as a partner in Mill Grove. Brings with him all drawings he did abroad (profiles in pencil and pastel—the earliest still extant) and presents them to his fiancée, Lucy Bakewell.

YEAR	AGE	ACTIVITY
1807		During this period teaches himself to wire up freshly killed birds in lifelike positions and begins to use some watercolor in eyes, bills, and feet of birds.
August 31	22 yrs.	Departs for Louisville with Rozier for joint commercial venture.
1808 April 5	23 yrs.	Marries Lucy Bakewell in Pennsylvania; departs for Louisville with her.
1809 June 12	24 yrs.	First son, Victor Gifford, is born in Louisville.
1810 March	25 yrs.	Meets Alexander Wilson for first time while in Louisville.
Summer		Audubon and Lucy settle in Henderson, Kentucky.
December		Audubon and Rozier depart for Sainte Geneviève, Missouri.
1811 April 6	26 yrs.	Dissolves partnership with Rozier. Returns to Lucy in Henderson and with her brother, Thomas Bakewell, establishes commission business to sell flour, pork, and lard and speculate in real estate.
1812 February	27 yrs.	Audubon returns to Pennsylvania.
June 18		United States declares war on Britain. American ports are blockaded.
July		Audubon granted American citizenship on July 3.
		At least 200 drawings destroyed by rats.

YEAR	AGE	ACTIVITY
		Second meeting with Alexander Wilson in Philadelphia.
August		Failure of Audubon's and Bakewell's business in New Orleans.
November 30		Second son, John Woodhouse, born.
1813	28 yrs.	Audubons move to log house in Henderson, Kentucky.
August 23		Alexander Wilson dies.
1815 December		Daughter, Lucy, is born.
1816	31 yrs.	Saw mill erected, but business never materializes; partners Pears and Bakewell withdraw from partnership.
1817	32 yrs.	Daughter, Lucy, dies.
1818	33 yrs.	Audubon's father dies in Nantes.
1819 April–May	34 yrs.	Travels by boat to New Orleans to settle financial suit. Returns to Kentucky by boat.
		Business in Henderson fails. Audubon sells all his possessions, goes to Louisville, is arrested and imprisoned, and declares bankruptcy. Daughter, Rose, born. Audubon supports himself by teaching art and doing black chalk portraits on commission. Moves to Louisville. Continues to draw chalk portraits until about 1826, producing about 100, of which about one-third survive.
		Financial panic in United States.
1820 January	35 yrs.	Infant Rose dies. Moves to Cincinnati to take temporary job as taxidermist and background scene painter at the Western Museum. Lucy joins him. Gives art classes and continues to draw birds.
October 12		Departs with his student assistant Joseph Mason on cargo boat down Ohio and Mississippi rivers to augment his collection of American birds.

YEAR	AGE	ACTIVITY
1821 January 7	36 yrs.	Arrives in New Orleans where he teaches drawing and paints portraits.
February		Sends twenty bird drawings to Lucy in Louisville.
March		Visits painter John Vanderlyn.
		Makes copies in watercolor of Vanderlyn and John Trumbull works. Birds now shown in a variety of positions in both horizontal and vertical formats. Increasing complexity of composition. Begins use of mixed media: watercolor, pastel, pencil, collage, etc.
Summer		Tutors at James Pirrie's plantation, Oakley, about 130 miles north of New Orleans.
October 20		Departs Oakley with Mason for New Orleans.
December 18		Lucy arrives in New Orleans with two sons, bringing back drawings. Mason adds botanical elements to some.
		Exploration of upper Missouri River encouraged by state of Missouri.
1822	37 yrs.	Audubon and Mason to Natchez. Audubon's sons join him, followed later by Lucy. She gets job teaching at Beech Woods Plantation in West Feliciana. Lucy supports herself and her sons until 1830.
July 23		Mason stops working with Audubon.
		Audubon studies oil painting with itinerant Pennsylvania painter John Steen, a teacher of Thomas Cole's.
Winter		Lives in Shippingport, Kentucky, where he does sign painting and steamboat murals.
1824		To Philadelphia to seek support for publication and is unsuccessful. Receives commission to make drawing for engraving on a New Jersey bank note—his first published work. Publishes two papers in Annals of Lyceum of Natural History.
Autumn		Visits Albany, Niagara Falls, and Pittsburgh.
November 24		Reunited with Lucy at Beech Woods in Louisiana.

YEAR	AGE	ACTIVITY
		Teaches drawing, dancing, and fencing in order to raise money for trip to England to find publisher for The Birds of America.
1825	*40 yrs.*	*Experiments with use of metallic paint.*
1826	*41 yrs.*	*Departs for New Orleans and then sails to England to find engraver. Arrives in Liverpool.*
		Begins to copy his bird drawings in oil and watercolor to earn money.
Autumn		*Exhibition of bird drawings in Liverpool, Manchester, and Edinburgh. Writes papers for Wernerian Society.*
November 1		*Trial agreement with William H. Lizars and first proofs result in contract. Drafts prospectus.*
1827	*42 yrs.*	*Exhibition at Royal Institution, Edinburgh. Publication of first prospectus. To London in May. Lizars resigns in June after finishing ten plates and Audubon hires R. Havell & Son.*
1828	*43 yrs.*	*Audubon tours England in search of subscribers. Meets William Swainson.*
September		*Visits Paris with the Swainsons.*
		Robert Havell, Jr., takes over publication when Havell, Sr., withdraws. Audubon continues to publish papers in England and Philadelphia.
1829	*44 yrs.*	*To America after three years in England. Paints in Camden and Great Egg Harbor, New Jersey, and the Great Pine Forest of Pennsylvania, and later in Philadelphia with assistant George Lehman. Reunited with Lucy at her new teaching post in Beech Grove.*
		In five months completes forty-two bird paintings, some with backgrounds by Lehman.
1830	*45 yrs.*	*Goes with Lucy to Kentucky, New York, and Washington. Received by President Andrew Jackson. The House of Representatives subscribes to* The Birds of America. *Audubons sail together for England. Audubon works on Ornithological Biography, with Lucy as copyist and William*

YEAR	AGE	ACTIVITY
		MacGillivray as scientific editor. Contract with Joseph Kidd to copy the bird paintings in oil so they can be exhibited.
1831	*46 yrs.*	*Publication of first volume of* Ornithological Biography *and arrangement of duplicate American edition.*
July 15		*Elected to American Philosophical Society. Returns to New York. To South with taxidermist Henry Ward and George Lehman.*
October		*In Charleston, he meets John Bachman who becomes his host and then collaborator, and Bachman's sister-in-law, Maria Martin, who becomes Audubon's assistant.*
November December		*Travels through Florida.*
1832	*47 yrs.*	*Cruise up St. John's River in Florida and then through Florida Keys.*
June		*After revisiting Bachman in Charleston, joins family in Philadelphia, and they travel to New England and New Brunswick.*
August		*Victor prepares to sail for England to represent his father while Audubon, Lucy, and John remain in Boston for winter.*
November 21		*Robert Havell, Sr., dies.*
1833 *March*	*48 yrs.*	*Audubon, Lucy, and John arrive in New York to plan new expedition and seek subscribers.*
June 6–August 31		*Audubon and John take boat trip to Labrador to paint the birds of that area.*
September		*Returns to Lucy in New York.*
October 24		*Arrives in Charleston with Lucy.*
1834 *March 1*	*49 yrs.*	*Audubon, Lucy, and John travel from Charleston to New York and sail for England on April 1.*
May 7		*Family arrives in Liverpool. Audubon seeks subscribers in area, then goes to London.*

YEAR	AGE	ACTIVITY
1835		
June	50 yrs.	Lucy and Audubon return to Edinburgh to continue work on Ornithological Biography. American edition burns in a Boston fire.
1836		
January	51 yrs.	Fire in New York destroys drawing kits and guns needed for future expedition.
		Begins to include more than one species in a single drawing and continues to paste earlier versions of birds onto later compositions as collage.
August 2		Audubon sails to America with John, who had just completed a visit to the Continent with Victor.
September 13		Travels to Philadelphia to acquire Townsend-Nuttall collection of Western bird skins whose purchase is negotiated by Edward Harris.
November 17		Arrives in Charleston to draw skins.
		Economic depression in United States.
1837	52 yrs.	Travels with John and Harris to Pensacola, Florida, and then takes spring cruise from New Orleans to Houston, Texas.
May		Returns to Charleston with John.
July 17		Audubon, John, and his bride, Maria Bachman, depart for Liverpool and London.
1838		
Mid-April	53 yrs.	Last of 100 new drawings completed.
June 20		Fourth and last folio volume of engravings for The Birds of America completed except for some final details.
October		Beginning of work on Synopsis for The Birds of America.
December		Victor returns to America to prepare for the arrival of his family.
1839		
May	54 yrs.	Publication of fifth and final volume of Ornithological Biography.

YEAR	AGE	ACTIVITY
July		Publication of the Synopsis.
September		Audubon and Lucy leave England, following John and Maria and settle at 86 White Street in New York.
1840	55 yrs.	Audubon, assisted by Victor and John, plan The Viviparous Quadrupeds of North America. Begins work on seven-volume octavo edition of The Birds of America lithographed by J. T. Bowen of Philadelphia with John Bachman as "junior editor" of text and J. B. Chevalier as copublisher.
Autumn		Victor marries Eliza Bachman in Charleston. Audubon seeks subscribers for Quadrupeds.
1841		
Spring	56 yrs.	Audubon purchases land in upper Manhattan.
1842		
April	57 yrs.	Audubon family moves to their new estate, Minnie's Land.
September 12		Audubon seeks subscribers in Canada and then New England.
October 20		Prospectus of Quadrupeds published.
1843		
March 11	58 yrs.	Audubon leaves for St. Louis.
April		Audubon, Harris, and party depart for the upper Missouri and Fort Union, North Dakota, and remain at Fort Union drawing and hunting until mid-August.
November 6		Audubon returns to Minnie's Land.
1844	59 yrs.	Octavo edition of The Birds of America completed.
1845	60 yrs.	First imperial folio volume of Quadrupeds engravings published.
1846	61 yrs.	Second volume of Quadrupeds published. Audubon abandons work as his sight fails.
June 10		John goes to London in search of mammal skins in collections.

YEAR	AGE	ACTIVITY
1847	62 yrs.	Audubon suffers from stroke and increasing senility.
1848	63 yrs.	Third and last volume of Quadrupeds published.
1849 February 8	64 yrs.	John leads a California gold rush expedition hoping to improve family's dwindling finances.

YEAR	AGE	ACTIVITY
1850	65 yrs.	Foundry acquired by John and Victor to improve family finances opens but soon fails.
1851 January 27	66 yrs.	John James Audubon dies at Minnie's Land. Work on octavo edition of Quadrupeds in three volumes published 1851–54.

Selected Watercolors and Catalog Entries

Orchard Oriole

ICTERUS SPURIUS (LINNAEUS)

Audubon's nomenclature: Black throated Oriole, *Icterus spurius**

Medium: pastel, graphite, trace of watercolor? on paper; 9⅛ × 11⅝ in.; 23.2 × 29.5 cm.

Inscription (bottom center): wild cherry—black throated Male Oriole—

Identification: immature male

Seasonal distribution: breeds in most of eastern United States, winters through Central America to northern South America

Flora: wild cherry, *Prunus serotina*

Acc. no. 1863.18.001

In his studio in Natchez, Mississippi, on April 12, 1822, Audubon completed a lively depiction of five Orchard Orioles—two adult males, two immature males in different plumages, and a female, all perched around a nest in the branches of a honey locust tree. Audubon sent the picture to Robert Havell, who engraved it for *The Birds of America.* Later he sent it to Joseph Kidd, the young Scottish artist whom he hired to copy his paintings in oil. About ten years before making that final image, Audubon drew this pencil and pastel portrait of a young male Orchard Oriole, which, with its position reversed, may well have served as the model for the young bird in the upper right of the published picture. Audubon had already portrayed an adult male and female Orchard Oriole near the Falls of the Ohio in 1808,[1] but, as he indicated in the *Ornithological Biography,* a complete vignette of this species had to include the immature male, which, over the course of several years, changes from a yellowish-green plumage resembling the female's to the adult male's black and chestnut. As Audubon pointed out, the male's successive differences in plumage are sufficiently marked to cause some observers considerable confusion. Indeed, *spurius* (or illegitimate), the Latin name of the species, arose from an initial confounding of the male Orchard Oriole and the female Northern Oriole, formerly known as the Baltimore Oriole. As a result, the Orchard Oriole was once called the Bastard Baltimore Oriole.

The name of the Orchard Oriole, unlike the common names of some other species, appropriately describes this bird's preferred habitat. Rather than deep woods, the bird frequents areas planted with fruit trees—nurseries as well as orchards—and likes cultivated places by roads or streams, often near human habitation. There it rarely descends to the ground but flits around the tree branches, dexterous and active, effectively controlling the resident worms, caterpillars, beetles, wasps, and other harmful insects, of which, as Audubon wrote, it sometimes eats hundreds each day. It also likes fruits and berries but does not consume enough to damage crops.

The young male Orchard Oriole here, whose profile image is distinctly inert compared to Audubon's later, more animated figures, exhibits the plumage typical of a bird of its age: a brownish-olive back and yellowish rump; pale brown wings with two indistinct dull white wingbars; a yellowish-olive tail; bright yellow underparts; and black chin, throat, and cheeks. The male bird does not acquire its adult plumage until its third year but can breed in the immature plumage in which it is shown here. At nesting time it energetically displays for the female, as Audubon noted, and sings a clear melodic, warbling song. The Orchard Oriole, which sometimes breeds close to others of its species, builds a carefully woven, cup-shaped grass nest, in which the female usually deposits four to six pale blue eggs. In such a nest Alexander Wilson once found a grass fiber that was thirteen inches long and had been woven through the body of the nest no fewer than thirty-four times.

The continuing support, on many levels, of Annette Blaugrund, Robin J. Brown, Gerald B. Rosenband, and Martin C. Sloane was invaluable to me in the completion of this project. My lifelong gratitude goes to my mother, Regina Slatkin, and my late father, Charles E. Slatkin, who inspired in me a passion for the natural world and for the power of words, and to my sister,

Laura M. Slatkin, whose unswerving dedication to the humanities and to humaneness is an everpresent source of strength and inspiration for me.

1. Both of these pictures are now in the collection of the Houghton Library, Harvard University.

wild cherry – black throated male Oriole

Dickcissel

SPIZA AMERICANA (GMELIN)

Audubon's nomenclature: Black throated Bunting, *Emberiza Americana*

Painted May 14, 1813, in Henderson, Kentucky.

Medium: pastel and graphite on paper; 9¼ × 11½ in.; 23.4 × 29.2 cm.

Inscription: Black throated Bunting A. Willson—/ (*across bottom, starting in 1. left corner*): 192 & 193 Henderson 14 May 1813 Male & Femelle

Emberiza Americana (*upper left, above male bird, graphite*) 12.

Identification: male above, female below

Seasonal distribution: breeds in central United States, winters through Central America south to northern South America

Flora: wild strawberry, *Fragraria virginiana*

Acc. no. 1863.18.002

Audubon composed the watercolor of two Dickcissels that he published in *The Birds of America* about ten years after completing this pencil and pastel drawing, one of the earliest in The New-York Historical Society's collection. As effective as this portrayal is in rendering the characteristics of the Dickcissel, and as modern as it is in its approach compared, for instance, to much of Wilson's work, Audubon was able, with added artistic and ornithological experience, to make his later picture even more effective compositionally than this one. Like this picture, the later one shows perched male and female birds. However, in the published image, Audubon reversed the position of the male so that both birds face in the same direction. The artist also simplified this background in the later picture, eliminating the rocks and much of the vegetation and using plants that are more graceful and delicate and provide less visual competition for the birds. The crouched postures of the Dickcissels here turn into more upright stances in the final work, a change that gives the subjects a more alert appearance than these somewhat hunched birds exhibit. Also notable in the later picture are more coloristic details of plumage in both male and female than appear here, and keener facial expressions.

The name of the Dickcissel derives from the sound of the incessant, unmusical song that the bird utters throughout the day, often from the top of a weed stalk, during breeding season. The species nests in the fields, meadows, and pastures of the Midwest, usually close to the ground but sometimes up in a tree, frequently in loose colonies. Such groups, "very partial to particular localities,"[1] as Audubon noted, are known for changing the site of their breeding grounds from year to year. The birds occupy the same habitat as Bobolinks and meadowlarks, and indeed, the males, with yellow breast and black patch below the throat, resemble half-sized meadowlarks with stubby bills. As birds that nest low, Dickcissels are often the victims of weasels, minks, raccoons, skunks, and opossums, as well as cats. In addition, they fall prey to hawks and owls. But arguably a greater threat to their numbers comes from mowing machines that destroy countless nests of both their first and second broods.

Dickcissels are ground feeders, consuming weed seeds, waste grain, and copious numbers of insects. In 1918, in Illinois, these birds were estimated to have eaten about 100 million grasshoppers during a single day in nesting season, enough insects to have destroyed 156 tons of hay that summer alone.[2] Dickcissels used to occur commonly in the Mid-Atlantic states, where Audubon described them as abundant (although, even in his day, not as common as in the prairies). He wrote of seeing many of these finches in New Jersey in late July, congregating in preparation for migration, which they perform, as he observed, in flocks of thirty or forty. The species is now scarce as a breeder in the East, for reasons that are not entirely clear.

1. John James Audubon, *Ornithological Biography*, vol. II (reprint of 1840–44 ed.; New York: Volair Books, 1979), p. 59.

2. Arthur Cleveland Bent, *Life Histories of North American Cardinals, Grosbeaks, Buntings, Towhees, Finches, Sparrows, and Allies*, part I (New York: Dover Publications, 1968), p. 179.

Black Throated Bunting A. Wilson—
Emberiza Americana

192 & 193.   Henderson 14 May 1812   Male & female

Audubon's nomenclature: 1. Goshawk, *Falco palumbarius* Linnaeus 2. Stanley Hawk, *Falco stanleii* Audubon

Cooper's Hawk painted December 5, 1809, in Louisville, Kentucky; adult Northern Goshawk painted between 1810 and 1819 in Henderson, Kentucky; immature goshawk painted c. 1829.

Medium: watercolor, pastel, graphite, gouache, selective glazing, collage on paper; 39 × 25⅞ in.; 99 × 65.7 cm.

Inscription (on lower goshawk, lower left, mostly cut off in cut for collage): . . . de ? fa/ . . . un/ . . . 83—

Identification: Adult Northern Goshawk, left; immature goshawk, above; immature Cooper's Hawk, right

Seasonal distribution: 1. breeds widely in northern and western North America, winters south of breeding range 2. breeds and winters widely across the United States

Havell plate number: CXLI in *The Birds of America*

Acc. no. 1863.17.141

A number of Audubon's pictures include birds that Audubon illustrated at different periods and subsequently assembled on a single sheet, but few demonstrate as dramatically as this one the differences in style and conception between his early pastels and his later watercolors. The Cooper's Hawk,[1] lower right, and the adult Northern Goshawk, lower left, are portrayed in the static, stylized manner that characterized much ornithological illustration before Audubon's time.[2] The figures have not shed the stiffness and severity of the stuffed, mounted skins that served Audubon as models. The birds' basic field marks are apparent, and a limited amount of differentiation and texturing is evident in the feathers, but the rigidity of the poses, the monolithic quality of the delineations, and the dullness of the birds' expressions predominate. The immature goshawk at the top, illustrated from a specimen taken in the Great Pine Forest near Mauch Chunk, Pennsylvania, probably in 1829, represents Audubon's mature style, based on years of experience in observing and depicting birds. Over the course of time he had transformed his illustrations from what were essentially portraits of dead specimens to vignettes of birds alive with activity.

When the original engraving of this work appeared, Audubon identified the bird on the lower right, which he believed to be new to science, as the Stanley Hawk, after Lord Stanley, later the fourteenth earl of Derby, a member of Parliament and a lover of natural history. A controversy arose when the ornithologist Charles Lucien Bonaparte claimed, rightly, that he had previously named and described the bird as a Cooper's Hawk in 1828, in honor of William Cooper, a founder of the New York Lyceum of Natural History, who had shot the specimen. In the octavo edition engraving of 1840–44, Audubon repositioned the goshawks. The figure of this bird was omitted from the engraving, and two figures of the same species, which he had originally called Stanley Hawks, were included in another plate and renamed Cooper's Hawks.

Both the Cooper's Hawk and the goshawk are members of a family called accipiters, a name derived from the Latin word *accipere*, to take or seize. Both species prey swiftly and efficiently on birds and mammals, using their relatively short, broad wings for speedy chase and their long tails for maneuvering through the woods. They detect prey animals by surveying the woods from a perch on a secluded branch or by flying low over the ground, and capture them in a surprise attack whose strike may last less than a second. When flying through open country, both birds characteristically alternate several rapid wingbeats with a glide. The female bird is considerably larger than the male in both the goshawk (characterized by its slate-blue back, the strong white line over its eye, and its finely barred underparts) and the Cooper's (with dark back, rusty barred breast, and well-rounded tail).

1. A depiction of a Cooper's Hawk dated November 29, 1810, probably made in Henderson, is in the collection of the Houghton Library, Harvard University.
2. Audubon made another watercolor of two young Cooper's Hawks which was published separately as Havell plate no. XXXVI. An oil painting of a Cooper's Hawk from 1825 was formerly in the collection of the Gilcrease Foundation, Tulsa, Oklahoma.

Painted in New Orleans on January 28–29, 1821. The landscape background, in oil, may have been added by Audubon's son Victor.

Medium: watercolor, graphite, oil paint, and pastel on paper; 23½ × 37 in.; 59.6 × 94.1 cm.

Identification: immature

Seasonal distribution: breeds and winters on southern Pacific and southern Atlantic coasts

Havell plate number: CCCCXXI in *The Birds of America*

Acc. No.: 1863.17.421

*I*n the early days of Audubon's career as a self-employed artist, his fortunes fluctuated wildly. On Thursday, January 18, 1821, his journal entry from New Orleans reads in part, "the time has been so Long and dull during these days ... by the time We receive the pay for [a recent commission] We will be penny Less."[1] But ten days later his mood had changed: "Drawing a Brown Pelican," he wrote on Sunday, January 28, "fatigued, Wearied of Body but in good Spirits having plenty to do at good Prices, and my Work much admired—only sorry that the Sun Sets."[2]

The immature Brown Pelican that this 1821 journal entry describes appears as gawky as the adult in plate CCLI (painted about ten years later) appears majestic, even iconic. Many young birds look more ungainly than their parents, and pelicans—among the largest of all living birds—generally seem clumsy on land. But other elements also contribute to the awkwardness of this image. In it, Audubon demonstrates a considerably less sophisticated treatment of composition and plumage texture than in the later one. Here he depicts his subject (males and females look alike in both the immature and adult plumages) in a less graceful pose than the later bird's, with mouth agape to emphasize its capaciousness and its unfeathered wrinkled pouch, both of which seem oversized in relation to its slender neck. The dark head of the immature bird (on which some of the white feathers of the adult plumage are just beginning to appear) exhibits a muddier texture than the adult's head, as do the immature's whitish underparts. The immature's dark eye (the adult's is yellow) appears small in relation to the massiveness of the bill and pouch.

Audubon described Brown Pelicans as being "as well aware of the time of each return of the tide, as the most watchful pilots,"[3] so that although the birds may be standing quietly asleep on one foot, soon thereafter, as the tide advances, "the slumbers of the Pelicans are over; the drowsy birds shake their heads, stretch open their mandibles and pouch by way of yawning, expand their ample wings, and simultaneously soar away."[4] It is perhaps this moment that Audubon depicted here, his subject, still balancing on one foot, having awakened, now yawning in preparation for a fishing foray.

Brown Pelicans usually feed on herring, which mass in large schools near the water's surface. The pelicans fly in small groups just above the water, which must be sufficiently clear for them to see into it to a certain depth. Audubon observed that when the waves are high, the pelicans engage in what the sailors call "troughing,"[5] gliding on stiff wings in the hollows between the waves. A pelican's skeleton weighs only about nine ounces, so the bird is able to remain aloft on the air currents for long periods, with only occasional flapping, until it sights prey and plunges in after it, the only member of its family to dive for food.

1. Howard Corning, ed., *Journal of John James Audubon Made During His Trip to New Orleans, 1820–21* (Boston: The Club of Odd Volumes, 1929), p. 120.
2. Ibid.
3. John James Audubon, *Ornithological Biography*, vol. VII (reprint of 1840–44 ed.; New York: Volair Books, 1979), p. 34.
4. Ibid.
5. Ibid., p. 5.

Whooping Crane

GRUS AMERICANA (LINNAEUS)

Painting probably begun in New Orleans in late 1821; alligators added in April 1822; background completed some years later.

Medium: watercolor, oil paint, graphite, gouache, selective glazing, and pastel on paper; 37 1/4 × 25 11/16 in.; 94.7 × 65.2 cm.

Inscriptions (lower right, over landscape, in graphite): No. 46—p. 236 *(verso, brown ink over original graphite inscription):* Length 5 feet 5/12/Breadth 7—"—8/12./Weight 13 to 3/4 avoir du poid/Male Bird—*(verso, graphite, partially under and partially below brown ink inscription):* Length ../Breadth ../Weight .. A.S.P./1820 Louisiana/Male

Identification: adult

Seasonal distribution: breeds in north central Canada, winters on Texas Gulf coast

Havell plate number: CCXXVI in *The Birds of America*

Acc. no. 1863.17.226

When Audubon's double elephant folio edition of *The Birds of America* was completed in 1839, with pages more than three feet long and more than two feet wide, it was the largest book ever produced up to that time. But even a work of such size could not accommodate the full-length image of a standing Whooping Crane, the largest crane—indeed, the largest wading bird, and the tallest bird of any species—in North America. The crane measures almost five feet tall if standing erect, as when "it stalks . . . with all the majesty of a gallant chief,"[1] through the grass with long, rapid strides, hunting marsh animals.

Whooping Cranes are voracious eaters; at one time they were bred domestically and used to reduce populations of frogs and other garden creatures. (One at Aransas National Wildlife Refuge was recorded to have eaten 800 grasshoppers in 75 minutes.) Audubon, who had observed the species avidly preying on young alligators—a scene he illustrates here—could therefore feel free to portray as highly characteristic the crane's curved feeding posture, a position that his picture surface was able to encompass. In fact, such a depiction of the species bent over and apparently compressed by the picture plane actually emphasizes the crane's commanding size and powerful form. The crane's prodigious white body fills the pictorial space, its riveting red face contrasting vividly with its sleek, black flight feathers and mighty legs. Audubon uses the bird's intense colors, together with the expressively sharp angles of its open bill

and potent feet and their proximity to the luckless alligators, to create a vignette of rapaciousness and helplessness.

Male and female Whooping Cranes look alike, although males are somewhat larger. Pairs mate for life and in the course of their courtship perform a complex and dramatic mating dance. They also deliver unison calls in a haunting and protracted duet. The windpipe inside the bird's massive neck, which curves around to a length of five feet, is responsible for the resounding cry—which can be heard over a distance of several miles—that gives the Whooping Crane its name.

Audubon had seen Whooping Cranes as early as 1810 (in fact, he describes showing the species to Alexander Wilson), so he was familiar with them at the beginning of his career. But because he believed another species, the Sandhill Crane, to be the young of the Whooping Crane, some of his information about the Whooping Crane's distribution must be questioned. Nevertheless, it is clear from his reports and those of others that this bird, now almost extinct, once nested in open marshes from Illinois to North Dakota and in Louisiana as well. As settlers drained the wetlands, this wild and wary crane, which shuns the human presence, gradually disappeared, and by the 1930s its numbers were reduced to no more than fifteen. Only strenuous captive breeding and management programs to counter habitat loss and the effects of natural disasters, pollution, and disease have now raised the population of this rare, severely endangered species to about two hundred birds.

1. John James Audubon, *Ornithological Biography*, vol. V (reprint of 1840–44 ed.; New York: Volair Books, 1979), p. 189.

Northern Parula

PARULA AMERICANA (LINNAEUS)

Audubon's nomenclature: Blue Yellow-backed Warbler, *Sylvia americana* Latham

Painted on March 27, 1821, in New Orleans.

Medium: watercolor, touches of gouache, pastel, graphite, and ink on paper; 18 7/16 × 11 9/16 in.; 46.8 × 29.4 cm.

Inscription (black ink, lower center): Blue Yellow-Back Warbler No. 1. male. No 2 female/Sylvia Pusilla/*(black ink, lower left):* Drawn from

Nature by John J. Audubon/March 27, 1821 plant by Joseph Mason

(graphite, upper right): 15 *(erased graphite, lower right):* Engraver . . . ?/?

Identification: male above, female below

Seasonal distribution: breeds in southeastern Canada and throughout most of eastern United States in coniferous or mixed woodlands near

wet areas, often where Spanish moss *(Tillandsia usneoides)* or old man's beard *(Usnea* lichen) is present on trees; winters in south Florida,

Mexico, and south to the Caribbean

Flora: red or copper iris, *Iris fulva,* painted by Joseph Mason

Havell plate number: XV in *The Birds of America*

Acc. no. 1863.17.015

During the first week of spring—on March 27, 1821—Audubon painted this pair of parula warblers in New Orleans, just at the season when he had observed the species arriving in Louisiana during its migration. The diminutive Northern Parula is most closely associated with wet woods and generally breeds near ponds, lakes, and rivers where insects are abundant and the trees are covered with the *Usnea* lichen with which, Audubon notes, it makes its nest. Here the parulas perch on a colorful and decorative water-loving plant, the copper iris or Louisiana flag, which Audubon had seen blooming in masses outside New Orleans at the time that the parulas were making their way north.

The iris in this composition is drawn by Audubon's gifted young assistant Joseph Mason, who also apparently shot the male bird portrayed in the picture.[1] From October 1820, when Audubon boarded a Mississippi River flatboat in Cincinnati bound for New Orleans, until July 1822, when he was living in Natchez, Mississippi, he had the able collaboration of Mason, who, he believed, could draw flowers better than probably any man in America. During those two years, Mason provided Audubon with flower backgrounds for more than fifty bird paintings, a fact to which Audubon subsequently gave less than full acknowledgment.

In observing the habits of the Northern Parula, Audubon noticed that the birds feed closer to the ground when they first arrive in the spring than later, when the trees are fully leafed out and the insects that they eat, no longer forced low by the cold weather, are more numerous up in the forest canopy. Like other warblers, the Northern Parula engages in considerable acrobatics when searching for food; the artist shows the lower bird here at the split second before it "raises its body (which is scarcely larger when stripped of its feathers than the first joint of a man's finger) upward to the full length of its legs and toes, and is thus enabled to seize insects otherwise beyond its reach."[2] Parulas often engage in flycatching as well, sallying out to pick up an insect from the air, and returning "suddenly to nearly the same place, as if afraid to encounter the dangers of a prolonged excursion."[3]

Audubon conveys a sense of the warbler's upward flight ("it ascends for a while in a very zigzag manner"[4]) by causing the viewer's eye to duplicate that upward motion, traveling from the long, spearlike plant leaves at the bottom of the composition to the vibrant flower blossoms at the top. The repetition of V-shapes produced by plant leaves and stems, punctuated by the two warblers, creates a spare and appealing decorative design that is emphasized by the extensive white background.

1. Howard Corning, ed., *Journal of John James Audubon Made During His Trip to New Orleans, 1820–21* (Boston: The Club of Odd Volumes, 1929), p. 141.
2. John James Audubon, *Ornithological Biography,* vol. II (reprint of 1840–44 ed.; New York: Volair Books, 1979), p. 189.
3. Ibid., p. 58.
4. Ibid., p. 57.

Blue Yellow Back Warbler. No 1 Male. No 2 female
Sylvia Pusilla

Drawn from nature by John J. Audubon
March 27th 1831   plant by Joseph Mason

Cerulean Warbler

DENDROICA CERULEA (WILSON)

Audubon's nomenclature: Azure Warbler, *Sylvia azurea*

Probably painted in Louisiana or Mississippi in 1822.

Medium: watercolor, graphite, and selected glazing on paper; 18⅞ × 11¾ in.; 47.9 × 29.8 cm.

Inscription (lower left): No 10. plate 48 *(bottom center):* Cerulean Warbler. Male 1. F. 2 / Sylvia Azurea

Plant Vulgo Bear Berrie/Ilex Dahon. *(bird in center labeled "1." A "2" at lower right indicates Audubon's planned placement of the female.)*

Identification: adult male

Seasonal distribution: breeds in southern Canada and eastern and southeastern United States, winters in northern South America

north to Bolivia

Flora: dahoon, yaupon, or cassena, *Ilex cassine,* painted by Joseph Mason

Havell plate number: XLVIII in *The Birds of America*

Acc. no. 1863.17.048

Cerulean Warblers feed, sing, and nest at the very tops of trees. They undergo four different plumage changes between hatching and their second winter, and can be difficult to see even with good optical equipment. Often an observer must locate the species by ear rather than eye, as its rolling, trilling song drifts through the summer woods. For these reasons, studying the Cerulean Warbler poses numerous problems, and it is perhaps not surprising that Audubon (like Alexander Wilson before him) demonstrates some confusion about this bird, which he depicted twice, in the present picture correctly identifying the adult male as a Cerulean Warbler, but in another, made at about the same time, calling an immature male a "Blue Green Warbler."[1]

When Havell engraved this adult male cerulean, Audubon instructed him to add a female bird to the picture. Havell used as a model a Cerulean Warbler by Alexander Wilson, who had first painted and described the species. In the engraving, however, the position of Wilson's bird has been altered to create a more streamlined, energetic image. By 1844, when Audubon produced his book in the octavo edition—smaller and more affordable than the double elephant folio—he recognized that the "Blue Green Warbler" and the Cerulean Warbler were the same species and recomposed the picture to include the adult male from the present image and the young male from the "Blue Green Warbler" composition. Having observed it clinging "to the extremities of bunches of leaves or berries, on which it procures the insects or larvae of which its food is principally composed,"[2] Audubon portrayed the Cerulean Warbler here in the midst of such activity. The bird's characteristic blue, white, and black plumage is set off by the enticing red of the berries above and beneath him, as well as by the lively greens of the healthy leaves near which he perches and the muted yellow-brown of the dying leaves on a neighboring branch. The warbler is eyeing a spider that sits on one of these fading leaves, the bird's interest perhaps an indirect reference by Audubon to the beneficial effect that the insectivorous birds have in ridding trees and plants of the pests that would otherwise decimate them. The warbler's angled posture, echoed by the forked twig behind him, suggests his flitting movements, as does his bent right leg, which is momentarily withdrawn from its supporting branch to reveal its delicate curved toes. Even the presence of the spider, a creature associated with rapid activity, adds a sense of vivacity to the scene.

This was not the first time that Audubon had represented the Cerulean Warbler. He tells us that a drawing he made of this species was among the large group of pictures destroyed by rats in about 1812 when he was still in Henderson, Kentucky. In 1831, Audubon included this picture in the group he sent to the painter Joseph Kidd in Edinburgh to copy in oil.

---

1. Although Audubon was an attentive observer who collected a vast amount of significant information about the birds he studied, he lacked the resources of field guides, specimen collections, and sophisticated optics that we have today, and not all of his conclusions have been substantiated by later ornithologists.

2. John James Audubon, *Ornithological Biography*, vol. II (reprint of 1840–44 ed.; New York: Volair Books, 1979), p. 45.

N°. 10. plate 48.— Cerulean Warbler. Male 1. F. 2
Sylvia azurea.
Plant Vulgo Bear berrie
Ilex Dahon

Summer Tanager

PIRANGA RUBRA (LINNAEUS)

Audubon's nomenclature: Summer Red Bird, *Tanagra aestiva*

Center bird and habitat painted at Bayou Sara, Louisiana, August 27, 1821; other two birds may have been added later.

Medium: watercolor, pastel, graphite, traces of gouache, and ink on paper; 18⅞ × 11⅝ in.; 47.9 × 29.5 cm.

Inscription (lower center): Summer Red Bird/Tanagra Aestiva *(lower left):* Drawn from Nature by John J. Audubon/Bayou Sarah Louisiana,

August 27th 1821 *(lower right, in graphite almost entirely erased):* No. ?9? . . 44/ . . Old 1. Young 2. F3/Aestiva plant vulgo—. . . ? . . ./

plant . . ? . . *(upper right, graphite):* 44

Identification: adult male above, adult female center, immature male below

Seasonal distribution: breeds in southeastern and southwestern United States, winters in central Mexico and central South America

Flora: muscadine vine, *Vitis rotundifolia,* painted by Joseph Mason

Havell plate number: XLIV in *The Birds of America*

Acc. no. 1863.17.044

Determined to carry through his project of depicting every American bird, and needing to earn a living while doing so, Audubon produced an average of one picture every three days in the year between leaving Cincinnati on October 12, 1820, and October of 1821: "62 drawings of *Birds and Plants,* 3 quadrupeds, 2 snakes, 50 portraits of all sorts . . ."[1] His pace was particularly remarkable since, during that period, he was also traveling from town to town by boat or on foot, teaching, supporting himself by doing commissioned work and other jobs, and searching for and observing birds in the field. The summer of 1821 was especially productive for "Hunting and Drawing My Cherished Birds of America."[2] Among those he depicted was the Summer Tanager, a "beautiful species of solitary habits, preferring at all times the interior of the forests, but not the densest parts of them"[3] (a notably meticulous observation of its habitat).

While Audubon usually represented only the adult male and female of a species in his compositions, in cases where the immature birds demonstrate considerable variation in plumage from the parents, he showed that difference as well. In this instance, as Audubon noted, "the alterations of plumage which appear in the young birds between the period at which they leave the nest, and the ensuing spring are . . . great,"[4] and he included the figure of an immature male Summer Tanager to demonstrate the striking combination of red and green patches that characterizes such birds at that age.

Audubon knew that this species feeds principally on insects, and here he has shown the adult male struggling to swallow a beetle of substantial proportions, "some of which are often of larger size than a bird of the dimensions of the Summer Red-bird might be supposed capable of swallowing."[5] Although Summer Tanagers do consume small fruits, Audubon does not report having seen them eat the grapes of the muscadine vine on which he represented them here and which he observed to be abundant in Louisiana, but he does point out that he himself "seldom lost an opportunity of refreshing my palate"[6] thus. "I am equally confident," he added, "that their juice would make an excellent wine."[7]

The image of the Summer Tanagers is less lively than some of Audubon's other pictures, perhaps because of the rigid poses of the three birds. This relatively static quality may reflect the rather sluggish behavior of the tanager as compared, for instance, to a Wood Warbler, or it may result from the fact that Audubon felt considerable pressure to produce the largest possible number of pictures in the shortest period of time and was less inclined, here, to depict an elaborate vignette than to provide an accurate representation of all three plumages of this elegant bird, whose colors alone, he may have felt, provided drama enough. In fact, the birds' showy hues may have prompted Audubon to include the Summer Tanager among the pictures he sent to Joseph Kidd in Edinburgh on July 29, 1831, to be copied in oil.

1. Howard Corning, ed., *Journal of John James Audubon Made During His Trip to New Orleans, 1820–21* (Boston: The Club of Odd Volumes, 1929), p. 199.

2. Ibid., p. 190.

3. John James Audubon, *Ornithological Biography,* vol. II (reprint of 1840–44 ed.; New York: Volair Books, 1979), p. 222. He had also made an earlier depiction of the Summer Tanager at the Falls of the Ohio on June 20, 1808, now in the collection of the Houghton Library, Harvard University.

4. Ibid., p. 223.

5. Ibid., p. 222.

6. Ibid., p. 224.

7. Ibid.

Summer Red Bird
Tanagra Aestiva

Drawn from Nature by John J. Audubon
Bayou Sarah, Louisiana, about 20th 1821

Boat-tailed Grackle

QUISCALUS MAJOR VIEILLOT

Painted near New Orleans at Bonnet Carré's Church on January 4, 1821.
Medium: watercolor, pastel, gouache, graphite on paper; 22⅜ × 17⁵⁄₁₆ in.; 56.8 × 43.5 cm.
Inscription (lower left): Drawn from Nature by John J. Audubon/Bonné Caré's church Jany 4th 1821 *(bottom center):* Boat tailed
Grakles/Gracula Barita *(lower right, in graphite):* No 27
Identification: female above, male below
Seasonal distribution: breeds and winters on Atlantic and Gulf coasts
Flora: live oak, *Quercus virginiana,* and Spanish moss, *Tillandsia usneoides*
Acc. no. 1863.18.032

After "examining their Manners very Closely"[1] —during a stop that he made toward the end of his Mississippi River trip in January 1821—Audubon drew this pair of watchful Boat-tailed Grackles. Having observed a male boat-tail carrying what the artist thought might be nesting material into a live oak tree hung with Spanish moss, Audubon depicted the birds in such a moss-festooned tree. He noted in his journal that the boat-tails' "walk is Elegant and Stately carrying their Long concave tails rather high,"[2] and he showed each perched bird gracefully elevating its conspicuous, spatulate tail, which grows to a length of seven inches in the male, and from which the species' name derives. In his composition of boat-tails made about ten years later, from which Havell produced the engraving for *The Birds of America,* Audubon again showed the male with tail raised and long, heavy bill open, perched in a live oak below the female, each bird again with a keenly alert expression. In the later picture, however, the position of the male is reversed, and that of the female has been altered as well to create a more varied and graceful composition.

Male and female boat-tails differ so significantly in appearance that beginning students sometimes mistake them for separate species. The female is considerably smaller than the male, her distinctively tawny-brown coloring contrasting markedly with the male's purplish-black iridescence. During courtship, the male shows off this rich plumage by antic posturing in which he assumes a number of different poses, spreading his wings and tail, bobbing up and down, jumping, bowing, and, intermittently in the midst of all this activity, raising his head straight up with the bill pointing vertically and remaining motionless for several minutes. Pairs like the one here may be seen together during breeding season, but boat-tails are not monogamous. Rather, males are polygynous, mating with several females, each of which then chooses a nest site, constructs her nest, lays and incubates the eggs, and tends the young without assistance from the male. Boat-tailed Grackles are gregarious, generally nesting in colonies, almost exclusively near water. They often feed on mud flats and near swamps and salt marshes, consuming fish, shrimp, and other aquatic creatures, but they do not hesitate to plunder cultivated fields for rice and corn or to pluck insects from the backs of cattle. They also prey on the eggs and nestlings of other birds.

In this depiction the bills of both grackles are open, an evident reference to the fact that, as Audubon noted in his journal when he made this picture, "their voice is Loud and Sweet."[3] Later in the *Ornithological Biography,* he wrote that "the notes of these birds are harsh, resembling loud shrill whistles . . . [but] in the love season they are more pleasing."[4] Indeed, boat-tails have a large and varied repertoire of vocalizations, ranging from a screech that resembles a gate swinging on a rusty hinge to an energetic yodel.

1. Howard Corning, ed., *Journal of John James Audubon Made During His Trip to New Orleans, 1820–21* (Boston: The Club of Odd Volumes, 1929), p. 105.
2. Ibid., p. 106.
3. Ibid., p. 105.
4. John James Audubon, *Ornithological Biography,* vol. IV (reprint of 1840–44 ed.; New York: Volair Books, 1979), p. 55.

Boat-tailed Grakles.
Gracula Barita

Drawn from Nature by John J. Audubon
Bomé Caré's church Janu.y 4.th 1821.

N.o 27

95

Eastern Bluebird

SIALIA SIALIS (LINNAEUS)

Audubon's nomenclature: Blue-bird, *Sylvia sialis*

Female and young painted c. 1820; male probably painted in Louisiana in 1822.

Medium: watercolor, pastel, gouache, and graphite on paper; 18⅞ × 11¹⁵⁄₁₆ in.; 47.9 × 30.3 cm.

Identification: adult male above, adult female left, immature right.

Seasonal distribution: breeds in southeastern Canada and eastern United States, winters in middle eastern North America, south to Mexico

Havell plate number: CXIII in *The Birds of America*

Acc. no. 1863.17.113

An observer with some knowledge of bluebird behavior, witnessing in nature the vignette that Audubon has depicted here, could draw certain interesting conclusions about the scene.

Bluebird young leave their nest at the age of about three weeks. Even though fledglings may be able to travel as far as a hundred yards on their first flight, their parents continue to feed them for another three or four weeks. A few days after a brood has fledged, the female may start a second or third brood, and, in that case, the male alone continues the feeding of the young. The presence in this scene of both parents with a fledged juvenile indicates that the young bird is between about three and seven weeks old and that the mother is between broods or has finished breeding. The presence of spots on the juvenile's breast indicates that the fledgling has not yet undergone the partial molt that occurs in August and September, in which the young bird loses these markings and comes to resemble the adult.

Because the tame, handsome Eastern Bluebird frequents backyards, gardens, parks, and orchards, it is a familiar and gladdening sight to many. Audubon made affectionate notations in his journal about the species, declaring:

It adds to the delight imparted by spring, and enlivens the dull days of winter. Full of innocent vivacity, warbling its ever pleasing notes, and familiar as any bird can be in its natural freedom, it is one of the most agreeable of our feathered favorites.[1]

Eastern Bluebirds were considerably more numerous in Audubon's day than they are in ours, especially in the northern states. The species' population decline has been attributed to many factors, including the introduction to the United States from Europe of the House Sparrow in 1851 and of the starling in 1890. Each of these birds competes with the much less aggressive bluebird for nesting sites, as does the native Tree Swallow. The chemical spraying of trees also takes its toll, as does severe weather. But the introducing of bluebird boxes in hospitable locations—a custom practiced even in Audubon's day before environmental hazards were as extreme as they are today—is slowly helping to stabilize the Eastern Bluebird population.

Audubon drew the expressive feeding scene at the bottom of this composition in approximately 1820, about the time that he traveled down the Mississippi River and wrote in his journal, "Many *Blue Birds*, these were pleasing to me, the poorest note of these is always wellcome to Mine ears."[2] He reworked the drawing at a later period and probably added the male bird at the top in Louisiana in 1822.[3] That figure not only completes the composition but also provides an accurate description of the adult male's plumage. However, it has the somewhat flattened aspect of a scientific specimen, and its stiffened claws and partially closed eye contribute to that effect, detracting to some extent from the appealing image of a bluebird singing its sweet song on the wing.

1. John James Audubon, *Ornithological Biography*, vol. II (reprint of 1840–44 ed.; New York: Volair Books, 1979), p. 171.

2. Howard Corning, ed., *Journal of John James Audubon Made During His Trip to New Orleans, 1820–21* (Boston: The Club of Odd Volumes, 1929), p. 80.

3. Audubon made another watercolor of the bluebird when he was in England in 1827, which was formerly in the collection of Mr. Bayard Ewing, East Greenwich, R. I. Its present location is unknown.

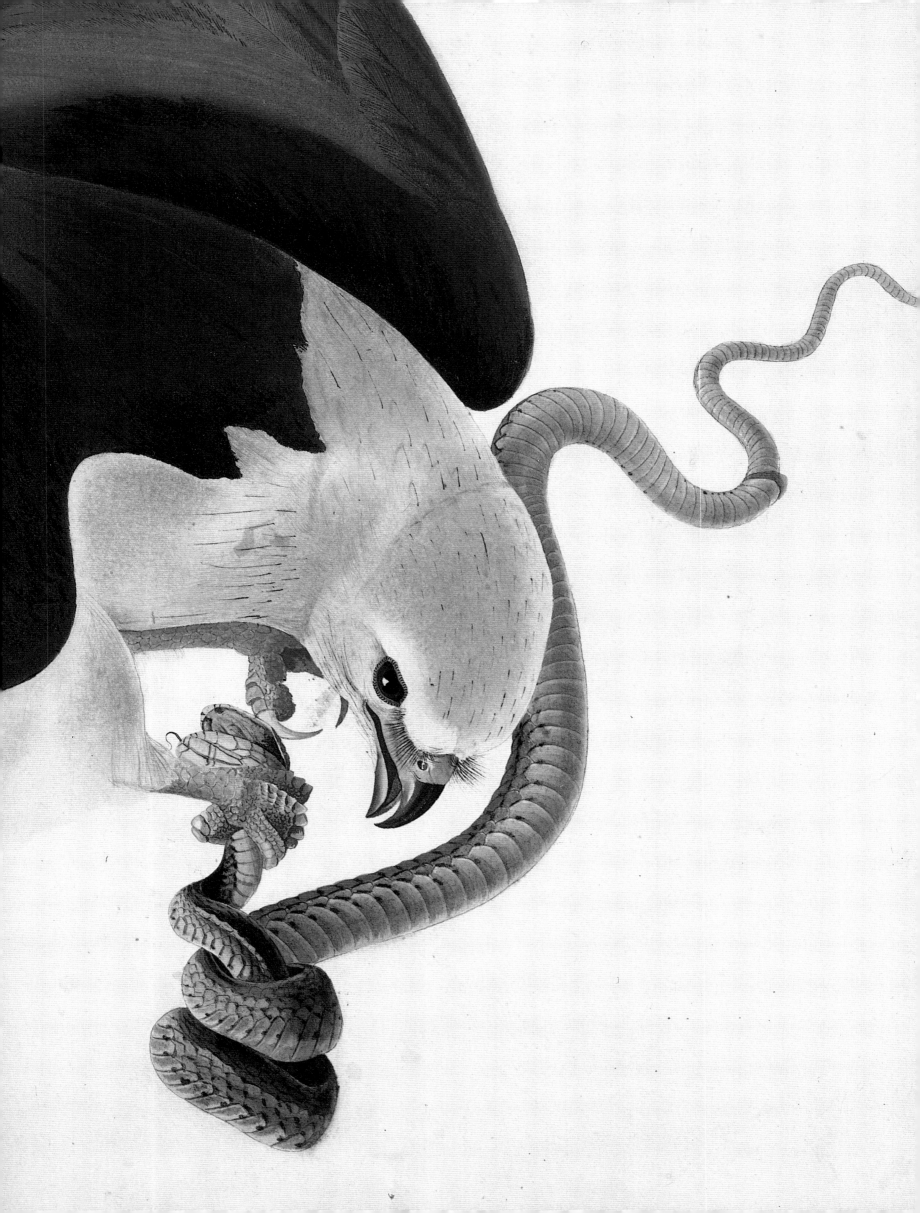

Audubon's nomenclature: Swallow-tailed Hawk, *Falco furcatus* Linnaeus

Painted at Oakley Plantation during the summer of 1821.

Medium: watercolor, pastel, graphite, and selective glazing on paper; 20⅝ × 28⅞ in.; 52.5 × 73.6 cm.

Inscription (lower left): No. 15. Plate 72./Published 1829. *(lower center):* Swallow-tailed Hawk. Male - Feml/The same./Falco F. furcatus/reptile vulgo—Garter Snake.—

Identification: adult carrying garter snake

Seasonal distribution: a disappearing species, much more widespread and populous in Audubon's day; formerly bred as far north as Minnesota, Virginia, and Kentucky, now breeds only locally in open woods and wetlands in extreme southern states and along Gulf Coast

Havell plate number: LXXII in *The Birds of America*

Acc. no. 1863.17.072

The thrill of discovering a habitat entirely new to him on his five-mile walk from Bayou Sara to Oakley Plantation was sufficiently strong, Audubon writes in his journal entry of June 18, 1821, to distract him at least temporarily from missing Lucy and his sons back in Louisville. "The Rich Magnolia covered with its Odoriferous Blossoms, the Holy [sic], the Beech, the Tall Yellow Poplar, the Hilly ground, even the Red Clay I Looked at with amazement."[1] The walk to Oakley was to produce greater delights still, including the American Swallow-tailed Kite sailing overhead, a bird Audubon says he yearned to find, and which he would paint that summer.

The kite's graceful flight is legendary—as buoyant as that of a swallow, of which the kite resembles a larger version. In his *Ornithological Biography*, Audubon took pleasure in describing the effortless glides, swift dives, and spiraling ascensions of this unparalleled avian aerialist. The swallow-tail is commonly seen as Audubon saw it near Oakley that day: silhouetted against the sky, its rakish wings pulled back, and its deeply forked tail spread for easy maneuvering. But in hunting, it swoops low over grasslands, tilting from side to side in search of the snakes, insects, frogs, lizards, and small birds that it eats, usually on the wing.

The appeal for Audubon of the kite's splendid form, sleek proportions, and elegant, efficient flight is augmented by the bird's bold coloring—its snowy head, hindneck, and underparts contrasting starkly with the blue-black wings and tail. This combination of graceful shape and intense color pattern inspired the artist to create an image as timeless and powerful as an emblem. Audubon emphasizes the swallow-tail's refinement by focusing on the sweeping curves of its head, wings, and tail as it glides into our field of vision. His spare treatment of the streamlined silhouette against the blank background effectively communicates the buoyancy of the kite by giving it the appearance of hanging weightlessly in the air. With a consummate sense of design, Audubon reduces the kite's contours to their essence, repeating their pristine lines in the rippling patterns of the bird's feathers. The same sweeping rhythms are again repeated in the expressive shapes of the white neck plumage, which echo the angular and rounded forms of the slender wings and tail and the spaces between them.

For all the purity of the kite's abstract form, however, its image is not insubstantial but solid, corporeal. Audubon has included every important physical detail, down to the correct number of flight feathers. He stresses the physical tension in the bird's neck as it bends to consume its prey. He juxtaposes the smooth, fluid curves of the bird's body with the tight, wriggling convulsions of the hefty garter snake. And, within a concentrated space, he contrasts the kite's sharp beak and talons with the helpless pink gape of the snake's open mouth, an anonymous but momentous scene of ferocity and struggle.

1. Howard Corning, ed., *Journal of John James Audubon Made During His Trip to New Orleans, 1820–21* (Boston: The Club of Odd Volumes, 1929), p. 160.

Nº 15. Plate 72.—
Publithd 1829.

Swallow-tailed Hawk
Falco F furcatus
reptile
Snake vulgo — Garter S

Fem. the same.

Red-tailed Hawk

BUTEO JAMAICENSIS (GMELIN)

Painted in Louisiana in 1821 and later reworked.

Medium: watercolor, pastel, graphite, and selective glazing on paper; 37⅝ × 25½ in.; 95.6 × 64.8 cm.

Inscription (across bottom, in graphite—extremely faint): Red Shouldered Hawk Male 1./ . . . gua . . .

Identification: male above, female below

Seasonal distribution: breeds widely throughout North America, winters throughout the United States

Havell plate number: LI in *The Birds of America*

Acc. no. 1863.17.051

During courtship, a male Red-tailed Hawk sometimes swoops down from above at the female, who rolls over in midair and exposes her claws to him in a feigned gesture of resistance. At nesting season this ritual ends with the hawks flying to a tree and mating. But Audubon observed that red-tail pairs, closely bonded before raising their young, sometimes engage in genuine, prolonged fights after the young are fledged. Indeed, Audubon described seeing these birds enmeshed in vicious, unrelenting battles for food. After watching two mated red-tails vying ruthlessly for the same rabbit, Audubon depicted that event in a scene of startling drama and pathos.

Making this image posed a multifaceted problem: to create a compelling composition; to fit two life-sized hawks on a single sheet of paper; to display as many of the birds' physical attributes as possible together with characteristic behavior; and to communicate the species' elegance, speed, and unrestrained power.

In Audubon's solution, two wild-eyed red-tails are locked in a brutal struggle, their taut bodies bursting with energy. The male bird plunges toward the female, his wings retracted for speed (and so they will fit on the page), his chestnut tail outspread and flashing, his claws stretched wide. The larger female twists her body around to defend herself and protect her food. Her own claws, one of which has pierced through the male's right foot, run with the blood of her wounded prey.

Confined by the limited space of the picture plane (in which they seem to have been arrested only momentarily), the birds' forms are joined by a continuous sharp outline that circumscribes their compact bodies. Enlivening that two-dimensional shape are the diverse textures and autumnal hues of each bird's plumage and its underlying musculature, rendered with the subtlest of gradations. Audubon artfully posed the birds' bodies so they would not only reveal maximum descriptive detail but would also stand out boldly against the boundless sky and fit easily into the space of the picture plane.

In depicting a full view of the female's underside, Audubon juxtaposed with great poignancy the vulnerable but powerfully defended white belly of the massive bird with that of the stricken rabbit, her prey, which nearly matches the hawk in hue. The rabbit's form is mostly surrounded by that of the red-tail, its engagement with and victimization by the hawks a grim but inevitable ingredient of their life cycle.

Audubon's picture, while romantic in its evocation of the dark side of nature—where survival is hard-won and unpredictable and life is often lived in extremes—is also filled with specific documentary information about such details as the fine feathers on the back of the female's head, the translucence of the red tail feathers seen from below, the subtle modulations in the shades of the brown and white back feathers, and the patterning on the female bird's right underwing.

Audubon also made an 1810 watercolor and an 1825 oil painting of the Red-tailed Hawk.[1]

1. The 1810 picture is in the collection of the Houghton Library, Harvard University and the 1825 oil in the collection of the Yale University Art Gallery.

Barred Owl

STRIX VARIA (BARTON)

Painted in about 1821.

Medium: watercolor, pastel, graphite, and ink on paper; 37 ½ × 25 ⅜ in.; 95.3 × 64.5 cm.

Inscription (lower center): Barred Owl Male adult./Strix nebulosa-/Grey Squirel./Sciurius cinereus.—*(lower right, faint, in graphite):* [W]eight

14 oz—

Identification: male

Seasonal distribution: breeds and winters widely in eastern and northwestern North America

Havell plate number: XLVI in *The Birds of America*

Acc. no. 1863.17.046

$\mathcal{S}$uch persons as conclude, when looking upon Owls in the glare of day, that they are, as they then appear, extremely dull, are greatly mistaken,"[1] cautions Audubon on the subject of the Barred Owl. "How often [when spending the night in the woods] have I seen this nocturnal marauder alight within a few yards of me, expose his whole body to the glare of my fire, and eye me in such a curious manner that, had it been reasonable to do so, I would gladly have invited him to walk in and join me in my repast, that I might have enjoyed the pleasure of forming a better acquaintance with him. The liveliness of his motions, joined to their oddness, have often made me think that his society would be at least as agreeable as that of many of the buffoons we meet with in the world."[2]

The intimate knowledge of and thorough delight in his subjects that produce such an exuberant reaction, linked with Audubon's innate sense of composition and sharp eye for detail, are responsible for his success in making pictures. Audubon sought to convey to his viewers that same sense of wonder, but such a goal provided endless frustrations. In the case of the owl, for instance, an accurate portrayal involves depicting, among other features, the rounded wing-feathers with especially soft edges, which enable the bird to fly in virtual silence,

and thus to be a deadly predator. Audubon had seen Barred Owls in every part of the country to which he traveled and had closely observed their feather structure, so elegantly adapted to hunting. Indeed, he makes one of the owl's extended, superbly designed wings a primary focus of his image. But, as Audubon explained, "For a long time I was dispirited, particularly when vainly trying to imitate birds of soft and downy plumage such as Owls,"[3] discouraged that his "first drawings, made entirely in watercolors, wanted softness and finish."[4] Ultimately, however, he discovered—by accident, as he describes it—that introducing the use of pastel to certain parts of his bird figures produced the subtle texture that he sought.

Here, the owl appears to be looking at an unknown object beyond the picture plane. In fact, Audubon had separately drawn a gray squirrel, which he instructed Havell to depict in the final engraving, where it appears clearly befuddling the owl; and he here illustrates a phenomenon he had noted and described without knowing the physiological basis for it: that the Barred Owl, so keenly able to track prey at night, sees the same animal less well during the day because the bird's retinas, composed of more rods than cones, are highly sensitive in low-light conditions but lose resolution in strong light.

1. John James Audubon, *Ornithological Biography*, vol. I (reprint of 1840–44 ed.; New York: Volair Books, 1979), p. 133.
2. Ibid., p. 132.

3. "My Style of Drawing Birds," in Maria R. Audubon, ed., *Audubon and His Journals* (New York: Dover Publications, 1986), vol. II, p. 527.
4. Ibid.

Barred Owl. Male adult.
Strix nebulosa.
Grey Squirrel.
Sciurus cinereus.

Chuck-will's-widow

CAPRIMULGUS CAROLINENSIS GMELIN

Painted in Natchez, Mississippi, on May 7, 1822.

Medium: watercolor, graphite, oil paint, and selective glazing on paper; 23⅝ × 18¾ in.; 60 × 47.6 cm.

Inscription (lower center): Chuck Wills widow/Caprimulgus Carolinensis/Spanish Whipper Will common name *(lower right):* Drawn from Nature by John J. Audubon/Natchez May 7th 1822 Weight of Male. 3¾ oz Female—3¼ . . ./Length of (male) 12¾ in. (female) Eggs siz/Breadth—26. of a cherry . . .

Identification: male above, female below, coral snake on branch

Seasonal distribution: breeds in southeastern United States, winters mostly in South America south to Colombia

Havell plate number: LII in *The Birds of America*

Acc. no. 1863.17.052

The open mouth of the Chuck-will's-widow is so large—a full two inches from corner to corner—that the species has been known to ingest warblers, hummingbirds, and sparrows as well as its usual diet of insects. In depicting the female's mouth fully agape as she hisses at an intruding snake, and in showing her mouth below the viewer's eye level, Audubon draws the observer's gaze to the cavernous opening with which this largest American member of the nightjar family scoops insects out of the air while on the wing. The long filamented bristles at the base of its bill help to funnel the insects in, and the mouth snaps shut suddenly when the prey hits the top of the palate. Audubon contrasts the large size of the chuck's mouth to the species' surprisingly diminutive bill, which the male perched above shows closed, pointing directly down at the female's mouth. Since a chuck catches insects in its open mouth while flying, usually close to the ground, it has no need for a bill large enough to pick up food from the earth. By focusing on the species' mouth Audubon also refers indirectly to the four-syllable song that the bird repeats insistently, and from which its name derives.

Depicting a scene that he actually witnessed, Audubon showed the snake here producing such tumult among the chucks that they spread their tails in alarm, revealing their distinctive patterns.[1] The white on the inner webs of the male's long, rounded outer tail feathers—which is rarely evident when the bird is at rest—differentiates him both from the female chuck, whose tail lacks white altogether, and from its close relative the Whippoorwill, a very similar smaller species, whose tail feathers show more extensive white than the chuck's. The fanned tails emphasize the mothlike appearance of this large-eyed, nocturnal species, which flies on virtually silent wings.

In the spring, chucks arrive in the southeast United States from their wintering grounds in South America. Males display before the females in courtship flights and by waddling awkwardly on their short, weak legs. Females lay their two eggs directly on the ground.

During the day, chucks, which are locally common in the pine and mixed woodlands of the southern United States, sleep perched on a branch, in a tree hollow, or on the ground. The intricate pattern of their mottled buff, reddish-brown, and black protective coloring disguises them so effectively in the shady woods that it is possible to look directly at them and fail to see them. At dusk they begin to whistle their loud song, less rapid and vigorous than a Whippoorwill's but repeated equally often. Audubon described it as "bringing to the mind a pleasure mingled with a certain degree of melancholy, which I have often found very soothing."[2] As the light dims, chucks swoop gracefully over the open fields and the woodland edges that border them, sometimes in groups of a dozen or more.

1. Audubon had previously portrayed the chuck near the Red River in June, 1821, in a picture now in the collection of the Houghton Library, Harvard University. On July 15, 1831, he sent the present picture to Joseph Kidd in Edinburgh to be copied in oil.

2. John James Audubon, *Ornithological Biography*, vol. I (reprint of 1840–44 ed.; New York: Volair Books, 1979), p. 151.

Chuck-Wills widow
Caprimulgus Carolinensis
Spanish Whippers Will common name

Drawn from Nature by John J. Audubon
Natchez May 7th 1822

Weight of Male. 33/4   Female - 3 7/16
Length of ..   12 3/4 in   Egg
Breadth --   26.   9 a Wing

107

Audubon's nomenclature: Bird of Washington, *Falco washingtonii* Audubon; the Bird of Washington or Great American Sea Eagle, *Falco washingtoniensis;* Sea Eagle, *Falco ossifragus;* Washington Sea eagle, *Haliaeetus washingtonii* Audubon

Painted in New Orleans in early 1822.

Medium: watercolor, graphite, collage, and selective glazing on paper; 38 5/16 × 23 5/8 in.; 97.3 × 60 cm.

Inscription (black ink, lower left): Sea EAGLE FALCO Ossifragus/Drawn from Nature/by/John J. Audubon/New Orleans 1822. *(black ink, lower right of center):* Male./Total length 3 Feet 6½/12/Bredth/——10'——1/12/Weight——14 12/16

Identification: immature

Seasonal distribution: Widespread in forests and along coasts and large rivers in Audubon's day. In modern times, many populations diminished and some extirpated because of pesticide use, disturbance of habitat, and killing of birds. Current recovery programs are producing a marked increase in numbers. Now breeds in scattered populations of varying concentrations from Newfoundland, northern Canada, and Alaska south to Florida, south Texas, and southern California. Winters throughout breeding range.

Havell plate number: XI in *The Birds of America*

Acc. no. 1863.17.011

"he name which I have chosen for this new species of Eagle [is] 'The Bird of Washington,'" Audubon announced exultantly.

As it is indisputably the noblest bird of its genus that has yet been discovered in the United States, I trust I shall be allowed to honor it with the name of one yet nobler, who was the saviour of his country, and whose name will ever be dear to it. . . . He was brave, so is the Eagle; like it, too, he was the terror of his foes; and his fame, extending from pole to pole, resembles the majestic soarings of the mightiest of the feathered tribe.[1]

George Washington had been dead for only fifteen years and was still greatly venerated when the young artist-naturalist, during an 1814 trading trip on the Upper Mississippi River, first observed the bird that he would name after the president.

During his career, Audubon described twenty-three valid new species and twelve subspecies of birds. In several instances, however, birds he believed newly discovered were in fact known species that he had observed in an immature or unusual plumage. The Bald Eagle does not acquire its familiar white head and tail until the age of four or five, and the immature bird sometimes shows white on the underside of the wings and occasionally cream or white blotching, which is absent in the adult.

Audubon's early sightings of immature bald eagles convinced him that he had found a new species.

Audubon believed that the eagle he documented was related to the Bald Eagle (already the emblem of the United States) and evidently considered it a powerful icon, a symbol appropriate to the Father of his adopted country. Ever the zealous entrepreneur and showman, Audubon may also have seen a fine opportunity for good personal public relations in such a gesture.

Audubon made at least four other images of the Bald Eagle. Two represent the adult bird: a first version, from 1820, in which a voracious eagle is depicted with a dismembered Canada Goose, and a second, copied from the first in 1828, substituting a catfish for the goose,[2] both versions evidently related to, and intended to surpass, Alexander Wilson's 1812 image of the Bald Eagle. A picture of another immature bald eagle—somewhat older than the present bird and correctly identified in the plate[3]—was probably painted in 1829. The later image is more animated but less dramatically monumental than this rather stiff, though majestic, profile. This picture, from 1822, is cut out from an earlier work and pasted down, as was sometimes Audubon's custom; it is either a copy of, or perhaps the same work as, the one the artist made before 1819, when his birds were less exuberantly lively than in his later work.[4]

1. John James Audubon, *Ornithological Biography,* vol. I (reprint of 1840–44 ed.; New York: Volair Books, 1979), p. 55.
2. Maria R. Audubon, ed., *Audubon and His Journals* (New York: Dover Publications, 1986), vol. I, p. 282, and vol. II, p. 215.
3. Interestingly, while in the species account of the Bald Eagle published in the *Ornithological Biography* in 1831, Audubon recognizes that the eagle takes at least

four years to change from the brown immature plumage to the adult plumage with white head and tail, and while even in his *European Journal* of 1828, he assures us that he has "seen enough [young White-headed Eagles] to know [what they look like]" (*op. cit.* vol. 1, p. 282), in his *Labrador Journal* of 1833, nonetheless, Audubon still refers to "a female Washington Eagle."
4. See *Ornithological Biography,* vol. I, p. 56 for a reference to the pre-1819 work.

SEA EAGLE,
FALCO Ossifragus

Drawn from Nature
by John J. Audubon
New Orleans 1822

White-breasted Nuthatch

SITTA CAROLINENSIS LATHAM

Audubon's nomenclature: White-breasted Black-Capped Nuthatch, *Sitta carolinensis* Brisson
Painted in 1822 in Louisiana or Mississippi.
Medium: watercolor, graphite, and red pastel, on paper; 23¾ × 17⅝ in.; 60.3 × 44.8 cm.
Identification: males upper left and lower right, females lower left and upper right
Seasonal distribution: breeds and winters widely throughout southern Canada and the United States
Havell plate number: CLII in *The Birds of America*
Acc. no. 1863.17.152

"Tree mouse," "devil down-head," and "upside-down bird" are all common names that the White-breasted Nuthatch has earned for its habit of climbing head down around trees in search of insects. The only bird that feeds on tree trunks and branches in such a fashion, the white-breast is especially adapted to occupy this niche (a foraging position that other species scarcely even attempt) because of its particularly long, sharp claw on each hind toe that enables the bird to grip the tree solidly. Audubon subtly emphasizes this feature in the upper-right-hand bird by highlighting one of its hind claws against its white breast and the other against the blank background of the page. The nuthatch navigates by placing one foot forward under its breast and the other back toward its tail, turning the rear foot at right angles to the body, and hitching about quickly, constantly, and with great agility. Audubon shows the bird at the far left in a typical upside-down position, and underscores its posture by placing the other nuthatches so that they lead the viewer to focus on it. Audubon also punctuates the composition by placing the upside-down bird at the extreme left of the group so that it forms a visual stopping point on which the viewer's gaze rests before moving up and right to the bird above and then clockwise around to the others.

White-breasts feed by probing their long, pointed, slender bills into the crevices of trees—usually deciduous ones—for the insects and larvae that, together with nuts and seeds, comprise their diet. Their head-down feeding position enables them to investigate these cracks from an angle different from the one that woodpeckers see when they feed in the opposite direction. Nuthatches often occur in groups like this one when they wander into overlapping territories. Both pairs here look animatedly off to the left, as though they have detected a predator that they are about to mob.

Nuthatches do not support themselves with their tails as woodpeckers do (Audubon reveals this by clearly showing the space between the tail of the bird farthest to the left and the tree trunk). Without tail support, the nuthatch cannot produce the same sturdy strike with its bill that a woodpecker does from its solidly anchored upright position. Instead, it forces soft-shelled nuts like chestnuts or acorns into the crevices of trees and hacks them open, as with a hatchet—hence its name. White-breasts also avidly take seeds from bird feeders, which they may frequent from dawn to dusk, familiar with them as a source of food in a territory where they are generally resident all year long. Members of a pair maintain a close relationship throughout the year, whether they inhabit forest, a farm lot, a country town, or even a park.[1]

---

1. Two other versions of this picture exist: an early one in pencil, pastel, and watercolor made on February 16, 1815, in Henderson, Kentucky, before Audubon undertook the *Birds of America* project, is now in the collection of the Houghton Library, Harvard University; a later oil is in the collection of Princeton University.

Red-eyed Vireo
VIREO OLIVACEUS (LINNAEUS)

Probably painted in Louisiana or Mississippi in 1822.

Medium: watercolor, graphite, selective glazing on paper; 18 7/16 × 11 11/16 in.; 46.8 × 29.7 cm.

Inscription (lower left): No. 15. Plate 74./Published/1829. *(upper right corner graphite):* 50

Identification: adult

Seasonal distribution: breeds across central and southeastern North America, winters in Amazon Basin of South America

Flora: honey locust, *Gleditsia triacanthos,* probably by Joseph Mason

Havell plate number: CL in *The Birds of America*

Acc. no. 1863.17.150

An observer rarely has the opportunity to see a Red-eyed Vireo as clearly as Audubon provides the chance to do here. Red-eyes spend most of their time feeding in the high canopy of open woods, where they hop about constantly among the leaves, well camouflaged by their greenish plumage. (The name *vireo,* in Latin, means "I am green.") They move about more actively than most treetop birds except warblers, and although they are common, they are far less often seen than heard. They sing more persistently than any other North American species: throughout the day, while they are feeding, even in intense heat, during the entire summer and into the fall. Their song consists of numerous short phrases uttered as frequently as 60–80 times per minute, which, in at least one recorded instance, reached a total of more than 22,000 in a single day. Many of the phrases end on a high note and sound like a question. They have a truncated quality and produce the effect of exhortatory speech rather than melody. Some of the phrases have been transliterated as "you see it—you know it—do you hear me?—do you believe it?" and have earned the red-eye the sobriquet "preacher bird."

Audubon began his written description of the Red-eyed Vireo by discussing its insect diet, and, indeed, red-eyes do consume six times as many spiders and insects as fruits, including many injurious pests such as tent caterpillars and gypsy moths. Both male and female vireos feed the young, often taking them orb weaver spiders—such as the one included in this picture—that spin their webs between the branches of trees up to twenty feet in the air. Indeed, the female vireo may also make use of the spider's web in building her neat, elegant nest.

Audubon noticed that "this bird . . . is often called to nurse the young of the Cow-bird,"[1] and, in fact, the red-eye is one of the most common hosts chosen by the parasitic Brown-headed Cowbird, which builds no nest, to hatch its eggs and feed the nestlings, often at the expense of the vireo's own much smaller babies.

To call attention to two of the Red-eyed Vireo's most important identifying characteristics, Audubon has framed the vireo's head within two small branches that bifurcate from the main one on which the bird stands. He has placed the vireo's red eye, which gives it its name, in the center on a direct diagonal between the closest node on each bifurcating branch; and the bird's white eye-line seamlessly continues the line of the main branch. Since adult Red-eyed Vireos are essentially identical in plumage there is no way to distinguish here whether this is a male or a female bird.[2]

1. John James Audubon, *Ornithological Biography,* vol. IV (reprint of 1840–44 ed.; New York: Volair Books, 1979), p. 157.

2. A copy of this painting in oil is in the collection of the American Museum of Natural History.

5

№ 15. Plate 74.
Published
1829.

Audubon's nomenclature: Snow-Bird, *Fringilla hyemalis;* Common Snow-bird, *Nephaea hyemalis,* Linnaeus

Painted in February, most likely in Louisiana in 1822.

Medium: watercolor, pastel, graphite, and selective glazing on paper; 19 × 11¾ in.; 48.4 × 29.8 cm.

Inscription (lower left, faint, in graphite): J. J. Audubon/February

Identification: female above, male below

Seasonal Distribution: breeds across Alaska, Canada, and the northern United States; winters across much of United States

Flora: cotton-gum tree, *Nyssa aquatica,* painted by Joseph Mason

Havell plate number: XIII in *The Birds of America*

Acc. no. 1863.17.013

Like many observers, Audubon, who knew the Dark-eyed Junco by its vernacular name of "snow bird," was most familiar with the species from observing flocks on their wintering grounds. Indeed, the species' Latin name, *hyemalis,* means wintry, and is related to the Sanskrit word *hima,* meaning snow. Although Dark-eyed Juncos are known for their tameness, Audubon noticed that in these winter flocks they often engage in aggressive behavior in which "their little bills are instantly opened, their wings are extended, their eyes are seen to sparkle, and they emit a repelling sound peculiar to themselves on such occasions."[1] The artist enlivened this image by showing the male junco engaged in such a frequently observed display.[2] Depicting the bird in this position (although here on a tree branch rather than the ground) enabled Audubon to show much of the junco's plumage, described as "leaden skies above, snow below."[3]

At the time that Audubon made this picture he was "drawing birds strenuously, and . . . applying coats of water-color under the pastels, thereby preventing the appearance of the paper that in some instances marred my best productions."[4] To depict the junco's plumage, Audubon worked here primarily in blacks, grays, whites, and browns, a color range of which he was extremely fond. Even in describing part of the junco's spring courtship behavior, Audubon remarks on the visual excitement created by the bird's color pattern: "The males chase each other on wing, when their tails being fully expanded, the white and black colours displayed in them present a quite remarkable contrast."[5]

Audubon's restrained palette in this image, combined with the spare setting of birds perched on bare cotton-gum branches and visually balanced by the tree's glossy oval fruit, creates an austere quality particularly pleasing to our modern eye. Both the image's stability and its dynamism derive from carefully constructed diagonals that run through each bird's body and intersect in the fruit stem above the male bird's head. The composition is anchored by a strong vertical line that runs through the upright twig above the female bird's eye and down through the demarcation between the male bird's head and body. This combination of stability and dynamism is essential to the vignette, in which Audubon has telescoped two moments of junco behavior: the aggressive posture of the male toward others and the momentary dispersal of startled birds into a tree close to the feeding ground, "where, however, they remain only for a few minutes, after which they return to their avocations"[6]—picking up seeds that larger wild or domestic scratching birds or squirrels uncover.

In Audubon's day, the "Slate-colored" Junco, shown here, was considered a separate species from the "Oregon" Junco, the "White-winged" Junco, and the "Gray-headed" Junco, populations generally distributed in different parts of North America. Some of these birds were subsequently found to interbreed, and all are now known as forms of the Dark-eyed Junco.

1. John James Audubon, *Ornithological Biography,* vol. II (reprint of 1840–44 ed.; New York: Volair Books, 1979), p. 88.
2. Donald and Lillian Stokes, *A Guide to Bird Behavior,* vol. III (Boston: Little, Brown, 1989), p. 329.
3. Arthur Cleveland Bent, *Life Histories of North American Cardinals, Grosbeaks, Buntings, Towhees, Finches, Sparrows, and Allies* (New York: Dover Publications, 1968), p. 1029.
4. Maria R. Audubon, ed., *Audubon and His Journals,* vol. I (New York: Dover Publications, 1986), p. 51.
5. *Ornithological Biography,* vol. II, p. 89.
6. Ibid., p. 88.

Audubon's nomenclature: Crested Titmouse, *Parus bicolor*

Painted in Louisiana or Mississippi in 1822.

Medium: watercolor, graphite, gouache, and selective glazing on paper; 18⅝ × 11⅝ in.; 47.3 × 29.5 cm.

Inscription (lower left): No 8 Plate 39. *(lower center):* Crested Titmouse Male 1. F. 2./Parus bicolor./Plant Pinus Strobus.

Identification: male above, female below

Seasonal distribution: breeds and winters throughout most of eastern United States (except in southern Florida) and into southern Canada

Flora: white pine, *Pinus strobus*, painted by Joseph Mason

Havell plate number: XXXIX in *The Birds of America*

Acc. no. 1863.17.039

*I*n March of 1810, while working in his store in Louisville, Kentucky, Audubon received a visit from Alexander Wilson, author of *American Ornithology*, the first extensive work on North American bird life. Wilson was traveling around the country seeking subscriptions to his book. Ferdinand Rozier, Audubon's business partner, discouraged him from signing up, according to Audubon, reproaching him in Wilson's presence—in French—that his own drawings were superior and his ornithological knowledge equal to Wilson's. Audubon was persuaded and did not subscribe. At the time he was only twenty-five years old and interested in birds primarily as a hobby. Wilson was forty-four and far more experienced in ornithology, having already published two volumes of his important reference work. Audubon clearly recognized the fine caliber of Wilson's depictions, however, and in the course of preparing his own work for publication, he based several drawings on Wilson's, which he then sought to eclipse. Such is the case with the Tufted Titmouse: Audubon made a drawing of the bird in Red Banks, Kentucky, on July 1, 1810, a few months after seeing Wilson's work;[1] he recomposed his picture in 1822, adding a second bird to show the ventral plumage together with another typical titmouse position, and gave Havell the image to publish. In 1827, while in Great Britain, he made a copy of the second bird from the 1822 picture, perhaps for an exhibition publicizing the *Birds of America* project.[2]

A comparison between Wilson's published picture and Audubon's image demonstrates the leap that Audubon made in ornithological illustration when compared with his predecessor. Wilson's titmouse (shown in a group of similar birds on a bare branch) possesses the species' diagnostic crest and dark

flanks and is depicted bending in a characteristic feeding position. The image is unquestionably graceful and appealing. However, to our modern eye, trained by later bird illustration, the crest of Wilson's titmouse appears overly long and pointed, its feathers undifferentiated; the contrast between back and wing color seems too great; the curve of the bird's head, neck, back, and tail seems distortedly sinuous; the tail appears too lobed; and the bird's expression looks weak. By contrast, Audubon's Tufted Titmouse—shown with its mate, busily feeding on the cone-laden branches of a white pine tree—assumes a distinctly naturalistic posture, with crest and tail in proportion, plumage color subtly rendered, and expression more intent than in Wilson's bird. Audubon copied Wilson's elegant but rather wooden, stereotyped titmouse, and then infused it with lifelike form, vigor, and energy.

Audubon's composition captures the titmouse in the midst of its distinctive habit: inspecting twigs, buds and bark for insects as it

> moves along the branches, searches in the chinks, flies to the end of twigs and hangs to them by its feet, whilst the bill is engaged in detaching a beech or hazel nut, an acorn or a chinquapin, upon all of which it feeds, removing them to a large branch, where, having secured them in a crevice, it holds them with both feet, and breaks the shell by repeated blows of its bill. They are to be seen thus employed for many minutes at a time.[3]

Audubon's placement of the birds' bodies at the top and bottom of a circle that curves around the two intersecting diagonal pine branches adds energetic movement to the page.

1. Formerly in the collection of Mrs. F. Abbot Goodhue, Hewlett, Long Island.
2. The two latter drawings are in the collection of The New-York Historical Society.

3. John James Audubon, *Ornithological Biography*, vol. II (reprint of 1840–44 ed.; New York: Volair Books, 1979), p. 143.

Crested Titmouse Male 1. F. 2.
Parus bicolor.
Plant Pinus Strobus.

N° 8. Plate 39.

117

Painted in New Orleans on February 7, 1822. Habitat added later.
Medium: watercolor, graphite, oil paint, and pastel on paper; 19⅞ × 28⅞ in.;
50.5 × 73.3 cm.
Inscription (across bottom, from left to right): Drawn by John J. Audubon/from
Nature—New Orleans Feb 7—1822/Weight of Male 12 Ounces/Total Length 16
In./Breadth 24¾—/16 Tail feathers Legs equal/Blue Winged Teal/Anas
Discors/Weight of Female 11 Ounces/Length 15 In./Breadth 23½. *(upper left, in
graphite):* Weight of the Male ¾ of a Pound/Total length 16 Inches Legs
equal/Breadth 24¾ do./Tail feathers 16 in number *(upper right, graphite):* Weight of
female 11 ozs/—15 inches—/(erased): . . 23½
Identification: male below, left; female above, right
Seasonal distribution: breeds widely in North America, winters along Atlantic, Pacific,
and Gulf coasts
Havell plate number: CCCXIII in *The Birds of America*
Acc. no. 1863.17.313

When the Blue-winged Teal is resting or swimming, the distinctive wing patch that gives the species its name is usually hidden from view. It was partly in order to depict this patch and partly to allude to the rapid flight of one of our swiftest and smallest ducks that Audubon showed his blue-wings in the air, where

> when flying in flocks in clear, sunny weather, the blue of their wings glistens like polished steel . . . when advancing against a stiff breeze, they alternately shew their upper and lower surfaces, and you are struck by the vivid steel-blue of their mantle, which resembles the dancing light of a piece of glass suddenly reflected on a distant object.[1]

In this picture, the teal's wings are sufficiently spread to reveal their blue feathers, bordered by a band of white-tipped ones. But to some viewers this wing position appears awkward for birds that are flying aloft. The awkwardness seems particularly pronounced in the engraving made from this composition, in which Havell altered the original background to illustrate a distant landscape far below the birds, which are thus shown in midair. The teal's wings are not extended as much as they should be for birds in full flight. But in the context of the present composition with the background as originally conceived, this wing position is explicable. Audubon observed that "before alighting . . . these Teals pass and repass several times over the place, as if to assure themselves of the absence of danger."[2] The birds shown here are gliding low over the water as he described, approaching a potential destination, their feet ex-

Blue Winged Teal
Anas Discors

Weight of Female 11 Ounces
Length 15 In
Breadth 23½

tended in preparation for landing, and their wings allowing them to coast downward, instead of propelling them.

Shorelines, rather than open water, are the Blue-winged Teal's preferred habitat. The species frequents shallows in the prairie states where abundant grasses, mollusks, insects, and crustaceans on or near the surface provide them with food. Blue-wings build well-concealed nests in the tall grass or reeds of potholes or shallow freshwater marshes. Unsuspicious, they often breed near human habitation, where their nesting grounds are continually lost to drainage and agricultural development, and their young to minks, foxes, raccoons, and skunks. The species' lack of wariness and its willingness to be lured by

decoys make it an easy target for hunters, who have always considered it a delicacy. It suffered a severe decline in numbers after 1880.

Blue-winged Teals migrate in small, compact flocks or single pairs, one of the last species to travel north in the spring and one of the first to move south in the fall. Males in flight are recognizable at a considerable distance by the white facial crescent that Audubon portrays here, which he emphasizes by framing it between two curving blades of marsh grass seen behind the bird's head. Most members of this nonhardy species winter in northern South America, farther south than any of our other shallow-water ducks.

1. John James Audubon, *Ornithological Biography*, vol. VI (reprint of 1840–44 ed.; New York: Volair Books, 1979), p. 290.

2. Ibid.

Red Knot

CALIDRIS CANUTUS (LINNAEUS)

Audubon's nomenclature: Red-breasted Sandpiper, *Tringa islandica* Linnaeus

Painted in Louisiana c. 1821.

Medium: watercolor, graphite, collage, and traces of charcoal on paper; 12 × 18⅝ in.; 30.5 × 47 cm.

Inscription (upper left, in graphite): Red-breasted Sandpiper. 1. Male Spring plumage/2. Female in Winter/Tringa islandica, L. *(middle left, in graphite):* Spring plumage/2. Winter plumage—*(along upper left side, diagonal, in graphite):* 4th volume *(recto shows strikethrough of inscription on verso just above collaged bird's head)*

Identification: breeding-plumaged male above, winter-plumaged female below

Seasonal distribution: breeds in northernmost arctic of Old and New Worlds, winters along Atlantic, Pacific, and Gulf coasts south to temperate South America

Havell plate number: CCCXV in *The Birds of America*

Acc. no. 1863.17.315

*I*n naming this species *canutus*, the Swedish naturalist Linnaeus was apparently recalling Canute, the Danish king known for attempting to hold back the tide. And indeed, when groups of hundreds or thousands of Red Knots mass on coastal beaches during migration in compact bunches of birds all moving together, the whimsical observer may be tempted to imagine that the knots actually possess the power that Canute desired.

Red Knots, the largest of the North American beach sandpipers, and once the most abundant of all North American shorebirds, commonly gather, fly, and roost in enormous groups. This habit, together with their generally unskittish nature, made them vulnerable to substantial depredations on their numbers by hunters who found them, as Audubon explained, "always welcome to the palate of the connoisseur in dainties."[1] The knots could be lured easily to decoys and entire flocks destroyed with a single volley. Not until they were protected by law in our century did their population begin to recover.

Audubon described seeing Red Knots in migration along the Gulf and Atlantic coasts from Texas to the Bay of Fundy, both in spring and autumn, and observed them wintering in east Florida as well. He described one of the species' most notable habits—that of flying swiftly and restlessly, wheeling in unison in huge, tight groups. He watched them feeding on sandy or rocky beaches (as here) or in salt marshes, probing their bills repeatedly into the earth with a sewing machine–like motion, digging for mollusks, crab eggs, grass seeds, worms, and insects. But he never found a Red Knot's nest, which the species (both in the Old World and the New) builds on higher gravelly plateaus in lichen-lined shallow depressions: not until 1909 during Admiral Peary's expedition to the North Pole was the first Red Knot nest discovered. (Because the species winters mostly in South America, some individuals make an annual round trip of about 19,000 miles.)

Audubon does not specify whether he ever saw a knot in full spring plumage with rufous head, neck, breast, and underparts, together with one in gray and white winter plumage as he shows them in this composition (the winter-plumaged bird in front was cut out of another sheet and pasted onto this one). But such an observation would have been possible: as with other shorebird species, some adult knots change into summer plumage as early as March and some remain in winter plumage as late as May; some adults, moreover, remain in breeding plumage until September, when others are already changing into winter plumage. (The two plumages are so different that, as Audubon did not hesitate to point out, Alexander Wilson believed the spring- and winter-plumaged birds to represent two separate species.) Audubon does note that the breeding-plumaged knot illustrated here is a young bird, since "those of the first year have their markings at that season handsomer than at any other period in their lives."[2]

---

1. John James Audubon, *Ornithological Biography,* vol. V (reprint of 1840–44 ed.; New York: Volair Books, 1979), p. 254.

2. Ibid., p. 256.

Red breasted Sandpiper. 1 Male Spring plumage
2. Female in Winter.
Tringa islandica, L.

4 Volume

1 Spring plumage
2 Winter plumage —

Anhinga

ANHINGA ANHINGA (LINNAEUS)

Audubon's nomenclature: *Bec à Lancette*, Black-Bellied Darter, *Plotus melanogaster*, Snake Bird

Painted in New Orleans in 1822.

Medium: watercolor, pastel, graphite, oil paint, and gouache on paper; 28½ × 20¼ in.; 72.4 × 51.4 cm.

Inscription (left side, in graphite): Length 2^{11}/12/Breadth 3^{11}/12/Tail feathers 12—/Weight—2^{15}/16 *(left side):* Length 2^{11}/12 feet

Breadth 3^{11}/12 12 Tail feathers Weight—2^{15}/16 *(bottom center):* Black Bellied Darter or Snake Bird/*Plotus melanogaster* Bec à Lancette

Common name *(along branch):* Drawn by John J. Audubon from Nature/New Orleans 1822 *(upper right, in graphite):*

Bec à Lancette Louisiana

Identification: male in front, female behind

Seasonal distribution: breeds and winters in the southeastern United States

Acc. no. 1863.18.034

Audubon took full advantage of the Anhinga's gangly neck, elongated body, and lengthy, fan-shaped tail as well as its singular prenuptial behavior to create the graceful, repetitive patterns in this image. The "Snake-bird . . . by its habits, rarely fails to attract the notice of the most indifferent observer,"[1] he wrote, and here he showed adult male and female Anhingas perched on a dead snag, their necks partially extended in courtship display. Apparently Audubon became dissatisfied with the lack of features visible on the female here, and with the somewhat unnatural position of the birds' bodies, shown aligned parallel to the perch in a posture that is pictorially elegant but actually unusual for the species. For the published vignette he redrew the image, depicting each bird sitting separately at differents heights on the tree, so that the viewer sees both birds in full. He also altered the position of the birds' bodies in the final image so that they are no longer seen from the side, as here, but perpendicular to the branch, as the birds most commonly perch. He showed the female from the front, exhibiting her black-and-tan plumage, which contrasts clearly with the black-and-white feathering of the male; and he depicted the male from the back with his wings spread, to reveal as much as possible of the intricate dark-and-silvery pattern of his plumage and to capture a typical posture of the species.

Just prior to breeding, Anhingas engage in the act of "peer-ing around," in which the birds, sitting upright, partially extend their heads and necks and then look slowly and repeatedly to the left and right. The S-shaped curve clearly visible in this species' neck exists because of a modification in the Anhinga's eighth and ninth vertebrae, which, together with specialized musculature, allows the bird to dart its neck out quickly, while swimming underwater with its large, fully webbed feet, and spear a fish. It impales the prey on its straight, pointed bill—which is nearly twice as long as its head—and then rises to the surface, flips the fish up in the air, and catches it in its mouth headfirst between finely serrated mandibles in order to swallow it most easily. Anhingas do their fishing in quiet bodies of fresh or salt water, diving from the surface, from the air, or from a perch. To prevent water from being forced in during the dive their nostrils have no openings. Often when they swim along in search of prey, Anhingas submerge their bodies so that only the small head and snaky neck are visible, and the bird's appearance harks back to its reptilian ancestors.

Anhingas' feathers are not waterproof, and the birds must dry them out frequently to keep them from becoming waterlogged. Thus they choose feeding areas near trees with open branches where they can conveniently perch and roost, spreading their wings to allow the water to disperse.

1. John James Audubon, *Ornithological Biography*, vol. VI (reprint of 1840–44 ed.; New York: Volair Books, 1979), p. 443.

Length 2 ½ feet
Breadth 3 ½
12 Tail feathers
Weight 2 lb 14 oz

Black Bellied Darter or Snake Bird
Plotus Melanogaster
Bec à Lanette Commune

Willet

CATOPTROPHORUS SEMIPALMATUS (GMELIN)

Audubon's nomenclature: Semi-palmated snipe, *Scolopax Semi-palmata*

Painted in Philadelphia, Pennsylvania, on May 9, 1824.

Medium: watercolor, black and brown pastel, graphite, and selective glazing on paper; 11½ × 18¹⁵⁄₁₆ in.; 29.2 × 48 cm.

Inscription (lower left, in black ink): Drawn from nature by John J. Audubon/Philadelphia May 9 1824 *(lower center, in black ink):*

Semi-palmated Snipe Female/Scolopax semi-palmata *(lower right, in black ink):* Weight 1 lb ½ oz Troy/Eggs = shot w. 1

(lower right, graphite): 21

Identification: breeding-plumaged female

Seasonal distribution: breeds in west-central North America and along Atlantic and Gulf coasts, winters along southern Atlantic,

Pacific, and Gulf coasts

Acc. no. 1863.18.016

When Audubon first drew the Willet on May 8, 1815, in Henderson, Kentucky, he depicted a breeding-plumaged bird perched on a rock, facing left, with a wriggling worm in its partly open beak. He made the present picture of the Willet exactly nine years and one day later, in Philadelphia, showing the bird in a similar posture, and adding surrounding vegetation. Interestingly, while he rendered the plumage with greater detail and subtlety in this later picture than in the first one and expressed the plasticity of the bird's body more effectively here, some of the liveliness in the original bird's facial expression and posture are lacking in this depiction. About ten years later, when Audubon made the final composition for *The Birds of America*, in which he included the figures of three Willets, he used a position very similar to this one but in reverse for one of two foreground birds, and once again accentuated the species' bright-eyed, energetic appearance. In that final image the bird in the reversed position as well as another bird in the background appear in winter plumage, with a third bird in breeding plumage. One reason to add the background bird was to show the Willet with its wing raised, displaying the unique, elegant, dramatic, dark-and-light underwing pattern that is not evident in this picture. Because of their even, gray-brown coloring and uniform heavy mottling, Willets appear rather drab and inconspicuous at rest, but when they fly, and as they land, they flash their striking underwing plumage, often while giving the "pill-will-willet" call from which their name arose.

Audubon did not include the rock in this composition arbitrarily. He noticed—as have countless field observers to this day—that, unlike many other shorebirds, Willets use numerous perches besides the ground, among them trees, fences, bushes, and posts, as well as rocks. Indeed, they have been observed on pine limbs as high as fifty feet above the ground.

In this picture (although less so than in the one he redrew for publication) the Willet's straight, heavy bill and long bluish-gray legs with their half-webbed feet, are prominent. On the coasts, mud flats, lake edges, and grasslands that the species frequents, its long bill enables it to probe into the earth as well as pick up prey from the surface—fish, mollusks, insects, worms, and especially crabs. Its long legs enable it to wade in comparatively deep water in search of food, and its partially webbed feet make it a good swimmer.

Audubon wrote of Willets that they "grow rapidly, become fat and juicy, and by the time they are able to fly, afford excellent food."[1] Indeed, Willets were shot so extensively and their eggs so heavily collected for the market that by the early twentieth century they were decimated along the Atlantic coast north of Virginia. A ban on hunting shorebirds has now allowed them to repopulate some of their former haunts.

1. John James Audubon, *Ornithological Biography*, vol. V (reprint of 1840–44 ed.; New York: Volair Books, 1979), p. 327.

Drawn from Nature by John J. Audubon
Philadelphia May 9th 1824

ated. Snipe.

ax. Semi-palmata

21

Weight 1 lb, 1½ oz, Troy.
Eggs Shot or. 1–

American Goldfinch

CARDUELIS TRISTIS (LINNAEUS)

Probably painted in New York in August, 1824.

Medium: watercolor, gouache, and graphite on paper; 18½ × 11¾ in.; 47 × 29.8 cm.

Inscription (in graphite, top male): 1 *(bottom female):* 2

Identification: male above, female below

Seasonal distribution: breeds across most of central North America, winters widely across the United States

Flora: bull thistle, *Cirsium vulgare*

Havell plate number: XXXIII in *The Birds of America*

Acc. no. 1863.17.033

*I*n the spring of 1824, Audubon went to Philadelphia, a center for the study of natural history, to try to arrange for the publication of his bird drawings. In spite of making some good contacts, he failed to interest an engraver and a publisher in his project, and his friends advised him to take the drawings abroad. He first persisted in the United States, however, visiting New York City at the beginning of August. He went from there by steamer up the Hudson River to Albany, where he hoped to see potential sponsors to whom he had letters of introduction. Unable to make those contacts, he traveled west to Niagara Falls along the Mohawk River. It was on that river trip that he was able to observe the largest number of goldfinches he had ever seen.

In watching the finches feed, Audubon noticed that they "tear up the down and withered petals of the ripening [thistle] flowers with ease, leaning downwards upon them, eat off the seed, and allow the down to float in the air. The remarkable plumage of the male . . . [is] at this season very agreeable; and so familiar are these birds that they suffer you to approach within a few yards, before they leave the plant on which they are seated."[1]

Audubon depicted the birds balancing delicately, as they typically do, on the slender thistle plants that provide them with both food and nesting material. The compositional rhythms produced by the birds and plants complement those generated by the spaces between the many-pointed thistle leaves. Audubon painted the thistles with particular elegance, emphasizing the circular and angular patterns of their fluffy, round flowers and spiky leaves, contrasting the leaves' sharp points with the diaphanous thistledown. The thistle on which the male goldfinch has alighted bends, even under his slight weight, and arches down, nearly touching the body of the female bird, where it underscores the subtle contrast between the fuzzy softness of the thistledown and the sleek softness of the female's feathers. The male fans the flashy pointed feathers of his tail for balance—Audubon creates a particularly intriguing passage by silhouetting the striking black-and-white tail pattern against the green points of the thistle leaves—as the bird considers the ripe blossom on the plant already accommodating the female. The yellow in the male's back and the female's undersides contrasts brightly with the near-complementary color of the deep pink thistle blossoms.

The undulating curve described by the bodies of the two finches not only shows a characteristic posture of the species but may also include a suggestion of the goldfinch's flight, "performed in deep curved lines, alternately rising and falling."[2]

1. John James Audubon, *Ornithological Biography,* vol. III (reprint of 1840–44 ed.; New York: Volair Books, 1979), p. 130.

2. Ibid., p. 129.

Painted about 1824.

Medium: watercolor, graphite, gouache, and selective scraping on paper; 19 ⅛ × 11 ⅝ in.; 49.6 × 29.4 cm.

Inscription (lower left): No. 17. Plate 83 *(lower center):* House Wren. Male 1. F.2. Young 3.4.5 *(lower center, graphite has been erased):*

Troglodytes aedon? . . . don/? Aedon?

Identification: male above, female left, young right.

Seasonal distribution: breeds across much of North America, winters across southern United States

Havell plate number: LXXXIII in *The Birds of America*

Acc. no. 1863.17.083

An old hat is not an unusual place for a House Wren to nest. In fact, wrens have been known to nest in a surprising variety of man-made objects that form cavities, including a fishing creel hanging in a shed, the nozzle of a pump, and even in an area near the axle of an automobile in daily use. In the wild, House Wrens nest in tree holes, but they adapt readily to, and sometimes even seem to prefer, nesting boxes and other constructed items. Historically, the wren's tolerance of human activity has made it much beloved of people who are cheered by its presence, its bubbly song, its plucky manner, and, not least, its insect-consuming capacities. Audubon knew that bird lovers often were eager to attract it.

> It delights in being near and about gardens, orchards, and the habitations of man, and is frequently found in abundance in the very center of our eastern cities, where many little boxes are put up against the walls of houses, or the trunks of trees, for its accommodation, as is also done in the country.[1]

In the spring of 1812, Audubon was able to study the House Wren at close range when he and his wife were in Pennsylvania. A pair of wrens nested in the hole of a wall just a few inches from the room in which Audubon worked, and he often watched the male searching the garden for insects with which it returned to the hole and fed its mate. Audubon tamed the male by feeding it flies and spiders, and eventually the bird grew brave enough to enter the room through the open window; it even sang there. Audubon could not resist the proximity of such an appealing subject, and one day closed the window, caught the bird, held it in his hand, and drew its portrait. Once he had finished he released the bird but observed that it never again entered his room.

Audubon probably used that pencil and pastel drawing as a model for the male bird in this picture, made about a dozen years later.[2] In both, the male is shown cocking his tail as wrens do in situations of excitement or disturbance such as territorial disputes or the approach of danger. The female here perches on a twig, the primary material with which wrens typically build, and feeds her young a spider. That prey may have been passed to her by the male, who does not feed the young directly at first.

The positions of the male and female birds combine to form a reverse S-curve that leads the viewer's eye into the hat where two of the young are still ensconced. The third juvenile has fledged but, characteristically, stays close to the nest and the other two young, clinging to the side of its makeshift home. Its extended wing provides both a lively detail of young wren plumage and a delicate, finely textured shape to complement the rough sturdiness of the hat.

1. John James Audubon, *Ornithological Biography,* vol. I (reprint of 1840–44 ed.; New York: Volair Books, 1979), p. 125.
2. The 1812 picture is now in the collection of the Houghton Library, Harvard University. There is also an oil copy of the present picture, made by Kidd, in the Pennsylvania Academy of Fine Arts.

No 17. Plate 83.

House Wren. Male 1. F. 2. Young 3. 4. 5.

Audubon's nomenclature: Green-blue or White-bellied Swallow, *Hirundo bicolor*

Painted on May 17, 1824 in Philadelphia.

Medium: watercolor, graphite, and gouache on paper; 18⅞ × 11⅝ in.; 47.9 × 29.5 cm.

Inscription (lower left, in black ink): Drawn by John J. Audubon/from Nature—Philadelphia May 17th 1824 *(lower center, in black ink):*
Green-blue or White-bellied Male 1. F. 2/Swallow Hirundo iridis *(crossed out)* bicolor *(lower right, in black ink):* No. 20/Plate 100 *(left, in
graphite, below egg):* Usually 5. *(graphite, mostly erased):*—M . . . P . . . P eig—s . . . *(indecipherable)*

Identification: male above, female below

Seasonal distribution: breeds widely over most of North America, winters in southeastern and southwestern United States,
Central America, and Cuba

Havell plate number: C in *The Birds of America*

Acc. no. 1863.17.100

At the time that he made this picture, in May 1824, Audubon was in Philadelphia seeking an engraver for his bird drawings. He formed a number of important connections on that trip, among them one with Napoleon Bonaparte's nephew, Charles Lucien Bonaparte, a distinguished young ornithologist. He also met a gentleman farmer and naturalist, Edward Harris, who became his benefactor. These men remained Audubon's lifelong friends (and both have species of American birds named after them); but Audubon also made certain enemies among the members of Philadelphia's ornithological community and, in the end, was advised to go abroad to publish his work. During the course of his stay in Philadelphia, Audubon took some time out from making personal contacts to make bird portraits, among them that of the Tree Swallow, a species actively breeding in the Philadelphia area at that season.

The Tree Swallow is an agile flyer, engaging in dramatic dives and other nimble aerial feats; it defends nest sites, catches insects, and performs courtship displays, all on the wing. Audubon wrote admiringly, "Its flight is easy, continued, and capable of being greatly protracted. It is seen sailing, circling, turning, and winding in all directions."[1] Although Tree Swallows may seem to be gentle, peaceful birds, they can become very pugnacious, particularly when competing for a tree cavity or nesting box in which to breed. On such occasions, two Tree Swallows may confront each other in the air and then do battle, falling to earth as they fight.

Once a Tree Swallow has established dominance in a territory, nest building begins. That activity is accomplished principally by the female, who is sometimes aided by the male in collecting materials, including grasses and, for the nest lining, feathers (preferably white ones, often from chickens). The swallows occasionally spar for the feathers, sometimes stealing the ones that other birds have gathered. Egg laying begins as soon as the nest is completed.

In this balletic image, Audubon alludes to several aspects of Tree Swallows' nesting behavior. He depicts one adult swallow attacking another, perhaps in pursuit of the white feather that drifts off to the right. To the left appears a tiny, white, life-sized swallow's egg, the future contents of the nest that the feather will help to line.[2]

The opposite-curving lines of the swallows' wings and the reverse thrust of their tails create opposing forces that lead the viewer's eye in different directions, generating keen pictorial tension that underscores the tension in the birds' bodies and the threatening approach of their nearly touching open bills. The composition produces a powerful description of the intense conflict in which Tree Swallows engage every nesting season.

1. John James Audubon, *Ornithological Biography*, vol. I (reprint of 1840–44 ed.; New York: Volair Books, 1979), p. 175.

2. Audubon sent this picture to Joseph Kidd in Edinburgh on July 29, 1831, to be copied in oil.

Chimney Swift

CHAETURA PELAGICA (LINNAEUS)

Audubon's nomenclature: Chimney Swallow or American Swift, *Cypselus pelagius* Temminck

Painted in the East, c. 1824; composition completed in 1829.

Medium: watercolor, graphite, touches of gouache, and collage on paper; 18⁵⁄₁₆ × 11⁷⁄₁₆ in.; 46.5 × 29 cm.

Inscription (lower left, in graphite): Nest front view/unglued from a chimney—/J. J. Audubon/July 18th *(lower right, in graphite):* Nest

profile/view *(upper right, in graphite):* 50

Identification: adults

Seasonal distribution: breeds in northeastern North America, winters in upper Amazon Basin, South America

Havell plate number: CLVIII in *The Birds of America*

Acc. no. 1863.17.158

$\mathcal{I}$n St. Francisville, Louisiana, Audubon counted more than one thousand Chimney Swifts entering a single chimney in one evening. In Louisville, Kentucky, he removed part of the base of a tree and spent a number of weeks observing some nine thousand swifts roosting inside. (Five years later, he returned to the same tree and noted swifts still roosting there.)

Acquiring knowledge about Chimney Swifts took perseverance because they "never alight on trees or on the ground. If one is caught and placed on the latter, it can only move in a very awkward fashion."[1] Indeed, Chimney Swifts spend more time flying than virtually any other land bird; essentially their entire outdoor existence—feeding, drinking, bathing, courting, and gathering nesting materials—occurs exclusively on the wing. Even copulation often takes place in midair. Moreover, swifts, as their name implies, have the speediest flight of any small perching bird, twisting and turning so rapidly and agilely that scientists used to think they sometimes flapped each wing alternately instead of together, an optical illusion that the birds create with their erratic movements. Although resembling swallows, as Audubon referred to them, swifts are actually physiologically more closely related to hummingbirds.

The Chimney Swift is notable for several physical characteristics that Audubon illustrates in detail, and for certain unusual behaviors as well. The swift's protracted flight, combining shallow wing beats with glides, is accomplished by

means of long, slender, pointed wings, which, as Audubon shows, extend well beyond the tail. The bird's diminutive bill is counterbalanced by a large mouth with strong jaw muscles (its size apparent in the bird on the left) that enable it to consume multitudes of insects. Its small, weak legs—almost useless for walking or sitting on tree branches—are equipped with sturdy claws, visible in the bird on the right, that allow it, even very soon after birth, to cling upright to the vertical surface on which it builds its nest, braced by its spiny tail, which it can fan out at will.

The nest of the Chimney Swift is distinctive and is such a remarkable part of the bird's life cycle that Audubon includes two graceful examples in his composition. Historically, Chimney Swifts nested in hollow trees, but now, as one of the few species that have adapted well to the human presence, the birds largely inhabit such man-made structures as chimneys, open well shafts, open silos, and the inside walls of buildings. The swift's nest, as Audubon shows, is a shallow half-round cup built of short, dried twigs that the birds snatch on the wing from dead trees. Audubon describes in his text how the birds break the twigs off with their feet and bring them to the nest site, where they fasten them to its vertical surface and then to each other with a gluey, salivalike substance secreted in their mouths. This organic cement hardens so effectively when it dries that the nest can withstand many a summer downpour.

1. John James Audubon, *Ornithological Biography*, vol. I (reprint of 1840–44 ed.; New York: Volair Books, 1979), p. 165.

Painted in Pittsburgh in the autumn of 1824.

Medium: watercolor, gouache, graphite, pastel, and black chalk (?) on paper; 26 3/16 × 18 1/4 in.; 66.5 × 46.4 cm.

Inscription (lower left): No. 13. Plate 62./Published 1829 *(lower left corner):* Drawn from Nature/Pittsburgh Pena/J.J. Audubon *(lower center):*
Passenger Pigeon Male 1. Female 2 Columba migratoria *(upper right corner, in graphite):* 63

Identification: female above, male below

Seasonal distribution: extinct; formerly bred widely in eastern North America and wintered widely in the southern United States

Havell plate number: LXII in *The Birds of America*

Acc. no. 1863.17.062

There is no bird in America today that we can observe in the multitudes in which Audubon beheld the now-extinct Passenger Pigeon, at one time more numerous than all other species of birds in this country combined. Indeed, it is nearly impossible to conceive that "almost solid masses"[1] of these "Wild Pigeons" (as they were then commonly known) once flew over the banks of the Ohio River for three days in succession, making a noise like "a hard gale at sea."[2] It is virtually unimaginable that shooting parties brought down so many that for a week in the autumn of 1813 a town's population "fed on nothing but pigeons and talked of nothing but pigeons";[3] that "numbers of birds immense beyond conception"[4] weighed down the trees in their roosting areas so heavily that "many trees two feet in diameter . . . were broken off at no great distance from the ground";[5] that in Audubon's day an estimated 5 billion of these birds inhabited Kentucky, Ohio, and Indiana alone. For, after mass destruction of the birds and their habitat, the last captive Passenger Pigeon died on September 14, 1914, in the Cincinnati Zoo.

In Audubon's observation, Passenger Pigeons traveled not to escape cold weather or to breed in a particular locality but to find food. They depleted the supply in one location, gleaning all the nuts, berries, seeds, or worms they could, and then moved on, sometimes at speeds of up to sixty miles an hour, their unusually acute vision apparently enabling them to determine even from a very great height what places afforded abundant pickings.

Audubon wrote that "the tenderness and affection displayed by these birds toward their mates, are in the highest degree striking."[6] Scientists today consider the attributing of such emotions to wild creatures anthropomorphizing, but they do note that courtship displays of members of the pigeon family are some of the most frequently observed aspects of the birds' behavior. Since Audubon's purpose was to depict Passenger Pigeons in detail rather than in hordes, he chose a courtship scene through which to describe them.[7]

In his interpretation, painted during a stay in Pittsburgh in 1824, a pair of the pigeons engages in the premating activity known to ornithologists as billing, in which the female inserts her beak into the male's and receives regurgitated food. The tapering forms and graceful movements of the birds are echoed in the curving branches that support them, repeating and emphasizing the lines and color tones of the pigeons themselves. The prominently displayed "long well-plumed tail" and "well-set wings"[8] of the richly colored male recall courting acts in which the birds drag their spread tails along the ground or clap their wings together in flight, "producing a smart rap, which may be heard at a distance of thirty or forty yards."[9]

1. John James Audubon, *Ornithological Biography*, vol. V (reprint of 1840–44 ed.; New York: Volair Books, 1979), p. 27.
2. Ibid., p. 29.
3. Ibid., p. 27.
4. Ibid., p. 29.
5. Ibid.
6. Ibid., p. 31.

7. Two other versions of Audubon's Passenger Pigeon exist: a much earlier one of a single bird made in Louisville, Kentucky, on December 11, 1809, now in the collection of the Houghton Library, Harvard University, and an oil copy of the present picture by Joseph Kidd, now in the collection of Harvard University's Museum of Comparative Zoology.
8. *Ornithological Biography*, vol. V, p. 26.
9. Ibid., p. 25.

No 13. Plate 62.
Published 1829.

Passenger Pigeon Male 1. Female 2
Columba migratoria

Drawn from Nature
Pittsburgh, Penn.
J. J. Audubon

Eastern Phoebe

SAYORNIS PHOEBE (LATHAM)

Audubon's nomenclature: Pewee Flycatcher or Pewit Flycatcher, *Musicapa fusca* Gmelin

Painted in Louisiana c. 1825,

Medium: watercolor, pastel, graphite, and gouache on paper; 18 13/16 × 11 1/2 in.; 47.8 × 29.2 cm.

Inscription (above male bird): 1 *(below female bird):* 2 *(top corner, in graphite):* 20

Identification: male above, female below

Seasonal distribution: breeds in north central and northeastern North America, winters in southeastern and south central

United States and south to Mexico

Flora: probably sea-island cotton, *Gossypium barbadense*

Havell plate number: CXX in *The Birds of America*

Acc. no. 1863.17.120

Many people who are drawn to birds recognize certain species for which they feel a special fondness because the birds evoke happy associations—with certain places, companions, or periods of life. For Audubon, such a species was the Eastern Phoebe, with which he became closely acquainted during his early days in Pennsylvania.

Perkiomen Creek runs through Mill Grove, Audubon's first residence in America. Audubon reminisced about wandering beside it, full of joyous ruminations about the natural world. "These impressive, and always delightful, reveries often accompanied my steps to the entrance of a small cave scooped out of the solid rock by the hand of nature. It was, I then thought, quite large enough for my study."[1] In early spring, Audubon discovered in his hideaway a nest of the Eastern Phoebe, which likes to build in niches with overhanging protection such as ledges or bridges, often around human habitation—in this case, "the rock immediately over the arched entrance of this calm retreat."[2] To his delight, Audubon found a pair of hardy phoebes already taking up residence in the cave nest, even though "the ground was still partially covered with snow, and the air retained the piercing chill of winter."[3] Audubon made daily visits to his retreat, and the phoebes, with characteristic tameness, became accustomed to his presence. He observed them refurbishing the nest, and eventually saw six eggs there. As the young hatched, he watched the parents feed them so fre-

quently that "I thought I saw the little ones grow as I gazed upon them."[4] He began to handle the young and, in time, attached little threads to their legs, which they or the parents always removed. But just before the fledglings left the nest, Audubon carefully fastened on new, silver threads. He describes his pleasure, the following spring, upon examining the phoebes that returned to nest at Mill Grove, when he found that two of them retained the little silver rings. In the years since this first American bird-banding experiment, professional and amateur ornithologists have undertaken thousands of banding studies to learn whether birds return to their nesting and wintering sites of previous years.

The phoebe is so called because its insistent, often-repeated song resembles the sound of that name—originally given to a daughter of Gaea in Greek mythology. It is generally the male who sings, from his arrival on the breeding ground until nest building begins. He is portrayed here announcing his presence while raising his crown in response to danger or excitement. The female lifts her wings over her back, perhaps about to flutter them as she does just before mating. The cotton plant on which the birds are perched adds to the scene the heightened sense of tactility produced by its palpable, contrasting textures, and the buff, brown, ocher, gray, and white tones that harmonize with and set off the phoebes' restrained plumage.

1. John James Audubon, *Ornithological Biography*, vol. I (reprint of 1840–44 ed.; New York: Volair Books, 1979), p. 224.
2. Ibid.
3. Ibid.
4. Ibid., p. 227.

The flight of the bird now before you is rapid, silent, and horizontal, as it moves from one tree to another, or across a field or river . . . it occasionally inclines the body to either side, so as alternately to shew its whole upper or under parts."[1] In his writings, Audubon noted that the cuckoo's grace in the air contrasts vividly with its awkwardness on the ground,[2] and when he came to paint the species in 1821 or 1822 in Louisiana, he used to good advantage the cuckoo's habit of turning itself in flight. Audubon chose for the subject of his picture the moment of such a turning maneuver—also capturing the instant in which the bird launches itself from its perch—in order to lend vitality to his composition as well as to show the bird at the angle from which its dramatic black-and-white tail pattern and the rich cinnamon tones of its wing linings are fully visible. Audubon had occasion both to study individual cuckoos (even in the nest) and to witness many of them migrating. "While travelling with great rapidity on a steamboat, so as to include a range of a hundred miles in one day, I have observed this Cuckoo crossing the Mississippi at many different points in the same day."[3]

Yellow-billed Cuckoos are often recognized by their song, "the frequent repetition of their dull and unmusical notes, which are not unlike those of a young bull-frog. These notes may be represented by the word *cow, cow* repeated eight or ten times with increasing rapidity."[4] Indeed, in the wild, the species is more frequently heard than seen. Audubon draws attention to the features for which the cuckoo is named[5]—its yellow bill and the distinctive cry that it emits, even well beyond the breeding season—by centering the bird's open beak in the composition and highlighting it against a light background. Several of the species' notable characteristics, including its song, its flight, and its habit of frequenting woodland thickets are all empha-

142

sized here in the close juxtaposition of the bird's bill with the dense foliage through which it flies and the bronze-brown plumage of its feeding companion, whose meal it seeks to share.[6]

The pawpaw tree, with its pendulous, pulpy, rusty-brown fruit (painted in a subtle and carefully observed manner that suggests the hand of the young Joseph Mason, who was assisting Audubon at the time) serves as a fine visual foil to the cuckoos' bronze plumage. The ragged edges of its partially eaten leaves call attention to the caterpillars that feed on them voraciously and that the cuckoos so effectively control, while at the same time adding an impressive element of abstract design to the composition. The birds' white tail spots flash brilliantly against other leaves, which echo the shape of the birds' tails and thus further integrate and enrich the picture's design.[7]

1. John James Audubon, *Ornithological Biography*, vol. IV (reprint of 1840–44 ed.; New York: Volair Books, 1979), p. 294.
2. Ibid., p. 295.
3. Ibid., p. 294.
4. Ibid.
5. The poetic name "rain crow," by which the bird is sometimes known, particularly among farmers who believe that its repetitive notes signal rain, also appears in Audubon's account.
6. Although Audubon describes Yellow-billed Cuckoos as feeding on "insects such as caterpillars and butterflies, as well as on berries of many kinds," and indeed depicts the lower bird in the act of eating a tiger swallowtail butterfly, modern ornithologists observe that the species consumes caterpillars almost exclusively.
7. A very early Audubon study of the Yellow-billed Cuckoo, signed and dating from about 1806, is in the collection of the Houghton Library, Harvard University.

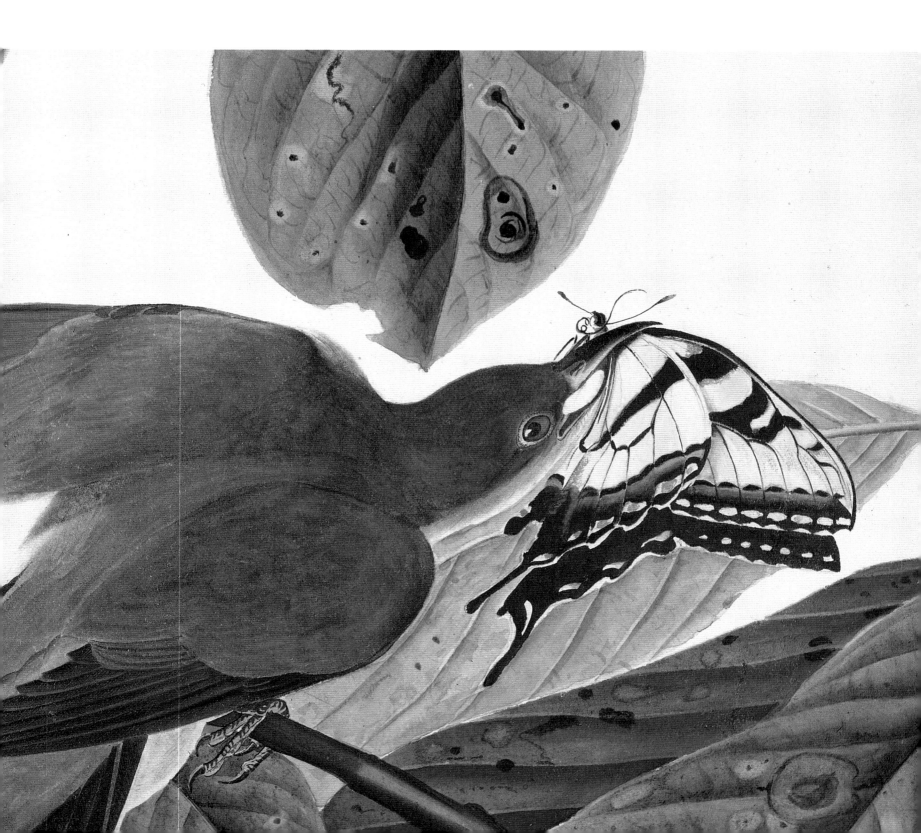

Peregrine Falcon

(FALCO PEREGRINUS) TUNSTALL

Audubon's nomenclature: Great-footed Hawk, *Falco peregrinus* Gmelin

Female drawn on December 26 and 27, 1820, on the Mississippi River, cut out and pasted down on sheet containing male and two
ducks, which were painted several years later.

Medium: watercolor, pastel, graphite, selective glazing, and collage on paper; 24 3/16 × 37 1/8 in.; 61.4 × 94.9 cm

Identification: male left, feeding on Green-winged Teal; female right, feeding on Gadwall

Seasonal distribution: breeds across northern and western North America, in South America, winters along all United States coasts

Havell plate number: XVI in *The Birds of America*

Acc. no. 1863.17.016

"I had the pleasure of seeing Mr Aumack Killed a *Great Footed Hawk*," wrote Audubon in his Mississippi River journal on Christmas Day 1820, "the *Bird* Alexander Wilson heard so many wonderful Tales of."[1] And when, in the course of the following two days, Audubon drew that bird in pastel—the large female Peregrine Falcon on the right of his composition ("a very Old Bird and a beautiful one"[2])—he used the pose in Wilson's depiction of the peregrine as the basis for his own more piercing portrayal. As in Wilson's earlier rendering of the peregrine, Audubon's falcon is crouched on the ground facing left, with mouth open; but Audubon's image portrays the bird's features as more vivid and palpable—as well as more streamlined—than those of Wilson's accurate but rather ungainly rendering. While Wilson depicted his peregrine with the tail drooping below the wings, bulky and rather hunched, peering into the distant landscape, Audubon showed a sleek voracious hunter consuming her ravaged kill. The body of Audubon's bird is slanted in a dramatic diagonal over which the viewer's eye travels from the bird's open beak dripping with blood, on the lower left, to the taut, raised tail and pointed wings on the upper right. The peregrine's position recalls its habit of diving or "stooping" upon its prey from high in the air, plummeting onto it at speeds that can approach two hundred miles an hour.

As impressive, if grisly, an image as Audubon portrayed in that vignette, his male peregrine on the left (painted in watercolor probably about four years later[3]) is even bolder and more formally expressive. It vividly demonstrates the maturation that Audubon's style underwent. Avoiding the static symmetry produced by illustrating two birds in profile, Audubon depicted the male twisting over his prey in an image markedly more sophisticated than that of the female. Bird faces viewer head-on, its fierce eyes and gaping bill aligned directly over those same, lifeless features of the Green-winged Teal that it is about to pluck. The falcon's pointed wings—one of its most prominent features—are half-raised, creating a complex, aggressive, jagged silhouette. The peregrine's tail is splayed to balance its twisting body, the feathers arrayed in a series of sharp points. Individual feathers are detailed more carefully than in the earlier bird (which Audubon cut out and pasted down onto the later composition that includes the male), its sharp talons more highly visible and the texture of the feathers more subtly delineated. The falcon's form merges with that of the dead teal (whose breast its left foot visibly penetrates), emphasizing the relationship that binds hunter and hunted.[4]

One of the fastest birds on earth, nearly worldwide in distribution, and a favorite of falconers to this day, the peregrine became a poignant symbol of the American conservation movement when, by the 1960s, organochlorines like DDT extirpated it as a breeder in the eastern United States. It was the first species placed on the U.S. Rare and Endangered Species list when the government authorized that protection. Elaborate captive breeding programs together with the banning of DDT are gradually demonstrating success in reestablishing Peregrine Falcons in some of their former breeding locations.

1. Howard Corning, ed., *Journal of John James Audubon Made During His Trip to New Orleans, 1820–21* (Boston: The Club of Odd Volumes, 1929), pp. 86–87.

2. Ibid., p. 87.

3. Audubon describes in the *Ornithological Biography* (vol. I, p. 87) having "shot a pair in the month of August near the Falls of Niagara," and the style of this bird is consistent with the work he was doing at that time.

4. An oil painting of Peregrine Falcons that Audubon probably made in Great Britain in 1826–27 is in the collection of the Cleveland Museum of Art.

Audubon's nomenclature: 1. Virginian Partridge, *Perdix virginiana* Latham 2. Red-shouldered Buzzard, *Falco lineatus* Gmelin

Painted about 1825. The blades of grass in the foreground were painted separately and pasted on as collage pieces.

Medium: watercolor, oil paint, pastel, graphite, collage, and selective glazing on paper; 25¾ × 39¼ in.; 65.4 × 99.6 cm.

Inscription (upper right): No 16. Plate 76. Published 1829 *(crossed out)* 1830/Virginian Partridge/Male adult 1./Do—2. Female adult

3.—Do—young 4. very young birds 5. Perdix Virginia

Identification: covey of male, female, and young Northern Bobwhites (males have white throats) attacked by immature Red-shouldered Hawk

Seasonal distribution: Northern Bobwhite breeds and winters throughout most of eastern United States; Red-shouldered Hawk breeds throughout eastern United States and in California and winters in the southern part of its breeding range

Havell plate number: LXXVI in *The Birds of America*

Acc. no. 1863.17.076

This is Audubon's only painting in which the prey species constitutes the primary subject. The Red-shouldered Hawk appears in another image that illustrates its plumage more fully with a pair of adult birds,[1] but this picture, in which the hawk is an immature, contains Audubon's only depiction of the Northern Bobwhite published in the double elephant folio.

Bobwhites were common throughout the United States in Audubon's day, and the naturalist frequently came upon them while walking in the woods. Audubon noticed that when a covey of these quail flies off of its own accord the birds remain in a flock, but when surprised by an enemy they disperse in different directions to confuse their predator, and they seek cover separately. Audubon observed that the birds roost in a close circle with their heads facing outward, and that "this arrangement enables the whole covey to take wing when suddenly alarmed, each flying off in a direct course, so as not to interfere with the rest."[2]

Here, the young red-shoulder surprises the quail during feeding (in an unusually open area), and they scramble for safety in different directions but with perhaps more jostling than normal. While Audubon may have exaggerated the birds' terrified expressions and physical upset to some extent for the sake of effect, his depiction admirably captures the explosive quality of such an encounter.

A comparison of this image with the significantly less dynamic portrayals of the bobwhite by Catesby and Wilson clearly demonstrates the vigorous new artistic approach of Audubon at his most expressive. Here he combines the active quality of the hunting scene with a remarkably audacious treatment of his subjects. The quail, dashing off wildly, twisting in panic, and bursting into flight, are frozen in a variety of unconventional positions, which we see from the hawk's level and perspective. The foreshortened and unusual views of the bobwhites provide a number of pictorial challenges to the artist and enable him to illustrate many details of five different plumages: the adult males with white throats that punctuate and enclose the group on the ground; the young males on the left, scattering into the air, legs dangling, their overlapping images creating a sense of visual confusion that emphasizes the confusion of the event; an adult female about to take flight just below them; and, at the back of the circle, a young female and a group of very young birds.

The frontal, foreshortened image of the hawk is bold and fearsome. The bird's wings and tail slice the air at intersecting diagonals that are extended by its rapacious claws, stretched to the limit for quick and effective grabbing, and lunging directly at us. Its glinting eye, on which we initially focus, startles us as it does the quail. The bird's sudden, purposeful movement contrasts vividly with the chaos of the quail; the hawk, though young, is learning to use his power.

1. That image was published in *The Birds of America* as plate LVI. Audubon also represented an immature Red-shouldered Hawk in plate LXXI but identified it as a "Winter Hawk" because he had seen it only at that season. He made an early drawing of the Red-shouldered Hawk, now at Princeton University, on November 29, 1809. A copy of the present picture is owned by the University of Liverpool.

2. John James Audubon, *Ornithological Biography*, vol. V (reprint of 1840–44 ed.; New York: Volair Books, 1979), p. 61.

N°16. plate 76.   Published 1830. 1830

Virginian Partridge.
Males adult 1.
Do — Young 2.
Females adult 3.
Do Young 4. Very Young birds 5.

Perdix Virginiana

Painted in Louisiana in 1821. Female in nest added c. 1825.

Medium: watercolor, graphite, pastel, and collage on paper; 38 1/16 × 25 3/4 in.; 96.6 × 65.5 cm.

Inscription (middle right, in graphite): The circle around the/eye, and the upper Mandible as in the Male/above—.

Identification: males left, above and below; females right, above and below

Seasonal distribution: breeds and winters in eastern and southeastern North America and along Pacific coast

Flora: sycamore, *Platanus occidentalis,* and resurrection fern, *Polypodium polypodioides*

Havell plate number: CCVI in *The Birds of America*

Acc. no. 1863.17.206

"Few birds are more interesting to observe during the love season than Wood Ducks," exulted Audubon.

The great beauty and neatness of their apparel, and the grace of their motions, always afford pleasure to the observer; and, as I have had abundant opportunities of studying their habits at that period, I am enabled to present you with a full acount of their proceedings.[1]

In his portrait of this woodland-loving duck, Audubon celebrated some of the species' remarkable aerial and arboreal feats. "I have sat beside a gigantic sycamore, on the watch for it,"[2] wrote the naturalist, who had observed the generally trusting and tame Wood Duck nesting and foraging for grapes, berries, beechnuts, and hickory nuts in the woods. In 1821, shortly after his flatboat trip to New Orleans, Audubon drew a male and female Wood Duck perched on such a sycamore branch. He completed his image by cutting the figure of a flying male out of a separate sheet and glueing it onto this one, finally adding the nesting female about four years later. His picture was based on the observations he made in the wild and on closer investigations as well. Audubon and his wife had cared for Wood Ducks at their home in Henderson, Kentucky, clipping their wings to keep them nearby and providing them with nesting boxes and nest materials, which the birds used successfully.

The Wood Duck's capacity to exploit such man-made structures has been an important advantage in its survival. The species breeds more widely throughout the United States than any other duck, and lives and migrates mainly within America's borders. Around 1900 it was threatened with extinction because of overhunting, the widespread cutting of hollow trees, in which it nests, and the draining of swamps, in which it feeds on water plants, snails, and frogs. Conservation measures including the use of nesting boxes, as well as regulations protecting the species and its environment helped to stabilize its population, but now loss of habitat threatens it once again.

Audubon's scene of paired Wood Ducks highlights the birds' magnificent appearance, portrays them from a variety of angles, emphasizes the diverse patterns and textures of their plumages, and identifies different aspects of their courtship behavior. At the apex of the triangular composition, the female approaches the male's bill with her own. The angles, proximity, and juxtaposition of the bills convey a lively sense of movement, repeated more actively in the flying male beneath, who, in a more advanced stage of mating, swoops by the female—already in her down-lined, tree-hollow nest—uttering his courtship calls.

Watercolor is Audubon's primary medium here, and he used it to depict a variety of textures, including the males' minute flank feathers and their downy undertail feathers outlined against the white background; he used pastel to suggest the softness of the breast feathers. Audubon's range of linear and painterly effects does full justice to this dazzling duck species.

1. John James Audubon, *Ornithological Biography,* vol. VI (reprint of 1840–44 ed.; New York: Volair Books, 1979), p. 275.

2. Ibid., p. 271.

Audubon's nomenclature: Carolina Parrot, *Psitacus carolinensis;* Parakeet, *Psitacus carolinensis*

Painted in Louisiana, probably in 1825.

Medium: watercolor, graphite, gouache, crayon/pastel, and selective glazing on paper; 29 11/16 × 21 3/16 in.; 75.4 × 53.9 cm.

Inscription (lower right side, in graphite): The upper Specimen was shot near Bayou Sarah/and appeared so uncommon having 14 Tailfeathers all 7 sizes distinct and firmly affixed in 14 different recepticals that I drew it more to verify one of those astonishing fits of nature/than any thing else—it was a female—/the Green heads also a singular although (. . . ?)/. . . mm (?) a Variety of the above one—Louisianna—December—J.J. Audubon *(lower right, in faint graphite):* No. 6—/Plate 26—*(lower left center):* Carolina Parrot—Psitacus carolinensis/Males 1. F. 2 Young 3 *(bottom center, in graphite):* Plant vulgo Cockle Burr—

Identification: bottom center bird immature, others adults

Seasonal distribution: extinct; formerly bred in eastern United States from the Great Lakes south to Florida and from Colorado to the Atlantic Coast

Flora: cocklebur, *Xanthium strumarium*

Havell plate number: XXVI in *The Birds of America*

Acc. no. 1863.17.026

*J*n 1920 the Carolina Parakeet—the only parrot native to the United States—was sighted for the final time in the wild.[1] On February 21, 1918, the last captive bird died in the Cincinnati Zoo. The once-abundant species became extinct, slaughtered for sport, food, and for its feathers. Engagingly antic, Carolina Parakeets were sold by the thousands as cage birds but rarely bred in captivity. Audubon warned that "the woods are the habitation best fitted for them, and there the richness of their plumage, their beautiful mode of flight, and even their screams afford welcome intimation that our darkest forests and most sequestered swamps are not destitute of charms."[2] But after farmers cleared the forests, the parakeets came to feed on their crops. "The stacks of grain put up in the field are resorted to by flocks of these birds, which frequently cover them so entirely that they present to the eye the same effect as if a brilliantly coloured carpet had been thrown over them."[3] The farmers lacked Audubon's appreciation of this captivating sight and, viewing the birds as pests, killed them in droves. Early in his field work Audubon saw countless parakeets but subsequently noticed that "our Parakeets are very rapidly diminishing in number; and in some districts, where twenty-five years ago they were plentiful, scarcely any are now to be seen."[4]

Audubon's poignant description of the parakeet's habits includes observations on their rapid flight and vociferous cries. He wrote of their aerobatics in circling, "and then gradually lowering until they almost touch the ground, when suddenly re-ascending, they all settle on the tree that bears the fruit of which they are in quest."[5]

The parakeets were awkward on the ground, but when they perched together in trees as Audubon shows them here, "they are quite at ease . . . moving sidewise, climbing or hanging in every imaginable posture, assisting themselves very dexterously in all their motions with their bills."[6] This composition provides an almost cinematic rendering of a scene that Audubon beheld frequently and that we will never witness: these luxuriantly hued, intelligent, playful birds deftly feeding.

The parakeet's flamboyant habit of spreading its tail appears here in two figures that frame the composition, the upper figure illustrating a parakeet unusually possessed of fourteen tail feathers. The bottom bird is a particularly bold, elegant example of ornithological illustration, shown full face, with head foreshortened and body in profile. The right wing is dramatically raised and the tail fanned as if the bird were about to fly into the viewer's space. Between the top and bottom birds, the eye travels in a sinuous reverse S-curve over parakeets in a variety of postures in which beaks, claws, outstretched necks, wings, and tails are all employed in the service of feeding.

1. Arthur Cleveland Bent, *Life Histories of North American Cuckoos, Goatsuckers, Hummingbirds and Their Allies,* part I (New York: Dover Publications, 1964), p. 3.
2. John James Audubon, *Ornithological Biography,* vol. IV (reprint of 1840–44 ed.; New York: Volair Books, 1979), p. 309.
3. Ibid., p. 307.
4. Ibid., p. 309.
5. Ibid., p. 308.
6. Ibid.

Blue Jay

CYANOCITTA CRISTATA (LINNAEUS)

Painted c. 1825.
Medium: watercolor, pastel, graphite, and selective glazing on paper; 23¾ × 18⅞ in.; 60.4 × 48 cm.
Inscription (lower right): Blue Jay Male 1. F. 2. &3/Corvus cristatus/Plant *(upper right corner, in graphite):* 2
Identification: females top and left, male right
Seasonal distribution: breeds and winters throughout northeastern North America
Flora: unfinished leaves of cross vine or trumpet flower, *Bignonia capreolata*
Havell plate number: CII in *The Birds of America*
Acc. no. 1863.17.102

*C*ommon names for the Blue Jay, such as nest-robber, belie the fact that the bird actually eats only one-third as much animal as vegetable matter. In fact, much of its animal diet includes harmful insects such as tent caterpillars, fruit-eating beetles, and the caterpillars of the gypsy moth rather than birds' eggs. But, perhaps because it combines certain of its habits with exhibitions of raucousness, showiness, and boldness, the species has established a reputation for being lawless and has tempted some of its observers into accusations of Blue Jay immorality. It is, of course, an outdated notion to ascribe human characteristics and motives to birds, which in fact act out of an instinct for survival and certain learned responses to their environment rather than premeditated maliciousness. But anthropomorphizing is practiced even in some quarters today and, as evidenced by Audubon's words, was much more prevalent in the nineteenth century.

> The Blue Jay . . . is more tyrannical than brave, and like most boasters, domineers over the feeble, dreads the strong, and flies even from his equals. In many cases in fact, he is a downright coward. . . . Many [birds] although inferior in strength, never allow him to approach their nest with impunity; and the Jay, to be even with them, creeps silently to it in their absence, and devours their eggs and young whenever he finds an opportunity. I have seen one go its round from one nest to another every day, and

suck the newly laid eggs of the different birds in the neighborhood, with as much regularity and composure as a physician would call on his patients.[1]

Even though such behavior is relatively infrequent among Blue Jays, it clearly attracts attention and seems appropriate to associate with a bird whose primary characteristics are intelligence, vociferousness, and inquisitiveness. Certainly, the activity makes a very dramatic subject for a picture.

Audubon has accentuated what he considered the unsavory nature of this scene by showing the Blue Jays taking apparent delight in their marauding. They plunge into the stolen eggs with gusto, actively enjoying their feast. For emphasis, the artist treats each egg as a focal point in the composition: the egg at the right—painted in a color complementary to the birds' plumage and thus appearing especially bright—forms an important visual connection between the female jay who has broken into it and the male eagerly sucking up its spilling contents. The other egg, beginning to drip juicily from the penetration of the bird's bill, forms a bright highlight on the left side of the picture both because of its color and because its consumer looks captivatingly out at the viewer.

Audubon's distaste for the jays' predatoriness was tempered by his admiration for their grace and splendid colors, which he has caught, along with three typical jay postures, in a composition that expresses the Blue Jays' verve and panache.[2]

1. John James Audubon, *Ornithological Biography*, vol. IV (reprint of 1840–44 ed.; New York: Volair Books, 1979), p. 112.
2. Audubon represented the Blue Jay on at least two other occasions: in an early pencil, pastel, and watercolor drawing from about 1811, now in the Munson-Williams-Proctor Institute in Utica, New York, that shows a single bird perched on a twig, and in a picture that Audubon sold in November 1828. It is unclear whether that is the same work as the oil in the Morris Tyler collection, New Haven, Connecticut.

Blue Jay Male 1. F. 2 & 3
Corvus cristatus
Plant

Loggerhead Shrike

LANIUS LUDOVICIANUS LINNAEUS

Probably painted in Louisiana, c. 1825.

Medium: watercolor, pastel, graphite, and selective glazing on paper; 26 13/16 × 18 3/4 in.; 68.1 × 47.6 cm.

Inscription (lower left): No 12 Plate 57/Published 1829/Loggerhead Shrike/Lanius Carolinensis—Plant. Smilax rotundifolia *(lower right, old, very faint, in graphite previously erased [JJA]):*? Lanius carolinensis *(upper left corner, in graphite):* 57

Identification: adults

Seasonal distribution: breeds locally throughout most of United States, winters across southern United States

Flora: probably hagbrier, *Smilax hispida,* growing around a dead tree

Havell plate number: LVII in *The Birds of America*

Acc. no. 1863.17.057

The flurried profusion of leaves among which the Loggerhead Shrikes squabble increases this scene's visual intensity and underscores the agitated mood produced by the birds' commotion. Audubon highlighted what he considered the pugnaciousness of the species by depicting a mated pair of loggerheads fighting over a dead rodent. Actually, shrikes—the only genuinely predatory songbirds—are not unusually combative with one another. But when they catch small animals such as the field mouse Audubon portrays here, or the reptiles, small birds, and insects that they also favor, interspecific aggression does take place from time to time. Audubon apparently had relatively limited experience with this species, which he described as occurring in Louisiana (where he evidently depicted it). It appears there for no more than a few weeks during the winter. Audubon supplemented his rather brief biographical account of the loggerheads with notes by John Bachman, several of whose observations of this species actually disagree with Audubon's own. For instance, Bachman's experience differed from that of Audubon, who stated that he had never observed a Loggerhead Shrike engaging in what is one of the species' most characteristic behaviors: the impaling of dead prey on a thorn or on the barbs of a wire fence. This habit of creating a storage larder by hanging prey on convenient nearby spiky objects, sometimes for long periods of time, has earned this species (as well as its close relative, the Northern Shrike)

the name Butcher Bird. Since, unlike raptors, the robin-sized shrike has no talons and relatively weak feet and legs, it sometimes wedges the animals it eats into the crotch of a tree branch as the bird has done here with its mouse, in order to tear off manageable pieces with its hooked beak. In hunting for such animals—which it does only by daylight—the shrike sits immobile on a wire, fencepost, or exposed branch in an open or brushy area, scanning the ground with eyes that can detect a running rodent at a distance of 250 feet. When it spots potential prey, it dives down close to the ground and, with its rapid flight, dashes directly toward its victim, alternating quick wingbeats with short glides. Sometimes it hovers over the ground as it hunts, pouncing suddenly upon its prey. If hunting is unsuccessful, it swoops up swiftly to its next perch. When it catches an animal, it kills it by biting the neck and severing the vertebrae. Unlike the raptors, it does not attempt to dispatch the animal with its feet, which are weak and which the animal might bite and injure.

The positions of these loggerheads—the only shrike species confined to North America—reveal the field marks that differentiate the large-headed, sleek-tailed, gray, black, and white birds from the very similar, if larger, Northern Shrike. The loggerhead is darker, and its facial mask extends above the eye and all the way across the bill, which is shorter than a northern's, and has a smaller hook.

N° 12. Plate 57.

Loggerhead Shrike.
Lanius Carolinensis.
Publish'd 1829. Plant. Smilax rotundifolia

Bald Eagle

HALIAEETUS LEUCOCEPHALUS (LINNAEUS)

Audubon's nomenclature: White Headed Eagle, *Falco leucocephalus*

Painted at Little Prairie, Mississippi, on November 23, 1820.

Medium: watercolor, pastel, and graphite on paper; 25⅜ × 38¼ in.; 64.6 × 97.3 cm.

Inscription (left side, in graphite): No 9 Plate 41—/White headed Eagle—Male—/Falco Leucocephalus/. . . cat? (*lower right side, in brown ink*
and converted lead white [?]): White Headed Eagle/Falco Leucocephalus/Drawn from Nature by J. J. Audubon/Litt Prairie

Mississippi, November 14, 182 . . .

Identification: male

Seasonal distribution: breeds in northern North America and Gulf Coast states, winters along all United States coasts and in
southern part of breeding range

Acc. no. 1863.18.040

During his 1820 flatboat trip down the Ohio and Mississippi, bound for New Orleans, Audubon observed numerous Bald Eagles, perched, in flight, nest-building, and hunting. He saw them pursuing two species of ducks, a Mallard that he had just shot and a Bufflehead. On Thursday, November 23, he shot the "Beautifull *White headed Eagle*"[1] here, and worked on this drawing of it for the next four days. In his November 27 journal entry he provided details about the "Noble Bird," which he described as a male with an extremely large heart that weighed eight and one-half pounds. It had a wingspan of a little more than six feet seven inches, and was slightly over two feet seven inches long. Audubon depicted the bird standing over a dismembered Canada Goose, a scene that he may actually have witnessed since, in the same journal entry he recounted,

> [an eagle] this morning took up the head of a Wild Goose thrown over board, with as much ease as a man could with the hand . . . to secure a Goose, the Male & Femelle, Dive alternatively after it and give it so little time to breath that the poor fellow is forced in a few Minutes.[2]

While the Bald Eagle is generally a fish eater, it also consumes carrion, small mammals, and, especially in the South during the later months of the year, waterfowl.

Bald Eagles probably mate for life, and once they establish a territory they generally frequent it year after year. Some birds even occupy the same area year-round. In the South, the eagles may begin breeding as early as September or October, perhaps so that their young, which spend more than two months in the nest before fledging, have time to develop sufficient plumage after they hatch to afford them protection by spring when the weather grows hot. Once the young are hatched, both parents hunt for them actively, bringing prey animals to the nest and tearing them apart into pieces that the small birds can swallow. Eventually the young are taught to tear the meat for themselves, spreading their bodies over the carcass and ripping it with bill and talons as Audubon shows the adult doing here. The artist has placed the bird's bill on the same diagonal as its feet and the beheaded goose to highlight the eagle's specialized feeding devices and emphasize the predator-prey connection.

The largest native eagle of North America, this species is not a close relative of the Golden Eagle but belongs to a group called sea eagles, birds that live close to large bodies of water. No more than thirty years ago, hunters were still collecting bounty payments for killing Bald Eagles, which were thought to be destructive to the animals and fish consumed by humans (an untrue assumption). The eagle population was so debilitated by such slaughter, in combination with the use of pesticides and the destruction of its habitat, that the species became endangered in the continental United States. Intensive recovery programs have succeeded in raising its numbers.

1. Howard Corning, ed., *Journal of John James Audubon Made During His Trip to New Orleans, 1820–21* (Boston: The Club of Odd Volumes, 1929), p. 37.

2. Ibid., p. 41.

Audubon's nomenclature: White-headed Eagle, *Falco leucocephalus* Linnaeus

Painted in London in 1828.

Medium: watercolor, pastel, graphite, selective glazing, and selective scraping on paper; 25⅜ × 38¼ in.; 64.6 × 97.2 cm.

Inscription (middle right, in rock): White-headed Eagle, male adult/*Falco leucocephalus* (*lower right*): Drawn from nature by/John J. Audubon/Little Prairie/Mississippi River

Identification: breeding-plumaged male feeding on a catfish

Seasonal distribution: breeds in local populations of different sizes from southeastern Alaska and Canada south to the northern and northwestern United States and along the East Coast. Winters from southern part of breeding range to the Gulf Coast.

Havell plate number: XXXI in *The Birds of America*

Acc. No. 1863.17.031

This morning I took one of my drawings from my portfolio and began to copy it, and intend to finish it in better style. It is the White-headed Eagle which I drew on the Mississippi some years ago, feeding on a Wild Goose; now I shall make it breakfast on a Catfish, the drawing of which is also with me, with the marks of the talons of another Eagle, which I disturbed on the banks of that same river, driving him from his prey. I worked from seven this morning till dark.[1]

Audubon's journal entry of February 10, 1828, written in London, does not specify in any greater detail why the artist chose to redraw the "White-headed" Eagle he had made eight years previously.[2] Indeed, Audubon often reworked earlier bird images when he felt that his knowledge of a particular species or his mastery of technique had substantially improved after the original picture was made. Perhaps Audubon had come to know that Bald Eagles feed more commonly on fish than on birds, and had thus decided to substitute his portrayal of a catfish for the goose. Perhaps he felt that the decapitated goose was too much of a visual distraction from the powerful image of the eagle and that the fish would simplify the composition. Unquestionably, his 1828 eagle is a stronger picture than the earlier one: the draftsmanship is more accomplished, the bird's expression more animated, the definition in the feathering, bone structure, and muscles of the head and scales on the legs and feet more detailed. The figure of the fish, clearer and simpler than that of the goose, produces greater visual impact. Even the sweep of the bird's left wing (which Audubon carefully depicted as shorter than the tail, a characteristic that he described in the *Ornithological Biography*) is more streamlined.

But Audubon may also have wished to rework the eagle in order to produce a more convincing image than that of his rival, Alexander Wilson, whose 1810 eagle Audubon had seen when he called on Wilson in Philadelphia.[3] That image was published in Wilson's *American Ornithology*, and both Audubon's 1820 and 1828 eagles are based on it. Audubon's bird is clearly more robust and vigorous than Wilson's, with more accurate proportions and a livelier expression. Audubon's image is more forceful and less stiff: the eagle's raised tail emphasizes its length and massiveness, and the exposed right leg, in a slightly altered position, produces a more persuasive spatial relationship and highlights the bird's determined posture and fierce possessiveness of its prey.

Audubon's vigilant eagle contrasts eloquently with the bloated, lifeless figure of the enormous catfish it has subdued. The juxtaposition of the eagle's taut, outstretched wing with the dead fish's flopped tail is particularly poignant. Audubon has placed the eagle's bright, glinting eye, ferocious, open beak, and lethal talons on a direct diagonal with the overturned, dismembered head of an eviscerated, open-mouthed fish to dramatize, by intense comparison, the bird's rapacious power.

---

1. Maria R. Audubon, ed., *Audubon and His Journals*, vol. I (New York: Dover Publications, 1986), p. 282.

2. The earlier drawing is also in the collection of The New-York Historical Society.

3. John James Audubon, *Ornithological Biography*, vol. II (reprint of 1840–44 ed.; New York: Volair Books, 1979), p. 203.

White Headed Eagle
Falco Leucocephalus
Drawn from Nature by J.J. Audubon
Little Prairie Mississippi Novr 14, 182

White-headed Eagle. Male adult.
Falco Leucocephalus.

Drawn from Nature by
John J. Audubon
Little Prairie
Mississippi River

Osprey

PANDION HALIAETUS (LINNAEUS)

Probably painted in Great Egg Harbor, New Jersey, in June 1829.

Medium: watercolor, pastel, and graphite on paper; 37 11/16 × 25 1/8 in.; 95.7 × 63.8 cm.

Inscription (faint graphite, middle right center): Begun Friday/at 11 o'clock/Finished Sunday evening *(lower left):* No 17. Plate 81 *(lower left of center):* Fish Hawk. Male/Falco haliaetus/Fish. Vulgo. Weak-Fish/

Identification: male osprey carrying weakfish

Seasonal distribution: breeds widely across northern and northwestern North America and along Atlantic and Gulf coasts; winters in southern United States and South America south to Peru and Brazil. Precipitous decline in population due to use of DDT and related pesticides, disturbance of habitat and shooting of birds now reversing as pesticides are eliminated and man-made nesting platforms are erected.

Havell plate number: LXXXI in *The Birds of America*

Acc. no. 1863.17.081

On a mid-June morning in 1829, while traveling to Great Egg Harbor, New Jersey, by horse and wagon, Audubon noticed a number of Osprey nests in the tallest trees at the edge of open woods on either side of the road. During his three-week stay at the shore he was able to count more than fifty such nests in a single day of walking and to watch Ospreys fishing actively.

The male Osprey begins to bring fish for the female soon after the pair has arrived on their breeding grounds in the spring, and continues to catch her food and that of the chicks until the sixth week of nesting, when the female starts to hunt again for herself. Even then, the male helps fish for the young, which do not catch their own food until a month or two after learning to fly.

The Osprey is almost exclusively a fish eater. When feeding, it flies over a body of fresh or salt water and, upon sighting a fish, usually pauses in midair, hovers with beating wings, dangles its legs, and then plunges into the water, feet and head first, sometimes disappearing almost entirely below the surface.

On rising with its prey, it is seen holding it in the manner represented in the Plate. It mounts a few yards into the air, squeezes the fish with its talons, and immediately proceeds towards its nest, to feed its young, or to a tree, to devour the fruit of its industry in peace. . . . The Fish Hawk has a great attachment to the tree to which it carries its prey, and will not abandon it, unless frequently disturbed.[1]

After the bird has risen with its catch, it shakes the water from its wings in midair and always positions the fish facing forward to reduce wind resistance during its flight. Sometimes it is harassed by an eagle, which forces it to drop its prey, and then often seizes the fish before it reaches the water. Ospreys, which weigh four or five pounds, have been observed to fly off with fish as heavy as they are. Audubon believed that the weak-fish depicted here weighed more than five pounds.

To Audubon, the Osprey was particularly majestic and impressive in the air, and he depicted it here flying off vigorously with its catch, emitting its characteristic cry.[2] Its strongly curved beak—ideally suited to tearing a fish's flesh—and its bright eye form a provocative contrast with the fish's gaping mouth and glazed stare. The depiction of the underside of the Osprey's left wing, shown from a boldly foreshortened angle, is not only a meticulously accurate rendering of plumage but a masterpiece of pure design. The upraised right wing, with its smooth, crisp silhouette, forms a stable T-shape with the left wing and body and gives the composition a sense of both solidity and energy. It is hard to imagine a more powerful image of flight.

1. John James Audubon, *Ornithological Biography*, vol. I (reprint of 1840–44 ed.; New York: Volair Books, 1979), p. 66.
2. Osprey sightings were not new to Audubon on his New Jersey trip. He had been intrigued by the species since his early days at Mill Grove and had made a drawing there in 1806 of an Osprey with a fish, which is now in the Houghton Library, Harvard University.

Fish Hawk. *Male.*
Falco haliætus.
Fish, *Vulg.* Weak–Fish.

N.º 17. Plate 81.

Magnolia Warbler

DENDROICA MAGNOLIA (WILSON)

Audubon's nomenclature: Black and Yellow Warbler, *Sylvia maculosa* Latham

Painted in the Great Pine Forest, Pennsylvania, on August 12, 1829.

Medium: watercolor and graphite on paper; 18 ¼ × 11 ⁷/16 in.; 46.4 × 29 cm.

Inscription (lower left): Black & Yellow Warblers. Males.—/*Sylvia maculosa.*—/Great Pine Swamp/Aug—t 12th/J.J.A.

(upper right corner, in graphite): 23

Identification: adult males

Seasonal distribution: breeds across most of central North America, winters from southern Mexico through Central America

and South America to Panama

Flora: purple-flowering raspberry, *Rubus odoratus*

Havell plate number: CXXIII in *The Birds of America*

Acc. no. 1863.17.123

The Magnolia Warbler never nests in magnolia trees. On the contrary, it makes its home in young spruces, firs, or hemlocks in the overgrown clearings, woodland edges, and bogs of Canada and the northeastern and central United States—hardly an environment that we associate with the tree whose name the species bears. But when Alexander Wilson named the bird in 1811, he was near Ft. Adams, Mississippi, and saw these warblers feeding in great numbers in magnolia trees as they migrated north. Having observed the species closely associated with that habitat and lacking more extensive experience with the bird, he named it for the tree that it seemed to prefer.

Like any viewer who observes the Magnolia Warbler gleaming yellow against the bright green foliage of the spring woods, fanning its flashy black-and-white tail and displaying its white wing bars, Audubon was charmed by the bird's splendid appearance and lively behavior. He was equally impressed with its song, "clear and sweetly modulated," as he described it, "surpassing that of many other birds of its tribe. It sings in the interior of the low woods, to which it seems at all times to give a decided preference."[1] And it is in such undergrowth that, on August 12, 1829, Audubon depicted the two resplendent males here—flitting about a purple-flowering raspberry bush, probably painted by George Lehman, in the Great Pine Forest of Pennsylvania.[2]

During the late summer of 1829, Audubon left Philadelphia by coach at four o'clock in the morning to make the eighty-eight-mile trip northwest to the Great Pine Forest and study its birds. After riding all day, he arrived at eight o'clock at night, and stayed in the town of Mauch Chunk. Dissatisfied with the quantity of birds to be found in that vicinity—a logging area where many of the trees had already been harvested—he hired a cart to take him fifteen miles further, through the mountains, into the middle of the pinelands. A storm blew up as the cart wended its way, and both Audubon and his driver were drenched by the time they reached the cabin of Jediah Irish, the lumberman with whose family Audubon would live for the next six weeks. During his stay, Audubon spent time watching timbering operations, fishing innumerable trout from the streams, and drawing birds, including several warblers.

Here he shows the sprightly Magnolia Warblers inspecting the branches and leaves of their raspberry bush for the insects that constitute their diet. The artist has masterfully captured the birds' dazzling color patterns and animated movements as they dart through the foliage, rapidly drooping their wings or spreading their tails to call attention to their striking markings. The unusual twisting pose of the lower bird is characteristic of many warblers as they glean insects from branch to branch, but they maintain the pose for so brief a moment that it is rarely observed at length.

1. John James Audubon, *Ornithological Biography*, vol. II (reprint of 1840–44 ed.; New York: Volair Books, 1979), p. 66.
2. On October 20, 1821, in Louisiana, Audubon had drawn an immature Magnolia Warbler that he said he wished to include as part of the present plate. But, according to his explanation, while he was away from London and unable to supervise the engraving, the drawing of the immature was mistakenly engraved separately as plate L and labeled "Swainson's Warbler," a title that also appears in Audubon's handwriting on the painting itself. The Swainson's Warbler was subsequently painted separately by Audubon's son John, and engraved as plate CXCVIII.

Black & Yellow Warblers. males. —
Sylvia maculosa). —

Great Pine Swamp
Aug. 12th
J.J.A.

Painted in New Jersey on June 22, 1829.

Medium: watercolor, graphite, and gouache on paper; 18⅝ × 11⅜ in.; 47.3 × 27.9 cm.

Inscription (lower left): Marsh Wren Male 1 F. 2. 3. & Nest 4/Troglodytes. palustris./New Jersey June 22d J.J.A. *(lower right):* No 20./Plate

98 *(crossed out)* 100 *(numeral 4 next to nest) (very faint, mostly erased pencil, upper right).* J . . 14 . .

Identification: females top and left, male right

Seasonal distribution: breeds widely across central North America, winters coastally and across southern United States

Havell plate number: XCVIII in *The Birds of America*

Acc. no. 1863.17.098

Audubon combined in his work a naturalist's curiosity, an artist's eye, a teacher's enthusiasm, and a poet's expressiveness. The writings that accompany his pictures are filled with vivid, everyday images designed to evoke immediate recognition and actively engage his readers with the birds whose lives he so painstakingly researched. Audubon conveyed the extensive ornithological data he had collected in the liveliest possible style. Regarding the Marsh Wren, which "lives entirely amongst the sedges, flags, and other rank plants that cover the margins of the rivers, and the inlets of the sea," Audubon wanted to make his audience aware of the tiny bird's elaborate process of nest building. He included a detailed rendering of the nest in his Marsh Wren composition and described it picturesquely:

> The nest is nearly the size and shape of a cocoa-nut, and is formed of dried grasses, entwined in a circular manner, so as to include in its mass several of the stems and leaves of the sedges or other plants among which it is placed. A small aperture, just large enough to admit the birds, is left, generally on the south-west side of the nest. The interior is composed of small dry grasses, and is nearly the depth and width of a common bottle. The eggs . . . are of a deep chocolate colour, and, from the small size, resemble so many beads.[1]

The Marsh Wren builds its nest in a number of complex stages. First, it binds together the leaves of growing bulrushes or cattails and intertwines coarse sedges inside them to form a wall. Then it interlaces a layer of grasses inside the wall, allowing space for an entrance at the side of the nest. It also brings in wet cattail fluff, which, in drying, provides excellent insulation. Finally the wren builds a lining of feathers and thinly shredded plants in the nest's central hollow. When the male Marsh Wren forms his territory, before the arrival of the female, he builds a number of unlined nests known as "courting nests." After the female arrives, she may signal her choice of one of those by adding the final lining to it, or she may build her own.

Audubon's image shows two female birds with the male. Indeed, the male Marsh Wren is often polygynous with a pair of females, but in general these females inhabit nests at opposite ends of his territory. In the Marsh Wren composition, Audubon turns the bird's finely crafted nest into an intricate still life that depicts each sedge blade and dried marsh grass as an individual form. Such precise attention to detail provides the opportunity for great pictorial refinement and delicacy of handling, especially around the outer edges of the nest and in the few stray grasses that have escaped the circle. It also makes clear the amount of industry in which the wren engages just to survive.

1. John James Audubon, *Ornithological Biography*, vol. II (reprint of 1840–44 ed.; New York: Volair Books, 1979), p. 136. Two other versions of Audubon's Marsh Wren exist: an early pencil, pastel, and watercolor version from about 1812, in the collection of The New-York Historical Society, and an oil copy by Joseph Kidd, formerly in the collection of Dr. Michael Heidelberger.

Marsh Wren *male*, ^{2.3.} *F. 1. Nest.* 4.
Troglodytes palustris.
New Jersey June 23^d
J. J. A.

N°. 20.
Plate N°.
100

171

Audubon's nomenclature: Sharp Tailed Finch, *Fringilla caudacuta* Wilson

Probably painted at Great Egg Harbor, New Jersey, in the summer of 1829.

Medium: watercolor, graphite, and gouache on paper; 18³⁄16 × 11½ in.; 46.2 × 29.2 cm.

Inscription (lower left): Sharp tailed Finch/Fringilla caudacuta Males 1,2. F 3.—

Identification: males above, female on nest

Seasonal distribution: breeds in coastal northeastern North America and central Canada south to North Dakota, winters along Atlantic and Gulf coasts

Havell plate number: CXLIX in *The Birds of America*

Acc. no. 1863.17.149

In posing the upper male Sharp-tailed Sparrow in this image with his feet typically spread apart to hold him nearly vertical, and showing him evidently in full voice, Audubon gives us a clear view of his brownish-olive-green back, gray cheek patch, and buff-colored facial markings. This characteristic posture allows the artist to illustrate the subtleties of the species' plumage but is not meant to suggest that the bird generally makes itself conspicuous or that it sings a glorious song. The sharp-tail is a skulker. Difficult to observe in its marshy habitat, it seldom leaves the ground, on which it walks rather than hops. When alarmed, it prefers to run through the grass like a mouse instead of flying off to escape danger. If it does take to the air, it usually darts low, in a short zigzag pattern, and quickly drops back down into the grass of its salt- or freshwater marsh. The sharp-tail does not usually exhibit itself by fluttering high in the air or perching up in tall trees during the breeding season, nor does it attract attention with its voice; in fact, its song consists only of a short, raspy, insectlike trill. Its large-headed, stubby-tailed shape may be visible only when it briefly alights above the marsh floor.

The nest of the sharp-tail is also difficult to see. The bird builds it rather loosely of coarse, dried grasses that it weaves together just above the marsh's high-water line, sometimes raised a few inches from the ground among concealing vegetation. Here Audubon meticulously depicts a view of the nest that demonstrates how the opening is placed toward one side, creating a partly dome-shaped structure.

Male sharp-tails do not defend individual territories, and several may overlap in particular breeding areas. Females alone incubate the eggs. Because males range more widely than females within a broad territory, there may be more than one male for every female in a given breeding location, as Audubon indicates here.

In spite of living surrounded by grasses, sharp-tails eat largely animal matter—more so than any other sparrow during the warmer times of year. They consume beetles and other kinds of insects, spiders, sandfleas, and a substantial number of small snails.

In this picture, Audubon recalls the sharp-tails' ground-loving habits by showing two of the three birds in the midst of the marsh plants and the third perched just barely above them. The effectiveness of their coloration for camouflage is apparent. Audubon places the birds so that their characteristic proportions are clearly visible and their short, pointed tails are highlighted. The three birds together form an angle; that shape is reiterated in several spears of marsh grass and dead twigs and repeats the angle of the birds' tailfeathers—the identifying feature that gives the species its name.[1]

1. An oil copy of this Sharp-tailed Sparrow composition, probably by Joseph Kidd, is in the collection of the National Gallery in Washington, D.C.

Yellow-breasted Chat

ICTERIA VIRENS (LINNAEUS)

Painted on June 7, 1829, in New Jersey.

Medium: watercolor, graphite, white gouache, and (yellow) pastel(?) on paper; 29 ¼ × 21 in.; 74.3 × 53.3 cm.

Inscription (lower left): Yellow-breasted Chat Males 1,2,3,4.F.5/Icteria viridis—Plant vulgo Sweet Briar/From Nature by John J. Audubon

F.L.S./June 7th Jersey *(upper right corner, in graphite):* 37 *(very faint, upper center by #1, in graphite):* Not be . . . sgrau? *(crossed out)*

Identification: males above, female on nest

Seasonal distribution: breeds across southern Canada and most of United States, winters from southern Baja California,

central Mexico, and Yucatan south to west Panama

Flora: rose, possibly *Rosa virginiana*

Havell plate number: CXXXVII in *The Birds of America*

Acc. no. 1863.17.137

Anyone who has not seen a Yellow-breasted Chat caught up in the highly conspicuous, seemingly rhapsodic courtship display that, with the nesting that results, is the subject of this scene, may have difficulty imagining the bizarre series of activities in which this atypical—and largest—warbler engages.[1] The courtship behavior of the chat is especially noteworthy because the species is otherwise unobtrusive and even retiring, restricting its movements to the thickest parts of brier patches or other undergrowth where the bird is very difficult to observe. In the process of trying to attract a mate, however, the chat, in fact, behaves in a scarcely credible fashion. "Now the bird mounts in the air in various attitudes, with its legs and feet hanging," exclaims Audubon, ". . . and jerks its body with great vehemence, performing the strongest and most whimsical gesticulations; the next moment it returns to the bush."[2] Other ornithologists have described the display in similar terms. As P. A. Taverner wrote, "[the chat] flings himself into the air—straight up he goes on fluttering wings—legs dangling, head raised, his whole being tense and spasmodic with ecstasy. . . . As he reaches the apex of his flight his wings redouble their beatings, working straight up and down while the legs [hang] limply down."[3]

More frequently identified by its voice than its generally secretive actions, the chat is named for its song—an improbable series of whistles, squeals, clucks, sputters, gurgles, squawks, cackles, and other strange sounds, delivered in numerous series of long and short phrases interspersed with individual notes at different pitches. "Sometimes the sounds are scarcely louder than a whisper," Audubon pointed out; "now they acquire strength, deep guttural notes roll in slow succession as if produced by the emotion of surprise, the others clear and sprightly glide after each other, until suddenly, as if the bird had become confused, the voice becomes a hollow bass. The performer all the while looks as if he were in the humor of scolding, and moves from twig to twig among the thickets with so much activity and in so many directions that the notes reach the ear as it were from opposite places at the same moment."[4]

By depicting the nest below the viewer's eye level, Audubon unmistakably reminds us that Yellow-breasted Chats usually nest close to the ground. In order to show in detail that the nest "is large, and composed externally of dry leaves, small sticks, strips of vine bark and grasses, the interior being formed of fibrous roots and horse-hair,"[5] the artist has omitted much of the formidable tangle of growth in which the nest is constructed to provide protection for the vulnerable female and young birds. The open view of the nest allows us to watch the male feeding his mate one of the many varieties of insects that the species consumes, and to recognize that his energetic courtship ritual was successful.[6]

1. In fact, enough viewers of this picture questioned the veracity of the chats' poses that Audubon directed Havell to omit the uppermost bird from his engraving in order to stem such criticism.

2. John James Audubon, *Ornithological Biography*, vol. IV (reprint of 1840–44 ed.; New York: Volair Books, 1979), p. 161.

3. P. A. Taverner, as quoted in Arthur Cleveland Bent, *Life Histories of North American Wood Warblers* (New York: Dover Publications, 1963), p. 588.

4. John James Audubon, *Ornithological Biography*, vol. IV, p. 161.

5. Ibid.

6. An Audubon drawing in the collection of the Houghton Library, Harvard University, entitled *Chat*, inscribed "Le Traquet de Buffon," and made in Nantes in early 1806, does not represent the Yellow-breasted Chat but rather a European species of chat unrelated to the present species.

Yellow-breasted Chat. Males 1.2.3.4. F. 5.
Icteria viridis.— Plant Vulgo. Sweet Briar.

From Nature by John J. Audubon, F.R.S.
June 7th Jersey —

Audubon's nomenclature: American Sparrow Hawk, *Falco sparverius* Linnaeus
Painted in the East in 1829.
Medium: watercolor, pastel, and graphite on paper; 29 ½ × 21 ⅟16 in.; 79.4 × 53.5 cm.
Inscription (upper right, in graphite): 42
Identification: female above, males below
Seasonal distribution: breeds widely throughout North and South America, winters in or south of breeding range
Flora: butternut tree, *Juglans cinerea*
Havell plate number: CXLII in *The Birds of America*
Acc. no. 1863.17.142

Audubon knew that the American Kestrel—until recently known as the Sparrow Hawk—is more inclined to consume grasshoppers, crickets, lizards, and little snakes or rodents than to eat birds (which, in fact, form a relatively small part of its diet). But showing the taut form of the female kestrel here about to dismember the limp body of a sparrow produces a stronger impact than depicting her with an insect, and it is characteristic of Audubon to make his vignettes as dramatic as he realistically could.

Audubon notes the abundance of this little predator, which to this day is the commonest of our falcons and the one with the most extensive range and habitat. But Audubon's acquaintance with the species was not restricted to observations in the wild. He kept as a pet a young male kestrel that had fallen from its nest, which he named Nero, and whose behavior he took pleasure in observing. He carefully described the bird's habit of hunting for food by leaving its perch, circling around while alternating quick wingbeats with periodic glides, watching the ground below, and, if needing a closer look, hovering in one place on beating wings, a hunting technique characteristic of this species.

When a kestrel is not seen hunched over recently captured prey or perched on a tall overlook such as a utility wire or pole, scanning the open ground beneath (with eyes about eight times as strong as a human's), it is commonly observed gliding lightly and quickly down from its perch to make a capture. Audubon shows the right-hand male bird here descending buoyantly, with the slender, pointed wings typical of this smallest American falcon outstretched to reveal their metallic blue color. The blue contrasts strongly with the male's reddish-brown back and tail, and distinguishes him from the female, whose folded, barred, rufous wings are evident in the figure above. The male bird's position, as he dynamically launches himself out into the viewer's space, also enables Audubon to illustrate the black band and white tip at the ends of the bird's tail feathers, which differentiate him from the female with her black-barred rusty tail. In the figure on the left, Audubon shows the ventral view of the male's plumage with the scattered black spots on the breast also typical of the female. By depicting this short-necked species' habitual gesture of turning its head to the side, the artist also has the opportunity to illustrate the bird's strong black-and-white face pattern. The stubby, hooked bill of the right-hand male, together with the diagnostic rufous crown patch surrounded by a wide blue-gray band, form the apex of a triangle continued by the bird's wings, whose base is complete when the viewer visually connects the other two birds.

While adult kestrels like these are primarily solitary, there is considerable interaction between male and female during breeding season, when the male often transfers food to the female near the nest.

Gray Jay
PERISOREUS CANADENSIS (LINNAEUS)

Audubon's nomenclature: Canada Jay, *Corvus canadensis* Linnaeus

Painted on September 26, 1829.

Medium: watercolor, graphite, traces of black pastel/chalk, and traces of gouache on paper; 29 ¼ × 21 in.; 74.4 × 53.5 cm.

Inscription (upper right corner, in graphite): 7 *(lower left corner, in graphite):* Corvus canadensis—/Canada Jay/Sept 26th/J.J.A.

Identification: adults

Seasonal distribution: breeds and winters across northern North America

Flora: white oak, *Quercus alba,* probably painted by George Lehman

Havell plate number: CVII in *The Birds of America*

Acc. no. 1863.17.107

In juxtaposing the soft-plumaged Gray Jay with a brittle, papery wasps' nest of about the same size and color as the bird, Audubon both created a visually intriguing contrast of texture and hue and alluded to one of the jay's numerous food sources. The Gray Jay is a true omnivore, content to devour fruits, seeds, and buds as well as insects, but it is even more inclined to take human food and belongings, which it scavenges boldly from campgrounds and sometimes stores in crannies for later use. As Audubon noted, it is notorious for stealing meat from carcasses that hunters hang in trees—a habit that has resulted in its nicknames of "Carrion Bird," "Moose Bird," and "Grease Bird"—and it has been known to enter houses in the woods and take food from pots and plates, and even from people's hands. In the *Ornithological Biography,* Audubon related his friend Edward Harris's description of a Gray Jay that once landed on the end of Harris's birch-bark canoe when he was fishing in Maine and stole the bait from his can.

Audubon knew that this species, which inhabits the northern woods, usually breeds in spruce and fir forests and only less frequently in mixed woodland, but he chose to depict this pair among oak branches, complementing the subtle rusty tints in their plumage with the oak's burnished fall foliage. Gray Jays often begin to nest in March or April when there is still snow on the ground of their breeding areas, and when the temperature sometimes reaches as low as _30 degrees Fahrenheit. Un-

like various other species that do not begin to incubate their eggs until the last of the clutch is laid, Gray Jays must start incubation immediately to keep their eggs from freezing. When it is not emboldened in the presence of human habitation, the jay, which is called Whiskey Jack by woodsmen, generally remains in the deep forest, where it glides lightly and silently through the trees in direct, straight swoops, seldom flapping its wings. Its loose, fluffy plumage mutes the sound of its flight, and its gray, black, and white coloration gives it a ghostlike appearance. Audubon highlighted the jay's distinctive crestless head pattern, with its black patch across the nape and its white forehead, cheeks, and throat, and he clearly delineated its short, small bill, out of which periodically issues a range of sounds, some pleasing, some harsh, and some distinctly unjaylike.

In Labrador, on June 27, 1833, Audubon observed a pair of Gray Jays feeding their young. It was four years after he had made this drawing of two adult Gray Jays and the first time that he was able to identify the juveniles, which are much darker than the adults—sufficiently so for Audubon to have considered them a separate species, as other ornithologists before him had done. Audubon subsequently instructed Havell to alter the original plate that he had made from this painting so as to add the figure of a young bird to the composition.

Brown Thrasher

TOXOSTOMA RUFUM (LINNAEUS)

Audubon's nomenclature: Brown Thrush or Ferruginous Thrush, *Turdus rufus* Linnaeus; Ferruginous Mocking-bird, *Orpheus rufus* Linnaeus
Painted on the East Coast in 1829.
Medium: watercolor, pastel, graphite, and selective scraping on paper; 37¹¹/₁₆ × 25 in.; 95.8 × 63.6 cm.
Inscription (lower right, in graphite): ? Quercus sugna/(vulgo) Black jack oak *(lower left, in graphite):* 24 *(upper right corner, in graphite):*
16 *(middle right side, in graphite):* begun
Identification: two males above and two females below with black snake
Seasonal distribution: breeds in southern Canada and eastern United States, winters in south central and southeastern United States
Flora: probably blackjack oak, *Quercus marilandica*
Havell plate number: CXVI in *The Birds of America*
Acc. no. 1863.17.116

Audubon actually witnessed the agitated scene depicted here, which, he says, resulted in damage to the thrashers' nest and the loss of their eggs. The event ended happily for the thrashers, however, when they finally killed the snake. Audubon himself played a part in the drama by picking up the flagging female (shown drooped over the snake's body at the bottom of the composition) and holding her for a few minutes until she began to revive.

This is the second image in which Audubon shows nesting birds beset by a snake; earlier he had made a picture of a rattlesnake threatening a group of distraught mockingbirds. Here the thrashers are attacking a black snake, an excellent climber that invades the nests of such species as Wood Ducks and bluebirds as well as thrashers. During such an intrusion, thrashers—among songbirds some of the boldest defenders of their nests and young—respond frantically, screaming loudly, flying rapidly over the snake, and sometimes pecking at it viciously. "Few snakes come off with success when they attack its nest," relates Audubon, "when the least alarm is given by an individual, a whole party of them instantly rush forth to assist in chasing off the common enemy. . . . Both male and female sit on the eggs. Their mutual attachment, and their courage in defending their nest, are well known to children who live in the country."[1] Audubon wrote that he expected this scene to arouse compassion and sympathy in the viewer, and serve as a lesson that

innocence assisted by friendship can overcome misfortune. These are sentiments that were commonly derived from history paintings rather than ornithological illustration, and his suggestion of such an interpretation indicates Audubon's intention that his audience regard his bird scenes with the respect and seriousness they would accord to human dramas.

More than twenty years before making this picture, Audubon had done a watercolor of a Brown Thrasher near New York. That picture, made in 1807 when Audubon was twenty-two years old, shows a single bird in profile, perched on a branch. It is painted in the manner of Wilson and other earlier bird illustrators, and shows a rather stiff and bland figure of a thrasher that demonstrates the bird's essential physiological characteristics but gives no evidence of typical behavior.[2] Audubon's passionate study of bird habits and improvement in painting techniques in the ensuing twenty years allowed him to provide a much more complete visual account of each species' uniqueness than he did earlier on. The later work shows not only a masterful sense of composition and the details of thrasher plumage (identical in males and in females) but also the birds' extreme aggressiveness (thrashers have been reported to attack vigorously not only snakes but dogs and even people who threaten their nest sites). A comparison between the two pictures vividly demonstrates the advancement in sophistication that Audubon brought to the field of bird painting.

1. John James Audubon, *Ornithological Biography*, vol. III (reprint of 1840–44 ed.; New York: Volair Books, 1979), p. 12.

2. The picture is in the collection of the Houghton Library, Harvard University.

Probably painted in New Jersey c. 1827–30.
Medium: watercolor, graphite, gouache, (black) pastel/chalk, and selective glazing on paper; 28 ¹³⁄₁₆ × 21½ in.; 73.2 × 54.6 cm.
Inscription (lower left): No. 17. Plate 82. Drawn from Nature & Published/by John J. Audubon F.R.S. F.L.S. LC. *(lower center):* Caprimulgus
vociferus/Whip-poor-will Male 1. F. 2.3 Quercus tinctoria Vulgo Black Oak *(upper right corner, in graphite):* 82 *(upper left, next to large moth, in*
graphite): Taterina Cester . . . ? sa *(left, below small moth, in graphite):* Rorubina Io/male
Identification: male above, females below
Seasonal distribution: from southern Canada through eastern, southern, and southwestern
United States, winters in southeastern United States
Flora: black oak, *Quercus velutina*
Havell plate number: LXXXII in *The Birds of America*
Acc. no. 1863.17.082

Although Audubon had known the Whippoorwill since his early days at Mill Grove and had drawn it both in 1806 and 1812,[1] the present picture was most likely done when he visited New Jersey in 1829. "I have represented a male and two females, as well as some of the insects on which they feed. It is remarkable that even the largest moths on which the Whip-poor-will feeds, are always swallowed tail foremost."[2] Audubon shows the male, above, in a characteristic swooping dive, his white tail feathers flashing and his enormous mouth wide, pursuing an elegant cecropia moth. The female just below him has been distracted by a caterpillar. The io moth above the second female, which completes the circle of Whippoorwills and their prey, has escaped the attention of that bird, sitting lengthwise on the curving limb. Whippoorwills take this position because their rather weak feet do not easily support their bodies at a perpendicular angle. The position also affords them highly effective protective coloration for outwitting enemies.

Of all the legends associated with birds, the one that the Greek philosopher Aristotle relates about the family that includes the Whippoorwill—the Caprimulgids or Goatsuckers—is among the more bizarre: "Flying to the udders of she-goats, it sucked them and so gets its name. They say that the udder withers when it has sucked at it and that the goat goes blind."[3] The Whippoorwill's genus name, *Caprimulgus*, derives from the Latin word *caper, capri,* meaning goat, and *mulgere,* "to milk or suck." The origins of the legend are obscure but doubtless are connected to the fact that this bird, which is active at dusk and at night, feeds by flying close to the ground over country fields and woodlots. Ancient shepherds probably saw its shadowy form swooping close to their flocks in its distinctive, silent manner and associated it with nefarious occurrences:

> Its flight is very low, light, swift, noiseless and protracted, as the bird moves over the places which it inhabits, in pursuit of the moths, beetles, and other insects of which its food is composed . . . it passes . . . repeatedly and in different directions over the same field.[4]

Contributing to the mysterious legend about this species may be the fact that Whippoorwills sing their insistent, repeated song at night, when few other birds are active or vocal. They begin at dusk, sing until about 9:30 P.M., fall silent, and begin again at about 2:00 A.M., continuing until dawn. They sing at the remarkable rate of about one call per second. The naturalist John Burroughs noted one Whippoorwill making a record-breaking 1,088 successive calls.

1. The 1806 watercolor and wash picture is now in the John James Audubon Collection (C0006), Manuscript Division, Department of Rare Books and Special Collections, Princeton University Libraries; the 1812 watercolor and crayon drawing of a female Whippoorwill is in the collection of the Houghton Library, Harvard University. The Historical Society's watercolor was copied in oil by Joseph Kidd in 1829.

2. John James Audubon, *Ornithological Biography,* vol. I (reprint of 1840–44 ed.; New York: Volair Books, 1979), p. 158.

3. Quoted in Edward S. Gruson, *Words for Birds* (New York: Quadrangle Books, 1972), p. 152.

4. John James Audubon, *Ornithological Biography,* vol. I, p. 155.

Nº 17. Plate 82.   Caprimulgus vociferus

Drawn from Nature & Published   Whip-poor-will.   Male 1. F. 2. 3
by
John J. Audubon F. R. S. F. L. S. &c.   Quercus tinctoria
                                    Vulgo Black Oak.

Probably painted on the East Coast in 1829.

Medium: watercolor, pastel, and graphite on paper; 37⅞ × 25⅝ in.; 96.3 × 65 cm.

Inscription (lower left, in graphite over watercolor): No 25.

Identification: male above, female below

Seasonal distribution: breeds in the Arctic, winters south to northern United States and occasionally wanders as far south as Florida,

Texas, and southern California

Havell plate number: CXXI in *The Birds of America*

Acc. no. 1863.17.121

Since Audubon was aware that Snowy Owls typically hunt during the day or early evening, he likely wished the setting in this composition to represent the dusk of a gathering storm rather than a nightscape. The scene's dark clouds form an intense, dramatic background for the owls, accentuating the white-and-brown-barred plumage of the birds and the harshness of their environment. The dead tree trunk on which they are perched emphasizes their desolate surroundings. In their native Arctic, such a landing place would be uncharacteristic for Snowy Owls, which nest above the tree line and in that habitat more usually frequent hillocks, posts, or the roofs of buildings.[1] In the foreboding landscape of Audubon's image, the owls sit vigilant, alert to any movement of animal prey. The pupils in their bright yellow eyes are dilated to take advantage of all available light; they have swiveled their large, round heads (which lack the eartufts of some other owl species) in different directions to survey their territory.

The snowy is the strongest and heaviest North American owl and one of the biggest. The female, here shown sitting on the lower branch, is larger than the male (as with many birds of prey), and she and the juveniles are most heavily barred. This coloration provides the owls with effective camouflage on the often frozen tundra. Although Audubon believed it true of both sexes, only the older males attain the immaculate milky-white plumage washed with clear lemon yellow that students of

bird life sometimes observe. Like other denizens of the North that spend much of the year on snowy ground, these owls have also evolved other special means of protection against climatic extremes, such as the fine feathers that insulate their legs down to the toes and form an essential shield against the cold.

Snowy Owls are not common in the lower forty-eight states, but they do come down in numbers from the Arctic every four years or so when their preferred food source, the little rodents called lemmings, undergo a cyclical crash. During such years the owls may wander as far south as Alabama, and in unfamiliar locations they adapt themselves to whatever prey is available. Audubon had the remarkable good fortune to see a Snowy Owl in Louisville, fishing near the Falls of the Ohio. He says that it lay flat on a rock, lengthwise along the contour of a pool of water, with its head down and turned toward the water as if asleep. When a fish surfaced, the owl thrust out its closest foot and grabbed it.

Audubon's Snowy Owls are keenly watchful and seem particularly appealing to us in part because of their binocular vision, with both eyes in one plane of the face, as human beings' are. But although Audubon successfully caught the fluffiness of the birds' feathered toes and of some of the facial plumage, the owls appear somewhat stiff, as if carved from wood or ivory—handsome but perhaps less corporeal than decorative.[2]

1. When Snowy Owls move south during years of incursion—the circumstance in which Audubon saw them—they do use trees as perches on rare occasions.
2. Audubon made two earlier pictures of the Snowy Owl. One is a crayon drawing of a male bird that was done in France and is now in the Houghton

Library, Harvard University, and the other is a pencil and pastel drawing, very much more primitive in conception than the present picture, done near the Falls of the Ohio in Louisville on December 29, 1809. That drawing is now in the collection of The New-York Historical Society.

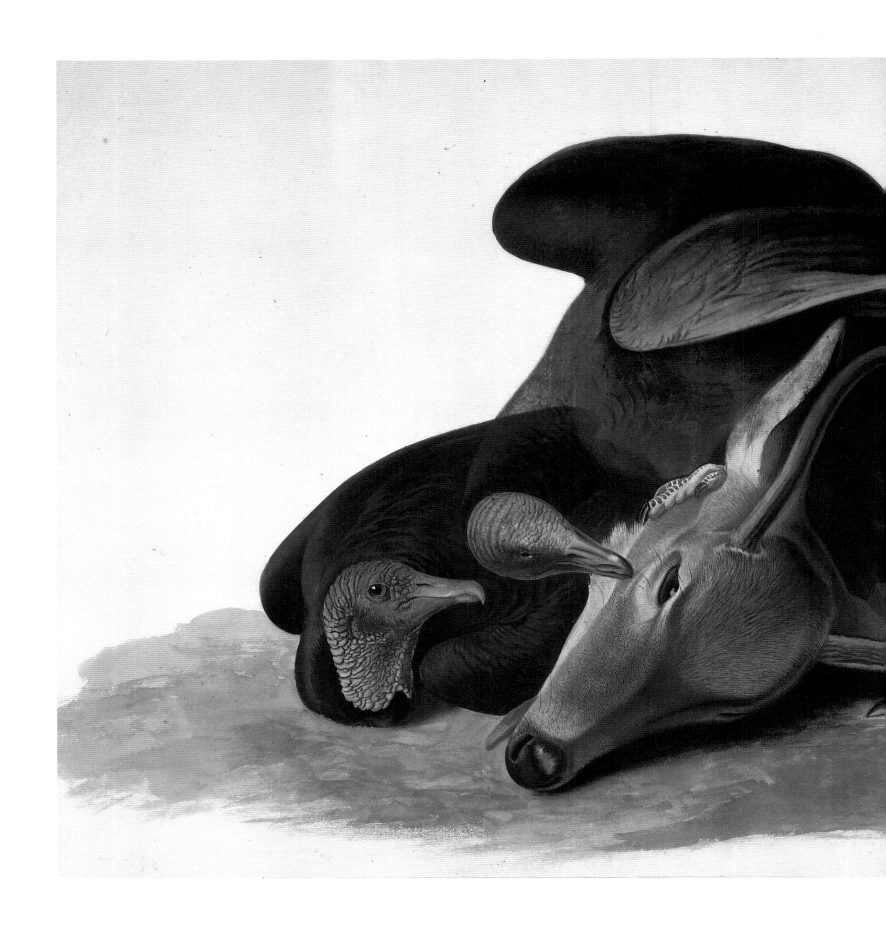

Bird on left and deer's head painted c. 1829; second bird added later.
Medium: watercolor, pastel, graphite, and collage on paper; 23⅜ × 36⅛ in.;
59.4 × 91.7 cm.
Identification: two adult Black Vultures and head of white-tailed deer,
Odocoileus virginianus
Seasonal distribution: breeds and winters in southeastern United States, south through
Mexico and southern South America
Havell plate number: CVI in *The Birds of America*
Acc. no. 1863.17.106

On Tuesday, December 12, 1826, Audubon presented some of his research to Dr. David Brewster, a physicist, the coeditor of a distinguished philosophical journal and a member of the University of Edinburgh's learned society, the Wernerians, in which Audubon was eagerly seeking membership. He noted the event in his journal: "This morning at ten I went to the house of Dr. Brewster. . . . He received me very kindly, and in a few minutes I began reading my paper on the habits of the Carrion Crow, *Vultur atratus*. . . . He was good enough to say it was highly interesting."[1] Audubon's discovery, based on his own experiments, showed that Black Vultures have a poor sense of smell and rely primarily on sight to find the carrion that they eat. This conclusion was upheld by subsequent experiments, including one in which Black Vultures avidly consumed a common skunk, apparently unaffected by its devastating odor.

Audubon had often seen Black Vultures close at hand. While on his trip down the Mississippi River, he had shot one on December 19, 1820, and made a drawing of it which he completed on December 21 at Mathews Bend, Mississippi, describing the process as follows: "Drawing nearly all day I finished the Carion Crow, it stunk so intolerably, and Looked so disgusting that I was very glad when I through it over Board."[2]

On December 26 he arrived in Natchez and "was surprised to see the immense number of vultures that strode along the streets or slumbered on the roofs."[3] In describing the prevalence of Black Vultures in the South, Audubon commented:

> Charleston, Savannah, New Orleans, Natchez, and other
> cities are amply provided with these birds, which may be
> seen flying or walking about the streets the whole day in
> groups. They also regularly attend the markets and
> shambles, to pick up the pieces of flesh thrown away by
> the butchers, and, when an opportunity occurs, leap from

one bench to another, for the purpose of helping themselves.[4]

Given the vulture's feeding habits, it was natural for Audubon to depict the birds with carrion. In his essay "Deer Hunting," he described how hunters in the woods would shoot and dress a deer and leave the less desirable parts for the vultures. In this scene, he shows a pair of birds prepared to feast on the head of a buck, which they surround like a mourning cloak. The movement of their own bare, wrinkled heads (devoid of feathers to reduce the possibility of infection from putrid flesh that might mat in the plumage) underscores the lifelessness of the deer. But in spite of its macabre subject matter and its initially shocking effect, the image is less sensationally bloodthirsty than objectively narrative, less a scene of gruesome frightfulness than a straightforward description of vulture behavior.

Audubon first painted the vulture on the left and the head of the deer, and subsequently added the second bird. He painted in the left bird's body and pasted on its head and feet, positioning them to envelop the deer and heighten the immediacy, veracity, and intensity of the scene.

1. Maria R. Audubon, ed., *Audubon and His Journals* (New York: Dover Publications, 1986), p. 181.
2. Howard Corning, ed., *Journal of John James Audubon Made During His Trip to New Orleans, 1820–21* (Boston: The Club of Odd Volumes, 1929), p. 82. The drawing is in the collection of The New-York Historical Society.
3. Maria R. Audubon, ed., *Audubon and His Journals*, p. 248.
4. John James Audubon, *Ornithological Biography*, vol. I (reprint of 1840–44 ed.; New York: Volair Books, 1979), p. 17.

Long-billed Curlew

NUMENIUS AMERICANUS BECHSTEIN

Painted in Charleston, South Carolina, in late October 1831.

Medium: watercolor, pastel, graphite, gouache, selective glazing, and selective scraping on paper; 24 15/16 × 37 5/8 in.; 63.4 × 95.7 cm.

Identification: adults

Seasonal distribution: breeds in western North America, winters in southern coastal United States

Havell plate number: CCXXXI in *The Birds of America*

Acc. no. 1863.17.231

"This bird is the largest of the genus found in North America. The great length of its bill is of itself sufficient to distinguish it from every other."[1] With this succinct description, Audubon characterizes the Long-billed Curlew, one of our stateliest shorebirds. The curlew's genus name, *Numenius,* is a late Greek word meaning "new moon" and refers to the curve of the bird's magnificent beak, which may reach a length of seven inches.

Studying the long-bill's habits was one of the many delights of Audubon's 1831 visit to Charleston, "as it was my good fortune to witness their departures and arrivals in the company of my friend BACHMAN."[2] Audubon noted that

> The Long-billed Curlew spends the day in the sea-marshes, from which it returns at the approach of night, to the sandy beaches of the sea-shores, where it rests until dawn. As the sun sinks beneath the horizon the Curlews rise from their feeding-grounds in small parties. . . . The flocks enlarge, however, as they proceed, and in the course of an hour or so the number of birds that collect in the place selected for their nightly retreat sometimes amounts to several thousands.[3]

During the day, long-bills frequent lake shores as well as river bars and salt marshes, feeding in groups of twos or threes on such aquatic creatures as crayfish, crabs, and mollusks. They also consume insects injurious to agricultural production—locusts, crickets, and grasshoppers—and it is therefore ironic that the spread of agriculture (as well as the massive slaughter of the curlews as game birds along the Atlantic coast) has extirpated the long-bills from their former breeding sites on the prairies and large areas of the plains where they nested abundantly in the open grasslands of dry upland fields and wet meadows.

The splendid bill for which the curlew is named is the focus of Audubon's image and a principal compositional feature with which the artist unites foreground and background, relates the birds to one another, and creates a sense of movement. The front bird's bill, whose curve is echoed in the spears of marsh grass that frame it, directs the viewer's eye from the bird on the mud flat, poised with its bill just above a blade of vegetation, to the city of Charleston so minutely detailed in the background.[4] The eye travels back and forth across the tiny space between bill tip and grass, evoking the imminent connection between them. The rear bird's bill, whose curve is repeated by some of the marsh grasses behind it, leads the eye down to the front bird's tail and bending legs, from which it travels back up to the rear bird's breast. The remarkable bill highlighted by Audubon is an appendage so distinctive that the artist evidently did not feel compelled to illustrate the long-bill's other diagnostic feature—its cinnamon wing linings.

1. John James Audubon, *Ornithological Biography,* vol. VI (reprint of 1840–44 ed.; New York: Volair Books, 1979), p. 36.
2. Ibid.
3. Ibid.
4. The marks among the grass to the left of the bill appear to come from smudged paint.

Black-crowned Night-Heron

NYCTICORAX NYCTICORAX (LINNAEUS)

Audubon's nomenclature: Night Heron or Qua Bird, *Ardea nycticorax* Linnaeus
Painted in June, 1832, in Charleston, South Carolina. The frog (pasted on) and the
habitat probably painted by George Lehman, who may also have helped
with the birds.
Medium: Watercolor, pastel, graphite, gouache, collage, selective glazing, and selective
scraping on paper; 25⅜ × 37⅞ in.; 64.4 × 96 cm.
Inscription (graphite, above right bird's head): 2 (*on head of lower bird*): 1
Identification: adult left, immature right
Seasonal distribution: breeds widely throughout the United States, winters in southeastern
and southwestern United States
Flora: zephyr lily, *Zephranthes atamasco*
Havell plate number: CCXXXVI in *The Birds of America*
Acc. no. 1863.17.236

$\mathcal{I}$n this Black-crowned Night-Heron vignette, Audubon effectively summarizes the species' life cycle, including the development of plumage and behavior. The juvenile Black-crowned Night-Heron on the right, whose feathering is characteristic of the species during its first few months of life, will attain the glossy black, gray, and white breeding plumage of the adult on the left at the age of three. Its rather vacant stare, often typical of young birds, contrasts vividly with the intent gaze of the adult, which focuses on "the frog . . . common in the retired swamps which the Night Heron frequents, and [which] is often devoured by it."[1] The adult bird (males and females have identical plumage) hunts the frog to nourish itself so it may continue to procreate. At the same time it teaches its progeny the survival skills needed to mature into adulthood and produce another generation. Through observing its parent feeding, the young heron learns to hunt the small creatures on which it will subsist: fish, shellfish, snakes, and even mice and young birds, as well as frogs.

Here, as the adult heron lunges toward its prey, the bird's taut body with its sharp, open bill assumes an aggressive diagonal posture. The heron's curved breeding plumes, horizontal feather patterning, angled legs and gripping feet, and its intense gaze emphasize the strong diagonal thrust toward the frog, which is also connected visually by its coloration to the young bird of similar hue standing near it. The frog thus forms a narrative and compositional link between the active, threatening adult about to catch it and the more passive chick learning

to do so. The young bird's hunched posture, withdrawn neck, and limp right foot are clearly juxtaposed with the outstretched neck and tense right foot of its active and more experienced parent. The viewer looks from the adult to the frog and then up to the young bird, whose bill points toward its parent and leads the eye to the bending marsh grasses (similar in hue to the young bird's bill) and then down to the adult. Audubon thus efficiently and deftly conveys the relationship between the birds, their environment, and their feeding habits.

The stocky Black-crowned Night-Heron is not, as its name implies, exclusively nocturnal, but it does feed chiefly during the darker hours, often flying distances of several miles from its nesting grounds to the meadows, lakes, and creekbeds where it hunts. Adaptable, it builds its large, flat stick nest in or near coastal marshes of fresh, brackish, or salt water, sometimes in enormous colonies, at heights varying from ground level to 160 feet in the air. In Audubon's day, it was subject there not only to the ravages of crows, hawks, vultures, and raccoons but also to "the planters who represent it as equalling any other bird in the delicacy of its flesh."[2]

1. John James Audubon, *Ornithological Biography*, vol. VI (reprint of 1840–44 ed.; New York: Volair Books, 1979), p. 87.

2. Ibid.

Audubon's nomenclature: Blue Heron, *Ardea caerulea*

Painted c. 1832. Background painted by George Lehman.

Medium: watercolor, pastel, graphite, traces of gouache, and small amount of selective glazing on paper; 20⅜ × 28⅞ in.; 51.8 × 73.4 cm.

Inscription (upper right, in graphite, most of it cut off): . . . crooked . . ./you will cut out and place near or on the outline/made on try to show a portion on the wha . . ./of *one leg and foot. (last four words underlined)*

Identification: breeding-plumaged adult

Seasonal distribution: breeds and winters along Atlantic and Gulf coasts

Havell plate number: CCCVII in *The Birds of America*

Acc. no. 1863.17.307

Admiring Audubon's imposing life-size figure of the Little Blue Heron, a viewer may find it hard to believe that the living bird weighs only fourteen ounces. But observers who have seen the little blue in the wild, as Audubon had the chance to do in Florida, Louisiana,[1] and South Carolina, will have noted the graceful flight that Audubon described in his biography of the species—the bird's wingbeats clearly faster than those of the bigger herons—and will realize the importance of lightness to a bird that achieves such buoyancy. On the ground, little blues walk gracefully as well, feeding quietly and deliberately near lakes and ponds or in such marshes, streams, and meadows as George Lehman, one of Audubon's assistants, depicts here. Although they may breed near brackish or salt water as well as fresh, they prefer to feed in fresh water. They often hunt at shallower depths than some other heron species, or seek their prey in the mud or on shore. Audubon remarked on their appetite for fiddler crabs and fish, which they consume in quantity; they also supplement their diet with a variety of frogs, lizards, snakes, turtles, shrimp, and spiders, as well as with various aquatic and terrestrial insects including grasshoppers, crickets, and beetles.

Little blues are the only herons to produce immaculately white young, and flocks of the birds are sometimes composed exclusively of these gleaming immatures, which show no blue until they grow their bluish-black-tipped flight feathers and then acquire increasing amounts of blue after their first winter.

Sometimes flocks include only the dusky blue adults, and sometimes they consist of a mixture: between the white immature plumage and the blue adult plumage the birds show every intergradation of the two shades.[2] Audubon discovered that some birds remain nearly white throughout their first breeding season, so that white, mottled, and blue birds may nest together. When the older blue adults molt into their breeding plumage, their heads and necks turn reddish-purple and their legs and feet black, as Audubon illustrates here. After breeding season, the heads and necks turn dark purple and the legs and feet dull green. Only the blue adults—never the young white ones—produce breeding plumes on the head and back, and thus the Little Blue Heron suffered less at the hands of plume hunters than some other species. But their populations, too, were substantially diminished by the beginning of the twentieth century. Little blues breed in large or small colonies, often in the company of other herons, in nests that vary in size from insubstantial to solid stick structures placed in water-loving trees or shrubs such as willows, swamp privets, or red maples. The nests are usually low but can be as high as forty feet above the ground or water. Both male and female, which are essentially identical in appearance, incubate the eggs. After breeding season many of the birds, especially the young white ones, disperse northward, sometimes as far as Labrador and Newfoundland.

1. Audubon described in his journal having made a drawing of a Little Blue Heron on March 18, 1821, in New Orleans. The present location of that work is unknown. See Howard Corning, ed., *Journal of John James Audubon Made During His Trip to New Orleans, 1820–21* (Boston: The Club of Odd Volumes, 1929), p. 137.

2. Audubon's inscription, now largely cut off, at the upper-right-hand corner of the painting, apparently instructs Havell to add to the engraving a second bird to the right of the one represented in the painting. A pencil outline of the head and neck of such a bird, standing erect, appears above the back of the present bird. Havell, in fact, did not add that figure but did portray a white immature Little Blue Heron in the background on the left.

Common Snipe

GALLINAGO GALLINAGO (LINNAEUS)

Audubon's nomenclature: American Snipe, *Scolopax wilsonii*
Probably painted near Charleston, South Carolina, in March 1832. The background is
by George Lehman.
Medium: watercolor, graphite, oil paint, gouache, black pastel/chalk, and collage on
paper; 14 13/16 × 21 3/8 in.; 37.6 × 54.3 cm.
Identification: male left, females center and right
Seasonal distribution: breeds widely throughout northern North America, winters across
southern United States
Havell plate number: CCXLIII in *The Birds of America*
Acc. no. 1863.17.243

The Common Snipe is best known for three of its habits: its airborne courtship display, including a tremulous
winnowing sound produced by the vibration of its two outer
tail feathers—a display executed at such an altitude that it is
barely perceptible to the naked eye; the erratic zigzag pattern of
its flight when it is flushed; and its custom of squatting or
crouching and "freezing" at the approach of danger, immobile
until almost touched. In a two-dimensional image intended to
convey typical aspects of snipe behavior, Audubon could most
effectively illustrate the last of these; here he organized his composition around two large female snipe in the awkward poses
they sometimes assume when they feel threatened, while a slim-
mer male bird scans for danger.[1]

The snipe's plumage, streaked and spotted in various shades
of black, brown, ocher, and buff, renders the bird virtually invisible against the darkened grasses of the bogs, marshes, and
swampy lake and pond edges on which it nests and feeds. An
ornithologist who studied the subtleties of this cryptic coloration pointed out that these markings are coarser on the throat,
lower breast, and sides than on the head, neck, and back, and
that if a snipe is seen by a predator at ground level against the
horizon, its coarser ventral markings will blend with the foreground shapes and shadows, while the finer dorsal patterns will
merge with the smaller-appearing objects in the background.

While it may seem incongruous that Audubon painted the
male snipe here—whose head is raised to investigate the same
danger that the females perceive—looking in the opposite direction from the other two birds, the male's position enables
Audubon to depict the full back view of the snipe's camouflag-
ing plumage while at the same time illustrating a feature of its
eyesight important to the bird in detecting danger. A snipe's

eyes are set sufficiently far to the rear of its head that the bird can see both forward and backward, and thus can raise its head, take advantage of the longitudinal dorsal stripes that disguise it among the marsh vegetation, and still focus on its enemy.

While the snipe may pick up food from the ground's surface, it often feeds in its water-soaked habitat by inserting its long bill deep into the mud to probe for earthworms, snails, and insect larvae. As Audubon illustrates in the center bird, the top half of the species' bill is longer than the bottom half to aid it in grasping prey. The bill is flexible, and the tips of both halves are equipped with sensitive nerve endings to help detect food. The snipe has powerful jaw muscles and can spread the end of its bill open while the rest of the bill remains closed, enabling the bird to extract food from the soil without expending the energy required to open its buried beak full-length against the resistance of the earth.

1. Audubon had depicted the Common Snipe in Henderson, Kentucky, on March 17, 1810, in an image now in the collection of the Houghton Library, Harvard University. He also represented the snipe on February 8, 1821, in New Orleans. In 1827, in Great Britain, Audubon made a pencil and watercolor copy of the original drawing of the snipe on the right that he had cut out and pasted down on the final composition engraved by Havell as plate CCXLIII. The 1827 picture was formerly in the collection of Kennedy Galleries, New York.

American Bittern

BOTAURUS LENTIGINOSUS (RACKETT)

Painted probably on the East Coast in 1832–33

Medium: watercolor, pastel, graphite, and selective scraping on paper; 21½ × 29³⁄16 in.;
54.6 × 74.2 cm.

Inscription (upper left, in graphite): No 68—Plate 337/American Bittern *(upper center, graphite):*
Male 1. *(and partially erased):* Female 2. *(upper right, in faint graphite):* Luin . . . /at/?ater . . .
p . . . off . . . e/a . . . /

Identification: adults

Seasonal distribution: breeds and winters widely throughout the United States

Havell plate number: CCCXXXVII in *The Birds of America*

Acc. no. 1863.17.337

A bird whose onomatopoetic nicknames, including "Plum Pudd'n," "Thunder-pump," or "Dunk-a-doo," are inspired by its vocalizations (liquid, guttural thumps and squelches, often uttered several times, and audible for half a mile or more) and whose features include a chunky shape, a height of two to three feet, and an almost four-foot wingspread would seem hard to miss. But the American Bittern is a furtive species, most active at dusk and at night, and its plumage and solitary, stealthy habits keep it well concealed in the marshes where it lives. Even Audubon, who by his own account had killed numerous bitterns, never observed all the bird's habits or ever found its nest. The bittern's yellowish-brown plumage, overlaid with darker brown and buff-colored streaks, spots, freckles, and bars, which help it blend almost invisibly into a shadowy swamp, and its habit of immobilizing itself or "freezing" when it senses danger (an attitude it can usefully assume even when very young and unable to fly) make the species difficult to discover.

The American Bittern hunts by standing completely still, looking down at the water, with bill parallel to the ground. When it sights such potential prey as frogs, snakes, or crayfish, mice, moles, or shrews, fish, or insects, it moves its bill infinitely slowly so as to remain inconspicuous, and at the last moment, thrusts it down to make its catch.

Found only locally within its range, this "genius of the bog," as Thoreau called it, protects itself by standing stock still and pointing its bill straight up so that its streaky neck plumage effectively camouflages it against tall, shaded water plants. From that hidden position it can focus directly on an approaching intruder, since its yellow eyes are placed low on its head. And unless the observer scares it up from virtually underfoot he rarely notices it. He is more likely to detect its ventriloquial call, produced when the bird swallows air and expresses it from an inflated esophagus. If he should flush the bird, however, he may have a good chance to observe it, because it flies low over the marsh, slowly and distinctively, with neck drawn in and legs extended, and it generally lands on the ground rather than in a tree or bush as other herons do.

During breeding season bitterns exhibit an otherwise concealed patch of white feathers that they raise over their backs and shoulders, sometimes simultaneously walking in a crouch with their backs arched and their necks retracted. The species does not nest colonially: the female builds a platform of dead marsh grasses, usually a few inches above the water, and lays three to five eggs, which are olive-buff like the nesting material surrounding them.

Audubon credits this work to his son John: it is not clear whether he himself had any significant role in it. The picture is more static than many of Audubon's compositions and demonstrates a less subtle relationship between birds and background than is characteristic of his vignettes.[1]

1. Audubon did draw an American Bittern in pastel on December 4, 1821, in New Orleans. (The bill, foot, and eye are done in watercolor and the background in oil.) The present location of that picture, formerly in the collection of Mrs. Seth Dennis, Weyhe Galleries, New York, is unknown.

Audubon's nomenclature: Great White Heron, *Ardea occidentalis*

Painted in Key West on May 26, 1832.

Medium: watercolor, pastel, graphite, gouache, and selective scraping on paper; 25¹¹⁄₁₆ × 38⁵⁄₁₆ in.; 65.2 × 98.7 cm.

Inscription (lower center, in graphite): Keep closely to the Sky in depth and colouring; have the water of a *Pea-green* tint. keep the division of the scales on the legs & feet white in your engraving—the colouring over these will subdue them enough/finish the houses better/from the original/which you have *(lower right):* scale lighter edges/have the upper back portion/only mellowing in the outline. *(lower right):* 57

(lower center): No 57. Plate 281. Ardea occidentalis. male adult spring plumage./View, Key-West

Identification: adult

Seasonal distribution: breeds and winters in Florida

Havell plate number: CCLXXXI in *The Birds of America*

Acc. no. 1863.17.281

In the Florida Keys, in April 1832, Audubon saw Great White Herons for the first time. He described them as "sedate," and "quiet," walking "majestically, with firmness and great elegance."[1] Indeed, unlike the members of their family who wade actively when they feed, great whites spend most of their time standing stock still in shallow coastal waters, waiting silently for a fish, shrimp, crab, or snail to come within reach. But it is characteristic of Audubon to animate his portrait of a species that he had generally seen quietly "perched like so many newly finished statues of the purest alabaster"[2] by choosing to depict it during the brief period of aggressive activity that the birds display after catching a meal, when they either swallow their prey alive or, if it is large, "beat it on the water, or shake it violently, biting it severely all the while."[3] Here Audubon's subject has just seized a fish in its broad, heavy bill. With neck still contorted, and mud-covered yellowish legs still bent, it begins to straighten up from its crouched fishing posture to prepare to swallow the fish. It hunts from an island near Key West, whose waterfront buildings gleam in the background and whose semitropical atmosphere the artist clearly conveys. Audubon's notes to Havell give directions not only about certain details of the representation of the bird but about the depiction of the intense hues of sky and sea as well.

Until 1973 the Great White Heron—which, as Audubon noted is pure white in every plumage—was considered the distinct species that Audubon described it to be. Today scientists believe that it is actually a color phase or subspecies of the Great Blue Heron, although it is in fact larger and has a longer wingspread. But while the great blue ranges extensively throughout North America, the great white is found only in southern Florida: our largest white heron has the most limited range of any of its family on this continent.

The great white's habitat includes the wide mud flats on which it feeds and the mangrove-covered islands where it nests—usually in areas safe from human disturbance—on bulky solid platforms that it constructs of large sticks in the crowns of low trees. It may use such a nest for a number of years, rebuilding and strengthening it each time so the nest can withstand winds of great velocity. The species was hunted until protective legislation intervened, but human disturbance has not been as devastating to its populations as to those of some other herons because the great white does not grow long breeding plumes and hence was not avidly sought by milliners. Young great whites were considered a delicacy by some Florida natives and were shot for the table, but more threatening to the species' population have been tropical storms. In 1935 a hurricane that destroyed a number of islands reduced the species population to a mere 150 birds.

1. John James Audubon, *Ornithological Biography*, vol. VI (reprint of 1840–44 ed.; New York: Volair Books, 1979), p. 115.

2. Ibid., p. 142.
3. Ibid., p. 115.

Keep closely to the Sky in depth and colouring ——
have the water of a Pea = green tint ——
Keep the division of the water in the
Legs of a dark white way now engraving
the colouring in and now will publish
mend enough ——

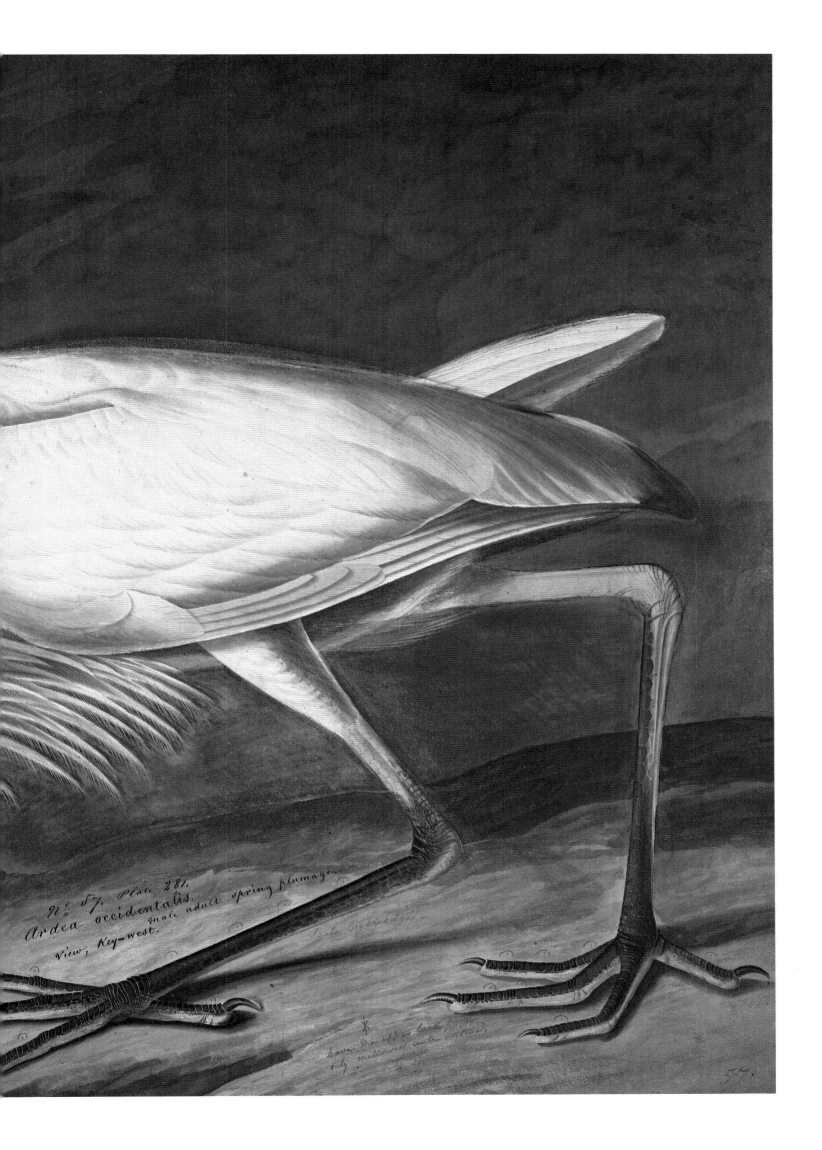

No 57, Plate 281.
Ardea occidentalis.
view, Key-west.　male adult spring plumage.

Snowy Egret
EGRETTA THULA (MOLINA)

Audubon's nomenclature: Snowy Heron or White Egret. *Ardea candidissima*
Painted in 1832, probably on March 25, in Charleston, South Carolina.
Medium: watercolor, graphite, gouache, selective glazing, and selective scraping on paper; 29 1/4 × 21 5/16 in.; 74.3 × 54.2 cm.
Identification: adult
Seasonal distribution: breeds along East Coast and widely throughout southern and western United States, winters along southern Atlantic,
southern Pacific, and Gulf coasts
Havell plate number: CCXLII in *The Birds of America*
Acc. no. 1863.17.242

While any life-size painting of an all-white bird covered with graceful plumes would produce a dramatic effect, Audubon's picture of the Snowy Egret—a bird that some consider the most delicate and ethereal of American herons—acquires added poignancy because of the species' near elimination through merciless slaughter.

Aigrettes (a word taken from the bird's French name) was the term plume hunters applied to the showy feathers that both male and female egrets grow on the head, breast, and back exclusively during nesting season. The snowies (as the birds are popularly known) display these feathers by raising, spreading, and lowering them during courtship. After the egrets have their young, the feathers are replaced with the birds' straight, short winter plumage. Thus, to obtain *aigrettes*, which were sold in immense quantities and at enormous prices for use on women's hats, hunters killed these small, slender herons in massive numbers during breeding season, often when there were young in the nest that were then left to die of starvation. Because snowies breed in colonies whose populations sometimes number in the thousands, with both parents taking part in nest building as well as incubating and feeding the young, countless numbers were easily destroyed. Only forceful conservation measures have restored the Snowy Egret to its former range.

Snowies inhabit a variety of wetland areas, from ponds, shorelines, and tidal flats to swamps, marshes, wet meadows, and fields such as the one on the plantation shown here. When feeding, they sometimes shuffle rapidly through shallow water—more actively than most other herons—to stir up fish, shrimp, crabs, and other shellfish as well as frogs and insects. But they also often take slow steps, as Audubon shows this bird doing, thus reducing the risk of forewarning potential prey.

Audubon's image[1] highlights the symmetry and contrasts of the bird's coloration: the immaculate feathers (white in all plumages) set off by the slender black bill and yellow lores at the top and the black legs with their yellow feet at the bottom. (In full breeding plumage the lores turn red and the feet bright orange.) Audubon emphasizes the bird's deliberate stalking at the water's edge by showing one foot in midstride and by including two flattened marsh plants over which the egret has just trodden. The spear of another marsh plant, curving downward just below the bird's breast (where a hunter would aim his shot) connects the scene's foreground and background, leading the eye to the tree bending over the pond in the distance, from there to the plantation house, and finally forward again to the tiny form of a hunter stalking the heron. In Audubon's day hunters did not yet kill snowies for their plumes but rather because they considered them fine eating. Yet the hunter's presence and the bird's wary expression ironically foreshadow the species' future plight and remind us of how close we came to losing this majestic creature.

1. Audubon reports having made an image of the snowy years earlier; on Sunday, April 22, 1821, he writes, "Finished to day a Drawing of a *Snowy Heron Ardea Candidissima* a beautiful Male" [Howard Corning, ed., *Journal of John James Audu-* *bon Made During His Trip to New Orleans, 1820–21* (Boston: The Club of Odd Volumes, 1929), p. 150], but the present location of that picture is unknown.

Great Egret

CASMERODIUS ALBUS (LINNAEUS)

Audubon's nomenclature: White Heron or Great White Heron, *Ardea alba*
Medium: watercolor, graphite, white pastel, white gouache, and selective glazing (eye) on paper; 37 7/16 × 25 1/2 in; 95.1 × 64.9 cm.
Identification: breeding-plumaged adult
Seasonal distribution: breeds along Atlantic and Pacific coasts and in east central United States, winters along Atlantic and
Pacific coasts and in southern United States
Acc. no. 1863.18.030

"The most difficult to Imitate of any bird I have yet undertaken,"[1] Audubon wrote of the Great Egret at the time that he first depicted it in New Orleans on March 25, 1821, from "a beautiful Specimen . . . in perfect order."[2] The artist's problems in rendering the species to his own satisfaction prompted him to make two other Great Egret compositions besides this one. The final picture that Havell published included far more detailed habitat than this image does and showed the bird in profile, feeding, rather than from behind, preening. Here the artist focused his attention on the bird's stark whiteness (the color of its feathers at all ages and seasons) and the sheer delicacy of its plumes. By positioning the egret above eye level, with its back toward the viewer, Audubon accorded greatest prominence to the elegant curves of the plumes and the translucence of their diaphanous filaments. The strength and solidity of the bird's neck and upper-body muscles, its mighty yellow bill (brightest during breeding season), and dark legs—both important field marks—provide a singular contrast to the filminess of the breeding plumes, "its silky train [which] reminded one of the flowing robes of the noble ladies of Europe."[3]

Audubon noted that Great Egrets, which feed during the day on aquatic animals, snakes, insects, and small mammals in fresh, brackish, or salt water, travel just before nightfall to roosts where they perch, clean their feathers, and then retire until daybreak. It is apparently such a scene of preening that Audubon depicted here, his stately subject undertaking its evening ritual against a darkening sky. Great Egrets are very much at home in the trees, where they not only roost—sometimes in very large numbers—but also build the bulky, flat platforms of their stick nests, which they construct either in individual sites or in colonies.

Great Egrets acquire their plumes at the beginning of breeding season in January or February and shed them after nesting in June or July. A single bird has been known to possess as many as fifty-four such plumes, which, with those of the Snowy Egret, were in great demand by plume hunters. In 1902 alone, about a ton and a half of Great Egret plumes were sold in London to decorate women's hats, a quantity that would have required the slaughter of close to 200,000 adult Great Egrets, and thus the destruction of two or three times that number of eggs and young to which the adults were devoting themselves during that season. The value of the plumes exceeded their weight in gold. Great Egrets were thus catastrophically reduced in numbers, and their population further eroded by drainage, by development of their habitat, and by prolonged droughts. The species required extensive conservation measures to restore its numbers. Through the efforts of the National Audubon Society, of which it was made the symbol, the species is now once again one of the most common and numerous of its family.

1. Howard Corning, ed., *Journal of John James Audubon Made During His Trip to New Orleans, 1820–21* (Boston: The Club of Odd Volumes, 1929), p. 141.
2. Ibid.

3. John James Audubon, *Ornithological Biography*, vol. VI (reprint of 1840–44 ed.; New York: Volair Books, 1979), p. 133.

White Heron Male Spring Dress
Ardea alba

Great Egret

CASMERODIUS ALBUS (LINNAEUS)

Audubon's nomenclature: Great White Heron, *Ardea alba*

Probably painted in Charleston, South Carolina, in June 1832.

Medium: watercolor, graphite, gouache, and collage on paper; 24-3/16 × 35½ in.; 61.4 × 90.5 cm.

Inscription (lower left, in graphite crossed out with heavier graphite wavy line): No. 69. Plate 341.

(lower left, in graphite): Great White Heron Male Spring Dress/Ardea alba—L. // Plate 356. *(Lower right, in graphite, faint):* 78 pl. 386

Identification: breeding-plumaged male

Seasonal distribution: breeds along Atlantic and Pacific coasts and in east central United States, winters along Atlantic and Pacific coasts and in southern United States

Havell plate number: CCCLXXXVI in *The Birds of America*

Acc. no. 1863.17.386

Great Egrets are especially fond of eating crayfish, among whose mud chimneys a member of the species appears here, searching for food. Audubon had witnessed "vast numbers"[1] of Great Egrets hunting in marshes and ponds at several sites in the southeastern United States and had commented on the bird's stalking behavior, "its steps measured, its long neck gracefully retracted and curved."[2] In this depiction Audubon portrayed a characteristically expressive posture, in which the egret pulls its neck back to prepare for lunging at nearby prey. By showing the bird in this expectant position, Audubon was able to give the scene a sense of immediacy, to emphasize the grace and flexibility of the egret's long neck, and, as a practical matter, to fit the bird's entire five-foot-long form onto the page. To create the most accurate and elegant possible rendering of the species, Audubon pasted onto this final image the drawing of the head and neck of a Great Egret from another of his pictures that he evidently considered a more successful portrayal than his initial one here.

The Great Egret is a widespread, versatile, gregarious bird. It nests colonially from Florida and Texas north to the Great Lakes and Maine and up into Canada, breeds in the Old World as well as the New, and seeks a variety of prey in fresh- as well as saltwater marshes and ponds. It is the longest and slenderest of the herons, and some observers regard it as the most graceful, with its light, agile movements and buoyant flight. The species is a year-long resident in the southern part of its breeding range, but numbers of the birds, perhaps in response to the south's intense summer heat, wander north in July and August. The Great Egrets that nest in more northerly areas migrate south in the fall.

Predominant in this image is the contrast between the comparative massiveness of the bird's body and of the crayfish chimneys, marsh plants, sea, clouds, and sky in the background and the extreme delicacy of the egret's evanescent breeding plumes, which Audubon rendered by means of fine, sensitive strokes. In the engraving of this image, Havell concentrated the marsh plants in the right rear of the composition to produce a dark mass of heavy, curving forms against which the gossamer-like breeding plumes appear all the whiter and more fragile. As Audubon suggested in the watercolor, the cascade of plumes in

the engraving is sufficiently translucent to reveal the dark marsh grasses behind them, lending the scene depth and formal interest. Havell changed the left rear of the composition, transforming the sea into a series of craggy hills under a lowering sky, and he added an element from another Audubon composition—the horned toad from his painting of the Swainson's Hawk. The specimen came to Audubon via Thomas Nuttall and Dr. Richard Harlan from the drier regions of the West, where it is more commonly found than on the southeastern coast.

1. John James Audubon, *Ornithological Biography*, vol. III (reprint of 1840–44 ed.; New York: Volair Books, 1979), p. 132.

2. Ibid., p. 133.

Roseate Spoonbill

AJAIA AJAJA (LINNAEUS)

Painted c. 1831–32 in Florida. Background probably by George Lehman.
Medium: watercolor, graphite, selective glazing, and gouache on paper; 23 1/8 × 35 11/16 in.; 58.7 × 90.6 cm.
Inscription (verso, revealed after backing removal, in graphite, right side, from edge down, top line trimmed away): to end of . . . / to end of
claws—36"—/ Alar extent—51"—/weight—3-lb 14 ozes./Florida Keyes May 23[d] 1832/J.J.A./drawn at London 1836
Identification: adult in breeding plumage
Seasonal distribution: breeds and winters along the Gulf coast south to Chile and Argentina
Havell plate number: CCCXXI in *The Birds of America*
Acc. no.: 1863.17.321

As the only spoonbill in the Western Hemisphere and the only pink spoonbill in the world, the roseate has always made a striking impression. During his trips to south Florida and Texas where the birds breed, Audubon watched flocks of spoonbills wheel in the sunlight, and he wrote exuberantly about the glowing color that their plumage produced. With its red eyes, its green head (which sometimes turns buff colored during courtship), its rosy and carmine wings, orange tail, and pink legs, the Roseate Spoonbill—the most sizeable North American member of the ibis family—is also the most brilliantly hued of all large North American waders.

Observations of spoonbills traveling from roosting to feeding areas enabled Audubon to describe their heronlike flight, with neck outstretched and trailing legs. Roseates are gregarious, and Audubon noted that they often associate with different species of herons. A later naturalist, coming upon a south Florida mangrove island whose trees were covered with Roseate Spoonbills together with white and blue herons, described the birds as "gems on a cushion of green velvet."[1]

Audubon shows the spoonbill's subtle colors and textures in careful detail: the feathered skin on the bird's bill, the bare skin on its head; even the round ear patch and the ear—an organ rarely visible except in the few species of birds with featherless heads—are both clearly apparent on the dark skin behind the eye. The spoonbill's wings, substantial for the size of the bird, are raised to reveal the burnished plumage of its tail.

Roseate Spoonbills breed in large, flat stick nests, mostly on mangroves and low bushes, and occasionally on the ground. The young spoonbills they produce are mainly white; it takes three years for them to acquire the adult plumage illustrated here, identical in male and female birds. The effect of that gorgeous plumage was not lost on the world of commerce. Milliners sent plume hunters into spoonbill rookeries to slaughter the birds for their wing and tail feathers, which were made into fans for the tourist trade in St. Augustine. By 1920 the species was all but extinct in the United States and survived only because the Audubon Society sent wardens to protect it. Some spoonbills that flew north across the Mexican border were then able to breed in a newly safe environment.

Audubon's spoonbill is about to wade into the water to search for the little fish, crustaceans, mollusks, and aquatic insects whose habitat it shares. Small flocks of Roseate Spoonbills hunt together in shallow salt and brackish water as well as fresh. The birds feed by moving their bills under the water from side to side in wide arcs, sometimes immersing the entire head. Nerve endings on the bill and tongue sense the presence of living prey and signal the bill to snap shut, trapping the food.

The swamp here was most likely sketched by George Lehman for Robert Havell to develop in his engraving.

1. Arthur Cleveland Bent, *Life Histories of North American Marsh Birds* (New York: Dover Publications, 1963), p. 14.

Probably painted in the Florida Keys in April or May 1832.

Medium: watercolor, pastel, graphite, gouache, and selective glazing on paper; 37½ × 26 1/16 in.; 95.4 × 66.3 cm.

Inscription (lower left): No 51 *(lower center):* BROWN PELICAN male, adult./PELECANUS FUSCUS *(lower right):* Pl. 251

(graphite, faint, lower left): No 51–251

Identification: adult male

Seasonal distribution: breeds and winters on southern Atlantic and southern Pacific and Gulf coasts, south to South America

Flora: mangrove, *Rhizophora mangle,* painted by George Lehman

Havell plate number: CCLI in *The Birds of America*

Acc. no. 1863.17.251

The Brown Pelican has the biggest bill pouch of any bird in the world. Audubon, who considered the species "one of the most interesting of our American birds,"[1] commented on the pelican's use of this pouch in feeding and remarked that—popular myth to the contrary—Brown Pelicans do not use their pouches to store fish or water or to bring these to their young. He observed the species performing twisting dives into the water from as high as fifty feet in the air (sometimes plunging entirely beneath the surface), scooping up fish, and immediately resurfacing. As Audubon reported, the birds then forced any accumulated water out of the bill and immediately swallowed the fish—if their catch was not stolen by one of the gulls that perch on pelicans to relieve them of their meal while the pelicans reposition it for swallowing. Later, if the pelicans fed young, they disgorged the fish in various stages of predigestion, depending on the age of their chicks.

Audubon depicted the "superb male whose portrait is before you and which was selected from among a great number"[2] sitting in a mangrove tree typical of the coastal Florida habitats frequented by the species. Brown Pelicans nest in bushes and low trees or on the ground on small islands or near shallow bays. In such vulnerable habitat, their colonies are often devastated by storms and floods. Their young are also subject to being eaten by gulls and other predators. But most destructive to their population have been the pesticides DDT and dieldrin.

Brown Pelicans eat saltwater fish almost exclusively—about four pounds a day. In the 1950s and 1960s, these pesticides found their way into coastal waters in enormous quantities and accumulated in the fish eaten by the pelicans. The resulting concentration of pesticides in the female pelicans' bodies caused them to lay eggs with shells so thin that they broke during incubation. In Louisiana, where the Brown Pelican is the state bird, the population of fifty thousand was completely wiped out in the early 1960s. Even today, the numbers of this species—the smallest member of the pelican family but, nonetheless, with a wingspread of about seven feet, one of the largest of living birds—are still diminished, although recovering.

Audubon commented on "how dexterously [Brown Pelicans] wield that great bill of theirs, as they trim their plumage," and gave a vivid description of the different textures he noticed, including the "stiff, hair-like and glossy" feathers on the front of the head and the "soft and downy" feathers on the hind neck. His image differentiates these distinctive features admirably: the sleek, smooth, white head feathers washed with yellow; the tiny fluffy feathers of the chestnut neck (which turn white in the postbreeding molt); and the larger, stiffer, silvery-brown back and wing feathers. Audubon ingeniously portrays those varied textures, as well as the contrasting surfaces of the bird's leathery, dark pouch and webbed feet, and its versatile, hard, smooth bill.

1. John James Audubon, *Ornithological Biography,* vol. II (reprint of 1840–44 ed.; New York: Volair Books, 1979), p. 32.

2. Ibid., p. 36. Audubon depicted an immature Brown Pelican in plate CCCCXXI.

BROWN PELICAN *Male, adult.*

No 51.

PELECANUS FUSCUS

Pl'e 251.

White-crowned Pigeon

COLUMBA LEUCOCEPHALA LINNAEUS

Audubon's nomenclature: White Headed Pigeon, *Columba leucocephala* Linnaeus; White-crowned Pigeon, *Columba leucocephala* Linnaeus

Painted at Indian Key, Florida, in April 1832.

Medium: watercolor, graphite, gouache, pastel(?), collage, selective glazing on paper; 29-3/16 × 21 in.; 74.2 × 53.4 cm.

Inscription (upper right corner, in graphite): 87

Identification: adults

Seasonal distribution: breeds and winters on southern tip of Florida

Flora: geiger tree, *Cordia sebestena*, painted by George Lehman

Havell plate number: CLXXVII in *The Birds of America*

Acc. no.: 1863.17.177

When the cargo ship *Delos* was sailing near Cuba on June 17, 1826, Audubon—who was making his first trip to England aboard the vessel—observed three White-crowned Pigeons circle the boat and head toward Florida. (The species breeds both in Cuba and in Florida, and some birds, as Audubon later wrote, commute between the two.) But although he described the incident in his journal, it was not until six years later that Audubon painted the white-crown.

Shortly after returning from a second voyage to England in September 1831, Audubon, together with his assistant George Lehman and his taxidermist Henry Ward, embarked on a trip to Florida and the Keys. They spent the winter in Charleston, South Carolina, where Audubon met the Rev. John Bachman, with whom he would remain friends for the rest of his life. In the latter half of April, after sailing on the *Spark* up Florida's St. John's River, they arrived in Key West aboard the cutter *Marion*.

Audubon described the White-crowned Pigeons that he observed in the Keys as being "at all times extremely shy and wary, more so in fact than any species with which I am acquainted. The sight of a man is to them insupportable, perhaps on account of the continued war waged against them, their flesh being juicy, well flavoured, and generally tender, even in old birds."[1] Indeed, droves of these gregarious, arboreal pigeons were slaughtered by hunters, especially near their breeding grounds, where they nest in large colonies, often in open sites in shrubs, trees, or cacti. Audubon noted that for protection the pigeons walk quietly through dense tree branches and then take flight silently to escape notice. They fly swiftly, and are indeed most often observed on the wing, frequently traveling between their coastal, woodland, or scrub nesting sites and the inland trees whose fruits, especially the pigeon plum and sea grape, together with seeds and some insects, provide the bulk of their diet.

Audubon chose not to show the large, dark pigeons in their characteristic unrestrained flight, but perched in similar—although deliberately asymmetrical—poses. Their wings are outstretched above their square tails for balance, and their bright white crowns are inclined toward each other as the female inserts her closed red-and-yellow bill into the male's open one, and the birds bob their heads up and down in the common courtship display called billing. White-crowns generally appear all dark to the observer; Audubon, however, has depicted their blue-green iridescence, visible only in excellent light. He has put them in a setting that is appropriate both ecologically and artistically: "I have placed a pair of these Pigeons on a low, flowering tree, which is rather scarce in the Keys. It is in full bloom during the whole year, and its leaves, I thought, correspond with the colour of the birds, while the brilliant hue of its flowers forms a strong contrast."[2]

1. John James Audubon, *Ornithological Biography*, vol. IV (reprint of 1840–44 ed.; New York: Volair Books, 1979), p. 316.

2. Ibid., p. 319.

Magnificent Frigatebird

FREGATA MAGNIFICENS MATHEWS

Audubon's nomenclature: Frigate Pelican, *Tachypetes aquilus*

Painted in the spring of 1832 in the Florida Keys.

Medium: watercolor, and graphite on paper; 38⅛ × 25⅛ in.; 97 × 64 cm.

Inscription (lower right): foot above *(lower right, closer to edge):* foot beneath

Identification: adult male

Seasonal distribution: breeds from Florida Keys and Gulf of Mexico south; seen occasionally throughout the year on Atlantic and Gulf coasts

Havell plate number: CCLXXI in *The Birds of America*

Acc. no.: 1863.17.271

This stunning asymmetrical image, whose sharp, angular, abstract form dynamically approaches the edges of the paper on three sides, conveys with great eloquence the combination of rapaciousness, speed, grace, and buoyancy that gives the Magnificent Frigatebird its name. A frigate was a fast, light sailing vessel, effective in war because of its maneuverability; its avian namesake, with the lightest skeleton in proportion to wing expanse of any living bird, itself seems to sail effortlessly, periodically descending through the air in dramatic dives to seize prey, often rapidly plundering the food, eggs, or young of other birds. With its long, slender hooked bill (shown open here to emphasize its owner's marauding habits) the frigatebird grabs other flying seabirds such as boobies or pelicans by the tail or wing, harassing them until they disgorge their new catch. Frigatebirds also fly down from great heights to seize the intended victims of predatory fish when the birds' keen eyesight detects feeding schools forcing their smaller prey to attempt escape above the surface of the water. The frigatebird has a narrow, deeply forked tail whose outermost feathers are longest to provide optimum aerodynamic flexibility. The bird is able to compress this tail into a point, and use it with its highly maneuverable, long, narrow angled wings that can expand to a length of almost eight feet while gliding on air currents or that can fold and turn down for swooping, as Audubon illustrates here. The

frigatebird's anatomy provides it with some of the finest aerial skills of any bird. From a slow glide it can instantaneously tilt to one side and plunge toward the water to grab fish attempting to elude piscine pursuers or swoop down to pluck jellyfish or squid from the surface of the sea; the bird controls its flight so precisely that it is able to stop just over the object and seize it without wetting its feathers or causing more than the slightest ripple on the water. Since the frigatebird's feathers are not waterproof, this skill is essential to its survival, and it rarely swims or even alights on the ocean. Frigatebirds are such accomplished gliders and weigh so little for their size (averaging only two and one half pounds, with an exceedingly strong, light, elastic skeleton), that they can sail for long periods without moving their wings, attaining speeds of up to twenty-two miles an hour even in totally calm air. Their aerial abilities also enable them to soar during raging storms, often flying above the clouds. The frigatebird's feet, on the other hand, are extremely weak—almost useless for any activity but perching. Those of a subadult bird that Audubon shows here apparently impressed him because of their unusual colors, and he relieved the starkness (but underscored the angularity) of his composition by including them. Curiously, he did not illustrate the distended throat pouch that turns from pale orange to bright red in breeding season when males inflate it like a balloon.

Crested Caracara

POLYBORUS PLANCUS (MILLER)

Audubon's nomenclature: Brazilian Caracara Eagle, *Polyborus vulgaris*

Painted near St. Augustine, Florida, on November 27, 1831.

Medium: watercolor, pastel, and graphite on paper; 38 ¼ × 24 ¹⁵⁄₁₆ in.; 97.1 × 63.4 cm.

Inscription (upper right, in graphite): 61

Identification: adults

Seasonal distribution: breeds and winters locally in Florida, parts of the Gulf coast, and the southwestern United States

Havell plate number: CLXI in *The Birds of America*

Acc. no.: 1863.17.161

Audubon finished this masterful picture in twenty-four hours, a stunning accomplishment given that he was completely unacquainted with the Crested Caracara[1] until the 1831 trip to Florida during which he painted it. His capacity to work rapidly was most important here because, even within the short period required to make this picture, the colors of his specimen had faded so as to become almost unrecognizable. Audubon worked quickly enough, however, to capture admirably the dramatic contrasts in the birds' rich plumage with its subtle shadings of brown-black, dark gray, buff, and white. He differentiated minutely between textures as well, emphasizing in the perched bird (which may be male or female—the plumage is identical) the smooth red skin covering its upper bill; the finely wrinkled skin on its lower face; the more coarsely textured feathers of the crest (which the species can raise at will) and the buff feathers covering the upper breast; and the appearance of the scaly feet against the rough tree bark. The bird's posture of self-defense, with head thrown back and open bill, also recalls the strange position the species assumes when emitting the raucous cry from which it takes its name.

In depicting the bird flying with its neck typically outstretched (and its four-foot-wide wings compressed), the artist clearly took delight in scrupulously reproducing the pattern of the fine barring on the tail and the primaries of the right wing, areas that appear translucent when the bird is in the air. In an especially subtle passage Audubon shows the contrast of the creamy white upper tail coverts with the dark rump feathers that lie above them and the delicately barred brown-and-white tail feathers beneath them.

As Audubon's depiction plainly shows, Crested Caracaras are strong birds, typically quarrelsome among themselves. They also exhibit aggressive behavior toward larger species such as Bald Eagles and Brown Pelicans, sometimes attacking them in midair and forcing them to relinquish their prey. While feeding on the carrion that is a staple of their diet they often fend off vultures from a carcass until they have eaten their fill. When hunting they may rapaciously attack large snakes, jackrabbits, and even young lambs, but they are primarily scavengers, highly effective in removing recently dead animals from open country and highways.

Caracaras generally are found in pairs. While they sometimes wheel in the air like vultures, they spend much time either flying low over the ground or walking or running on their long legs, looking for food. The caracara reaches the northernmost limits of its range in Florida, Texas, and Arizona. The birds mate early and, in Florida, often produce eggs by December. Considerably more numerous south of the border the species has been designated the national bird of Mexico; but in Florida its numbers are quickly diminishing, and today Crested Caracaras breed there only in scattered locations.

1. In 1865 this bird was named Audubon's Caracara by John Cassin (1813–69), a Philadelphia businessman and ornithologist who became curator of birds at the Philadelphia Academy of Natural Sciences. Recently, however, it has come to be considered a subspecies, and the name was changed to reflect its new taxonomic status.

Barn Swallow

HIRUNDO RUSTICA LINNAEUS

Audubon's nomenclature: Barn Swallow, *Hirundo americana*

Probably painted in New Jersey in June 1832.

Medium: watercolor, graphite, gouache, and traces of black pastel/chalk on paper; 21 × 13 11/16 in.; 53.4 × 34.8 cm.

Inscription (upper right corner, in graphite): 73

Identification: adults

Seasonal distribution: breeds across much of North America, winters in South America as far south as Argentina

Havell plate number: CLXXIII in *The Birds of America*

Acc. no. 1863.17.173

In this image of one of North America's most beloved birds Audubon recalls the Barn Swallows' mutually attentive relationship, their adaptation to the human environment, and their cooperation in nesting. The artist suggests with his spare and elegantly fluid forms the agile, swooping flight for which swallows are so well known and to which he skillfully alludes even though the birds are perched. His picture is full of curving and sweeping lines; the undulating form created by the combined silhouette of the two birds, which the viewer's eye follows from lower left to upper right, duplicates the pattern of a swallow in flight; and the tapering wings and elongated tails of each bird, which enable them to fly so admirably, are set off against the plain background and provide much of the composition's visual impact.

While the Barn Swallows fly, they drink, bathe, and, above all, feed, dramatically reducing the surrounding area's insect population, particularly that of house flies and their relatives. Over fields, marshes, and ponds the birds swoop low, consuming quantities of flying insects stirred up by the movement of people, animals, or farm machinery.

Arriving on the breeding grounds together, male and female Barn Swallows, essentially indistinguishable in plumage, soon pair and begin courtship, perching near each other and rubbing heads and necks together as Audubon suggests in this scene. Nest building quickly follows. Originally, Barn Swallows nested on cave and cliff walls, but man-made structures of rough board or other materials with uneven surfaces to which they could equally firmly affix their nests provided better protection. Since Colonial times, Barn Swallows have been familiar around country buildings. With a shorthand notation, Audubon evocatively incorporated a wood plank in his composition, focusing attention both on the birds and on a characteristic location of their nest.

Both male and female swallows participate in repairing a previous year's nest (which they may do for several years in succession) or building a new one—a layered structure that they create with mud pellets, adding grasses for stability. Having found a mud source, the swallows make repeated trips to it from their nesting site, sometimes as much as half a mile away, gathering bits of mud that they attach to the horizontal or vertical surface of the building, bridge, or culvert chosen to support the nest. They may spend as much as two weeks completing the structure, working continuously, sometimes for fourteen hours a day. Both adults incubate the eggs, frequently exchanging places. At night, when the female stays on the nest, the male may perch near her. Audubon has rendered to great effect the nest's size, shape, and texture, contrasting these features to those of the man-made board on which it is constructed and of the delicate birds whose efforts created it.

Townsend's Bunting

EMBERIZA TOWNSENDI AUDUBON

Audubon's nomenclature: Townsend's Finch, *Fringilla townsendi*

Medium: watercolor, pastel, graphite, collage, gouache, and selective glazing on paper; 20 1/16 × 13 5/8 in.; 51 × 35.3 cm.

Inscription (lower right, in faint graphite): the crops of Bird/not to be noticed/in the Engraving *(lower left, in graphite):* No 73 (The 3 is over a 4)

(lower center, in graphite): Plate 369 *(crossed out)* 365./Townsends Finch *(partially trimmed off at bottom) (lower right):* Rosa Laevigata

Flora: rose, *Rosa laevigata*

Havell plate number: CCCC in *The Birds of America*

Acc. no. 1863.18.013

Species such as the Carbonated Warbler, the Blue Mountain Warbler, the Cuvier's Kinglet, and the Small-headed Flycatcher are not familiar to the average bird student, even though each is a species that Audubon painted from an existing specimen and included in *The Birds of America.* These species, like the Townsend's Bunting here, are mystery birds that ornithologists to this day have not been able to identify. Their presence in Audubon's work is a testament to the kinds of challenges that the artist-naturalist faced in his pioneering attempt to study and codify hundreds of American birds without access to major collections of books, bird skins, or photographs. Audubon wrote that he made the pictures of the Carbonated Warbler, the Cuvier's Kinglet, and the Small-headed Flycatcher from birds that he himself had shot[1]—species that he never saw subsequently and of which his specimens have since been lost. The Blue Mountain Warbler was described by Wilson, and Audubon depicted it from a skin in London's Zoological Society. For the Townsend's Bunting, a specimen source that should be equally unimpeachable exists: that of John Kirk Townsend, a distinguished young Quaker ornithologist and pharmacist from Philadelphia. In 1833, the year before Townsend set out on the famous Wyeth expedition to the Columbia River basin in the Pacific Northwest with the British immigrant botanist and ornithologist Thomas Nuttall, he shot a bird in Chester County, Pennsylvania, on May 11. The specimen of that bird is now in the collection of the Smithsonian Institution in Washington, D.C., with a label identifying it as a Townsend's Bunting, named by Audubon himself for the man who collected it. Audubon never sighted another bird like this one, nor has any ornithologist since positively identified the species. Much speculation exists about its possible relationship to a Dickcissel or a Blue Grosbeak, both members of the same family that might conceivably hybridize with one another, but scientists have had difficulty accounting for the anomalies of the bird's appearance even under those circumstances, unlike the case of Audubon's Bemaculated Duck, which Audubon and, later, other ornithologists ultimately recognized as the hybrid of a Mallard and a Gadwall.

Audubon had to have made this picture from the unique specimen that Townsend procured, speculating on how the bird would have appeared in life. He drew the specimen from three different angles to show views from both sides and back. He cut out the top and bottom birds from separate sheets of paper and pasted them down on this sheet that contains a wild rose and a butterfly painted by Maria Martin. Only the top bird in this picture appears in *The Birds of America*, in a slightly altered position, together with four other species, two of which are also the subjects of controversy because the locations in which Audubon describes having found them are out of the species' normal ranges.

1. Both Alexander Wilson and Audubon claim to be the original describers of the flycatcher.

Plate 369. 1865

Rosa Laevigata

Bachman's Warbler

VERMIVORA BACHMANII (AUDUBON)

Painted in the fall of 1833.

Medium: watercolor, graphite, and gouache on paper; 21½ × 14 1/16 in.; 54.6 × 35.7 cm.

Inscription (lower right—Maria Martin's handwriting?): Gordonia Pubescens *(upper right corner, in graphite):* 85

Identification: male above, female below

Seasonal distribution: on the verge of extinction; once bred throughout the southeastern United States; winters on Cuba and Isle of Pines

Flora: franklinia, *Franklinia alatamaha,* painted by Maria Martin. The plant was discovered in the South in 1765 by the distinguished botanists William and John Bartram, who named it in honor of Benjamin Franklin and took slips of it home to cultivate. It was restricted to a very small area in the vicinity of the Altamaha River in Georgia, and has not been found in the wild since 1790.

Havell plate number: CLXXXV in *The Birds of America*

Acc. no. 1863.17.185

Today, less than 160 years after its discovery, and less than 100 years after the identification of its nest, the Bachman's Warbler is close to extinction. It was a victim first of the millinery trade (a specimen now in the American Museum of Natural History had originally been prepared for decorating a lady's hat) and then of the draining and cutting of the low, wet forests in the southeast where the birds bred. The species was found in 1833 by Audubon's close friend John Bachman, the Lutheran pastor and scientist, who collected the first individuals and in whose honor Audubon named the bird. By the 1940s the warbler was already considered the rarest songbird in North America. The last published sighting was that of a male, in 1975.

Even when more numerous, the Bachman's Warbler was not easy to observe. In the spring it migrated from its wintering grounds on Cuba and the Isle of Pines through local parts of the southern United States, and took up residence among the dense bushes, cane stands, and blackberry and grape vines of heavily timbered southeastern river bottoms. It bred in these swampy woods, apparently near the ground, mostly in small colonies. Shy and difficult to approach, the warbler must have been easily overlooked as it moved through the brush or, when flushed, flew close to the ground for long distances, often amid impenetrable tangles. Audubon never saw the bird in life and painted it only from specimens that Bachman sent him. Bachman himself never saw the bird's nest, which was not found until sixty-four years after he had first discovered the species.

The friendship that brought about the naming of this bird (and two others that Audubon named for Bachman) was a particularly close, productive one. It began in the autumn of 1831 when Audubon, who had already published the first volume of his *Ornithological Biography,* was in Charleston, South Carolina, on his way to Florida. He was invited to stay with the Rev. Bachman, who later described the period as "one of the happiest months of my life"[1] and Audubon as "communicative, intelligent, and amiable to an extent seldom found associated in the same individual."[2] The two men remained friends and colleagues for life. Bachman collected and studied southern species for Audubon and collaborated with him on *The Viviparous Quadrupeds of North America.* Audubon's two sons married Bachman's daughters, and Bachman's sister-in-law (and second wife), Maria Martin, painted the backgrounds for about twenty of Audubon's birds.

Compared to Maria Martin's lush franklinia bush onto which Audubon painted the Bachman's Warblers here, the birds are relatively stiff and formulaic. Their field marks are apparent—the most important being the yellow face and black crown and bib of the male and the dusky crown and bib of the female—but their poses lack individuality and betray the fact that Audubon had never observed this particular species' behavior. It is poignant to think that we will probably never have a chance to do so either.

1. Quoted in John P. S. MacKenzie, *Birds in Peril* (Boston: Houghton Mifflin, 1977), p. 154.

2. Ibid.

Gordonia Pubescens

Painted in early 1833.

Medium: watercolor, pastel, graphite, and selective glazing on paper; 38 × 25½ in. 96.6 × 64.7 cm.

Inscription (bottom center, in black ink over watercolor): Aquila Chrysaetos Sen r/ Golden Eagle Female Adult/ . . . J. A.

Identification: adult female

Seasonal distribution: breeds across northern and western North America, winters widely across the United States

Havell plate number: CLXXXI in *The Birds of America*

Acc. no. 1863.17.181

A diminutive figure in buckskins and hunting cap makes his laborious way over a tree-trunk bridge that spans a treacherous precipice. This figure, depicted in the lower left of Audubon's Golden Eagle painting, has long been considered a self-portrait.[1] The hunter seems to have slung across his back not only his gun but the body of a (presumably recently shot) Golden Eagle that he has procured from the nearby cliffs at the risk of much evident personal danger. Interestingly, while we know that these were not the circumstances under which Audubon obtained the Golden Eagle depicted here, we also know that the artist's creation of this image was a great ordeal for him.

Audubon writes that he worked with such intensity and for so long on this picture of the Golden Eagle—a task that he variously describes as having taken sixty hours or two weeks, longer than any other bird picture except the Wild Turkey (the very first image in *The Birds of America*)—that he nearly paid for his efforts with his life. He had bought a live adult Golden Eagle in Boston in February of 1833, agonized about whether to liberate it or kill it, and, having finally taken its life after several attempts to do so without harming the glorious bird's appearance, worked on its image in such a frenzy that he became ill and had to be attended by three physicians.

Why Audubon experienced such a crisis with this picture is open to speculation, but the reasons may be connected to the fact that he seems to have felt a kinship with this "king of birds"[2] in a particularly powerful way. By juxtaposing an image of the eagle's hard-won but triumphant seizure of the rabbit—the source of the bird's sustenance and that of its progeny—with a depiction of his own struggle to capture the eagle physically (and, by extension, to capture it on the page)—the artist may be referring to the difficulties he underwent to create this picture. In a larger sense, the image may be emblematic of Audubon's desire to satisfy through his art his hunger—and that of his public—for knowledge and achievement. It is intriguing to discover from his account in the *Ornithological Biography* that Audubon was afflicted with a type of seizure in the course of making this picture. Did he wonder, at the time, whether some higher force was seizing him, as he had seized the eagle, and the eagle had the rabbit?

Audubon does not depict his Golden Eagle in the midst of a stately and effortless glide. Rather, the bird strains with all its power to carry off its prey, its body tense with the dead weight of the rabbit, its neck muscles taut, its wings working strenuously to provide sufficient lift. The picture is an image of struggle in ascent, struggle to attain a goal that, for eagle and artist, will have to be gained time and time again.[3]

1. See the compelling analysis in Mary Durant and Michael Harwood, *On the Road with John James Audubon* (New York: Dodd, Mead, 1980), pp. 413–14.

2. John James Audubon, *Ornithological Biography*, vol. I (reprint of 1840–44 ed.; New York: Volair Books, 1979), p. 50.

3. Mysteriously, the figure hitching himself across the log is absent from Robert Havell's engraving of the Golden Eagle, and the anecdote about Audubon's illness does not appear in the octavo edition of the *Ornithological Biography*.

Aquila Chrysaëtos
Golden Eagle

Painted in Labrador in June 1833.
Medium: watercolor, graphite, and selective glazing on paper; 29 5/16 × 21 3/8 in.; 74.5 × 54.3 cm.
Inscription (graphite, left side of rock, over watercolor): . . . ? . . . tundra *(lower right edge, previously erased graphite):* Dilo . . . b . . .
Identification: adult
Seasonal distribution: breeds widely throughout North America, winters along Atlantic, Pacific, and Gulf coasts.
Havell plate number: CCLVII in *The Birds of America*
Acc. no. 1863.17.257

Audubon's expressive and dignified portrait of the Double-crested Cormorant, with its clean lines and uncluttered background, provides a detailed image of this singular bird. Understandably, however, the artist gave no hint here of the atmosphere that he found pervading a colony of such cormorants that he visited off Labrador:

> The noise produced by the multitudes on the island was not merely disagreeable, but really shocking . . . the whole surface of the rock resembled a mass of putridity: feathers, broken and rotten eggs, and dead young, lay scattered over it; and I leave you to guess how such a place must smell in a calm warm day.[1]

In such colonies, in spring, male Double-crested Cormorants place the foundations of their nests directly on the rock ledges or ground, or on trees or bushes near the water. The males then continue to supply nesting materials to the females, who finish the nest building. In the first season the pair produces a relatively insubstantial nest, to which, however, the male continues to add throughout the season. The two birds then sometimes use it for several years more. Cormorants are known for the distinctiveness of the nesting materials that they employ: seaweed, for which they dive, and which is pliable when wet but hardens when dry to become an effective cementing material, sticks, moss, earth, feathers, evergreen twigs, and even trash that the birds collect from the water's edge. In one instance, cormorants nesting near a sunken ship included in their nests pocket knives, tobacco pipes, hairpins, and hair combs from the wreckage.

The double crest for which this cormorant is named, and which Audubon depicts with such delicacy, is rarely seen. It consists of two tufts of soft, curved feathers less than two inches long—one behind each eye—which grow only during nesting season and are shed after a matter of weeks. More conspicuous are the adult's bright yellow-orange throat patch and its long, curved bill, which the cormorant uses when fighting and defending territory as well as for capturing fish, shrimp, salamanders, and reptiles, and sometimes mollusks and sea worms. Their fish-eating habits have given cormorants the reputation of threatening the commercial and sport fishing industries. In fact, studies have shown that the fish they consume are generally not of value to people and often actually compete with those that are. Moreover, the nitrogen- and phosphorus-rich droppings that the cormorants produce encourage luxuriant growth of the algae on which the fish depend. Thus, cormorant colonies probably actually help to produce more fish than they consume—in the case of the double-crest, in fresh water as well as salt.

These visually striking, greenish-black birds, whose short, stout webbed feet are placed far to the rear to aid the species in diving, often strike a pose that makes a memorable impression on observers: because their feathers lack complete waterproofing and get soaked when the birds dive for food, cormorants frequently sit with wings stretched out on either side to dry, producing an odd, antediluvian appearance.

1. John James Audubon, *Ornithological Biography,* vol. VI (reprint of 1840–44 ed.; New York: Volair Books, 1979), pp. 424–25. Audubon first depicted the Double-crested Cormorant during his Mississippi River trip of 1820–21, and painted a subspecies, the Florida Cormorant, on April 26, 1832.

Audubon's nomenclature: Puffin, *Mormon arcticus*

Painted in Labrador in 1833.

Medium: watercolor, graphite, gouache, selective glazing, and traces of pastel on paper;
14½ × 21⅜ in.; 36.8 × 54.3 cm.

Identification: two adults in breeding plumage

Seasonal distribution: breeds along northern Atlantic coast, winters offshore

Havell plate number: CCXIII in *The Birds of America*

Acc. no. 1863.17.213

Audubon rarely depicted birds frontally as he did the Atlantic Puffin on the left, and generally, when he did show birds from that angle, they were owls, whose eyes, like those of humans, are both located in the front plane of the face. But he was intent on illustrating where and how puffins nest—a notable aspect of their behavior—and for that purpose, a full-face view is effective both narratively and artistically.

As Audubon suggests in the background of his picture, great rafts of puffins congregate in breeding season on the sea beneath their rocky, coastal nesting grounds. Males fight and pairs court, billing with the impressive beaks that they will partly shed in the fall. The scene Audubon portrays here he doubtless saw repeatedly on June 28 and August 12, 1833, during his trip to Labrador, when his party visited two islands known for their puffin colonies. Audubon writes that the first island was "pleasant to the eye, on account of the thick growth of green grass with which it was covered."[1] He describes the "abundance of Puffins"[2] there: "some . . . flew past us with the speed of an arrow, others stood erect at the entrance of their burrows, while some . . . withdrew within their holes."[3]

Puffins nest in large groups; pairs build burrows several feet long in the loose soil of turf-covered slopes or the tops of cliffs, as well as on islands, often concealing the entrance under a flat rock. The male does most of the digging, using his bill to break up the earth and his feet and sharp claws (clearly visible in the bird on the right) to excavate and scatter it. The puffin uses grass, seaweed, and feathers to line the back of its burrow, and there the female usually lays a single egg. She does most of the incubating, tucking the egg under a wing and leaning over it to keep it warm. Because the egg is well hidden, the parents, who remain together through the season, may spend a few hours a day outside the burrow, as the male does here. Sometimes they strut erectly up and down, which, unlike other members of their

family, they do with considerable ease. They maneuver with even greater facility in the air or water, flying quickly and low over the sea, "diving with the swiftness of thought,"[4] and swimming underwater with their wings.

In the bird at the right, Audubon depicts the bold accents of bill, eye plates, and feet framing and punctuating the bird's stark black-and-white plumage. In the bird at the left he juxtaposes thin stripes of those primary colors with alternating bands of black and white in a compelling abstract pattern.

Puffins are curious and trusting by nature, and their populations near inhabited areas have been decimated by hunters as well as by predators such as dogs, cats, rats, foxes, and Great Black-backed Gulls. Audubon himself commented on the diminishing size of some of the puffin breeding colonies.

1. John James Audubon, *Ornithological Biography*, vol. VII (reprint of 1840–44 ed.; New York: Volair Books, 1979), p. 238.
2. Ibid., p. 239.
3. Ibid.
4. Ibid., p. 238.

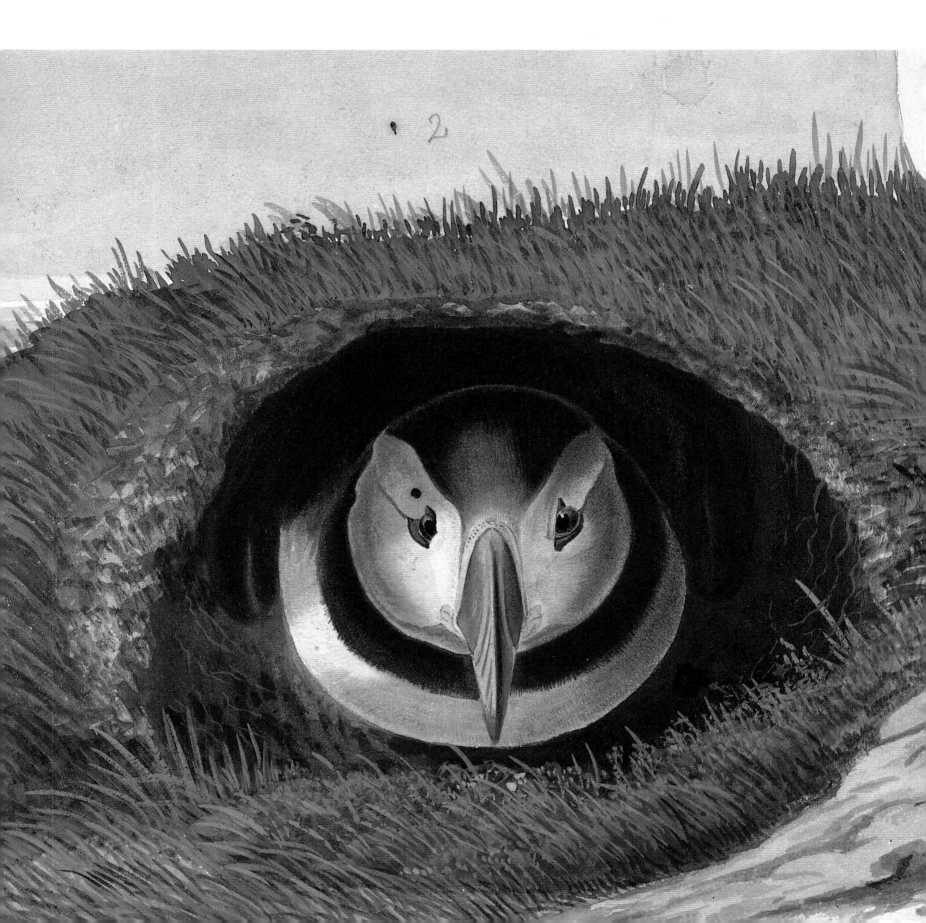

Northern Gannet

SULA BASSANUS (LINNAEUS)

Audubon's nomenclature: Gannet, *Sula bassanus*
Painted on June 22 and 23, 1833, off Gannet Rock in the Gulf of St. Lawrence.
Medium: watercolor, pastel, graphite, gouache, collage, selective glazing, and selective scraping on paper; 24¾ × 37⅝ in.; 62.8 × 95.6 cm.
Inscription (lower center, in graphite): No 66—326 (6) *(crossed out "6")* (lower right, in graphite): No 65 *(lower center, in graphite):* Gannet
Identification: immature in front, adult behind
Seasonal distribution: breeds along northeast Atlantic coast and in northern Europe, winters off Atlantic and Gulf coasts
Havell plate number: CCCXXVI in *The Birds of America*
Acc. no. 1863.17.326

"No man who has not seen what we have this day can form the least idea of the impression the site made on our minds."[1] It was June 14, 1833. The boat carrying Audubon and his party arrived at the Canadian "Bird Rocks" in the Gulf of St. Lawrence, where the passengers witnessed more than 100,000 Northern Gannets, some nesting and others filling the air with a blizzard of white bodies. Gannets are coastal marine birds, seldom seen either inland or farther than three hundred miles out at sea. Audubon had previously observed some wintering in the Gulf of Mexico, but mostly immature birds and only in small numbers. Here, at one of the few sites in the western Atlantic where the birds breed, he beheld hordes of them on the three-hundred-foot-high rock, nesting no farther apart than a beak's length. Legions flew gracefully overhead on updrafts or low close to the ocean with stiff, rapid wingbeats, bills pointing down. Huge flocks dove into the sea from a height of about one hundred feet for capelins and other fish, plummeting at sixty miles an hour, submerging themselves completely, and producing fifteen-foot-high spray. In their carefully controlled dives, gannets hit the water like lances. The birds' large pointed bills break the surface first, their nostrils closed to prevent filling with water. The blow is cushioned by air sacs under the birds' skin and by a specially reinforced skull; their plumage is waterproof for protection.

Audubon knew that fishermen often climbed the rock to slaughter the tame birds for cod bait, but stormy weather pre-vented his boat from coming ashore. He was, however, able to watch the inaccessible colony from close by, to hear the din that arose from the island, and to smell the rank odor. He noted that the birds (which mate for life, reinforcing their bond with complex breeding rituals) compete fiercely for their small nest sites and defend them aggressively with their bills. To prevent landing at another bird's nest and being attacked, gannets learn to recognize each others' individual landing calls. The birds hollow their nests out of the earth and surround them with seaweed—sometimes procured from islands many miles away—that dries as it hardens and strengthens the nest, which the gannets renovate annually. Sexes appear identical, and both male and female incubate, wrapping their fully webbed feet around the (usually single) egg for warmth. Parents feed the young until they are fully grown. The chicks are black and naked upon hatching but "become gradually downy and white and . . . look like great lumps of carded wool."[2] Soon they acquire the dark grayish-brown plumage with small white spots that the immature here exhibits. It takes several years for the young to acquire the blue-gray bill, buff-colored head, white plumage, and black upper wing tips of the adults; during that time they remain at sea all year. In spite of cold, wet weather and seasickness, Audubon finished painting these two birds in a single day—June 22—and painted the background on the following day.

1. Howard Corning, ed., *Journal of John James Audubon Made During His Trip to New Orleans, 1820–21* (Boston: The Club of Odd Volumes, 1929), p. 362.

2. John James Audubon, *Ornithological Biography*, vol. III (reprint of 1840–44 ed.; New York: Volair Books, 1979), p. 46.

Gannet

Audubon's nomenclature: Common Cormorant, *Phalacrocorax carbo* Dumont

Female and young at left painted in Labrador in July 1833; male added later, perhaps in March 1834.

Medium: watercolor, graphite, gouache, and selective glazing on paper; 25½ × 38½ in.; 64.9 × 97.8 cm.

Inscription (lower right, in faint graphite): The young when . . ./grown exhibit the/Nostril quite open/Common Cormorant . . ./corax carbo.

Du . . ./. . . 54/. . . *(indecipherable) (upper right, in graphite):* The young when half grown/exhibit the nostrils quite open—

Identification: adult female and young at left, adult male in breeding plumage at right

Seasonal distribution: principally a European species but found generally throughout the Northern Hemisphere; in North America, breeds only along the North Atlantic coast; winters south of breeding range

Havell plate number: CCLXVI in *The Birds of America*

Acc. no. 1863.17.266

Newly hatched cormorants, like the two seen here begging for food, resemble "little, animated, greasy rubber bags,"[1] in the eyes of one ornithologist. Audubon himself remarked on their "uncouth appearance, their legs and feet seeming enormous"[2] and took pains in this picture to show his viewers what he meant. Powerful legs and large, webbed feet enable cormorants to swim efficiently both on the surface of the water and underneath it in pursuit of fish; indeed, young cormorants learn to swim before they learn to fly, so rapid development of the legs and feet is essential.

The chicks are entirely dependent on their parents for several weeks before they can leave the nest. They are naked at birth and do not open their eyes until four or five days after hatching. Not until about a week after birth do they begin to develop a covering of downy feathers. Throughout this period they are attended by the adults, both of whom have participated in their incubation and feeding, even bringing water on hot days to spill over them in a stream and to pour into their open bills. The young feed initially on regurgitated food: the parents disgorge it into their mouths or the chicks thrust their bills inside the parents' to obtain the partially digested fish. Audubon noted that the young "ate . . . certainly more than their own weight each day, and appeared always ready to receive more."[3] Once having left the nest, the young begin by walking, looking awkward on the ground as they hop from stone to stone; after learning to fly, however, they move impressively through the sky, joining together in distinctively long strings of V-formations. Cormorants often fly close to the surface of the water, touching it with the tips of their wings at each downward beat.

When young Great Cormorants molt into adult breeding plumage, they acquire the white face and flank patches and the fine white head feathers that cause them, when standing in their colonies, to "look like a crowd of black dominoes,"[4] in Audubon's words. They retain the flank patch and white head feathers from February or March until June, and then shed them. Thus the male bird on the right of this scene, perhaps painted in March of 1834, still shows the flank patch and head feathering, whereas the female in the nest with her young, whom Audubon had observed and painted in July of the previous year (subsequently successfully integrating the male into the composition), has already molted out of that plumage.

The Great Cormorant's expertise in catching fish has not been lost on its human neighbors. The species has been domesticated and trained for fishing in England, parts of Europe, and the Orient since at least the sixteenth century. A strap or ring is placed around the cormorant's neck so that it cannot swallow its catch, and the fisherman then retrieves it from the bird's gullet, periodically removing the device so that the bird can eat.

1. T. Gilbert Pearson, ed., *Birds of America*, vol. I (New York: Garden City Books, 1936), p. 97.
2. John James Audubon, *Ornithological Biography*, vol. VI (reprint of 1840–44 ed.; New York: Volair Books, 1979), p. 414.
3. Ibid.
4. Ibid., p. 416.

Black Guillemot

CEPPHUS GRYLLE (LINNAEUS)

Probably painted in Eastport, Maine, during the summer of 1833. The chick at the left is most likely the work of Audubon's son John.

Medium: watercolor, pastel, graphite, selective glazing, and gouache (?) on paper; 14¾ × 21⁵/16 in.; 37.5 × 54.1 cm.

Inscription (upper left, near top, in graphite): Note/S(T) ur? cent/?

Identification: winter-plumaged adult above, downy young lower left, breeding-plumaged adult lower right

Seasonal distribution: breeds along northern Atlantic coasts and off northern Alaska, winters in North Atlantic

Havell plate number: CCXIX in *The Birds of America*

Acc. no. 1863.17.219

It would be unusual, but not impossible, to observe assembled together at one time a group of Black Guillemots such as the adult in summer plumage, the adult in winter plumage, and the downy chick here. Some breeding-plumaged Black Guillemots, like the one on the right, keep their summer feathering into the fall when the young, like the chick on the left, have been born, and most mature birds have begun molting into their winter plumage like that of the flying bird above.

Black Guillemots are sufficiently hardy to be able to survive even during the winter near their nesting grounds in the North Atlantic, as long as food is available. After breeding in protected cliff crevices or on shores above the high-water line—where they do not construct lined nests but lay their eggs directly on bare rocks, pebbles, or shells they have collected—and after watching over their chicks' first flight down into the water, they often remain in the vicinity of their breeding areas, even during the cold months, feeding on fish, crustaceans, shellfish, rock eels, and marine worms. They swim buoyantly in the water, holding their heads high, like the bird on the right here, or "shoot past you on fluttering wings"[1] like the top bird, flying strongly and swiftly, often in a wide circle not far above the water.

"Go to the desolate shores of Labrador,"[2] Audubon instructed those of his audience eager to verify his portrayal of the Black Guillemot. For so Audubon had done, sighting this species all along the way north from Massachusetts. When he arrived in Labrador he found "a regular nursery of these birds"[3] and observed "the young . . . at first quite black, . . . covered with soft down . . . their legs, feet, and bill . . . black"[4] in contrast to "the red colour of the legs of the old birds [which] is much brighter during the breeding season than at any other time, and the mouth also is bright red."[5] To illustrate this description, Audubon portrays here the progression of plumage changes that the birds undergo: the black downy chick crouched on the white ice at the left will grow up to boast impressive white-on-glossy-black feathering as a breeding-plumaged adult and, with molting, will reverse those tones in winter to show black on a predominantly white field, patterns that Audubon was particularly adept at using as abstract compositional elements in his images. The red mouth—or gape—of the swimming adult bird and the red legs (now rather faded in this picture) of that bird and the one flying above it provide the only highlights of bright color in this image of powerful dark and light contrasts. The stark beauty of the birds' plumage patterns, which Audubon plays off against one another in portraying the guillemot's life cycle, reflects the solitary atmosphere of the isolated northern coasts where the Black Guillemots make their home.

1. John James Audubon, *Ornithological Biography*, vol. VII (reprint of 1840–44 ed.; New York: Volair Books, 1979), p. 274.
2. Ibid.
3. Ibid., p. 273.
4. Ibid., p. 275.
5. Ibid.

Common Goldeneye

BUCEPHALA CLANGULA (LINNAEUS)

Audubon's nomenclature: Golden eyed Duck, *Fuligula clangula*

Painted probably c. 1832–34 on the Atlantic coast.

Medium: watercolor, and black and brown (and blue?) pastel on paper; 21 ³/₁₆ × 29 ⅝
in.; 53.6 × 75.3 cm.

Inscription (lower left, in graphite): Plate 342 *(lower center, in graphite):* Golden eyed
Duck/Male 1. Female 2—*(last line partially trimmed along bottom edge of paper)*

Identification: male left, female right

Seasonal distribution: breeds across northern North America, winters throughout the
United States

Havell plate number: CCCXLII in *The Birds of America*

Acc. no. 1863.17.342

The Common Goldeneye is one of the best known, most plentiful, most widely distributed American ducks. Audubon described it as "spreading over the whole country, as if it seemed not to care in what region it spends its time, provided it find abundance of water."[1] The medium-sized, stout, compact species breeds in tree cavities near northern lakes and ponds and engages in perhaps the most spectacular, elaborate courtship display of any native waterfowl. The male puffs up his head feathers, thrusts his large head with its stubby bill forward and up, throws it back to touch his tail, gives a quick jerk, returns to a normal position, and ends by spurting forward, exhibiting his bright orange feet. After mating, the female lays about ten eggs in a nest cavity, whose entrance may be as high as sixty feet off the ground, and which may be as much as fifteen feet deep.

During the winter this hardy species sometimes remains north and inland where there is open water, but often in late fall it moves south and to the coast, where it feeds in relatively shallow water by dabbling or diving for aquatic animals and plants. The birds fly to the open ocean at dusk, where hundreds may sleep in dense floating rafts. Audubon saw them wintering in South Carolina and Florida.

The swift, strong flight of the Common Goldeneye, which Audubon called "powerful, extremely rapid and wonderfully protracted . . . with a speed equal to that of any . . . Duck,"[2] has been clocked at fifty miles an hour. As it flies, its rapidly beating wings produce a vibrant whistling sound that can be heard at a distance of half a mile, and that has earned it such local names as "Merry-wing," "Whistle Diver," and "Spirit Duck." On their breeding and wintering grounds, Common Goldeneyes generally travel singly or in pairs; they migrate in small flocks at considerable heights. In flight, the male shows more white in its

body and wings than almost any other North American duck.

Although Audubon, the enthusiastic hunter, described the Common Goldeneye's flesh as "fishy, and in my opinion unfit for being eaten,"[3] the birds are a popular sportsman's target. Here he shows a pair in midflight, the male (in a rare although not unique Audubon motif) having just been wounded in the left wing. As the male stops and begins to plummet forward, the female brakes in midair, her left foot nearly touching his tail. The ducks' palpable corporeality, asymmetrical shapes, and strong dark-and-light contrasts—particularly the complex pattern in the male's plumage—are arresting in their starkness and power. That Audubon set himself the challenge of showing such rapid flyers instantaneously and involuntarily changing speed and direction while hurtling through space with tilting bodies and feet askew, is testimony to his surpassing originality and unflagging inventiveness. Seventy-five years later this picture inspired no less an artist than Winslow Homer in his painting *Right and Left*.[4]

1. John James Audubon, *Ornithological Biography*, vol. VI (reprint of 1840–44 ed.; New York: Volair Books, 1979), p. 362.

2. *Ibid.*, p. 364.

3. Ibid., p. 365.

4. In the collection of the National Galley of Art, Washington, D.C.

Pacific Loon

GAVIA PACIFICA (LINNAEUS)

Audubon's nomenclature: Black-throated Diver, *Colymbus arcticus*

Painted c. 1834, perhaps from a drawing made on November 13 and 14, 1820, and from specimens procured in Great Britain.

Medium: watercolor, pastel, graphite, selective glazing, and selective scraping on paper; 25¼ × 38⅛ in.; 64.1 × 96.9 cm.

Inscription (across bottom, in graphite): J. J. A. No 70 Plate 346/Black-throated Diver/Colymbus arcticus Linn./1. Adult male spring plumage

2. female 3 young? bird? Autumn

Identification: winter-plumaged bird center, breeding-plumaged birds left and right

Seasonal distribution: breeds in northern North America, winters along Pacific coast; rare on Atlantic coast

Havell plate number: CCCXLVI in *The Birds of America*

Acc. no. 1863.17.346

This is the rarest of the three species of loons in eastern North America. Audubon had less experience with it in the wild than with other species because in this hemisphere it breeds in northern Alaska and Canada and winters on the Pacific Ocean.[1] Audubon wrote, "whilst in Labrador, I saw a few pairs courting on wing . . . but all our exertions failed to procure any of the nests."[2] The bird specimens that Audubon used here may have come from Great Britain, where the species also breeds.[3]

In his vignette, Audubon positioned the figures so that the most visually startling bird—the breeding-plumaged loon seen from behind—is at the left, where most viewers begin their observation of the composition, and where it therefore produces its greatest impact. Of the three birds, this one occupies the largest compositional area. In simultaneously illustrating the bird's characteristic features and using the dark-and-light contrasts and variegated forms in its elaborate plumage as predominant elements of design, Audubon has brought great dynamism to the composition. He highlights the smooth, tapered shape created by the bird's distinctive sleek, dark head, with its ruby eye and straight, dark bill, and its typical silvery-gray nape; the expressive irregular forms of the diagnostic purplish-black throat patch and elegantly striated neck; the rhythmically repetitive black and white shapes in the four checkered dorsal areas that alternate with uneven sections of deep black feather-

ing along the back and short tail; and the curving dark wings dappled with elliptical white spots. Framing the picture on the right is a bird of the same plumage to which the left-hand bird's bill leads the viewer's eye. The right-hand bird is seen from the front, where its fine neck striations and dappled wings contrast impressively with its white underparts, and are closely juxtaposed with the patterns of the winter-plumaged juvenile bird behind it, down to which the right-hand bird's bill points. Unlike the other two birds', the young bird's eye is brown and its bill blue-gray. Characteristically, its plumage contains less contrast than that of the others, but the gray-tipped feathers on its upper back give it its identifying scaly appearance.

Pacific Loons nest at lake and pond edges and must spend their time close to water. They cannot take flight from land and walk only with difficulty, because their legs are placed far back on their bodies for optimal swimming and diving. In the water, however, they propel themselves easily with their fully webbed feet, searching for crustaceans, mollusks, small fish, aquatic plants, and insects, which they seize rather than spear. They are capable of remaining submerged for more than three minutes and at a depth of thirty feet, and they come ashore mostly to rest and preen or attend their young. Anyone in the vicinity is alerted to their presence by their eerie vocalizations, which range from high yelps to piercing shrieks and expressive squeals.

1. Today taxonomists consider the loon that Audubon knew as the Arctic Loon to comprise two distinct species, the Arctic Loon and the Pacific Loon. The bird that Audubon portrayed is the latter.

2. John James Audubon, *Ornithological Biography*, vol. VII (reprint of 1840–44 ed.; New York: Volair Books, 1979), p. 295.

3. Audubon had depicted the bird earlier in an 1820 drawing that he made on the Mississippi River, now in the collection of The New-York Historical Society. An oil copy of the later picture was formerly in the collection of Mrs. F. J. Laiser.

Black-throated Diver
Colymbus arcticus

Painted c. 1834, with greater detail than Audubon's 1821 picture from which it was copied

Medium: watercolor, graphite, and traces of gouache (on beak) on paper; 21½ × 14⅝ in.; 54.6 × 37.3 cm.

Inscription (lower left, in graphite): Common Tern/Sterna Hyrundo

Identification: breeding plumage

Seasonal distribution: breeds in northeastern United States, winters in southeastern United States, Caribbean, and South America to Peru

Havell plate number: CCCIX in *The Birds of America*

Acc. no. 1863.17.309

Audubon observed Common Terns at sites from Labrador to Texas during both spring and fall. The species breeds in the Northern Hemisphere of the Old World and the New and is the tern most widely distributed and frequently seen along our eastern seaboard. Audubon had numerous occasions to watch the terns diving and giving their harsh, rolling calls—as he depicts here—while they hunted small fish, shrimp, and insects or drove intruders from their nests.

Common Terns, whose pair bonds are strong, return to the same nest site year after year. Their colonies, where other terns or gulls may also breed, sometimes include thousands of nests that the females make on the ground on a sandspit, salt marsh, river or lake edge, a patch of floating vegetation (like a muskrat house), coastal island, or rocky ledge. The birds scrape shallow depressions in the soil and enlarge them by sitting in them and turning around repeatedly, then usually lining them with plant materials, feathers, or seashells. Common Terns are fiercely protective parents. Their colonies are subject to destruction not only by humans who encroach on their sandy beach habitat but also by cats, dogs, foxes, and possums as well as weasels, raccoons, skunks, and owls. Rats can destroy several thousand chicks in a colony, and even ants sometimes enter the terns' eggs and kill the hatching young. Tern parents, both of which incubate the eggs, vociferously attack any creature they perceive as a danger, sometimes even striking people and killing young gulls or other small animals. High storm tides that inundate thousands of eggs and young, destruction for the millinery trade, changes in marine conditions that deplete their food supply, and chemical pollution have also threatened Common Tern populations, which have diminished markedly since Audubon's time.

Terns hover over fish, suddenly plunging into the water to seize them. Males bring food to incubating females, and after the eggs are hatched, both parents feed the young—first in the nest, and later on the wing or on the water. Fishermen often set nets at Common Tern feeding sites, aware that the small fish that the terns eat are forced to the surface by larger ones under the water. In the fall, Common Terns sometimes also dive after insects on the wing.

Audubon emphasizes the tern's pointed wings and deeply forked tail that produce its agile flight, and give the bird its Latin name, *Sterna hirundo*, the swallow tern. The artist shows the wings' silvery color (although not the characteristic dark wedge near the tip of the upper wing), the black cap, which in breeding season extends to the lower level of the eyes, the orange-red bill with black tip, and the white rump and tail (although not its dark outer edges). He angles the tail in the same direction as the dashingly turned head, both to create a sense of dramatic movement and to reveal the striking orange-red leg and foot.

Common Tern
Sterna Hirundo.

255

Black-shouldered Kite

ELANUS CAERULEUS (DESFONTAINES)

Audubon's nomenclature: Black-winged Hawk, *Falco dispar* Temminck
Painted on February 8, 1834. Beetle probably painted by Maria Martin.
Medium: watercolor, graphite, traces of gouache, selective glazing, and pastel/chalk on paper; 28⅜ × 21³/₁₆ in.; 72 × 53.8 cm.
Inscription (lower center, in graphite): Black winged Hawk/Male 1. Female 2 *(second line of inscription partially trimmed at bottom edge) (lower right, in graphite, very faint):* indecipherable
Identification: male above left, female below right
Seasonal distribution: breeds and winters in Texas and California
Havell plate number: CCCLII in *The Birds of America*
Acc. no. 1863.17.352

Swerving suddenly upward from a rushing dive is a maneuver at which Black-shouldered Kites excel. Audubon's male kite, having just turned his head up, is about to change direction dramatically in this way, an imminent movement that animates Audubon's composition through the viewer's anticipation. Black-shouldered Kites sometimes engage in this behavior when harrying large birds in their territory or, as here, when a potential food item abruptly catches their attention. In nesting season the male, who remains paired with the larger female throughout the year, does all the hunting both during the period of incubation and while the young are fledging. He searches for food in open woodlands, marshes, savannahs, or fields, often reconnoitering from an exposed perch or circling slowly overhead. When he sights an appropriate reptile, mammal, bird, or insect, he sometimes hovers in midair, raises his wings vertically, and then drops down in a controlled descent, wings above his head and legs dangling, to capture his meal. He may then pass the food to the female in flight or present it to her as she perches in a tree. No other North American kite hovers in this way, and, indeed, the black-shoulder spends only about two and one half hours a day hunting while hovering because that activity uses so much energy—in the case of this kite accounting for about half of its total energy consumption.

Audubon shows the perched female kite apparently reacting to the male's rushing onslaught by bending away and raising her wings, a reaction that connects her visually to the male bird. The whiteness of her face and undersides shades into gray and black under her long, pointed flight feathers, her black shoulders appearing as dark patches within the gray. Her relatively small yellow legs and feet, and black claws grasping the branch, form the base of two intersecting triangles that also unite male and female birds: the apex of one is formed by the female's rounded head with its dark-rimmed amber eyes and yellow mouth, and the other is created by the same features in the male. The species' black shoulders are fully apparent in the figure of the male bird, as are its rich gray back and long, slightly notched tail, white except for the characteristic gray central feathers.

In spite of sometimes appearing fierce, these birds are gentle and docile by nature, a fact Audubon learned firsthand from the live kite on which he based the male in this picture. Audubon had received the bird as a gift and was particularly delighted because it was the first Black-shouldered Kite he had seen alive. The species may have been more common in the southeast in Audubon's day than it is today: it suffered a massive decline early in this century, possibly due in part to its being hunted because of the incorrect belief that it preys on game birds.

Audubon's nomenclature: Great Cinereous Owl, *Strix cinerea* Gmelin

Painted probably in London, c. 1834–36.

Medium: watercolor, graphite, brown and black pastel on paper; 34³⁄₁₆ × 25⅛ in.; 86.8 × 63.8 cm.

Inscription (in graphite, bottom center): No 71/raise the Bird about 4 inches, in The Copper higher than/in this Drawing and put a Landscape below of Wild Mountains/and Woods/Great American Owl Ne . . . Plate 351 *(in graphite, on right side):* . . . 11 along . . . 1½ in-1 . . . gap 1¾ in- Bredth of . . . 1½– height . . . to claw lin-1 . . . claw ⅞ in/5 primary . . . rgest-/ . . . from root /" . . . ng . . . y/"

Identification: adult

Seasonal distribution: breeds and winters widely across northwestern North America, winters south to northern United States

Havell plate number: CCCLI in *The Birds of America*

Acc. no. 1863.17.351

In a moment of intense concentration, the Great Gray Owl peers out, awesome, motionless, and silent. It seems to have heard a sound over its left shoulder and turned to respond, assuming a position typical of owls, which can rotate their heads 270 degrees or more to gain wide-ranging access to prey. Audubon employs this pose, in which the bird's body faces partly away from the viewer—its long, barred tail visible at an angle below its distinctively barred wings—to illustrate the plumage patterns on its dorsal and ventral sides and on its feathered toes. The complex, subtle markings in the bird's monochromatic brownish plumage, seen against a blank background (essentially unaltered by Havell in the engraving), create a series of irregular, rippling, changing rhythms that, together with the bird's recently changed position, introduce a subtle sense of movement to the scene.

The great gray is North America's largest owl, with a wingspan reaching five feet. Its body mass is actually smaller than that of the Snowy or Great Horned Owl, but its feathers are sufficiently bulky to create the larger overall size. Its tuftless head, with its inconspicuous bill, appears especially massive in relation to its body, partly because of its extensive, well-developed facial discs—surrounded by a border of short feathers and defined by patterns of concentric gray and brown circles—whose function is to conduct sound to the bird's ear openings located just below the level of its eyes, at the sides of the head.

Audubon, whose acquaintance with this relatively rare species was limited primarily to descriptive notes by the naturalist John Richardson, specimens,[1] and a bird he saw flying over Boston Harbor in the winter of 1832, was nonetheless able to conclude that "the comparatively small size of this bird's eyes renders it probable that it hunts by day, and the remarkable smallness of its feet and claws induces me to think that it does not prey on large animals."[2] In fact, in the Arctic, toward the northernmost limit of its range, the great gray does indeed generally hunt during daylight. On its more southern breeding grounds it tends to feed toward dusk, taking small mammals such as meadow mice and some of the smaller bird species—prey less sizable than that consumed by its cousin the Great Horned Owl.

The great gray is generally a trusting bird (its only enemy is man), and it can be seen searching for food from fence posts, low trees, and shrubs or the edges of northern coniferous or deciduous woods. Its dark, mottled plumage conceals it well in its arboreal surroundings. In winters when its northern food supply is depleted, it occurs—sometimes in comparatively large numbers—as far south as the northern United States. It breeds from twelve to fifty feet high, often in the abandoned nest of a crow or hawk that it repairs and deepens. While the female incubates, the male procures food for the nestlings.

1. On the subject of this picture, Audubon writes that "My drawing was taken from a remarkably fine specimen in the collection of the Zoological Society of London" [John James Audubon, *Ornithological Biography*, vol. I (reprint of 1840–44 ed.; New York: Volair Books, 1979), p. 131].

2. Ibid.

No 71

Black-billed Magpie

PICA PICA (LINNAEUS)

Audubon's Nomenclature: American Magpie, *Corvus pica*

Painted in Great Britain, c. 1835–36.

Medium: watercolor, graphite, traces of gouache, wet pastel, selective glazing, and selective scraping on paper;
28 15/16 × 20 1/4 in.; 51.4 × 73.4 cm.

Inscription (lower center in graphite, very faint): Pisc(?) (?) The . . . bird 2 Finches *(lower right, very faint, in graphite:* "Plate 357.—No. 72,/Male
1./Female 2. *(last line is partially trimmed away at bottom. Recto shows strikethrough image of brown [iron gall] inscription at verso top—presently illegible)*

Identification: adults

Seasonal distribution: breeds and winters widely in western North America

Havell plate number: CCCLVII in *The Birds of America*

Acc. no. 1863.17.357

Until his Missouri River trip in 1843, well after this picture was painted, Audubon had not seen a Black-billed Magpie in the wild in North America.[1] These birds inhabit open areas in the mountains and valleys of the western United States, to which Audubon did not travel until late in his life. He had read descriptions of magpies by Lewis and Clark, the first Americans to write about the species, and by the soldier and explorer Zebulon Pike, published in Alexander Wilson's *American Ornithology*. But Audubon's experience with the magpie in this country was limited enough for him to incorrectly describe those he saw on his trip to Europe in 1826 as "not the same bird that we have in America."[2] He subsequently changed his mind after discussions with other notable ornithologists; today scientists recognize the European and American species to be the same.[3]

Magpies are conspicuous, showy birds. Their black head with white breast and shoulders, white wing patches that flash in flight, and extremely long tail (accounting for more than half the bird's length) make them unmistakable as they swoop gracefully among the thickets, scattered trees, and streamside shrubs of western farms and ranches. In the top bird here (the sexes look identical), Audubon illustrated the glossy iridescence that can be seen at close range on the wings and tail and the impressive wedge-shaped silhouette of that tail when it is spread. He emphasized the species' sleek lines and eloquently captured its straight, even flight in the bottom bird, which

seems just to have streamed into view. He treated with particular delicacy the translucence of the light primary feathers in the left wing, through which the black secondary feathers can be seen, and the shadow that the branch on which the bird perches casts over its breast.

Jays, crows, and ravens are all relatives of the magpie, which shares with them a reputation for intelligence, resourcefulness, gregariousness, and aggressiveness. All are omnivores, sustaining themselves on a diet ranging from live insects and other animal prey such as mice, snakes, and young birds to eggs, carrion, fruit, and grain. The magpie frequently feeds on the ground, walking with sometimes jerky steps, continually twitching its raised tail. Like the other corvids mentioned above, magpies lack a tuneful song, expressing themselves instead (as the upper bird here is apparently doing) in a series of noisy chatterings and whistles. In captivity the species often imitates human speech.

Black-billed Magpies, which may mate for life, build massive domed stick nests, often with more than one entrance, sometimes close to the ground, sometimes as high as fifty feet up in a tree. Within the stick mass they create a cup of mud lined with fine grasses, roots, and hair. After the young are born, magpies travel around locally in loose family groups (they generally do not migrate) and they, or other species, may use their nests as shelters or reuse them to breed.

1. He was familiar with the bird in France, however, and had drawn one on his visit to Nantes in 1805–6. That picture was formerly in the collection of R. W. Shufeldt.

2. Maria R. Audubon, ed., *Audubon and His Journals* (New York: Dover Publications, 1986), p. 114.

3. The other species of American magpie, the yellow-billed, was named by Audubon. In its Latin binomial, *Pica nuttalli*, Audubon honored Thomas Nuttall. The yellow-billed is closely related to the black-billed and appears very similar.

261

American White Pelican

PELECANUS ERYTHRORHYNCOS GMELIN

Background (and possibly bird) painted by George Lehman, c. 1831.
Medium: watercolor, gouache, graphite, selective scraping, and selective glazing (tip of beak) on paper; 25¾ × 38½ in.; 65.5 × 97.6 cm.
Identification: adult
Seasonal distribution: breeds in west central North America, winters in southern California and along Gulf coast
Acc. no. 1863.18.036

Audubon described how, when he first moved to Kentucky in 1808, he frequently saw white pelicans on the Ohio River, particularly in the vicinity of Henderson. He wrote that "should one [bird] chance to gape, all, as if by sympathy, in succession open their long and broad mandibles, yawning lazily and ludicrously."[1] The pelican in this scene may be engaged in such activity or perhaps in pulsating its pouch to cool itself down in hot weather. The bird's pose provided the artist with the opportunity to focus on its bill, one of the species' most conspicuous and important features, which Audubon had carefully observed pelicans using in a variety of ways. Audubon noticed that, in spite of the enormity of its bill, the pelican is able to preen its feathers with surprising delicacy. He also remarked that sometimes, when white pelicans fish, only their upper mandible appears above the surface of the water. The lower one is spread laterally, as the artist shows it here, so that it can snare prey as the bird swims. (Later ornithologists have suggested that this activity may be more ceremonial than practical.) The white pelican's pouch can hold two or three times more than the bird's stomach and may be required to do so when the pelican scoops up as much as three gallons of water together with the fish that it catches. In contrast to its grace in the water—and in the air, where it is capable of sailing for long distances without flapping its wings, a fact to which Audubon alludes by showing a V-formation of pelicans soaring in the distance here—the species is rather clumsy on land. This picture emphasizes the bird's grotesque aspects: its short, stout legs and large feet bearing the massive, somewhat flattened body that the pelican holds horizontally, and its small, elongated head supporting a bill that is three times the head's length. Audubon measured the pouch of the white pelican's bill at seven inches deep opposite the bill's base and wrote that it extended down the bird's throat about eight inches, making it almost two feet long from the tip of the lower mandible to its end. When not in use, the pouch contracts so that it occupies very little space. In breeding season, the bill becomes brighter and develops a raised plate about halfway along the upper mandible.

While this image emphasizes many of the white pelican's most salient characteristics and illustrates them in a dramatically more lifelike fashion than any artist had done previously, Audubon may have felt that the bird in this portrayal was too ungainly to present to the public. The image of this species that Audubon chose to publish shows the bird in full profile and replaces the awkwardness here with stateliness and grandeur.

In spite of the fearsome appearance of this subject, pelicans actually have gentle dispositions and have been easily tamed.

1. John James Audubon, *Ornithological Biography*, vol. VII (reprint of 1840–44 ed.; New York: Volair Books, 1979), p. 21.

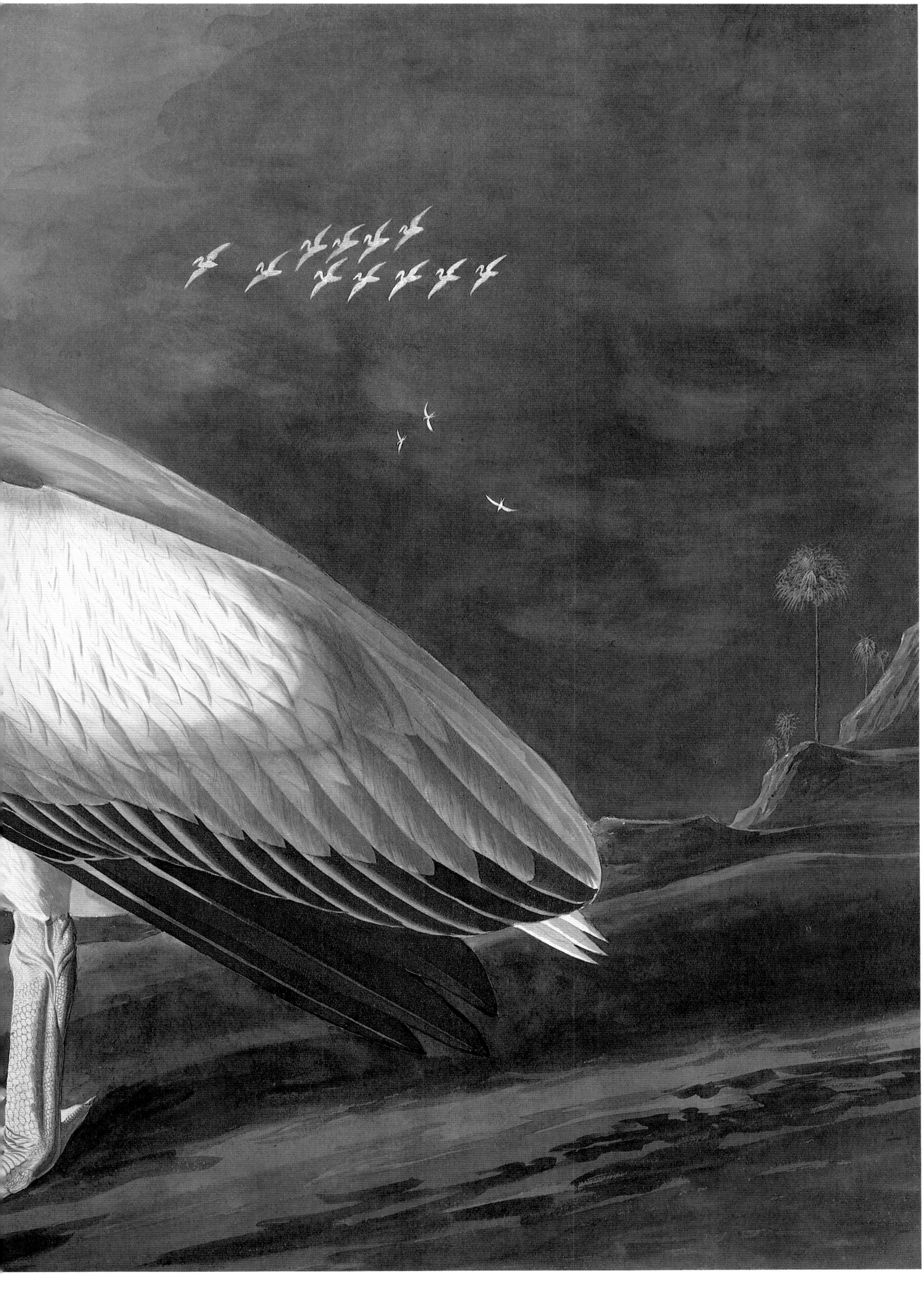

Painted c. 1831–32, possibly in Florida. Redrawn in London in 1836 from earlier sketches and purchased skins.

Medium: watercolor, pastel, graphite, and selective scraping on paper; 36 15/16 × 25 in.; 93.9 × 63.5 cm.

Identification: breeding plumage

Seasonal distribution: breeds in west central North America, winters in southern California and along Gulf coast

Havell plate number: CCCXI in *The Birds of America*

Acc. no. 1863.17.311

The *American White Pelican* exemplifies Audubon's capacity to depict the subtly different shades and textures of a bird's plumage and anatomical structure. Together with persuasively expressing in a majestic portrait what he called "the gravity and sedateness"[1] of one of America's largest birds, Audubon skillfully rendered the detailed structure of such specific body parts as the bird's finely wrinkled pouch—"thin, transparent, elastic, rugous, highly vascular, and capable of being expanded like a net,"[2] as Audubon described it in his extensive writing on the pelican's anatomy. The smooth hardness of the yellow-orange bill is meticulously differentiated from the comparably hued pouch and the stiff knobbiness of the protuberance on the upper mandible, as well as from the similarly textured osculature of the head, visible beneath the tiny, smooth white feathers behind the eye. The silkiness of the pelican's yellowish crest is distinguished from the slightly rougher shagginess of the similarly colored breast patch, as are the long black flight feathers from the shorter black secondaries.

Audubon described seeing a hundred white pelicans at a time on the sand bars of the Ohio River, at the mouth of the Mississippi, and in the Gulf of Mexico. "The White American Pelican," he wrote, distinguishing the species for the first time definitively from the white European pelican, "never descends from on wing upon its prey, as is the habit of the Brown Pelican."[3] He described the white pelicans feeding cooperatively in groups by swimming together in a semicircle and driving schools of fish toward the shallow water, where they are easily seized. White pelicans catch their food on or near the surface of the water by wading or by swimming buoyantly, periodically submerging their heads all at the same time, scooping up fish in their bills, and then draining out the water. They generally fish soon after sunrise and just before sunset, remaining largely inactive during the day. When flying, flocks often form into loose lines or Vs and soar on their nearly ten-foot-long wings, circling high on air currents, wheeling in unison, or performing "extended gyrations."[4] Although they may weigh as much as fifteen to twenty pounds, their light, hollow bones enable them to stay airborne for long periods, even in the face of a strong gale.

White pelicans nest colonially, in the western prairies, in groups of from a few to several hundred pairs, having withdrawn from the East in response to the disturbance of their nesting sites. On low islands in inland lakes the pelicans lay their eggs in depressions they form in the earth, often building a rim of dirt and debris around the outside. After breeding, the pelicans (both sexes identical in appearance) shed the horny excrescence on the bill. The feathery crest is replaced by a mottled gray cap, which itself is lost at the end of the season. Both sexes incubate, and later feed the young by regurgitating food that the small ones eat directly from the parents' pouches.

1. John James Audubon, *Ornithological Biography*, vol. VII (reprint of 1840–44 ed.; New York: Volair Books, 1979), p. 24.
2. Ibid., p. 27.
3. Ibid., p. 23.
4. Ibid., p. 25.

Audubon's nomenclature: Black Backed Gull, *Larus marinus*

Painted in Boston on December 31, 1832.

Medium: watercolor and graphite on paper; 11¼ × 8⅞ in.; 28.6 × 22.5 cm.

Inscription (upper right): Foot of Larus marinus   Boston 31 dec. 1832

Seasonal distribution: breeds on northern North Atlantic coasts, winters south to mid-Atlantic states

Havell plate number: CCXLI in *The Birds of America*

Acc. no.: 1863.18.028

After summering in Maine and New Brunswick, Audubon, Lucy, and their son John spent the winter of 1832 in Boston. It was there that Audubon made this carefully detailed drawing of the foot of a Great Black-backed Gull, one of relatively few individual studies of birds' body parts that he depicted. Audubon probably drew the image of the black-backed gull that he sent to Havell to engrave for *The Birds of America* during his summer stay on the North Atlantic coast, several months before he depicted this foot. The completed composition shows this highly aggressive species, which preys voraciously on the eggs and young, and sometimes even the adults, of seabirds, sinking to the ground, wounded, after being shot. The gull's black-mantled wing is fully outstretched and its bill gaping open in final agony, but its underside, crushed to the ground by the weight of its fall, obscures any view of its legs and feet. Audubon evidently felt that the lack of visible feet (which are apparent in virtually every other species that he depicted) was a serious omission. In the paintings of the Magnificent Frigatebird (shown diving headlong in flight), the Great Crested Grebe (shown half-immersed in water, swimming), and the Black-and-white Warbler (shown from above against a branch), where the species' feet are not clearly visible, Audubon added studies of the feet to his original compositions, which Havell then included in the engravings. Certain other Audubon compositions include details such as a feather drawn individu-

ally or an egg. In the case of the Great Black-backed Gull, Audubon drew the foot separately rather than on the same page as the full composition, and sent the drawing to Havell, who added it to the upper-right-hand corner of the Great Black-backed Gull engraving. The pink legs and large feet of this gull—one of the biggest of its family in North America—are a notable identifying feature. The yellow-orange tone of the foot's webbing and the pink hue of the leg and toes echo those same colors in the injured bird's open bill and extended tongue (with which the foot is placed on a direct diagonal), and thus draw attention to the dramatic plight of the bird. Audubon shows that the foot, webbed for swimming, contains four small claws, actually specialized scales that form a hard covering. In this species the claws grow, as they do in most birds, with three pointing forward and one pointing to the rear. Audubon clearly depicted the slightly arched shape of the claws and represented the expanded inner margin of the one on the middle toe. The gull's claws grow continuously throughout its life and are kept short through wear.

Like the feet of other birds, those of the Great Black-backed Gull consist primarily of tendons and lack musculature. There are relatively few nerves and blood vessels in the feet, which are thus less likely to freeze when exposed to low temperatures than parts of the body that are protected by feathers.

Foot of Larus Marinus
Boston 31. dec. 1832

269

Sabine's Gull

XEMA SABINI (SABINE)

Audubon's nomenclature: Fork-tailed Gull, *Larus sabini* Sabine

Probably painted in Great Britain in 1835.

Medium: watercolor and graphite on paper; 14 ½ × 21 9/16 in.; 36.8 × 54.2 cm.

Inscription (lower left): No 57/Plate 285. *(lower center, in graphite):* FORK TAILED GULL/LARUS SABINII, Sab. *(lower right, in graphite, very faint, previously erased, mostly indecipherable):* . . . Bird . . . / land . . . to M—(?) Bakewell *(brown stains lower right might be strikethrough of iron gall ink inscription on verso)*

Identification: breeding-plumaged adult

Seasonal distribution: circumpolar: breeds in the high Arctic, winters at sea

Havell plate number: CCLXXXV in *The Birds of America*

Acc. no.: 1863.17.285

*I*f this image of the Sabine's Gull is less animated than some of his other depictions, it is because Audubon was less well acquainted with this bird than with those he had been able to observe at length. Sabine's Gulls nest in the Arctic, to which Audubon never traveled, and, except for watching the species flying over the harbor of Halifax, Nova Scotia, on his return trip from Labrador in August 1833, Audubon did not have a chance to study it. Much of the description of the Sabine's Gull in the *Ornithological Biography* consists of information provided by Sir John Richardson, a Scottish naturalist of Audubon's acquaintance who lived in London and was the coauthor, with the zoologist William Swainson, of a work on North American fauna. But although Audubon may have painted this picture from a stiffly positioned specimen in a collection (perhaps on his visit to Great Britain in 1835), he was careful to enliven the image by showing the bird tucking one of its black legs under its breast, while standing on the other. This highly characteristic gesture, practiced by gulls and certain other species, of raising one leg underneath themselves enables the birds to conserve some of the body heat otherwise lost through their featherless extremities; it is a pose very often observed in the wild.

The British naturalist Joseph Sabine named this gull after his brother Edward, a physicist and astronomer who discovered the species. Edward Sabine found the birds on some low, rocky islands off the west coast of Greenland during the Ross and Perry arctic expeditions that he joined in 1818–19. Sabine's Gulls breed in the high Arctic, either singly or in small colonies—sometimes in the company of Arctic Terns—nesting on the low, wet tundra in shallow depressions that they may line with grasses or willow twigs. They feed on the tundra flats, picking up aquatic worms, insects, and larvae much in the manner of shorebirds. Their flight is gracefully erratic like a tern's, and while they never feed by submerging or even landing on the water, they may hover over its surface and dive or dip down to seize small fish. They migrate over the Pacific Ocean to winter mostly off the coast of South America from Panama to Chile and are rarely seen inland.

Audubon portrayed the solitary figure of this dapper gull in breeding plumage standing on a rock.[1] Its dark gray hood contrasts handsomely with the narrow black border around its neck, the narrow red border around its eye, and the yellow tip of its black bill. While Audubon does not show the bird's wings outstretched—and thus does not depict the characteristic strong black triangle on the outer wing or the contiguous white triangle on the inner wing that separates the black outer primaries from the bird's gray mantle—he does show, under the bird's folded wing tips, the distinctive forked tail, which in Audubon's day gave the bird its common name, "fork-tailed gull."

---

1. In the engraving that Havell made of the Sabine's Gull, he included a portrait of a Sanderling that Audubon had intended to depict with other shorebirds but had drawn on a separate piece of paper, which was overlooked in the engraver's studio.

N° 57.
Plate 285.

FORK-TAILED GULL
LARUS SABINII, SAB.

LATERALLUS JAMAICENSIS (GMELIN)

Audubon's nomenclature: Least Water hen, *Rallus jamaicensis* Gmelin
Painted in Philadelphia in October 1836.
Medium: watercolor, pastel, graphite, and selective scraping on paper; 11½ × 16¾ in.; 29.2 × 42.5 cm.
Inscription (lower left): No 70 Plate 349 *(lower center):* Least Water hen—Edwards Rallus jamaicensis, Gmel. 1 Adult Male—2 Youngling—
Identification: adult male and young
Seasonal distribution: breeds on Atlantic and Pacific coasts and parts of central United States, winters in southern part of breeding range
and along the Gulf coast
Havell plate number: CCCXLIX in *The Birds of America*
Acc. no.: 1863.17.349

Audubon was the first person in the United States to paint and scientifically describe the tiny, secretive Black Rail, and even he never saw the bird in life. He portrayed this adult and one of its young from specimens sent to him by the painter Titian Ramsey Peale, at first a critic of Audubon's who, by the fall of 1836, had softened his attitude sufficiently to provide Audubon with these specimens.

This smallest American rail, which lives and nests very locally in coastal and freshwater short-grass marshes and unmown wet meadows, is, as one observer put it, "about as difficult to observe as a field mouse."[1] It avoids detection by darting through the grass so swiftly, with its head held low and its neck extended, that the eye can scarcely follow it. It rarely exercises its powers of flight. Today field observers searching for the furtive Black Rail in breeding season often find that they must employ tape recordings of the bird's call to attract it into the open. Before the use of such equipment was possible, finding the rail could be an exhausting proposition. Not until forty years after Audubon made this picture (and more than twenty-five years after his death) was the bird's highly camouflaged nest first discovered. Thirty-three years after Audubon's death, an ornithologist checked a Black Rail nest at half-hour intervals throughout an entire day without being able to glimpse any sign of the bird, either on the eggs or moving through the grass,

although the eggs were warm enough each time to indicate that the bird had just been incubating them. Twenty-one years later, an ornithologist described how it took him and a colleague with his hunting dog four hours of incessant searching to procure a specimen in a meadow where the bird was constantly giving its metallic call.

The Black Rail builds a neat, small nest, a deep cup of fine, soft grasses on the ground or on a mat of the previous year's vegetation. It places the nest under a tuft of overhanging grass spears or a concealing canopy of standing weeds, which it weaves together into an arch to hide the nest from above. A passageway leads to an entrance in the nest's side. The rail hunts in the area for insects, seeds, and small marine creatures that themselves consume the dying and dead marsh plants.

Audubon, familiar with rail behavior from other species that he knew, depicted a downy Black Rail chick following behind its parent, imitating its surreptitious, skulking walk. In order to create pictorial balance and counterpoint, Audubon showed the chick raising the opposite foot from the parent. The subtle colorations of the parent's plumage—its slate-black head and neck, rusty nape, and blackish back barred with white and grayish white—are absent in the chick, which, like all young rails, is uniformly black. Because of this similarity in coloring, other young rails are often confused with the Black Rail.[2]

1. Frank M. Chapman, *Handbook of Birds of Eastern North America* (New York: Dover Publications, 1966), p. 257.

2. The marshy background that appears in the engraving of this composition was added by Robert Havell, Jr.

Nº 70. Plate 349.

Least Water hen - Edward.
Rallus Jamaicensis, Gmel. 1 adult Male. 2. Jüngling -

Black-bellied Plover

PLUVIALIS SQUATAROLA (LINNAEUS)

Medium: watercolor and graphite on paper; 14 13/16 × 21 1/8 in.; 37.6 × 53.7 cm.

Inscription (upper left, graphite): No 67 Plate 334/Black bellied Plover

Identification: breeding-plumaged adult left, young, right

Seasonal distribution: breeds in the Arctic, winters along all United States coasts

Havell plate number: CCCXXXIV in *The Birds of America*

Acc. no.: 1863.18.035

The unruffled, if watchful, demeanor of the adult Black-bellied Plover standing and facing left in this drawing bears no resemblance to that of the distressed bird that Havell included in his engraving—a crouching figure facing right. On the other hand, the downy chick here reappears in Havell's engraving in a form almost identical to this one. In the period between creating these images, Audubon made an intermediate image of two adult Black-bellied Plovers composed of a breeding-plumaged bird that he drew in about 1822 and pasted down onto a picture containing a winter-plumaged bird that he made in about 1833. When Havell made his engraving, he added the figure of the chick from the present image to the composition containing the two birds, thereby completing the vignette. In the engraving, the breeding-plumaged adult, unlike the one in this picture, not only faces the chick, but indeed stretches forward, nearly touching the young one with its bill, as the winter-plumaged bird looks on. Audubon had remarked on the adult plovers' "anxiety for their young,"[1] which are able to walk almost as soon as they are born and thus can readily wander into danger. In the image that was engraved, Audubon represented this parental vigilance by showing the adult engaged in a distraction display intended to lure a predator away from the chick; he created a relationship between breeding-plumaged adult and chick that, unlike the one here, is clearly intense. Yet, while the interaction between the two birds is effective, and the adult's protective posture enables Audubon to depict its characteristic white upper tail feathers and barred tail and the white stripe on its outstretched wing (although not the typical black "armpit" feathers by which many field observers recognize it), the figure of the adult in the engraving inevitably appears more mannered and contorted than does this simpler representation.

The stocky Black-bellied Plover, with its big head and heavy bill, is the largest American plover, a bird that nests in the high Arctic north of the tree line. (Ornithologists have puzzled over Audubon's contention that he found Black-bellied Plover nests in Pennsylvania, much farther south than the species has ever been thought to breed.) The species nests in both the Old World and the New, essentially circumscribing the North Pole, the only plover that is truly cosmopolitan. In nesting, adults scrape depressions in the ground, which they line with bits of moss. They generally produce four young, whose sulfur-yellow and black backs and gray-buff underparts help to camouflage them in the yellowish tundra grass, particularly when they hide by lying head down and tucking their legs under their bodies.

Black-bellied Plovers eat insects, worms, and mollusks, as well as grasshoppers, beetles, and sometimes seeds and berries that they pick up from coastal sand and mud flats, lake shores, and freshly plowed fields. They typically feed by standing still and erect, running forward for a few feet, bending for prey, and then resuming their former pose.

1. John James Audubon, *Ornithological Biography*, vol. V (reprint of 1840–44 ed.; New York: Volair Books, 1979), p. 200.

Rock Wren, Winter Wren

SALPINCTES OBSOLETUS (SAY), TROGLODYTES TROGLODYTES (LINNAEUS)

Rock Wren, the large center bird, painted in Charleston, South Carolina, in the winter of 1836–37. Winter Wren at lower right painted
on the Mississippi River in 1820; other two Winter Wrens painted in Eastport, Maine, in 1833.
Medium: watercolor, pastel, graphite, touches of gouache, selective glazing, and collage on paper; 20¾ × 13¹⁵⁄₁₆ in.; 52.7 × 35.4 cm.
Inscription (left, in graphite): No 73 Plate 360 *(lower center):* 1—Male - 2 Female 3 Young in autumn—*(lower right):* Plate 365 *(lower center):*
Winter Wren. Keep up . . . to . . . processing (?) *(lower left inscription on verso shows as strikethrough)*
Identification: Rock Wren, left center; Winter Wrens, remaining three
Seasonal distribution: Rock Wren breeds throughout southwestern North America, winters in much of its breeding range
Winter Wren breeds across northern portion of eastern, central, and western North America, winters in coastal breeding areas and in
southern and eastern United States
Havell plate number: CCCLX in *The Birds of America*
Acc. no.: 1863.17.360

The many specimens of newly discovered birds that Audubon acquired from Thomas Nuttall, and had to draw quickly during the winter of 1836–37 in Charleston, forced the artist into certain pictorial compromises. In this scene, for instance, he decided to save time by including two species of wrens, substantially different in size, that occupy entirely different habitats. The tiny Winter Wren, which Audubon observed often and depicted on at least three different occasions,[1] usually lives in moist forest underbrush; the much larger Rock Wren, which Audubon knew only from skins and written descriptions, inhabits the arid talus slopes and gulches of the southwest. Combining such different species, with which he had had widely different experiences, posed several compositional problems. These difficulties were heightened by the fact that although Audubon had originally drawn the Rock Wren perching on a stone, for this picture his son Victor had cut out and pasted down the image of the bird without including the perch beneath it. Havell then represented the bird, whose posture is that of a ground dweller, on a branch—an improbable situation for a wren that lives where there is hardly any vegetation. The proximity of the rather awkwardly placed Rock Wren to the three Winter Wrens that differ from it so markedly in size and habitat, and to which it relates only superficially in the composition, creates a jarring effect.

Depicting the Winter Wren in different positions helped Audubon to suggest the flitting, bustling, bobbing motions of the stub-tailed little bird as it scuttles through the undergrowth—movements that led Audubon (and many ornithologists subsequently) to compare it to a mouse. The Winter Wren is a skulker, easily concealing itself among the fallen timber, leaves, moss, and tree roots of the forest floor. Its dark brown coloring and miniature size—it is one of the tiniest songbirds in North America—provide excellent camouflage in the shadows of the cool forests, where it nests and feeds, hunting in crevices with its diminutive bill for insects. Most conspicuous about it is its surprisingly loud, high-pitched, energetic, and pleasingly musical song, which generally offers the best means of locating the species.

The Rock Wren is a much easier bird to spot, living as it does on open, barren, mountainous rock outcroppings and sunny, exposed cliff walls. Active and tame, it is liable to attract an observer by making short, jerky flights between nearby rock crannies to search for insects or by scolding vociferously from a close perch. It, too, has a loud, clear song, but one of repeated couplets, not nearly so captivating as that of the Winter Wren. The Rock Wren can also be located by its nest, whose presence in a crevice, unlike that of the Winter Wren—which is hidden among the upturned roots of a fallen tree in dense brush—is revealed by a little entrance path of pebbles, rock chips, and other objects that may extend for several feet.

1. Aside from the birds represented here, Audubon did a pencil and watercolor drawing of a Winter Wren in London in 1827 for his friend Hannah Rathbone. The picture is in the John James Audubon Collection (C0006), Manuscript Division, Department of Rare Books and Special Collections, Princeton University Libraries.

276

Sharp-tailed Grouse
TYMPANUCHUS PHASIANELLUS (LINNAEUS)

Probably painted in Charleston, South Carolina, during the winter of 1836–37. The background may have been painted by Audubon's son Victor.

Medium: watercolor, oil paint, graphite, and selective glazing on paper; 20-⅜ × 29¼ in.; 51.8 × 74.9 cm.

Inscription (lower right, in graphite): Sharp-tailed Grous. Male 1. Female 2—

Identification: adults

Seasonal distribution: breeds and winters in central North America

Havell plate number: CCCLXXXII in *The Birds of America*

Acc. no. 1863.17.382

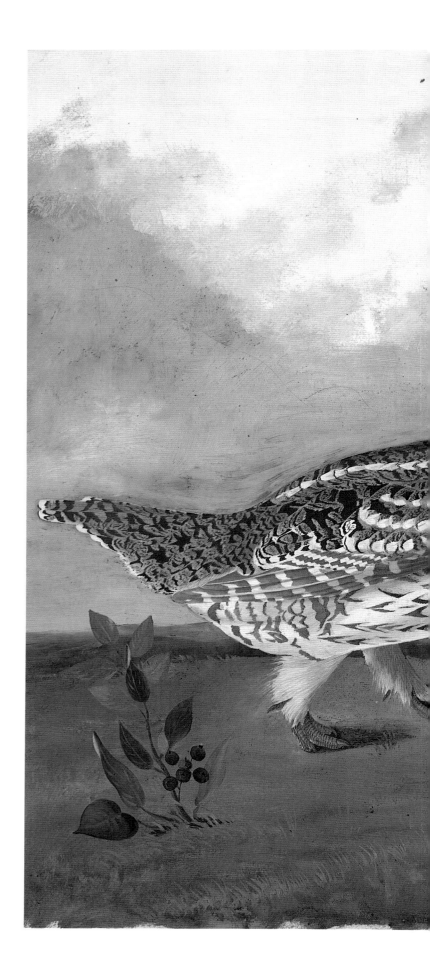

In his Missouri River journal of 1843, Audubon made a number of keen observations about this species, including one that he had "seen . . . a fine flock of Sharp-tailed Grouse, that, when they flew off from the ground near us, looked very much like large Meadow Larks,"[1] and that "Sharp-tailed Grouse are first-rate eating now, as they feed entirely on grasshoppers, and berries of different kinds."[2] But just a year earlier, when the octavo edition of *The Birds of America* appeared in print, Audubon's description of the Sharp-tailed Grouse began with the words, "This is another species of our birds with the habits of which I am entirely unacquainted." Audubon probably made this painting during the winter of 1836–37 in Charleston, before he had had a chance to see the Sharp-tailed Grouse in the wild. The species had been described by George Ord in 1815 from birds collected by Lewis and Clark, and subsequently by other ornithologists (including Townsend, who probably provided the specimens for this picture). Since this grouse primarily inhabits the brushlands, clearings, and forest edges of the Northwest, Audubon was not able to observe it until he took his final trip.

The Sharp-tailed Grouse's narrow tail from which the bird's name derives occupies the center of this composition. In flight the white outer tail feathers are a highly visible field mark of this large, brownish bird with its black and buff dorsal markings and scaled, spotted white underparts. By showing its feathered legs in midstep, Audubon has highlighted the jerky, chickenlike motions of the species, which prefers to walk rather than to fly.

At the beginning of the mating season, large groups of Sharp-tailed Grouse gather around a traditional dancing ground, or lek, which the birds may have used for generations. To start their mating display, one male grouse runs into the

circle and another comes to meet him. The birds partially open their wings, lower their heads, and raise and spread their tails. They inflate the purplish sac on each side of their head, rattle their bristly tail quills, and shuffle their feet back and forth while emitting a low cooing note that can be heard as far as two miles away. Sometimes males approach one another slowly and stand face-to-face with their eyes closed in a kind of trance. They may end the ritual by squatting flat on the ground for as much as twenty minutes, with their beaks almost touching.

Such elaborate displays can continue for weeks while the females come to the lek and mate with the first male that provides sufficient stimulation; couples do not form pair bonds, and the females nest and incubate on their own.

The process of turning brushy prairies into farmland together with the hunting of hundreds of thousands of these tame birds every year has taken a toll on their numbers. In several of the prairie states, their populations have declined or completely disappeared.

1. Maria R. Audubon, ed., *Audubon and His Journals* Vol. II (New York: Dover Publications, 1986), p. 26.

2. Ibid., p. 176.

Audubon's nomenclature: 5. Mourning Warbler, *Sylvia philadelphia* Wilson

Painted in Charleston, South Carolina, probably in the winter of 1836–37, with the assistance of Audubon's son John.

Medium: watercolor, graphite, and traces of black pastel on paper; 21⅞ × 14½ in.; 55.5 × 36.7 cm.

Inscription: (across bottom): No 77 Plate 383 1,2 Black-throated Green Warbler. 3,4 Golden-winged Warbler.— 5. Blackburnian W. female. 6,7 Mourning Warbler./Sylvia virens, Lath.—Sylvia chrysoptera, Lath.—Sylvia blackburnia (AE) Sylvia philadelphia, Wils./8,9 Cape May Warbler.— Sylvia maritima, Wils. P.S. The letter Engraver can easily place all these different names in one line. *(upper right corner, in graphite):* 399–414 *(graphite names by bird 3):* Golden-winged *(and 6):* Mourning wa . . .

Identification (clockwise from top): male Black-throated Green Warbler; female Black-throated Green Warbler; female Blackburnian Warbler; male and female MacGillivray's Warblers; female and male Cape May Warblers; female and male Golden-winged Warblers

Seasonal distribution: 1. breeds in northeastern United States, winters from the Yucatan Peninsula south to Colombia and Venezuela

2. breeds in northern North America, winters in Florida and the West Indies

3. breeds in central and eastern North America, winters from southern Texas and Florida to central Panama

4. breeds in northern North America, winters in South America

5. breeds in western North America, winters from southern Baja California to western Panama

Flora: water oak, *Quercus nigra,* painted by Maria Martin

Havell plate numbers: CCCXCIX and CCCCXIV in *The Birds of America*

Acc. no. 1863.17.399

These warblers, flitting among the thin branches of a treetop, illustrate an intriguing dimension of bird biology. All five species that Audubon portrayed here possess plumages with some combination of light, dark, and bright yellow hues. When these species are seen at a moderate distance, the feather patterns of each provide equally efficient camouflage as the birds feed surrounded by sun-dappled tree leaves: each variation of hues produces effective cryptic coloration that enables the bird to blend with its background and thus be protected from danger. At close range, however, the same color combinations that, at a distance, provide equal concealment in the foliage, produce highly individual patterns that the birds use for identification and display when among their own or other species.

Warblers are small, active birds whose thin, pointed bills are particularly adapted to their insect-eating habits. Indeed, these birds are responsible for ridding trees and shrubs of innumerable insect pests, such as aphids and their eggs. More than a hundred species of warblers exist—all in the New World— and of those, about half are found in North America. In fact, after finches, warblers constitute the largest family of North American songbirds. Most warblers migrate considerable distances to and from the woodlands or swamps in which they breed and, in the process, account for one of the most exhilarating of ornithological events, the warbler "waves" that move north in the spring and south in the fall and that observers await with anticipation each year. An especially appealing aspect of this phenomenon is that during migration many different species of warblers, which vary in habits from solitary to gregarious and in habitat from ground-dwelling to arboreal, may be seen together in the same tree, as here.

Audubon was able to observe in the wild only the three species represented at the top of this composition: the Black-throated Green Warbler (the male of which is the highest bird in the picture, with the female, here probably depicted for the first time, just below him to the right[1]), the Blackburnian Warbler[2] (only the female appears here, below and to the right of the female Black-throated Green), and the Golden-winged Warbler[3] (the male and female are the top two birds on the left-hand side). The two other warblers, the MacGillivray's (male and female appear at lower right) and the Cape May (male and female are shown at lower left), were drawn from specimens. Audubon depicted the MacGillivray's Warbler, which he named for his colleague and editor, from specimens collected by John Kirk Townsend (who discovered the bird and gave it its Latin name) after he had also referred to specimens collected by his friend Edward Harris. The specimens for the drawings of the Cape May Warblers came from Harris as well.

Havell created two separate engravings from this picture: one with the five birds on the right and the other with those on the left.

1. Audubon had depicted a Black-throated Green Warbler on May 7, 1812, in Pennsylvania, on a sheet on which he had already represented a Vesper Sparrow. That picture is now in the collection of The New-York Historical Society. An 1827 watercolor copy of the Black-throated Green Warbler in that picture was given to The New-York Historical Society in 1962.
2. Audubon had drawn a single Blackburnian Warbler on May 12, 1812, in Pennsylvania, which appears in Havell plate CXXXV. An oil copy of that painting exists in a New Brunswick collection.
3. Audubon cut out and pasted down a figure of a Golden-winged Warbler—which may have formed the basis of the top figure in Havell plate CCCCXIV—onto a sheet containing a picture of a Blue-winged Warbler made on April 20, 1815.

No 77.
Plate 383. —

1, 2. Black-throated Green Warbler. 3, 4. Golden-winged Warbler. — 5. Blackburnian W. (male. 6, 7. Mourning Warbler. —
Sylvia virens, Lath. — Sylvia chrysoptera, Lath. — Sylvia blackburniæ (Æ) Sylvia Philadelphia, Wils.

8, 9. Cape May Warbler. —
Sylvia maritima, Wils.

P.S. The letter engraver can easily place all the different names in our Print.

Audubon's nomenclature: 1. Black-capt Titmouse, *Parus atricapillus* Wilson

2. Chestnut-crowned Titmouse, *Parus minimus* Townsend 3. Chestnut-backed Titmouse, *Parus rufescens* Townsend

Painted in Charleston, South Carolina, during the winter of 1836.

Medium: watercolor, graphite, gouache, traces of black pastel, pastel on paper, selective glazing; 19 × 13 9/16 in.; 48.3 × 34.5 cm

Inscription: (lower left, black ink): "J. J. A. Chestnut-backed Titmouse 1. Male 2. Female Parus rufescens. Townsend. No. 71 *(lower center, black ink):* Black-capt Titmouse 3. Male 4 F. Parus atricapillus, Wils. Willow-oak. Quercus Phelloes, L. *(lower right, black ink):* "Chestnut crowned Titmouse 5. M 6. F Parus minimus, Townsend.-and Nest Plate 353" *(lower right side, graphite, faint):* "Total length 5 1/8 /. . . ins 8 1/4 /tail beyond wings. 1 5/8 /claws 5/8 shorter than any of/Phila C. . . . Garden (CBar . . . [trimmed off] Oct 30 1836-J.J.A." *(verso traces of brown ink inscription strikethrough, lower middle right)*

Identification (clockwise from upper right): Bushtit male, female; Black-capped Chickadee male, female; Chestnut-backed Chickadee male, female

Seasonal distribution: 1. breeds and winters widely across central North America

2. breeds and winters along most of Pacific coast

3. breeds and winters in western United States

Flora: willow oak, *Quercus phellos,* painted by Maria Martin

Havell plate number: CCCLIII in *The Birds of America*

Acc. no. 1863.17.353

These three species are related—they are all members of the titmouse family—but only one of them inhabits a part of the country with which Audubon was acquainted. The Black-capped Chickadee, illustrated at the bottom of the picture, is common all across the northern half of the United States. Specimens of the other two species, which occur in western North America, together with information about their habits, had to come to Audubon from the ornithologists John Kirk Townsend and Thomas Nuttall, who had discovered them during their expedition to the Pacific Northwest. Audubon bought many bird skins from Townsend and Nuttall as he was beginning the last stages of his *Birds of America* project, and in the interest of meeting his deadline, he illustrated more than one species on a single sheet.

Audubon has posed the birds in this scene as though he were making an animated drawing of a single individual changing position, rolling over counterclockwise. By thus depicting each bird clinging to a twig in a different but related posture, and by leading the viewer's eye in a swinging motion over each bird from upper right to upper left, Audubon physically engages the viewer in the species' acrobatic behavior. Voracious eaters,

chickadees and bushtits support themselves with their strong feet, twisting into innumerable positions to divest buds, leaves, twigs, cones, and trunk bark of many highly injurious insects (such as tent caterpillars, weevils, and scale), together with their eggs and larvae. Chickadees can change direction within 3/100 of a second, their wings can beat 30 times a second, and their hearts about 800 times a minute when they are active—compared to about 80 times in human beings. Each bird must eat continuously to support such a high metabolism. The birds also consume fruit and, especially in the winter, seeds.

During breeding season both parents participate in nest building. The chickadees generally excavate holes in rotting trees about ten feet above the ground, and the Bushtits construct an elaborate gourd-shaped hanging nest such as the one that Audubon acquired from Nuttall, which provides the central focus here. Bushtits build their nest from the top down, binding a rim of soft lichens and mosses to several twigs with spider webs, and adding leaves, flowers, and even feathers like those here of the Steller's Jay. The nest is thickest at the bottom, where the eggs will be laid and the greatest insulation needed.

Chesnut-backed Titmouse. 1. male. 2. female
Parus rufescens. Townsend.

Black-capt Titmouse 3. male. 4. ♀.
Parus atricapillus, Wils.
Willow Oak. Quercus phillos, L.

Chesnut crowned Titmouse. 5. m. 6. ♀.
Parus minimus. Townsend.—
and nest.

№ 71.

Plate 353.

Western Tanager, Scarlet Tanager

PIRANGA LUDOVICIANA (WILSON), PIRANGA OLIVACEA (GMELIN)

Audubon's nomenclature: 1. Louisiana Tanager, *Tanagra ludoviciana* Wilson

Painted in Charleston, South Carolina, during the winter of 1836–37.

Medium: watercolor, graphite, gouache, and selective glazing on paper; 21 9/16 × 13 3/4 in.; 54.8 × 34.9 cm.

Inscription (upper right side, in graphite): Mr Havell w . . ./please attend . . . /the Jaggings O . . . /Bills *(lower left):* 1. 2. Louisiana Tanager/Tanager ludoviciana. Wils./1 & 2 Males spring plumage *(lower right):* Scarlet Tanager. Tanager rubra, L./3 old male spring plumage/4 old female Do do [dittos] *(lower left corner):* No 71 *(bottom center):* J. J. A. *(lower right):* Plate 354—/Plant/Laurus carolinens

Identification: male Western Tanagers upper right and upper left; male Scarlet Tanager center; female Scarlet Tanager below

Seasonal distribution: 1. breeds in much of western North America, winters from southern California to Costa Rica

2. breeds in much of eastern United States, winters from Panama south to northwestern Bolivia

Flora: the redbay or laurel tree, *Persea borbonia*, painted by Maria Martin

Havell plate number: CCCLIV in *The Birds of America*

Acc. no. 1863.17.354

The Western and Scarlet Tanagers are two of the most colorful bird species in North America; combining them gave Audubon the opportunity to produce a visually dazzling picture. It also gave him the chance to outdo Alexander Wilson, who had previously depicted both birds and, in fact, had actually named the Western Tanager, which he had drawn from specimens collected by Lewis and Clark. (Wilson had named the species Louisiana Tanager, an appellation still retained in its Latin name, after the Louisiana Territory that Lewis and Clark explored. At the time of their expedition, that territory stretched from the Mississippi River to the Continental Divide and north to British Columbia; they found the tanager in what is now Idaho. It occurs only rarely in what is now the state of Louisiana.) Audubon acquired his specimens of the Western Tanager from Townsend and Nuttall[1] and collected his own specimens of the Scarlet Tanager, which he found "breeding abundantly in Louisiana,"[2] considerably farther south than they now nest, as well as in Texas and in Maine.

Tanagers are found only in this Hemisphere. The Western Tanager lives mainly in the coniferous woods of the western mountains and the scarlet generally in the mature deciduous woods of the east. Most tanagers are brightly colored and inhabit the upper canopy of the forest. Paradoxically, in spite of their vivid plumage, they are difficult to see because they move slowly and conceal themselves well among the high foliage, where they glean countless insects and consume wild fruits. The Scarlet and Western Tanagers often are most easily located by their songs, which sound similar to one another and resemble the phrases of an American Robin but are raspier.

Audubon made the male Scarlet Tanager (about which a bird painter of today has said, "it's impossible to paint that bird—there aren't the pigments to match it"[3]) the central focus of his composition. He depicted the bird on the wing, gliding through the woods with what he described as an even, swift flight. He could thus show the full length of its red back, mostly concealed when its black wings are folded. During courtship the tanager displays this scarlet plumage to the olive-yellow female, here pictured below him, by hopping underneath her on a branch and spreading his wings.

Both Western Tanagers here are males[4] whose red heads differ subtly in hue from the scarlet's, and contrast with their orange-yellow backs. This species is the only North American tanager with wing bars, and Audubon makes them conspicuous. However, his lack of experience with the bird is evidenced by the fact that he depicted both wing bars as equally orange-yellow. In reality the lower one is visibly lighter.

1. Audubon wrote in *Ornithological Biography* (vol. III, p. 231) that these were the first specimens taken since Lewis and Clark procured their birds, and that these were finer skins.

2. John James Audubon, *Ornithological Biography*, vol. III (reprint of 1840–44 ed.; New York: Volair Books, 1979), p. 227. He had figured a single male Scarlet Tanager in pencil and pastel during August 1810 when he was in Red Banks (later Henderson), Kentucky, a picture now in the collection of the Houghton Library, Harvard University.

3. As quoted in James Fenwick Lansdowne and John A. Livingston, *Lansdowne's Birds of the Forest*, vol. II *(Birds of the Eastern Forest)* (New York: Arrowwood Press, 1989), p. 420.

4. The female Western Tanager appears (with several other species) in the painting for Havell plate CCCC. Townsend and Nuttall did not collect a female, and Audubon acquired his specimen separately, from his friend Dr. Trudeau.

1.2. *Louisiana Tanager*
Tanagra ludoviciana, Wils.
 1 & 2. *Males Spring plumage.*

Scarlet Tanager. Tanagra rubra, L.
3. *Old Male spring plumage.*
4. *Old Female   do   do.*

Nº 71.

Plate 354.

J. J. A

Plant
Laurus caroline

Red-bellied Woodpecker, Northern Flicker, Yellow-bellied Sapsucker, Lewis's Woodpecker, Hairy Woodpecker

MELANERPES CAROLINUS (LINNAEUS), COLAPTES AURATAUS (LINNAEUS),

SPHYRAPICUS VARIUS (LINNAEUS), MELANERPES LEWIS (GRAY),

PICOIDES VILLOSUS (LINNAEUS)

Audubon's nomenclature: 2. Red Shafted Woodpecker, *Picus mexicanus* Swainson 3. Red Breasted Woodpecker, *Picus flaviventris* Vieillot
Upper four birds painted c. 1822; painting completed in Charleston, South Carolina, during the winter of 1836–37. Maria Martin
completed the dead tree limb at left.
Medium: watercolor, pastel, graphite, gouache, collage, and selective glazing on paper; 37⅛ × 24¼ in.; 94.3 × 61.7 cm.
Inscription (across bottom): Red Shafted Woodpecker./Picus mexicanus—Swain. 1. Male 2. female.—/Lewis Woodpecker. Picus torquatus,
Wils. 3. Male, 4. Female/Red breasted Woodpecker/Picus flaviventris, Viell./5. Male, 6. female/Red bellied Woodpecker, Picus
carolinus L. 7. Male, 8. Female/Hairy Woodpecker, Picus villosus L./9. Male, 10. Female/Red-cockaded Woodpecker *(crossed out):*
Red-cockaded Woodpecker Picus querulus, Wils.—/11. Male. 12 Do. 13 female/*(clockwise from 1, left, in graphite):* Picus ruber/This
species ../? L .. pr ../of all these C . . . specimens . . ./J / Sunday/Tuesday/Hairy/Hairy/Culla/Red bellied/46 Coloystes
rubricatus, Bouoys.
Identification: male and female Red-bellied Woodpeckers upper right; Northern Flickers (western race), center; Yellow-bellied Sapsuckers
below; male and female Lewis's Woodpeckers lower center; male and female Hairy Woodpeckers upper left
Seasonal distribution: 1. breeds and winters widely across the eastern United States
2. breeds and winters throughout most of North America 3. breeds in northeastern and western North America
4. breeds and winters across the western United States 5. breeds and winters across much of North America
Havell plate number: CCCCXVI in *The Birds of America*
Acc. no. 1863.17.416

A flock of woodpeckers such as is depicted here would not occur in nature. Woodpeckers generally feed either alone or in family groups rather than in aggregations like this one, since they vie for similar kinds of food (and, in the case of this particular group, the species occupy different habitats). But Audubon's composition does capture a sense of the purposeful and often conspicuous activities of this family.

Audubon centered his image around the two largest birds of the group: the male (middle right) and female (middle left) flickers. Courtship among flickers and other woodpeckers sometimes includes a display between sexes as Audubon depicted here, in which the flickers' tails are spread and their wings raised to reveal the rich coloring of the wing linings. The focal point of this central group is the birds' bills, natural attributes for Audubon to choose as a focus, since in this family they serve several unique functions. Woodpeckers use their strong, pointed bills during courtship, to establish territory and form a pair bond through repeated loud drumming on a hard surface, and to chisel into the bark of trees in order to feed or to excavate nesting holes, as the Red-bellied Woodpecker is doing here. In the male red-bellied (upper right), Audubon illustrated the startlingly long, thin tongue which woodpeckers can extend quickly and easily while feeding. They employ the barbed end and sticky saliva coating to gather insects and grubs. Red-bellieds dig their nest holes in dead trees such as the one this pair is clinging to, whereas Hairy Woodpeckers (the male and female appear at upper left), may make their holes in trees that are living. Audubon believed that his image of the female, which lacks the red head patch of her male counterpart, was the first depiction of that bird.

The Yellow-bellied Sapsucker (bottom left and right) and the Lewis's Woodpecker are colorful western species, whose behavior Audubon knew only from the writings of others, as his somewhat awkward illustrations of them attest.

Anna's Hummingbird

CALYPTE ANNA (LESSON)

Audubon's nomenclature: Columbian Humming-bird, *Trochilus anna* Lesson
Probably painted in London in 1838.
Medium: watercolor, graphite, and selective glazing on paper; 21⅜ × 14⁷⁄₁₆ in.; 54.3 × 36.7 cm.
Inscription (bottom center, in graphite): Trochilus anna, Lesson. *(bottom right, in graphite):* 1. Males—2. Female & nest
Identification: males, upper four; female below.
Seasonal distribution: breeds and winters along most of Pacific coast
Havell plate number: CCCCXXV in *The Birds of America*
Acc. no. 1863.17.425

The Anna's Hummingbird breeds in California, farther west than Audubon journeyed in his search for new species. Even so, using specimens from a Mr. Loddige in London for the four males and from Thomas Nuttall for the female and the nest on which she is sitting, Audubon was able to depict the bird's quick and delicate movements with lifelike accuracy because during his travels in eastern North America he had extensively observed the behavior of the Anna's close relative, the slightly smaller Ruby-throated Hummingbird; he admiringly described it as moving "from one flower to another like a gleam of light, upwards, downwards, to the right, and to the left."[1]

As with other members of its family—like the ruby-throat—the Anna's can fly backward and sideways as well as straight up and down, and can hover in midair like a helicopter when feeding with its long, slender bill on nectar from tree and flower blossoms and on the insects that the nectar attracts. The largest hummingbird to occur over most of its range and a member of the family with the highest metabolic rate of almost any warm-blooded vertebrate, the Anna's requires nectar from more than a thousand blossoms a day to sustain it. It is also more dependent on insect nourishment than any other North American hummer and needs to feed almost continuously during daylight hours.

As part of its courtship, the male Anna's performs a series of spectacular aerial displays. He springs from his perch, stops to sing briefly before the female (his high, squeaky song is the most clearly defined of any California hummer's), flies up almost out of sight to a height of one hundred feet or more, dives down precipitously and nearly vertically, and, before swerving up again, suddenly spreads his tail, causing his stiff outer feathers to vibrate and produce a sharp, loud popping sound. In these display dives, the male—unique among North American hummingbirds in having red on both crown and throat feathers—deliberately orients himself so that the sun shines brilliantly on his purple-red gorget.

Once courtship is completed, the female Anna's builds a neat, minute nest of plant down, spider webs, and lichens, often lined with feathers, in a bush or small tree up to thirty feet above the ground. Twice during the breeding season she lays two tiny white eggs.

In Paris, on September 10, 1828, Audubon met the duke of Rivoli, a twenty-nine-year-old collector and patron of natural history. The duke (after whom Rivoli's Hummingbird was named, and who assembled a collection of about twelve thousand bird skins, which was bought by the Academy of Natural Sciences of Philadelphia), became an admirer of Audubon's work and a subscriber to *The Birds of America*. In 1829, Audubon's colleague and friend, the distinguished French naturalist René Primevère Lesson, named Anna's Hummingbird after the duke's wife, whom Audubon described in his journal as "a beautiful young woman, not more than twenty, extremely graceful and polite."[2]

1. John James Audubon, *Ornithological Biography,* vol. IV (reprint of 1840–44 ed.; New York: Volair Books, 1979), p. 191.
2. Maria R. Audubon, ed., *Audubon and His Journals,* vol. I (New York: Dover Publications, 1986), p. 314. A pencil drawing that Audubon made below the upper-right-hand male Anna's Hummingbird duplicates that bird's position and indicates that Audubon experimented with two placements of the figure. In the end, either he or Havell decided to retain in the engraving the position of the completed bird in the drawing.

Gyrfalcon

FALCO RUSTICOLUS LINNAEUS

Audubon's nomenclature: Iceland falcon or Jer Falcon, *Falco islandicus* Latham

Painted in Great Britain in 1837.

Medium: watercolor, graphite, gouache, selective glazing, and selective scraping on paper; 38 ½ × 25 ⅝ in.; 97.8 × 65.2 cm.

Inscription (lower left, in graphite): No 75./Plate 371

Identification: adults

Seasonal distribution: breeds in Arctic, winters south to northern United States

Havell plate number: CCCLXVI in *The Birds of America*

Acc. no. 1863.17.366

From earliest times, this largest of all falcons has been regarded as the most majestic. During the Middle Ages, when the wealthy employed falcons in hunting, only royalty was allowed to use the powerful, long-winged, keen-sighted Gyrfalcon, considered by many the most magnificent of these swiftest birds of prey. Today the observation of a Gyrfalcon in the wild is all the more thrilling because of the species' rarity and inaccessibility.

Gyrfalcons live farther north than any other members of the falcon family. They breed in the arctic tundra on high rock ledges and in caves in the walls of towering cliffs, sometimes in old raven, hawk, or Golden Eagle nests. They range in color from largely white to entirely dark, with almost every intermediate shade possible. In August 1833, during the Labrador trip, Audubon's son John and two friends shot male and female dark-phase Gyrfalcons and brought them back to the boat for Audubon to draw. Audubon wrote that these were the first Gyrfalcons he had seen, and described the intense and arduous task of depicting them. In the 1833 picture, the female bird's posture and expression convey a sense of wildness, but the male bird appears more tame and docile. Four years later, in England, Audubon made this picture of two savage-looking white-phase Gyrfalcons from a single female bird that he had known only in captivity. According to the bird's owner, John Heppenstall, of Sheffield, England, Audubon and Lucy had visited him while the bird was alive (Heppenstall owned it for more than five years before it died) but at the time of the visit Audubon had an injured finger and could not draw it. Heppenstall averred that this depiction, made from the specimen, was an accurate representation but that Audubon would have preferred to have both a male and a female to draw. Since the sexes have essentially the same plumage, the only substantial difference would have been in size: the female is larger.

Gyrfalcons are the only birds of prey inhabiting the Arctic during the winter that are normally active during whatever daylight hours there may be. The birds usually survey their territory by perching horizontally on a rise in an open field or on an upright structure such as a fence post or stake. In flight they alternately flap and glide, stopping to hover if something attracts them. They fly fairly close to the ground to hunt their prey—mostly birds, particularly ptarmigan, which they often flush by hovering over willow thickets, and then generally capture in the course of powerful flight rather than with swooping dives such as Peregrine Falcons make. Their muscular legs, formidably hooked beak, and strong, sharp, curved talons are all adapted to efficient predation. Frequently they nest close to colonies of seabirds that provide them easy access to such prey as dovekies, murres, and kittiwakes. They also take small mammals such as lemmings and arctic hares.

Gyrfalcons occasionally wander as far south as the middle Atlantic states in the winter, where they frequent areas with large gull concentrations. The birds in their white phase, most of which come from Greenland, are the least often seen.

Audubon's nomenclature: Turkey Buzzard, *Cathartes atratus* or *Cathartes aura*

Probably painted in December 1820.

Medium: watercolor, pastel, graphite, and small amounts of gouache (in beak) on paper; 18⅝ × 18⁵⁄₁₆ in.; 47.4 × 46.5 cm.

Identification: downy young

Seasonal distribution: breeds throughout the United States, winters in the southern United States

Acc. no. 1863.18.022

urkey Vultures' nestlings, unlike those of many other hawks, open their eyes immediately after birth and in less than a week have begun to move actively around the nest site. By the time the babies are two weeks old, they have become substantially larger, heavier, and more aggressive than they were at birth. Already very alert, the young birds hiss and snap energetically at intruders, as Audubon's subject is doing. Their black flight feathers, visible in this image on the young bird's folded wings, have begun to show through their cottony natal down whose texture Audubon so effectively captured.[1] These flight feathers, on wings that will have a six-foot spread—almost that of an eagle—do not become fully developed until the birds are about two months old. It takes about ten weeks for the bird to assume the full juvenal plumage that it will possess throughout its first winter. Late that winter, the bird will begin to acquire its adult feathering, and the naked facial skin, black in the nestling bird as Audubon illustrates here, turns red.

Young Turkey Vultures spend a good deal of time sunning themselves in front of the place in which they were born. Their parents seek out nesting locations that are large, secluded, and as inaccessible as possible to predators: dark caves, crevices in cliff faces, or hollow trees (as shown). Once they have successfully raised a brood at such a site, the parents may return to the same location for a number of years. They do not actually construct a nest but generally lay their eggs directly on the earth, stone, or wood floor of the chosen site. Turkey Vultures may begin to breed as early as January in the South. The female lays two eggs, which both parents incubate for about a month until the chicks hatch. In captivity, young Turkey Vultures are reported to enjoy being handled by people, especially while feeding, and to have become devoted pets, following their owners around like puppies.

With a fine sense of both sight and smell, Turkey Vultures are expert scavengers, feeding almost exclusively on carrion. They have relatively weak bills and talons and are not capable of killing most live animals as other raptors do. They must thus find their food by chance and be satisfied with a variety of prey. For this reason, as the most widely distributed member of their family and the predominant avian scavenger in the United States, Turkey Vultures are helpful as agents of sanitation, eliminating dead animals from farms and roadsides. Their gliding flight enables them to scan enormous areas for prey with minimal effort. In spite of having been killed in large numbers in the past because of a fear that they spread disease, Turkey Vultures have actually been found to be very useful hygienically: a number of bacteria that produce serious animal diseases have been discovered to be destroyed by passing through the Turkey Vulture's digestive tract.

1. Audubon ultimately decided not to include this image in *The Birds of America* and published instead a composition showing two Turkey Vultures perched on branches—an immature bird with all-black plumage and an adult.

Audubon's nomenclature: Californian Vulture, *Cathartes californianus* Illiger
Painted in 1838, probably in London.
Medium: watercolor, graphite, and gouache on paper; 38½ × 25¼ in.; 97.8 × 64.2 cm.
Inscription (lower left): No 84 Plate 416—/John J. Audubon/1838 *(lower center):* California Vulture/Cathartes Californianus,
Illiger./Old Male
Identification: adult
Seasonal distribution: formerly bred and wintered in California
Havell plate number: CCCCXXVI in *The Birds of America*
Acc. no. 1966.042

The California Condor has become extinct in the wild during the past generation. In 1966, when The New-York Historical Society acquired this picture (the only painting for *The Birds of America* not included in the Society's purchase from Lucy Audubon), several dozen wild condors still ranged over the mountains of southern California where the species was breeding. Twenty-seven years later, the few condors that fly free in that area are products of a captive breeding program that is painstakingly raising them in two California zoos in the hope of reestablishing them in the wild.

Condors are highly sensitive to the intrusions of man, which have contributed substantially to the species' decline. The birds were formerly found in the West from Washington State to Baja California, Texas, and New Mexico. Lewis and Clark reported condors abundant at Deer Island, Oregon, in 1806. But the birds have been shot in large numbers because they were thought to prey on live farm animals. They have also been killed by eating coyotes poisoned because of their predation habits by ranchers on whose land the condors searched out dead livestock. In the Ice Age, when their population was much more plentiful, condors fed on the bodies of large mammals. More recently they probably subsisted on the carcasses of deer and other animals killed by mountain lions, grizzlies, and coyotes. But man has now effectively eliminated most of the predators that provided the condors' food supply. (In spite of popular belief, condors do not kill animals.) Loss of ranches to housing development has also been destructive to the species. The birds do not have a high reproductive rate; they lay only one egg, and the parents tend their single nestling until its second year. Further, a condor chick takes five to seven years before reaching breeding age. It is thus only the birds' longevity that may counteract assaults on its numbers (one bird in the National Zoo in Washington lived to age forty-five).

Audubon never ventured sufficiently far west to observe the California Condor in its natural setting. His reports came from Townsend, who saw condors near the Columbia River, feeding on dead salmon. Condors can weigh close to twenty-two pounds and may eat up to three pounds of carrion a day if it is available.

Condors can grow to be almost five feet long with a nearly ten-foot wingspread—the widest of any North American land bird. They have superb powers of flight, and once they leap into the air from a roosting tree, or flap along the ground until airborne, they can remain aloft for hours, soaring on rising currents of warm air. They dexterously manipulate their flight feathers to produce maximum wing surface, and can soar at high speeds, ranging widely, their pure white underwing feathers visible from afar. On the ground, however, they are less graceful, holding their naked red head, their neck with its purple patch, and their large black body in a slouching posture.

Nº 84. Plate 416.

John J. Audubon
1838

Californian Vulture.
Cathartes Californianus, Illiger.
Old Male.

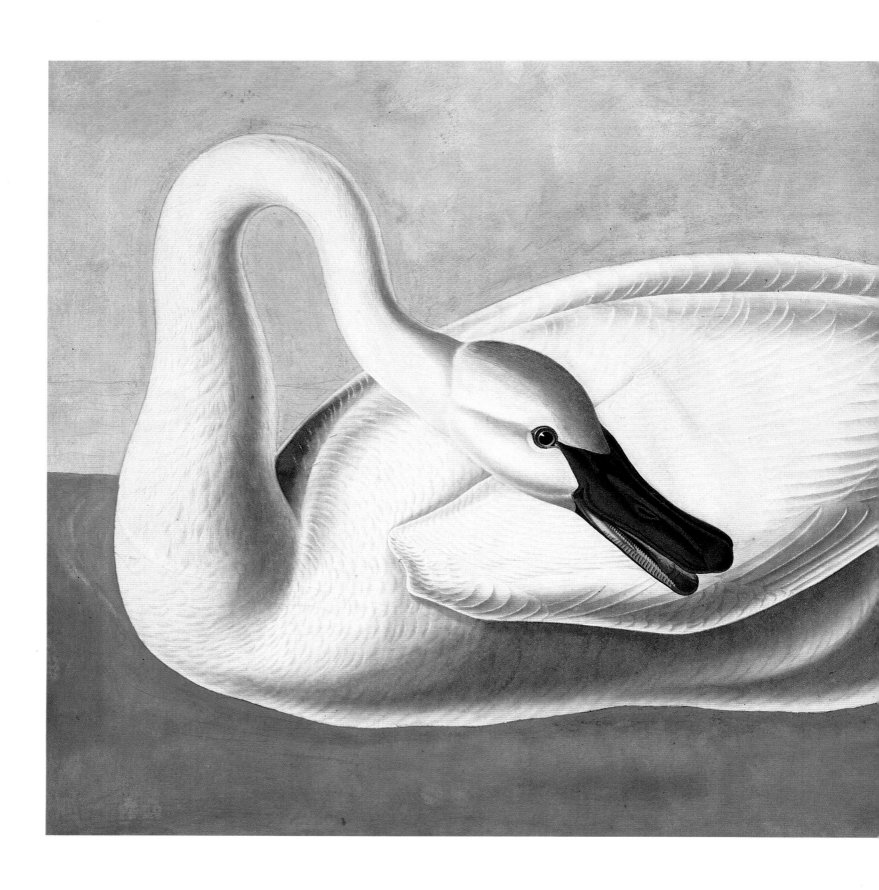

Trumpeter Swan

CYGNUS BUCCINATOR RICHARDSON

Probably painted c. 1836–37.
Medium: watercolor, pastel, oil paint, graphite, and selective scraping on paper;
23 × 37¾ in.; 58.5 × 95.9 cm.
Identification: adult
Seasonal distribution: breeds and winters in northwestern North America
Havell plate number: CCCCVI in *The Birds of America*
Acc. no. 1863.17.406

*T*he figure of this powerful, robust bird, with its predatory gaze and open bill, boldly contrasts with the conventional graceful, sentimental image of the swan. Audubon's composition emphasizes the length and massiveness of the trumpeter's muscular neck and its substantial breast, in which the breastbone is modified to accept the trumpeter's long, convoluted windpipe. It is the windpipe that produces the resonant cry for which the species is named, and which one writer compared to the sound of an old-fashioned French taxi's horn. The scene also highlights the species' characteristic all-black bill and its typical gesture, described by Audubon in his writings, of extending a single leg and foot. The artist leads the viewer's gaze from left to right over each feature in turn, and then up and around the mighty swan's carefully shaded and textured all-white back, evidently recalling the trumpeter's status not only as the largest North American waterfowl but as the largest swan in the world. A Trumpeter Swan can measure six feet long when fully extending its neck—as it does in flight—and can have a wingspan of ten feet.

Audubon made two pictures of the trumpeter based on frequent observations and on keeping a male as a pet for more than two years in Henderson, Kentucky. In December 1821, he drew a young bird in New Orleans (where, he tells us, they were sold in the markets) and, probably fifteen years later, made this image of a trumpeter foraging.

The species generally feeds by submerging its head and neck below the surface in sheltered, shallow, usually fresh water, after using its large, webbed feet and strong, flexible claws to dig deep holes in the bottom sediment and expose roots and growing plants. When swimming in deeper waters, trumpeters sometimes tip bottom-side up like certain duck species. They do not dive, although they are capable of swimming long distances underwater if necessary. While they are basically herbivorous, they do take aquatic insects, such as the one Havell depicts this bird eyeing in his engraving of the picture.

"As often as the howlings of the numerous wolves that prowled through the surrounding woods were heard," wrote Audubon, "the clanging cries of the swans would fill the air."[1] Before the arrival of Europeans in the New World (to which these birds are native), Trumpeter Swans ranged intermittently all the way from coast to coast. Even in Audubon's day the birds bred as far south as Missouri and wintered as far south as Texas. But their size made them desirable trophies and their feathers were prized (by artists including Audubon) as quills. The feathers were also used for down, powder puffs, and ornament, and the eggs and young were taken for food. Hundreds of thousands of the relatively tame birds were killed, and their population quickly retreated northwest. After nearing extinction the birds were protected, and now a population of about five thousand breeds in the western United States, Canada, and, primarily, Alaska. Conservationists are attempting to reestablish breeding populations in certain former nesting areas.

1. John James Audubon, *Ornithological Biography*, vol. VI (reprint of 1840–44 ed.; New York: Volair Books, 1979), p. 221.

Additional Watercolors
from
The New-York Historical Society

Plate I
Wild Turkey,
Meleagris gallopavo Linnaeus

Plate V
Canada Warbler, *Wilsonia canadensis* (Linnaeus)

Plate III
Prothonotary Warbler,
Protonotaria citrea (Boddaert)

Plate VI
Wild Turkey, *Meleagris gallopavo* Linnaeus

Plate IV
Purple Finch,
Carpodacus purpureus (Gmelin)

Plate VII
Common Grackle, *Quiscalus quiscula* (Linnaeus)

Plate VIII
White-throated Sparrow, *Zonotrichia albicollis* (Gmelin)

Plate XII
Northern Oriole,
Icterus galbula (Linnaeus)

Plate IX
Hooded Warbler, *Wilsonia citrina* (Boddaert)

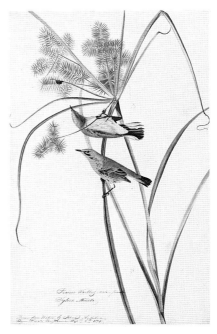

Plate XIV
Prairie Warbler,
Dendroica discolor (Vieillot)

Plate X
Water Pipit, *Anthus spinoletta* (Linnaeus)

Plate XVII
Mourning Dove,
Zenaida macroura (Linnaeus)

Plate XVIII
Bewick's Wren,
Thryomanes bewickii (Audubon)

Plate XXI
Northern Mockingbird,
Mimus polyglottos (Linnaeus)

Plate XIX
Louisiana Waterthrush,
Seiurus motacilla (Vieillot)

Plate XXII
Purple Martin,
Progne subis (Linnaeus)

Plate XX
Blue-winged Warbler,
Vermivora pinus (Linnaeus)

Plate XXIII
Common Yellowthroat,
Geothlypis trichas (Linnaeus)

Plate XXIV
Common Yellowthroat,
Geothlypis trichas (Linnaeus)

Plate XXVIII
Solitary Vireo,
Vireo solitarius (Wilson)

Plate XXV
Song Sparrow,
Melospiza melodia (Wilson)

Plate XXIX
Rufous-sided Towhee,
Pipilo erythrophthalmus (Linnaeus)

Plate XXVII
Red-headed Woodpecker,
Melanerpes erythrocephalus (Linnaeus)

Plate XXX
Pine Warbler,
Dendroica pinus (Wilson)

Plate XXXII
Black-billed Cuckoo, *Coccyzus erythrophthalmus* (Wilson)

Plate XXXVI
Cooper's Hawk,
Accipiter cooperii (Bonaparte)

Plate XXXIV
Worm-eating Warbler,
Helmitheros vermivorus (Gmelin)

Plate XXXVII
Northern Flicker,
Colaptes auratus (Linnaeus)

Plate XXXV
Yellow Warbler,
Dendroica petechia (Linnaeus)

Plate XXXVIII
Kentucky Warbler,
Oporornis formosus (Wilson)

Plate XL
American Redstart, *Setophaga ruticilla* (Linnaeus)

Plate XLIII
Cedar Waxwing,
Bombycilla cedrorum Vieillot

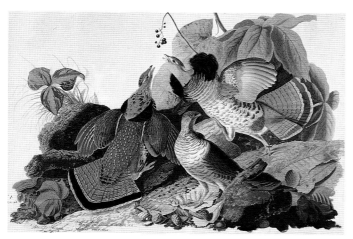

Plate XLI
Ruffed Grouse, *Bonasa umbellus* (Linnaeus)

Plate XLV
Willow Flycatcher,
Empidonax traillii (Audubon)

Plate XLII
Orchard Oriole, *Icterus spurius* (Linnaeus)

Plate XLVII
Ruby-throated Hummingbird,
Archilochus colubris (Linnaeus)

Plate XLIX
Cerulean Warbler,
Dendroica cerulea (Wilson)

Plate LIV
Bobolink,
Dolichonyx oryzivorus (Linnaeus)

Plate L
Magnolia Warbler,
Dendroica magnolia (Wilson)

Plate LV
Cuvier's Kinglet,
Regulus cuvieri Audubon

Plate LIII
Painted Bunting,
Passerina ciris (Linnaeus)

Plate LVI
Red-shouldered Hawk,
Buteo lineatus (Gmelin)

Plate LVIII
Hermit Thrush,
Catharus guttatus (Pallas)

Plate LXI
Great Horned Owl,
Bubo virginianus (Gmelin)

Plate LIX
Chestnut-sided Warbler,
Dendroica pensylvanica (Linnaeus)

Plate LXIII
White-eyed Vireo,
Vireo griscus (Boddaert)

Plate LX
Carbonated Warbler,
Sylvia carbonata Audubon

Plate LXIV
Swamp Sparrow,
Melospiza georgiana (Latham)

Plate LXV
Yellow Warbler,
Dendroica petechia (Linnaeus)

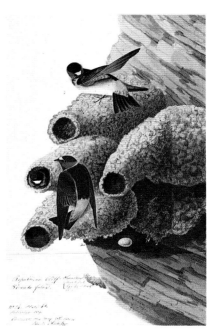

Plate LXVIII
Cliff Swallow,
Hirundo pyrrhonota Vieillot

Plate LXVI
Ivory-billed Woodpecker,
Campephilus principalis (Linnaeus)

Plate LXIX
Bay-breasted Warbler,
Dendroica castanea (Wilson)

Plate LXVII
Red-winged Blackbird,
Agelaius phoeniceus (Linnaeus)

Plate LXX
Henslow's Sparrow,
Ammodramus henslowii (Audubon)

Plate LXXI
Red-shouldered Hawk, *Buteo lineatus* (Gmelin)

Plate LXXV
Merlin,
Falco columbarius Linnaeus

Plate LXXIII
Wood Thrush, *Hylocichla mustelina* (Gmelin)

Plate LXXVII
Belted Kingfisher,
Ceryle alcyon (Linnaeus)

Plate LXXIV
Indigo Bunting, *Passerina cyanea* (Linnaeus)

Plate LXXVIII
Carolina Wren,
Thryothorus ludovicianus (Latham)

Plate LXXIX
Eastern Kingbird, *Tyrannus tyrannus* (Linnaeus)

Plate LXXX
Water Pipit, *Anthus spinoletta* (Linnaeus)

Plate LXXXV
Yellow-throated Warbler, *Dendroica dominica* (Linnaeus)

Plate LXXXVI
Red-tailed Hawk,
Buteo jamaicensis (Gmelin)

Plate LXXXVII
Scrub Jay,
Aphelocoma coerulescens (Bosc)

Plate LXXXVIII
Bay-breasted Warbler,
Dendroica castanea (Wilson)

Plate LXXXIX
Nashville Warbler,
Vermivora ruficapilla (Wilson)

Plate XCII
Merlin,
Falco columbarius Linnaeus

Plate XC
Black-and-white Warbler,
Mniotilta varia (Linnaeus)

Plate XCIII
Seaside Sparrow,
Ammodramus maritimus (Wilson)

Plate XCI
Broad-winged Hawk,
Buteo platypterus (Vieillot)

Plate XCIV
Vesper Sparrow,
Pooecetes gramineus (Gmelin)

Plate XCIX
Brown-headed Cowbird, *Molothrus ater* (Boddaert)

Plate XCV
Yellow Warbler,
Dendroica petechia (Linnaeus)

Plate XCVI
Black-throated Magpie-Jay,
Calocitta colliei (Vigors)

Plate CI
Common Raven, *Corvus corax* Linnaeus

Plate XCVII
Eastern Screech-Owl,
Otus asio (Linnaeus)

Plate CIII
Canada Warbler, *Wilsonia canadensis* (Linnaeus)

Plate CIV
Chipping Sparrow, *Spizella passerina* (Bechstein)

Plate CIX
Savannah Sparrow,
Passerculus sandwichensis (Gmelin)

Plate CV
Red-breasted Nuthatch, *Sitta canadensis* Linnaeus

Plate CX
Hooded Warbler,
Wilsonia citrina (Boddaert)

Plate CVIII
Fox Sparrow, *Passerella iliaca* (Merrem)

Plate CXI
Pileated Woodpecker,
Dryocopus pileatus (Linnaeus)

316

Plate CXII
Downy Woodpecker,
Picoides pubescens (Linnaeus)

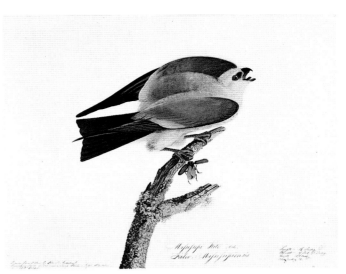

Plate CXVII
Mississippi Kite, *Ictinia mississippiensis* (Wilson)

Plate CXIV
White-crowned Sparrow,
Zonotrichia leucophrys (Forster)

Plate CXVIII
Warbling Vireo, *Vireo gilvus* (Vieillot)

Plate CXV
Eastern Wood-Pewee,
Contopus virens (Linnaeus)

Plate CXIX
Yellow-throated Vireo, *Vireo flavifrons* Vieillot

317

Plate CXXII
Blue Grosbeak,
Guiraca caerulea (Linnaeus)

Plate CXXVI
Bald Eagle,
Haliaeetus leucocephalus (Linnaeus)

Plate CXXIV
Wilson's Warbler,
Wilsonia pusilla (Wilson)

Plate CXXVII
Rose-breasted Grosbeak,
Pheucticus ludovicianus (Linnaeus)

Plate CXXV
Brown-headed Nuthatch,
Sitta pusilla Latham

Plate CXXVIII
Gray Catbird,
Dumetella carolinensis (Linnaeus)

318

Plate CXXIX
Great Crested Flycatcher,
Myiarchus crinitus (Linnaeus)

Plate CXXXII
Black-backed Woodpecker,
Picoides arcticus (Swainson)

Plate CXXX
Grasshopper Sparrow,
Ammodramus savannarum (Gmelin)

Plate CXXXIII
Blackpoll Warbler,
Dendroica striata (Forster)

Plate CXXXI
American Robin,
Turdus migratorius Linnaeus

Plate CXXXIV
Blackburnian Warbler,
Dendroica fusca (Müller)

Plate CXXXV
Blackburnian Warbler,
Dendroica fusca (Müller)

Plate CXXXIX
Field Sparrow,
Spizella pusilla (Wilson)

Plate CXXXVI
Eastern Meadowlark,
Sturnella magna (Linnaeus)

Plate CXL
Pine Warbler,
Dendroica pinus (Wilson)

Plate CXXXVIII
Connecticut Warbler,
Oporornis agilis (Wilson)

Plate CXLIII
Ovenbird,
Seiurus aurocapillus (Linnaeus)

Plate CXLIV
Acadian Flycatcher,
Empidonax virescens (Vieillot)

Plate CXLVII
Common Nighthawk,
Chordeiles minor (Forster)

Plate CXLV
Palm Warbler,
Dendroica palmarum (Gmelin)

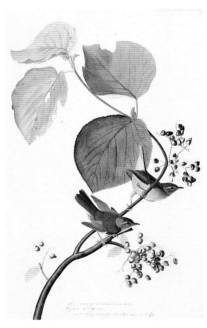

Plate CXLVIII
Black-throated Blue Warbler,
Dendroica caerulescens (Gmelin)

Plate CXLVI
Fish Crow,
Corvus ossifragus Wilson

Plate CLI
Turkey Vulture,
Cathartes aura (Linnaeus)

Plate CLIII
Yellow-rumped Warbler,
Dendroica coronata (Linnaeus)

Plate CLVII
Rusty Blackbird,
Euphagus carolinus (Müller)

Plate CLIV
Tennessee Warbler,
Vermivora peregrina (Wilson)

Plate CLIX
Northern Cardinal,
Cardinalis cardinalis (Linnaeus)

Plate CLVI
American Crow,
Corvus brachyrhynchos Brehm

Plate CLX
Carolina Chickadee,
Parus carolinensis Audubon

Plate CLXII
Zenaida Dove,
Zenaida aurita (Temminck)

Plate CLXV
Bachman's Sparrow, *Aimophila aestivalis* (Lichtenstein)

Plate CLXIII
Palm Warbler,
Dendroica palmarum (Gmelin)

Plate CLXVI
Rough-legged Hawk, *Buteo lagopus* (Pontoppidan)

Plate CLXIV
Veery,
Catharus fuscescens (Stephens)

Plate CLXVII
Key West Quail-Dove, *Geotrygon chrysia* Bonaparte

Plate CLXVIII
Fork-tailed Flycatcher,
Tyrannus savana Vieillot

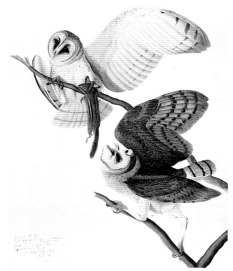

Plate CLXXI
Common Barn-Owl, *Tyto alba* (Scopoli)

Plate CLXIX
Mangrove Cuckoo,
Coccyzus minor (Gmelin)

Plate CLXXII
Blue-headed Quail-Dove, *Starnoenas cyanocephala* (Linnaeus)

Plate CLXX
Gray Kingbird,
Tyrannus dominicensis (Gmelin)

Plate CLXXIV
Olive-sided Flycatcher, *Contopus borealis* (Swainson)

Plate CLXXV
Sedge Wren, *Cistothorus platensis* (Latham)

Plate CLXXIX
House Wren,
Troglodytes aedon Vieillot

Plate CLXXVI
Spruce Grouse, *Dendragapus canadensis* (Linnaeus)

Plate CLXXX
Pine Siskin,
Carduelis pinus (Wilson)

Plate CLXXVIII
Orange-crowned Warbler, *Vermivora celata* (Say)

Plate CLXXXII
Common Ground-Dove,
Columbina passerina (Linnaeus)

Plate CXCIII
Lincoln's Sparrow,
Melospiza lincolnii (Audubon)

Plate CXC
Yellow-bellied Sapsucker, *Sphyrapicus varius* (Linnaeus)

Plate CXCI
Willow Ptarmigan, *Lagopus lagopus* (Linnaeus)

Plate CXCIV
Boreal Chickadee,
Parus hudsonicus Forster

Plate CXCV
Ruby-crowned Kinglet,
Regulus calendula (Linnaeus)

Plate CXCII
Northern Shrike, *Lanius excubitor* Linnaeus

Plate CXCVI
Gyrfalcon,
Falco rusticolus Linnaeus

Plate CXCIX
Northern Saw-whet Owl, *Aegolius acadicus* (Gmelin)

Plate CXCVII
Red Crossbill,
Loxia curvirostra Linnaeus

Plate CC
Horned Lark, *Eremophila alpestris* (Linnaeus)

Plate CXCVIII
Swainson's Warbler,
Limnothlypis swainsonii (Audubon)

Plate CCI
Canada Goose, *Branta canadensis* (Linnaeus)

Plate CCII
Red-throated Loon, *Gavia stellata* (Pontoppidan)

Plate CCV
Virginia Rail, *Rallus limicola* Vieillot

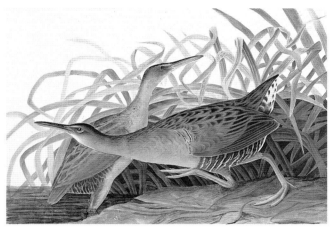

Plate CCIII
King Rail, *Rallus elegans* Audubon

Plate CCVII
Brown Booby, *Sula leucogaster* (Boddaert)

Plate CCIV
Clapper Rail, *Rallus longirostris* Boddaert

Plate CCVIII
Eskimo Curlew, *Numenius borealis* (Forster)

Plate CCIX
Wilson's Plover, *Charadrius wilsonia* Ord

Plate CCXII
Ring-billed Gull, *Larus delawarensis* Ord

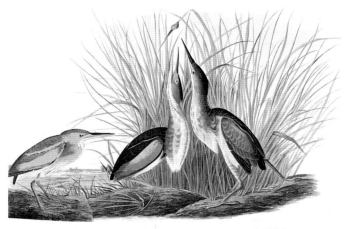

Plate CCX
Least Bittern, *Ixobrychus exilis* (Gmelin)

Plate CCXIV
Razorbill, *Alca torda* Linnaeus

Plate CCXI
Great Blue Heron, *Ardea herodias* Linnaeus

Plate CCXV
Red-necked Phalarope, *Phalaropus lobatus* (Linnaeus)

Plate CCXVI
Wood Stork, *Mycteria americana* Linnaeus

Plate CCXX
Piping Plover, *Charadrius melodus* Ord

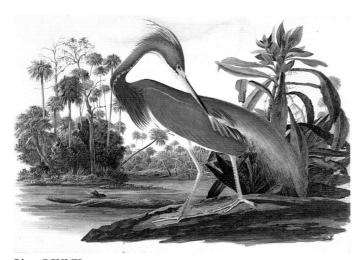

Plate CCXVII
Tricolored Heron, *Egretta tricolor* (Müller)

Plate CCXXI
Mallard, *Anas platyrhynchos* Linnaeus

Plate CCXVIII
Common Murre, *Uria aalge* (Pontoppidan)

Plate CCXXII
White Ibis, *Eudocimus albus* (Linnaeus)

Plate CCXXIII
American Oystercatcher, *Haematopus palliatus* Temminck

Plate CCXXVII
Northern Pintail, *Anas acuta* Linnaeus

Plate CCXXIV
Black-legged Kittiwake, *Rissa tridactyla* (Linnaeus)

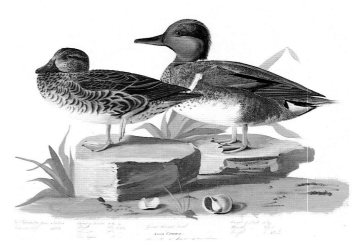

Plate CCXXVIII
Green-winged Teal, *Anas crecca* Linnaeus

Plate CCXXV
Killdeer, *Charadrius vociferus* Linnaeus

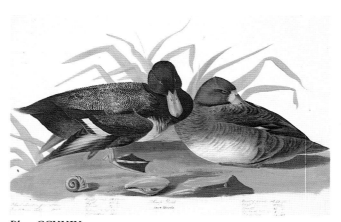

Plate CCXXIX
Greater Scaup, *Aythya marila* (Linnaeus)

Plate CCXXX
Sanderling, *Calidris alba* (Pallas)

Plate CCXXXIV
Ring-necked Duck, *Aythya collaris* (Donovan)

Plate CCXXXII
Hooded Merganser, *Lophodytes cucullatus* (Linnaeus)

Plate CCXXXV
Sooty Tern, *Sterna fuscata* Linnaeus

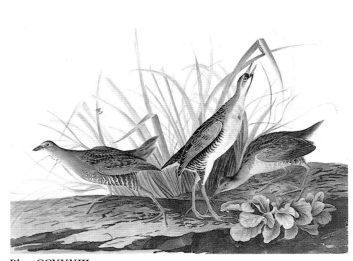

Plate CCXXXIII
Sora, *Porzana carolina* (Linnaeus)

Plate CCXXXVII
Whimbrel, *Numenius phaeopus* (Linnaeus)

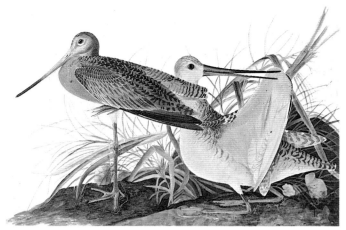

Plate CCXXXVIII
Marbled Godwit, *Limosa fedoa* (Linnaeus)

Plate CCXLI
Great Black-backed Gull, *Larus marinus* Linnaeus

Plate CCXXXIX
American Coot, *Fulica americana* Gmelin

Plate CCXLIV
Common Moorhen, *Gallinula chloropus* (Linnaeus)

Plate CCXL
Roseate Tern, *Sterna dougallii* Montagu

Plate CCXLV
Thick-billed Murre, *Uria lomvia* (Linnaeus)

Plate CCXLVI
Common Eider, *Somateria mollissima* (Linnaeus)

Plate CCXLIX
Tufted Puffin, *Fratercula cirrhata* (Pallas)

Plate CCXLVII
White-winged Scoter, *Melanitta fusca* (Linnaeus)

Plate CCL
Arctic Tern, *Sterna paradisaea* Pontoppidan

Plate CCXLVIII
Pied-billed Grebe, *Podilymbus podiceps* (Linnaeus)

Plate CCLII
Double-crested Cormorant, *Phalacrocorax auritus* (Lesson)

Plate CCLIII
Pomarine Jaeger, *Stercorarius pomarinus* (Temminck)

Plate CCLVI
Reddish Egret, *Egretta rufescens* (Gmelin)

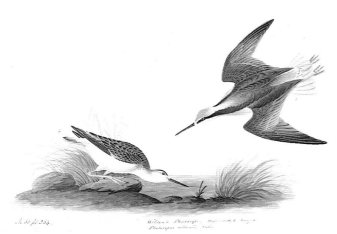

Plate CCLIV
Wilson's Phalarope, *Phalaropus tricolor* (Vieillot)

Plate CCLVIII
Hudsonian Godwit, *Limosa haemastica* (Linnaeus)

Plate CCLV
Red Phalarope, *Phalaropus fulicaria* (Linnaeus)

Plate CCLIX
Horned Grebe, *Podiceps auritus* (Linnaeus)

Plate CCLX
Leach's Storm-Petrel, *Oceanodroma leucorhoa* (Vieillot)

Plate CCLXIII
Curlew Sandpiper, *Calidris ferruginea* (Pontoppidan)

Plate CCLXI
Sandhill Crane, *Grus canadensis* (Linnaeus)

Plate CCLXIV
Northern Fulmar, *Fulmarus glacialis* (Linnaeus)

Plate CCLXII
White-tailed Tropicbird, *Phaethon lepturus* Daudin

Plate CCLXV
Buff-breasted Sandpiper, *Tryngites subruficollis* (Vieillot)

Plate CCLXX
Wilson's Storm-Petrel, *Oceanites oceanicus* (Kuhl)

Plate CCLXVII
Long-tailed Jaeger, *Stercorarius longicaudus* Vieillot

Plate CCLXXII
Parasitic Jaeger, *Stercorarius parasiticus* (Linnaeus)

Plate CCLXVIII
American Woodcock, *Scolopax minor* Gmelin

Plate CCLXIX
Common Greenshank, *Tringa nebularia* (Gunnerus)

Plate CCLXXIII
Royal Tern, *Sterna maxima* Boddaert

Plate CCLXXIV
Willet, *Catoptrophorus semipalmatus* (Gmelin)

Plate CCLXXVII
Canada Goose, *Branta canadensis* (Linnaeus)

Plate CCLXXV
Brown Noddy, *Anous stolidus* (Linnaeus)

Plate CCLXXVIII
White-rumped Sandpiper, *Calidris fuscicollis* (Vieillot)

Plate CCLXXVI
King Eider, *Somateria spectabilis* (Linnaeus)

Plate CCLXXIX
Sandwich Tern, *Sterna sandvicensis* Latham

Plate CCLXXX
Black Tern, *Chlidonias niger* (Linnaeus)

Plate CCLXXXVI
Greater White-fronted Goose, *Anser albifrons* (Scopoli)

Plate CCLXXXII
Iceland Gull, *Larus glaucoides* Meyer

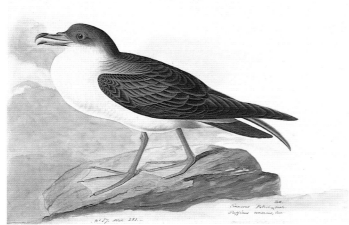

Plate CCLXXXIII
Greater Shearwater, *Puffinus gravis* O'Reilly

Plate CCLXXXVII
Ivory Gull, *Pagophila eburnea* (Phipps)

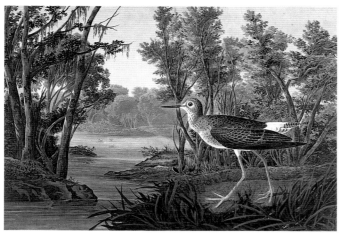

Plate CCLXXXVIII
Lesser Yellowlegs, *Tringa flavipes* (Gmelin)

Plate CCXCI
Herring Gull, *Larus argentatus* Pontoppidan

Plate CCLXXXIX
Solitary Sandpiper, *Tringa solitaria* Wilson

Plate CCXCII
Great Crested Grebe, *Podiceps cristatus* (Linnaeus)

Plate CCXC
Dunlin, *Calidris alpina* (Linnaeus)

Plate CCXCIII
Horned Puffin, *Fratercula corniculata* (Naumann)

Plate CCXCIV
Pectoral Sandpiper, *Calidris melanotos* (Vieillot)

Plate CCXCVII
Harlequin Duck, *Histrionicus histrionicus* (Linnaeus)

Plate CCXCV
Manx Shearwater, *Puffinus puffinus* (Brünnich)

Plate CCXCVIII
Red-necked Grebe, *Podiceps grisegena* (Boddaert)

Plate CCXCVI
Barnacle Goose, *Branta leucopsis* (Bechstein)

Plate CCXCIX
Audubon's Shearwater, *Puffinus lherminieri* Lesson

Plate CCC
1. Lesser Golden-Plover, *Pluvialis dominica* (Müller)
2. Greater Golden-Plover, *Pluvialis apricaria* (Linnaeus)

Plate CCCIII
Upland Sandpiper, *Bartramia longicauda* (Bechstein)

Plate CCCI
Canvasback, *Aythya valisineria* (Wilson)

Plate CCCIV
Ruddy Turnstone, *Arenaria interpres* (Linnaeus)

Plate CCCII
American Black Duck, *Anas rubripes* Brewster

Plate CCCV
Purple Gallinule, *Porphyrula martinica* (Linnaeus)

343

Plate CCCVI
Common Loon, *Gavia immer* (Brünnich)

Plate CCCXII
Oldsquaw, *Clangula hyemalis* (Linnaeus)

Plate CCCVIII
Greater Yellowlegs, *Tringa melanoleuca* (Gmelin)

Plate CCCXIV
Laughing Gull, *Larus atricilla* Linnaeus

Plate CCCX
Spotted Sandpiper, *Actitis macularia* (Linnaeus)

Plate CCCXVI
Anhinga, *Anhinga anhinga* (Linnaeus)

Plate CCCXVII
Surf Scoter, *Melanitta perspicillata* (Linnaeus)

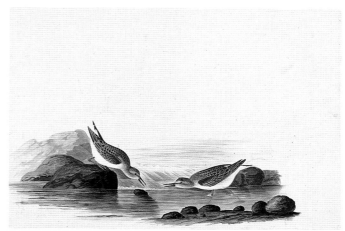

Plate CCCXX
Least Sandpiper, *Calidris minutilla* (Vieillot)

Plate CCCXVIII
American Avocet, *Recurvirostra americana* Gmelin

Plate CCCXXII
Redhead, *Aythya americana* (Eyton)

Plate CCCXIX
Least Tern, *Sterna antillarum* (Lesson)

Plate CCCXXIII
Black Skimmer, *Rynchops niger* Linnaeus

Plate CCCXXIV
Bonaparte's Gull, *Larus philadelphia* (Ord)

Plate CCCXXV
Bufflehead, *Bucephala albeola* (Linnaeus)

Plate CCCXXVII
Northern Shoveler, *Anas clypeata* Linnaeus

Plate CCCXXVIII
Black-necked Stilt, *Himantopus mexicanus* (Müller)

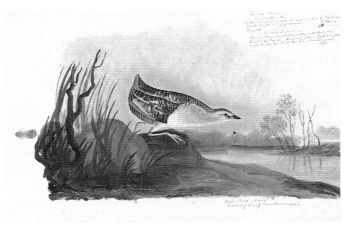

Plate CCCXXIX
Yellow Rail, *Coturnicops noveboracensis* (Gmelin)

Plate CCCXXX
Semipalmated Plover, *Charadrius semipalmatus* Bonaparte

Plate CCCXXXI
Common Merganser, *Mergus merganser* Linnaeus

Plate CCCXXXIV
Black-bellied Plover, *Pluvialis squatarola* (Linnaeus)

Plate CCCXXXII
Labrador Duck, *Camptorhynchus labradorius* (Gmelin)

Plate CCCXXXV
Short-billed Dowitcher, *Limnodromus griseus* (Gmelin)

Plate CCCXXXIII
Green-backed Heron, *Butorides striatus* (Linnaeus)

Plate CCCXXXVI
Yellow-crowned Night-Heron, *Nycticorax violaceus* (Linnaeus)

Plate CCCXXXVIII
Mallard × Gadwall hybrid, *Anas platyrhynchos × strepera*

Plate CCCXLI
Great Auk, *Pinguinus impennis* (Linnaeus)

Plate CCCXXXIX
Dovekie, *Alle alle* (Linnaeus)

Plate CCCXLIII
Ruddy Duck, *Oxyura jamaicensis* (Gmelin)

Plate CCCXL
British Storm-Petrel, *Hydrobates pelagicus* (Linnaeus)

Plate CCCXLIV
Stilt Sandpiper, *Calidris himantopus* (Bonaparte)

Plate CCCXLV
American Wigeon, *Anas americana* Gmelin

Plate CCCL
Mountain Plover, *Charadrius montanus* Townsend

Plate CCCXLVII
Smew, *Mergellus albellus* (Linnaeus)

Plate CCCLV
Seaside Sparrow, *Ammodramus maritimus* (Wilson)

Plate CCCXLVIII
Gadwall, *Anas strepera* Linnaeus

Plate CCCLVI
Northern Harrier, *Circus cyaneus* (Linnaeus)

Plate CCCLVIII
Pine Grosbeak, *Pinicola enucleator* (Linnaeus)

Plate CCCLXII
1. Scrub Jay, *Aphelocoma coerulescens* (Bosc)
2. Steller's Jay, *Cyanocitta stelleri* (Gmelin)
3. Yellow-billed Magpie, *Pica nuttalli* (Audubon)
4. Clark's Nutcracker, *Nucifraga columbiana* (Wilson)

Plate CCCLIX
1. Say's Phoebe, *Sayornis saya* (Bonaparte)
2. Western Kingbird, *Tyrannus verticalis* Say
3. Scissor-tailed Flycatcher, *Tyrannus forficatus* (Gmelin)

Plate CCCLXIII
Bohemian Waxwing, *Bombycilla garrulus* (Linnaeus)

Plate CCCLXI
Blue Grouse, *Dendragapus obscurus* (Say)

Plate CCCLXIV
White-winged Crossbill, *Loxia leucoptera* Gmelin

Plate CCCLXV
Lapland Longspur, *Calcarius lapponicus* (Linnaeus)

Plate CCCLXVII
Band-tailed Pigeon, *Columba fasciata* Say

Plate CCCLXVIII
Rock Ptarmigan, *Lagopus mutus* (Montin)

Plate CCCLXIX
1. Sage Thrasher, *Oreoscoptes montanus* (Townsend)
2. Varied Thrush *Ixoreus naevius* (Gmelin)

Plate CCCLXX
American Dipper, *Cinclus mexicanus* Swainson

351

Plate CCCLXXI
Sage Grouse, *Centrocercus urophasianus* (Bonaparte)

Plate CCCLXXII
Swainson's Hawk, *Buteo swainsoni* Bonaparte

Plate CCCLXXIII
1. Evening Grosbeak, *Coccothraustes vespertinus* (Cooper)
2. Black-headed Grosbeak, *Pheucticus melanocephalus* (Swainson)

Plate CCCLXXIV
Sharp-shinned Hawk, *Accipiter striatus* Vieillot

Plate CCCLXXV
Common Redpoll, *Carduelis flammea* (Linnaeus)

Plate CCCLXXVI
Trumpeter Swan, *Cygnus buccinator* Richardson

Plate CCCLXXVII
Limpkin, *Aramus guarauna* (Linnaeus)

Plate CCCLXXX
Boreal Owl, *Aegolius funereus* (Linnaeus)

Plate CCCLXXVIII
Northern Hawk-Owl, *Surnia ulula* (Linnaeus)

Plate CCCLXXXI
Snow Goose, *Chen caerulescens* (Linnaeus)

Plate CCCLXXIX
Rufous Hummingbird, *Selasphorus rufus* (Gmelin)

Plate CCCLXXXIII
Long-eared Owl, *Asio otus* (Linnaeus)

Plate CCCLXXXIV
Dickcissel, *Spiza americana* (Gmelin)

Plate CCCLXXXVIII
1. Northern Oriole, *Icterus galbula* (Linnaeus)
2. Tricolored Blackbird, *Agelaius tricolor* (Audubon)
3. Yellow-headed Blackbird, *Xanthocephalus xanthocephalus* (Bonaparte)

Plate CCCLXXXV
1. Violet-green Swallow, *Tachycineta thalassina* (Swainson)
2. Bank Swallow, *Riparia riparia* (Linnaeus)

Plate CCCLXXXIX
Red-cockaded Woodpecker, *Picoides borealis* (Vieillot)

Plate CCCLXXXVII
Glossy Ibis, *Plegadis falcinellus* (Linnaeus)

Plate CCCXC
1. Lark Bunting, *Calamospiza melanocorys* Stejneger
2. Lark Sparrow, *Chondestes grammacus* (Say)
3. Song Sparrow, *Melospiza melodia* (Wilson)

Plate CCCXCI
Brant, *Branta bernicla* (Linnaeus)

Plate CCCXCII
Harris's Hawk, *Parabuteo unicinctus* (Temminck)

Plate CCCXCIII and CCCXCV
1. Townsend's Warbler, *Dendroica townsendi* (Townsend)
2. Yellow-rumped Warbler, *Dendroica coronata* (Linnaeus)
3. Mountain Bluebird, *Sialia currucoides* (Bechstein)
4. Western Bluebird, *Sialia mexicana* Swainson
5. Black-throated Gray Warbler, *Dendroica nigrescens* (Townsend)
6. Hermit Warbler, *Dendroica occidentalis* (Townsend)

Plate CCCXCIV
1. Lazuli Bunting, *Passerina amoena* (Say)
2. Chestnut-collared Longspur, *Calcarius ornatus* (Townsend)
3. Lark Sparrow, *Chondestes grammacus* (Say)
4. Golden-crowned Sparrow, *Zonotrichia atricapilla* (Gmelin)
5. Rufous-sided Towhee, *Pipilo erythrophthalmus* (Linnaeus)

Plate CCCXCVI
Glaucous Gull, *Larus hyperboreus* Gunnerus

Plate CCCXCIX and CCCC
1. Smith's Longspur, *Calcarius pictus* (Swainson)
2. Lesser Goldfinch, *Carduelis psaltria* (Say)
3. Black-headed Siskin, *Carduelis notata* Du Bus de Gisignies
4. Western Tanager, *Piranga ludoviciana* (Wilson)
5. Hoary Redpoll, *Carduelis hornemanni* (Holböll)
6. Townsend's Bunting, *Emberiza townsendi* Audubon

Plate CCCXCVII
Scarlet Ibis, *Eudocimus ruber* (Linnaeus)

Plate CCCCI
Red-breasted Merganser, *Mergus serrator* Linnaeus

Plate CCCXCVIII
1. Dark-eyed Junco, *Junco hyemalis* (Linnaeus)
2. Clay-colored Sparrow, *Spizella pallida* (Swainson)

Plate CCCCII
1. Crested Auklet, *Aethia cristatella* (Pallas)
2. Ancient Murrelet, *Synthliboramphus antiquus* (Gmelin)
3. Marbled Murrelet, *Brachyramphus marmoratus* (Gmelin)
4. Least Auklet, *Aethia pusilla* (Pallas)
5. Rhinoceros Auklet, *Cerorhinca monocerata* (Pallas)

Plate CCCCIII
Barrow's Goldeneye, *Bucephala islandica* (Gmelin)

Plate CCCCVII
Light-mantled Albatross, *Phoebetria palpebrata* (Forster)

Plate CCCCIV
Eared Grebe, *Podiceps nigricollis* Brehm

Plate CCCCVIII
Black Scoter, *Melanitta nigra* (Linnaeus)

Plate CCCCV
Semipalmated Sandpiper, *Calidris pusilla* (Linnaeus)

Plate CCCCIX
1. Forster's Tern, *Sterna forsteri* Nuttall
2. Trudeau's Tern, *Sterna trudeaui* Audubon

357

Plate CCCCXVIII
1. Rock Ptarmigan, *Lagopus mutus* (Montin)
2. White-tailed Ptarmigan, *Lagopus leucurus* (Richardson)

Plate CCCCXXII
Rough-legged Hawk, *Buteo lagopus* (Pontoppidan)

Plate CCCCXIX
1. Hermit Thrush, *Catharus guttatus* (Pallas)
2. Townsend's Solitaire, *Myadestes townsendi* (Audubon)
3. Gray Jay, *Perisoreus canadensis* (Linnaeus)

Plate CCCCXXIII
1. Mountain Quail, *Oreortyx pictus* (Douglas)
2. Crested Bobwhite, *Colinus cristatus* (Linnaeus)

Plate CCCCXX
Red-winged Blackbird, *Agelaius phoeniceus* (Linnaeus)

Plate CCCCXXIV
1. House Finch, *Carpodacus mexicanus* (Müller)
2. Rosy Finch, *Leucosticte arctoa* (Pallas)

Plate CCCCXXVII
American Black Oystercatcher, *Haematopus bachmani* Audubon

Plate CCCCXXX
Marbled Murrelet, *Brachyramphus marmoratus* (Gmelin)

Plate CCCCXXVIII
Surfbird, *Aphriza virgata* (Gmelin)

Plate CCCCXXXI
Greater Flamingo, *Phoenicopterus ruber* Linnaeus

Plate CCCCXXIX
Steller's Eider, *Polysticta stelleri* (Pallas)

Plate CCCCXXXII
1. Burrowing Owl, *Athene cunicularia* (Molina)
2. Little Owl, *Athene noctua* (Scopoli)
3. Northern Pygmy-Owl, *Glaucidium gnoma* (Wagler)
4. Short-eared Owl, *Asio flammeus* (Pontoppidan)

Plate CCCCXXXIII
1. Northern Oriole, *Icterus galbula* (Linnaeus)
2. Northern Waterthrush, *Seiurus noveboracensis* (Gmelin)
3. Varied Thrush, *Ixoreus naevius* (Gmelin)
4. Lesser Goldfinch, *Carduelis psaltria* (Say)

Plate CCCCXXXV
American Dipper, *Cinclus mexicanus* Swainson

1863.18.003/004
1. Vesper Sparrow, *Pooecetes gramineus* (Gmelin) (left)
2. Black-throated Green Warbler, *Dendroica virens* (Gmelin) (right)

Plate CCCCXXXIV
1. Red-eyed Vireo, *Vireo olivaceus* (Linnaeus)
2. Small-headed Flycatcher, *Sylvania microcephala* Ridgway
3. Least Flycatcher, *Empidonax minimus* (Baird and Baird)
4. Black Phoebe, *Sayornis nigricans* (Swainson)
5. Blue Mountain Warbler, *Sylvia montana* Wilson
6. Western Wood-Pewee, *Contopus sordidulus* Sclater

1863.18.005
Sylvia Trochitus Delicata

1863.18.009
American Robin,
Turdus migratorius Linnaeus

1863.18.006
Rose-breasted Grosbeak,
Pheucticus ludovicianus (Linnaeus)

1863.18.010
Unidentified Sparrows

1863.18.007/008
Marsh Wren, *Cistothorus palustris* (Wilson) (left)
Eastern Wood-Pewee, *Contopus virens* (Linnaeus) (right)

1863.18.011
Yellow-rumped Warbler,
Dendroica coronata (Linnaeus)

1863.18.012
Bachman's Warbler,
Vermivora bachmanii (Audubon)

1863.18.017
Gadwall, *Anas strepera* Linnaeus

1863.18.014
1. Blue-winged Warbler, *Vermivora pinus* (Linnaeus)
2. Golden-winged Warbler, *Vermivora chrysoptera* (Linnaeus)

1863.18.018
American Black Duck, *Anas rubripes* Brewster

1863.18.015
Red-breasted Merganser, *Mergus serrator* Linnaeus

1863.18.019
Snowy Owl,
Nyctea scandiaca (Linnaeus)

1863.18.020
Long-billed Dowitcher, *Limnodromus scolopaceus* (Say)

1863.18.024
Common Black-headed Gull, *Larus ridibundus* Linnaeus

1863.18.021
Pectoral Sandpiper, *Calidris melanotos* (Vieillot)

1863.18.025
Unidentified Shorebird (Red Knot?), *Calidris canutus* (Linnaeus)

1863.18.023
Black Vulture, *Coragyps atratus* (Bechstein)

1863.18.026
Bonaparte's Gull, *Larus philadelphia* (Ord)

1863.18.029
Great Egret, *Casmerodius albus* (Linnaeus)
White Heron

1863.18.037
Steller's Eider, *Polysticta stelleri* (Pallas)

1863.18.031
Sharp-shinned Hawk, *Accipiter striatus* Vieillot

1863.18.038
Herring Gull, *Larus argentatus* Pontoppidan

1863.18.033
Common Tern, *Sterna hirundo* Linnaeus

1863.18.039
Little Blue Heron, *Egretta caerulea* (Linnaeus)

Descriptions of Watercolors

Plate numbers refer to *The Birds of America* prints. The last set of digits of the Historical Society's accession numbers 1863.17.001–435 are the same as the plate numbers, except for 1863.17.395, which is combined with 1863.17.393, and 1863.17.414, which is combined with 1863.17.399. There is no 1863.17.084 or 1863.17.426.

Watercolors not directly related to *The Birds of America* are numbered 1863.18.001–040. Audubon's nomenclature has been included where it differs from the current English and Latin names. The Historical Society does not have the watercolors for the Black-throated Blue Warbler, plate CLV, and the Blue-gray Gnatcatcher, plate LXXXIV.

Plates marked with an asterisk appear in the Selected Watercolors section.

1863.17.001
Wild Turkey, *Meleagris gallopavo* Linnaeus
39¼ × 26¼ in. (99.7 × 67 cm.)
Great American Cock Male

*1863.17.002
Yellow-billed Cuckoo, *Coccyzus americanus* (Linnaeus)
19¼ × 24⅛ in. (48.9 × 61.3 cm.)

1863.17.003
Prothonotary Warbler, *Protonotaria citrea* (Boddaert)
18¹⁄₁₆ × 11⅞ in. (45.90 × 30.1 cm.)

1863.17.004
Purple Finch, *Carpodacus purpureus* (Gmelin)
18¹⁵⁄₁₆ × 12 in. (48 × 30.5 cm.)

1863.17.005
Canada Warbler, *Wilsonia canadensis* (Linnaeus)
18¾ × 11⅝ in. (47.6 × 29.4 cm.)
Bonaparte Fly catcher

1863.17.006
Wild Turkey, *Meleagris gallopavo* Linnaeus
25⁷⁄₁₆ × 38¹³⁄₁₆ in. (64.7 × 98.6 cm.)
Great American Hen and Young

1863.17.007
Common Grackle, *Quiscalus quiscula* (Linnaeus)
23⅞ × 18½ in. (60.6 × 47 cm.)
Purple Grackle or Common Crow Blackbird

1863.17.008
White-throated Sparrow, *Zonotrichia albicollis* (Gmelin)
18¼ × 11⅛ in. (46.4 × 28.4 cm.)

1863.17.009
Hooded Warbler, *Wilsonia citrina* (Boddaert)
18½ × 11⁹⁄₁₆ in. (47.1 × 29.3 cm.)
Selby's Fly Catcher

1863.17.010
Water Pipit, *Anthus spinoletta* (Linnaeus)
11½ × 16¹⁵⁄₁₆ in. (29.3 × 42 cm.)
Brown Lark or Brown Titlark

*1863.17.011
Bald Eagle, *Haliaeetus leucocephalus* (Linnaeus)
38⁵⁄₁₆ × 23⅝ in. (97.3 × 60 cm.)
Bird of Washington or Great American Sea Eagle

1863.17.012
Northern Oriole, *Icterus galbula* (Linnaeus)
23¾ × 18⅝ in. (60.3 × 47.3 cm.)
Baltimore Oriole

*1863.17.013
Dark-eyed Junco, *Junco hyemalis* (Linnaeus)
19 × 11¾ in. (48.4 × 29.8 cm.)
Snow Bird or Common Snow-bird

1863.17.014
Prairie Warbler, *Dendroica discolor* (Vieillot)
18¹¹⁄₁₆ × 11⅝ in. (47.5 × 29.7 cm.)

*1863.17.015
Northern Parula, *Parula americana* (Linnaeus)
18⁷⁄₁₆ × 11⁹⁄₁₆ in. (46.8 × 29.4 cm.)
Blue Yellow-backed Warbler

*1863.17.016
Peregrine Falcon, *Falco peregrinus* Tunstall
24³⁄₁₆ × 37⅜ in. (61.4 × 94.9 cm.)
Great-footed Hawk

1863.17.017
Mourning Dove, *Zenaidura macroura* (Linnaeus)
26⅝ × 19 in. (67.1 × 48.3 cm.) sight
Carolina Pigeon or Carolina Turtle Dove

1863.17.018
Bewick's Wren, *Thryomanes bewickii* (Audubon)
18⅝ × 11⅜ in. (47.3 × 28.9 cm.) sight
Bewick's Wren or Bewick's Long-tailed Wren

1863.17.019
Louisiana Waterthrush, *Seiurus motacilla* (Vieillot)
18½ × 11⁵⁄₁₆ in. (47 × 29.4 cm.)

1863.17.020
Blue-winged Warbler, *Vermivora pinus* (Linnaeus)
19 × 11¾ in. (48.3 × 29.9 cm.) sight
Blue-winged Yellow Warbler

1863.17.021
Northern Mockingbird, *Mimus polyglottos* (Linnaeus)
29¹¹⁄₁₆ × 20⅞ in. (75.4 × 52.9 cm.)
Mocking Bird

1863.17.022
Purple Martin, *Progne subis* (Linnaeus)
22¾ × 18⅛ in. (57.8 × 46.2 cm.)

1863.17.023
Common Yellowthroat, *Geothlypis trichas* (Linnaeus)
18⅝ × 11⅝ in. (47.4 × 29.6 cm.)
Yellow-breasted Warbler or Maryland Yellow Throat

1863.17.024
Common Yellowthroat, *Geothlypis trichas* (Linnaeus)
18½ × 11¹¹⁄₁₆ in. (47 × 29.6 cm.)
Roscoe's Yellow-throat

1863.17.025
Song Sparrow, *Melospiza melodia* (Wilson)
19⅛ × 12 in. (48.5 × 30.5 cm.)

*1863.17.026
Carolina Parakeet, *Conuropsis carolinensis* (Linnaeus)
29¹¹⁄₁₆ × 21³⁄₁₆ in. (75.4 × 53.9 cm.)
Carolina Parrot or parakeet

1863.17.027
Red-headed Woodpecker, *Melanerpes erythrocephalus* (Linnaeus)
23⅜ × 18⅝ in. (59.3 × 47.4 cm.)

1863.17.028
Solitary Vireo, *Vireo solitarius* (Wilson)
19³⁄₁₆ × 11¾ in. (48.9 × 29.9 cm.)
Solitary Flycatcher or Solitary Vireo

1863.17.029
Rufous-sided Towhee, *Pipilo erythrophthalmus* (Linnaeus)
18⅞ × 11⅝ in. (48.2 × 29.2 cm.)
Towhe Bunting

1863.17.030
Pine Warbler, *Dendroica pinus* (Wilson)
16½ × 10½ in. (41.9 × 26.7 cm.)
Vigor's warbler or Vigor's Vireo

*1863.17.031
Bald Eagle, *Haliaeetus leucocephalus* (Linnaeus)
25⅜ × 38¼ in. (64.6 × 97.2 cm.)
White-headed Eagle

1863.17.032
Black-billed Cuckoo, *Coccyzus erythrophthalmus* (Wilson)
19⅜ × 24⅛ in. (49.2 × 61.3 cm.) sight

*1863.17.033
American Goldfinch, *Carduelis tristis* (Linnaeus)
18½ × 11¾ in. (47 × 29.8 cm.)

1863.17.034
Worm-eating Warbler, *Helmitheros vermivorus* (Gmelin)
19³⁄₁₆ × 11¹⁵⁄₁₆ in. (49.5 × 30.5 cm.) sight

1863.17.035
Yellow Warbler, *Dendroica petechia* (Linnaeus)
18¾ × 11¾ in. (47.7 × 29.8 cm.) sight
Children's Warbler

1863.17.036
Cooper's Hawk, *Accipiter cooperii* (Bonaparte)
19⅛ × 18⁹⁄₁₆ in. (48.6 × 47.2 cm.)
Stanley Hawk

1863.17.037
Northern Flicker, *Colaptes auratus* (Linnaeus)
26¾ × 18⅝ in. (67.9 × 46.2 cm.) sight
Gold-winged or Golden-winged Woodpecker

1863.17.038
Kentucky Warbler, *Oporornis formosus* (Wilson)
19 × 11¹¹/₁₆ in. (48.3 × 30 cm.) sight

*1863.17.039
Tufted Titmouse, *Parus bicolor* Linnaeus
18⅝ × 11⅝ in. (47.3 × 29.5 cm.)
Crested Titmouse

1863.17.040
American Redstart, *Setophaga ruticilla* (Linnaeus)
18¹⁵/₁₆ × 11⅝ in. (48.1 × 29.5 cm.)

1863.17.041
Ruffed Grouse, *Bonasa umbellus* (Linnaeus)
25¾ × 38⅛ in. (65.5 × 97.3 cm.)

1863.17.042
Orchard Oriole, *Icterus spurius* (Linnaeus)
23¹³/₁₆ × 18⅞ in. (60.5 × 47.9 cm.)

1863.17.043
Cedar Waxwing, *Bombycilla cedrorum* Vieillot
17½ × 11⁵/₁₆ in. (44.6 × 28.7 cm.)
Cedar Bird

*1863.17.044
Summer Tanager, *Piranga rubra* (Linnaeus)
18⅞ × 11⅝ in. (47.9 x 29.5 cm.)
Summer Red Bird

1863.17.045
Willow Flycatcher, *Empidonax traillii* (Audubon)
18 × 11¹¹/₁₆ in. (45.8 × 30 cm.) sight
Traill's Flycatcher

*1863.17.046
Barred Owl, *Strix varia* (Barton)
37½ × 25⅜ in. (95.3 × 64.5 cm.)

1863.17.047
Ruby-throated Hummingbird, *Archilochus colubris*
   (Linnaeus)
23¾ × 18¾ in. (60.3 × 47.6 cm.)

*1863.17.048
Cerulean Warbler, *Dendroica cerulea* (Wilson)
18⅞ × 11¾ in. (47.9 × 29.8 cm.)
Azure Warbler

1863.17.049
Cerulean Warbler, *Dendroica cerulea* (Wilson)
18⅞ × 11¾ in. (47.9 × 29.8 cm.)
Cerulean warbler or Azure Warbler

1863.17.050
Magnolia Warbler, *Dendroica magnolia* (Wilson)
18¾ × 11½ in. (47.6 × 29.2 cm.)
Swainson's Warbler (misidentified) or Black and
   Yellow Warbler

*1863.17.051
Red-tailed Hawk, *Buteo jamaicensis* (Gmelin)
37⅝ × 25½ in. (95.6 × 64.8 cm.)

*1863.17.052
Chuck-will's-widow, *Caprimulgus carolinensis* Gmelin
23⅝ × 18¾ in. (60 × 47.6 cm.)

1863.17.053
Painted Bunting, *Passerina ciris* (Linnaeus)
18⅝ × 11⅝ in. (47.4 × 29.5 cm.)
Painted Bunting or Painted Finch

1863.17.054
Bobolink, *Dolichonyx oryzivorus* (Linnaeus)

18¹³/₁₆ × 11⅞ in. (47.6 × 30 cm.)
Rice Bird or Rice Bunting

1863.17.055
Cuvier's Kinglet, *Regulus cuvieri* Audubon
14⅝ × 10⁹/₁₆ in. (36.8 × 26.7 cm.)
Cuvier's Regulus or Cuvier's Wren

1863.17.056
Red-shouldered Hawk, *Buteo lineatus* (Gmelin)
35⅛ × 25¹/₁₆ in. (89.2 × 65.1 cm.)

*1863.17.057
Loggerhead Shrike, *Lanius ludovicianus* Linnaeus
26¹³/₁₆ × 18¾ in. (68.1 × 47.6 cm.)

1863.17.058
Hermit Thrush, *Catharus guttatus* (Pallas)
17¼ × 11¼ in. (43.8 × 28.6 cm.)

1863.17.059
Chestnut-sided Warbler, *Dendroica pensylvanica*
   (Linnaeus)
17 × 10½ in. (43.4 × 26.7 cm.)

1863.17.060
Carbonated Warbler, *Sylvia carbonata* Audubon
18½ × 11¾ in. (47 × 29.8 cm.) sight

1863.17.061
Great Horned Owl, *Bubo virginianus* (Gmelin)
35⅛ × 24⅞ in. (89.2 × 63.2 cm.)

*1863.17.062
Passenger Pigeon, *Ectopistes migratorius* (Linnaeus)
26³/₁₆ × 18¼ in. (66.5 × 46.4 cm.)

1863.17.063
White-eyed Vireo, *Vireo griseus* (Boddaert)
18¹³/₁₆ × 11¾ in. (47.8 × 29.8 cm.) sight
White-eyed Flycatcher

1863.17.064
Swamp Sparrow, *Melospiza georgiana* (Latham)
18½ × 11⅞ in. (47 × 30.1 cm.)

1863.17.065
Yellow Warbler, *Dendroica petechia* (Linnaeus)
17¾ × 11⅝ in. (45.1 × 28.4 cm.)
Rathbone's Warbler

1863.17.066
Ivory-billed Woodpecker, *Campephilus principalis*
   (Linnaeus)
38 × 25 in. (96.6 × 63.5 cm.)

1863.17.067
Red-winged Blackbird, *Agelaius phoeniceus* (Linnaeus)
23¾ × 18½ in. (60.2 × 46.4 cm.)
Red-winged Starling or Marsh Blackbird

1863.17.068
Cliff Swallow, *Hirundo pyrrhonota* Vieillot
18¹³/₁₆ × 11⅞ in. (47.9 × 30.1 cm.)
Republican Cliff Swallow

1863.17.069
Bay-breasted Warbler, *Dendroica castanea* (Wilson)
18⅞ × 11⅞ in. (47.9 × 30.1 cm.)

1863.17.070
Henslow's Sparrow, *Ammodramus henslowii*
   (Audubon)
17³/₁₆ × 11¹/₁₆ in. (43.7 × 29.5 cm.)
Henslow's Bunting

1863.17.071
Red-shouldered Hawk, *Buteo lineatus* (Gmelin)
25 × 38½ in. (63.5 × 97.8 cm.)
Winter Hawk

*1863.17.072
American Swallow-tailed Kite, *Elanoides forficatus* (Linnaeus)
20⅝ × 28⅞ in. (52.5 x 73.6 cm.)
Swallow-tailed Hawk

1863.17.073
Wood Thrush, *Hylocichla mustelina* (Gmelin)
18¹³/₁₆ × 11¹¹/₁₆ in. (47.8 × 29.6 cm.)

1863.17.074
Indigo Bunting, *Passerina cyanea* (Linnaeus)
18¾ × 11¾ in. (47.6 × 29.8 cm.) sight
Indigo-bird

1863.17.075
Merlin, *Falco columbarius* Linnaeus
16⁷/₁₆ × 10½ in. (41.8 × 26.7 cm.)
Le Petit Caporal

*1863.17.076
1. Northern Bobwhite, *Colinus virginianus* (Linnaeus)
2. Red-shouldered Hawk, *Buteo lineatus* (Gmelin)
25¾ × 39¼ in. (65.4 × 99.6 cm.)
1. Virginian Partridge
2. Red-shouldered Buzzard

1863.17.077
Belted Kingfisher, *Ceryle alcyon* (Linnaeus)
29⁷/₁₆ × 20¹⁵/₁₆ in. (74.7 × 53.2 cm.)

1863.17.078
Carolina Wren, *Thryothorus ludovicianus* (Latham)
18¾ × 27½ in. (47.6 × 69.8 cm.)
Great Carolina Wren

1863.17.079
Eastern Kingbird, *Tyrannus tyrannus* (Linnaeus)
18⅞ × 11¹¹/₁₆ in. (47.9 × 29.7 cm.)
Tyrant Flycatcher

1863.17.080
Water Pipit, *Anthus spinoletta* (Linnaeus)
9¹¹/₁₆ × 16⁷/₁₆ in. (24.5 × 42 cm.)
Prairie Titlark

*1863.17.081
Osprey, *Pandion haliaetus* (Linnaeus)
37¹¹/₁₆ × 25⅛ in. (95.7 × 63.8 cm.)

*1863.17.082
Whippoorwill, *Caprimulgus vociferus* Wilson
28¹³/₁₆ × 21½ in. (73.2 × 54.6 cm.)

*1863.17.083
House Wren, *Troglodytes aedon* Vieillot
19⅛ × 11⅝ in. (49.6 × 29.4 cm.)

1863.17.085
Yellow-throated Warbler, *Dendroica dominica* (Linnaeus)
18¹³/₁₆ × 11⁹/₁₆ in. (47.8 × 29.4 cm.) sight

1863.17.086
Red-tailed Hawk, *Buteo jamaicensis* (Gmelin)
37⅛ × 25¾ in. (94.4 × 65.4 cm.)
Black Warrior

1863.17.087
Scrub Jay, *Aphelocoma coerulescens* (Bosc)
29⅛ × 20¾ in. (74 × 52.7 cm.) sight
Florida Jay

1863.17.088
Bay-breasted Warbler, *Dendroica castanea* (Wilson)
18¾ × 11⁷⁄₁₆ in. (47.6 × 29 cm.) sight
Autumnal Warbler

1863.17.089
Nashville Warbler, *Vermivora ruficapilla* (Wilson)
18¹³⁄₁₆ × 11½ in. (47.9 × 29.4 cm.)

1863.17.090
Black-and-white Warbler, *Mniotilta varia* (Linnaeus)
19¼ × 11⅝ in. (48.9 × 29 cm.) sight
Black and white Creeper

1863.17.091
Broad-winged Hawk, *Buteo platypterus* (Vieillot)
38⅛ × 25⅜ in. (96.9 × 64.5 cm.)

1863.17.092
Merlin, *Falco columbarius* Linnaeus
23⅛ × 18 in. (58.7 × 45.8 cm.) sight
Pigeon Hawk

1863.17.093
Seaside Sparrow, *Ammodramus maritimus* (Wilson)
18¹³⁄₁₆ × 11⁹⁄₁₆ in. (47.8 × 29.6 cm.)
Sea-side Finch

1863.17.094
Vesper Sparrow, *Pooecetes gramineus* (Gmelin)
18⅞ × 11⁹⁄₁₆ in. (47.9 × 29.5 cm.)
Grass Finch or Bay-winged Bunting

1863.17.095
Yellow Warbler, *Dendroica petechia* (Linnaeus)
18¹³⁄₁₆ × 11⅝ in. (47.7 × 29.7 cm.)
Blue-eyed yellow Warbler or Yellow-poll Warbler

1863.17.096
Black-throated Magpie-Jay, *Calocitta colliei* (Vigors)
37¼ × 24¹⁄₁₆ in. (94.6 × 61.2 cm.)
Columbia Jay

1863.17.097
Eastern Screech-Owl, *Otus asio* (Linnaeus)
27¹⁄₁₆ × 21 in. (68.8 × 53.4 cm.)
Mottled Owl or Little Screech Owl

*1863.17.098
Marsh Wren, *Cistothorus palustris* (Wilson)
18⅝ × 11⅜ in. (47.3 × 27.9 cm.)

1863.17.099
Brown-headed Cowbird, *Molothrus ater*
   (Boddaert)
11⅝ × 18¹⁵⁄₁₆ in. (29.4 × 48.3 cm.)
Cow Bunting or Cow-pen Bird

*1863.17.100
Tree Swallow, *Tachycineta bicolor* (Vieillot)
18⅞ × 11⅝ in. (47.9 × 29.5 cm.)
Green-blue or White-bellied Swallow

1863.17.101
Common Raven, *Corvus corax* Linnaeus
35¾ × 25⅜ in. (90.3 × 64.5 cm.)
Raven

*1863.17.102
Blue Jay, *Cyanocitta cristata* (Linnaeus)
23¾ × 18⅞ in. (60.4 × 48 cm.)

1863.17.103
Canada Warbler, *Wilsonia canadensis* (Linnaeus)
18⅝ × 11⁷⁄₁₆ in. (47.2 × 29 cm.)

1863.17.104
Chipping Sparrow, *Spizella passerina* (Bechstein)
18⁷⁄₁₆ × 11⁷⁄₁₆ in. (46.8 × 29 cm.)

1863.17.105
Red-breasted Nuthatch, *Sitta canadensis* Linnaeus
18⅜ × 11⁷⁄₁₆ in. (46.7 × 29.1 cm.) sight

*1863.17.106
Black Vulture, *Coragyps atratus* (Bechstein)
23⅜ × 36⅛ in. (59.4 × 91.7 cm.)

*1863.17.107
Gray Jay, *Perisoreus canadensis* (Linnaeus)
29¼ × 21 in. (74.4 × 53.5 cm.)
Canada Jay

1863.17.108
Fox Sparrow, *Passerella iliaca* (Merrem)
11½ × 17½ in. (29.2 × 44.5 cm.) sight
Fox-coloured Sparrow

1863.17.109
Savannah Sparrow, *Passerculus sandwichensis* (Gmelin)
17½ × 11½ in. (44.5 × 29.2 cm.) sight
Savannah Finch

1863.17.110
Hooded Warbler, *Wilsonia citrina* (Boddaert)
17⁹⁄₁₆ × 11¾ in. (44.6 × 29.9 cm.)

1863.17.111
Pileated Woodpecker, *Dryocopus pileatus* (Linnaeus)
37¹³⁄₁₆ × 25³⁄₁₆ in. (96.2 × 63.9 cm.)

1863.17.112
Downy Woodpecker, *Picoides pubescens* (Linnaeus)
23⅝ × 18¼ in. (59.8 × 46.4 cm.)

*1863.17.113
Eastern Bluebird, *Sialia sialis* (Linnaeus)
18⅞ × 11¹⁵⁄₁₆ in. (47.9 × 30.3 cm.)
Blue-bird

1863.17.114
White-crowned Sparrow, *Zonotrichia leucophrys* (Forster)
16⅜ × 10½ in. (41.3 × 26.7 cm.)

1863.17.115
Eastern Wood-Pewee, *Contopus virens* (Linnaeus)
18⅛ × 11⁷⁄₁₆ in. (47.3 × 29.1 cm.)
Wood Pewee

*1863.17.116
Brown Thrasher, *Toxostoma rufum* (Linnaeus)
37¹¹⁄₁₆ × 25 in. (95.8 × 63.6 cm.)
Brown Thrush or Ferruginous Thrush; Ferruginous
   Mocking-bird

1863.17.117
Mississippi Kite, *Ictinia mississippiensis* (Wilson)
18¼ × 23½ in. (46.4 × 60 cm.)

1863.17.118
Warbling Vireo, *Vireo gilvus* (Vieillot)
18³⁄₁₆ × 11⅜ in. (46.2 × 29 cm.)

1863.17.119
Yellow-throated Vireo, *Vireo flavifrons* Vieillot
18½ × 11⅜ in. (47 × 28.9 cm.)

*1863.17.120
Eastern Phoebe, *Sayornis phoebe* (Latham)
18¹³⁄₁₆ × 11½ in. (47.8 × 29.2 cm.)
Pewee Flycatcher or Pewit Flycatcher

*1863.17.121
Snowy Owl, *Nyctea scandiaca* (Linnaeus)
37⅞ × 25⅝ in. (96.3 × 65 cm.)

1863.17.122
Blue Grosbeak, *Guiraca caerulea* (Linnaeus)
29¼ × 20¹⁄₁₆ in. (74.3 × 52.2 cm.)

*1863.17.123
Magnolia Warbler, *Dendroica magnolia* (Wilson)
18¼ × 11⁷⁄₁₆ in. (46.4 × 29 cm.)
Black and Yellow Warbler

1863.17.124
Wilson's Warbler, *Wilsonia pusilla* (Wilson)
18¼ × 11½ in. (46.3 × 29.2 cm.)
Green black capt Flycatcher

1863.17.125
Brown-headed Nuthatch, *Sitta pusilla* Latham
19¹⁄₁₆ × 11½ in. (48.4 × 29.3 cm.)

1863.17.126
Bald Eagle, *Haliaeetus leucocephalus* (Linnaeus)
36½ × 24¾ in. (92.7 × 62.9 cm.) sight
White-headed Eagle

1863.17.127
Rose-breasted Grosbeak, *Pheucticus ludovicianus*
   (Linnaeus)
29¼ × 19⅜ in. (74.3 × 49.2 cm.) sight

1863.17.128
Gray Catbird, *Dumetella carolinensis* (Linnaeus)
18¾ × 11½ in. (47.6 × 29.2 cm.) sight
Cat Bird

1863.17.129
Great Crested Flycatcher, *Myiarchus crinitus* (Linnaeus)
18⁹⁄₁₆ × 11⁷⁄₁₆ in. (47.1 × 29 cm.)

1863.17.130
Grasshopper Sparrow, *Ammodramus savannarum* (Gmelin)
16¾ × 10¼ in. (42.8 × 26.2 cm.)
Yellow-winged Sparrow

1863.17.131
American Robin, *Turdus migratorius* Linnaeus
37 × 25¾ in. (94 × 65.4 cm.) sight

1863.17.132
Black-backed Woodpecker, *Picoides arcticus* (Swainson)
29³⁄₁₆ × 20¹⁵⁄₁₆ in. (74.1 × 53.2 cm.)
Three-toed Woodpecker

1863.17.133
Blackpoll Warbler, *Dendroica striata* (Forster)
18½ × 11⁷⁄₁₆ in. (47 × 29.1 cm.) sight

1863.17.134
Blackburnian Warbler, *Dendroica fusca* (Müller)
18⅜ × 11½ in. (46.8 × 29.3 cm.)
Hemlock Warbler

1863.17.135
Blackburnian Warbler, *Dendroica fusca* (Müller)
16⅞ × 10½ in. (40.3 × 26.2 cm.)

1863.17.136
Eastern Meadowlark, *Sturnella magna* (Linnaeus)
36½ × 26 in. (92.9 × 66 cm.)
Meadow Lark

*1863.17.137
Yellow-breasted Chat, *Icteria virens* (Linnaeus)
29¼ × 21 in. (74.3 × 53.3 cm.)

1863.17.138
Connecticut Warbler, *Oporornis agilis* (Wilson)
18⅜ × 11½ in. (46.7 × 29.2 cm.)

1863.17.139
Field Sparrow, *Spizella pusilla* (Wilson)
18⅛ × 11⁷⁄₁₆ in. (46 × 29 cm.) sight

1863.17.140
Pine Warbler, *Dendroica pinus* (Wilson)
18¼ × 11½ in. (46.4 × 29.2 cm.) sight
Pine Creeping Warbler

*1863.17.141
1. Northern Goshawk, *Accipiter gentilis* (Linnaeus)
2. Cooper's Hawk, *Accipiter cooperii* (Bonaparte)
39 × 25⅞ in. (99 × 65.7 cm.)
1. Goshawk
2. Stanley Hawk

*1863.17.142
American Kestrel, *Falco sparverius* Linnaeus
29½ × 21¹⁄₁₆ in. (79.4 × 53.5 cm.)
American Sparrow Hawk

1863.17.143
Ovenbird, *Seiurus aurocapillus* (Linnaeus)
18⁷⁄₁₆ × 11⅜ in. (46.8 × 28.9 cm.) sight
Golden-crowned Thrush

1863.17.144
Acadian Flycatcher, *Empidonax virescens* (Vieillot)
18½ × 11⁷⁄₁₆ in. (47 × 29 cm.) sight
Small Green Crested Flycatcher

1863.17.145
Palm Warbler, *Dendroica palmarum* (Gmelin)
17¼ × 11½ in. (44.5 × 29.2 cm.) sight
Yellow Red-poll Warbler

1863.17.146
Fish Crow, *Corvus ossifragus* Wilson
38 × 25½ in. (96.6 × 64.9 cm.)

1863.17.147
Common Nighthawk, *Chordeiles minor* (Forster)
29³⁄₁₆ × 20½ in. (74.2 × 52.1 cm.)
Night Hawk

1863.17.148
Black-throated Blue Warbler, *Dendroica caerulescens*
(Gmelin)
18⅜ × 11⁷⁄₁₆ in. (46.7 × 29 cm.)
Pine Swamp Warbler

*1863.17.149
Sharp-tailed Sparrow, *Ammodramus caudacutus*
(Gmelin)
18³⁄₁₆ × 11½ in. (46.2 × 29.2 cm.)
Sharp Tailed Finch

*1863.17.150
Red-eyed Vireo, *Vireo olivaceus* (Linnaeus)
18⁷⁄₁₆ × 11¹¹⁄₁₆ in. (46.8 × 29.7 cm.)

1863.17.151
Turkey Vulture, *Cathartes aura* (Linnaeus)
37³⁄₁₆ × 26 in. (95.8 × 66 cm.)
Turkey Buzzard

*1863.17.152
White-breasted Nuthatch, *Sitta carolinensis* Latham
23¾ × 17⅝ in. (60.3 × 44.8 cm.)
White-breasted Black-Capped Nuthatch

1863.17.153
Yellow-rumped Warbler, *Dendroica coronata* (Linnaeus)
16¹³⁄₁₆ × 10¾ in. (42.7 × 27.3 cm.)
Yellow-Crown Warbler, or Yellow rump Warbler

1863.17.154
Tennessee Warbler, *Vermivora peregrina* (Wilson)
18 × 11⅜ in. (45.7 × 29.9 cm.) sight

1863.17.156
American Crow, *Corvus brachyrhynchos* Brehm
38⅞ × 25¹¹⁄₁₆ in. (98.7 × 65.2 cm.)

1863.17.157
Rusty Blackbird, *Euphagus carolinus* (Müller)
29⅜ × 20¾ in. (74.6 × 52.7 cm.)
Rusty Grakle

*1863.17.158
Chimney Swift, *Chaetura pelagica* (Linnaeus)
18⁵⁄₁₆ × 11⁷⁄₁₆ in. (46.5 × 29 cm.)
Chimney Swallow or American Swift

1863.17.159
Northern Cardinal, *Cardinalis cardinalis* (Linnaeus)
18³⁄₁₆ × 11 in. (46.1 × 29.1 cm.)
Cardinal Grosbeak

1863.17.160
Carolina Chickadee, *Parus carolinensis* Audubon
18¹⁄₁₆ × 11½ in. (47.3 × 29.2 cm.) sight
Black-capped Titmouse or Carolina Titmouse

*1863.17.161
Crested Caracara, *Polyborus plancus* (Miller)
38¼ × 24¹⁵⁄₁₆ in. (97.1 × 63.4 cm.)
Brazilian Caracara Eagle

1863.17.162
Zenaida Dove, *Zenaida aurita* (Temminck)
29³⁄₁₆ × 20¹⁵⁄₁₆ in. (74 × 53.2 cm.)

1863.17.163
Palm Warbler, *Dendroica palmarum* (Gmelin)
21⁷⁄₁₆ × 14⅜ in. (54.5 × 36.5 cm.)
Yellow red poll Warbler

1863.17.164
Veery, *Catharus fuscescens* (Stephens)
21¼ × 13 in. (54 × 33 cm.) sight
Tawny Thrush

1863.17.165
Bachman's Sparrow, *Aimophila aestivalis* (Lichtenstein)
21 × 13¹¹⁄₁₆ in. (53.5 × 34.8 cm.) sight
Bachman's Finch

1863.17.166
Rough-legged Hawk, *Buteo lagopus* (Pontoppidan)
21⅛ × 13¾ in. (53.5 × 34.9 cm.)
Rough-legged Falcon

1863.17.167
Key West Quail-Dove, *Geotrygon chrysia* Bonaparte
19⅜ × 28¾ in. (49.2 × 73 cm.) sight
Key West Dove or Key-west Pigeon

1863.17.168
Fork-tailed Flycatcher, *Tyrannus savana* Vieillot
21½ × 14¹⁄₁₆ in. (54.7 × 35.8 cm.)

1863.17.169
Mangrove Cuckoo, *Coccyzus minor* (Gmelin)
21⅜ × 14⅜ in. (54.3 × 36.4 cm.)

1863.17.170
Gray Kingbird, *Tyrannus dominicensis* (Gmelin)
21⁷⁄₁₆ × 14⅜ in. (54.5 × 36.5 cm.) sight
Gray Tyrant or Pipiry Flycatcher

1863.17.171
Common Barn-Owl, *Tyto alba* (Scopoli)
37⅝ × 25½ in. (95.5 × 64.7 cm.)
Barn Owl

1863.17.172
Blue-headed Quail-Dove, *Starnoenas cyanocephala*
(Linnaeus)
20⁹⁄₁₆ × 27⅛ in. (52.3 × 68.9 cm.)
Blue-headed Pigeon

*1863.17.173
Barn Swallow, *Hirundo rustica* Linnaeus
21 × 13¹¹⁄₁₆ in. (53.4 × 34.8 cm.)

1863.17.174
Olive-sided Flycatcher, *Contopus borealis* (Swainson)
21½ × 14¹⁄₁₆ in. (54.6 × 35.8 cm.)

1863.17.175
Sedge Wren, *Cistothorus platensis* (Latham)
21½ × 14⁷⁄₁₆ in. (54.7 × 36.7 cm.)
Nuttall's lesser-marsh Wren

1863.17.176
Spruce Grouse, *Dendragapus canadensis* (Linnaeus)
25 × 35⅜ in. (63.5 × 90 cm.)
Spotted or Canada Grouse

*1863.17.177
White-crowned Pigeon, *Columba leucocephala* Linnaeus
29³⁄₁₆ × 21 in. (74.2 × 53.4 cm.)
White Headed Pigeon

1863.17.178
Orange-crowned Warbler, *Vermivora celata* (Say)
20⅛ × 12½ in. (51.2 × 31.7 cm.)

1863.17.179
House Wren, *Troglodytes aedon* Vieillot
19¹⁄₁₆ × 12¾ in. (48.4 × 32.4 cm.)
Wood Wren

1863.17.180
Pine Siskin, *Carduelis pinus* (Wilson)
21½ × 14⁷⁄₁₆ in. (54.7 × 36.7 cm.)
Pine Finch

*1863.17.181
Golden Eagle, *Aquila chrysaetos* (Linnaeus)
38 × 25½ in. (96.6 × 64.7 cm.)

1863.17.182
Common Ground-Dove, *Columbina passerina*
(Linnaeus)
29⅝ × 21⁵⁄₁₆ in. (75.3 × 54.2 cm.)
Ground Dove

1863.17.183
Golden-crowned Kinglet, *Regulus satrapa* Lichtenstein
21³⁄₁₆ × 13³⁄₁₆ in. (53.8 × 33.5 cm.) sight
Golden crested-Wren or American Golden-crested
Wren

1863.17.184
Black-throated Mango, *Anthracothorax nigricollis*
(Vieillot)
21 × 13¾ in. (53.3 × 35 cm.) sight
Mangrove Humming Bird or Mango Humming Bird

*1863.17.185
Bachman's Warbler, *Vermivora bachmanii* (Audubon)
21½ × 14 1/16 in. (54.6 × 35.7 cm.)

1863.17.186
Greater Prairie-Chicken, *Tympanuchus cupido* (Linnaeus)
25 × 35⅞ in. (63.5 × 91 cm.) sight
Pinnated Grous

1863.17.187
Boat-tailed Grackle, *Quiscalus major* Vieillot
29⅞ × 21⅛ in. (74.5 × 53.7 cm.)

1863.17.188
American Tree Sparrow, *Spizella arborea* (Wilson)
21½ × 14⅜ in. (54.7 × 36.6 cm.)
Tree Sparrow

1863.17.189
Snow Bunting, *Plectrophenax nivalis* (Linnaeus)
21 1/16 × 14⅛ in. (53.5 × 35.8 cm.)

1863.17.190
Yellow-bellied Sapsucker, *Sphyrapicus varius* (Linnaeus)
21⅛ × 13⅛ in. (53.7 × 33.3 cm.)
Yellow-bellied Woodpecker

1863.17.191
Willow Ptarmigan, *Lagopus lagopus* (Linnaeus)
24¾ × 38⅛ in. (62.9 × 96.8 cm.) sight
Willow Grous or Large Ptarmigan

1863.17.192
Northern Shrike, *Lanius excubitor* Linnaeus
29¼ × 20⅝ in. (74.3 × 52.4 cm.) sight
Great American Shrike or Great cinereous Shrike or
     Butcher Bird

1863.17.193
Lincoln's Sparrow, *Melospiza lincolnii* (Audubon)
21¼ × 14⅛ in. (54 × 35.8 cm.)
Lincoln Finch

1863.17.194
Boreal Chickadee, *Parus hudsonicus* Forster
21 3/16 × 14 1/16 in. (53.7 × 37.1 cm.)
Canadian Titmouses or Hudson's Bay Titmouse

1863.17.195
Ruby-crowned Kinglet, *Regulus calendula* (Linnaeus)
20 3/16 × 11⅞ in. (51.3 × 30.1 cm.)
Ruby-crowned Wren

1863.17.196
Gyrfalcon, *Falco rusticolus* Linnaeus
38⅛ × 25 1/16 in. (96.8 × 65.1 cm.) sight
Labrador Falcon

1863.17.197
Red Crossbill, *Loxia curvirostra* Linnaeus
29¼ × 21 in. (74.4 × 53.4 cm.)
American Crossbill or Common Crossbill

1863.17.198
Swainson's Warbler, *Limnothlypis swainsonii* (Audubon)
21⅛ × 14⅛ in. (53.6 × 35.9 cm.)
Brown headed Worm eating Warbler

1863.17.199
Northern Saw-whet Owl, *Aegolius acadicus* (Gmelin)
20½ × 13⅛ in. (52 × 33.3 cm.)
Little Owl

1863.17.200
Horned Lark, *Eremophila alpestris* (Linnaeus)

13⅜ × 20⅞ in. (34 × 53 cm.)
Shore Lark

1863.17.201
Canada Goose, *Branta canadensis* (Linnaeus)
38 × 25⅞ in. (96.5 × 65.7 cm.) sight

1863.17.202
Red-throated Loon, *Gavia stellata* (Pontoppidan)
21½ × 29½ in. (54.6 × 75 cm.)
Red-throated Diver

1863.17.203
King Rail, *Rallus elegans* Audubon
17⅞ × 21 7/16 in. (37.6 × 54.5 cm.)
Fresh-water Marsh Hen or Great Red breasted Rail

1863.17.204
Clapper Rail, *Rallus longirostris* Boddaert
21 5/16 × 14⅝ in. (54.2 × 37.1 cm.)
Salt-Water Marsh Hen

1863.17.205
Virginia Rail, *Rallus limicola* Vieillot
14½ × 21⅜ in. (36.8 × 54.3 cm.)

*1863.17.206
Wood Duck, *Aix sponsa* (Linnaeus)
38 1/16 × 25¾ in. (96.6 × 65.5 cm.)

1863.17.207
Brown Booby, *Sula leucogaster* (Boddaert)
28 11/16 × 21½ in. (75.3 × 54.6 cm.)
Booby Gannet

1863.17.208
Eskimo Curlew, *Numenius borealis* (Forster)
14 9/16 × 20 15/16 in. (36.9 × 53.1 cm.)

1863.17.209
Wilson's Plover, *Charadrius wilsonia* Ord
14⅝ × 21½ in. (37.2 × 54.6 cm.)

1863.17.210
Least Bittern, *Ixobrychus exilis* (Gmelin)
14 11/16 × 21⅝ in. (37.3 × 54.8 cm.)

1863.17.211
Great Blue Heron, *Ardea herodias* Linnaeus
36 × 25⅜ in. (91.6 × 64.5 cm.)

1863.17.212
Ring-billed Gull, *Larus delawarensis* Ord
21½ × 29½ in. (54.6 × 75 cm.) sight
Common Gull or Common American Gull

*1863.17.213
Atlantic Puffin, *Fratercula arctica* (Linnaeus)
14½ × 21⅜ in. (36.8 × 54.3 cm.)
Puffin

1863.17.214
Razorbill, *Alca torda* Linnaeus
14 9/16 × 21 7/16 in. (36.9 × 54.5 cm.) sight
Razor billed Auk

1863.17.215
Red-necked Phalarope, *Phalaropus lobatus*
     (Linnaeus)
14½ × 21⅜ in. (36.9 × 54.4 cm.)
Hyperborean phalarope

1863.17.216
Wood Stork, *Mycteria americana* Linnaeus
38 × 25¾ in. (96.7 × 65.4 cm.)
Wood Ibis

1863.17.217
Tricolored Heron, *Egretta tricolor* (Müller)
21 7/16 × 29½ in. (54.5 × 74.9 cm.)
Louisiana Heron

1863.17.218
Common Murre, *Uria aalge* (Pontoppidan)
14¾ × 21 7/16 in. (37.5 × 54.4 cm.) sight
Foolish Guillemot

*1863.17.219
Black Guillemot, *Cepphus grylle* (Linnaeus)
14¾ × 21 5/16 in. (37.5 × 54.1 cm.)

1863.17.220
Piping Plover, *Charadrius melodus* Ord
14⅝ × 21 in. (37.2 × 53.4 cm.)

1863.17.221
Mallard, *Anas platyrhynchos* Linnaeus
25⅝ × 38¼ in. (65.1 × 97.3 cm.)
Mallard Duck

1863.17.222
White Ibis, *Eudocimus albus* (Linnaeus)
20 13/16 × 25½ in. (52.8 × 64.7 cm.)

1863.17.223
American Oystercatcher, *Haematopus palliatus*
     Temminck
14½ × 22½ in. (36.8 × 57.2 cm.) sight
Pied oyster-catcher

1863.17.224
Black-legged Kittiwake, *Rissa tridactyla* (Linnaeus)
14½ × 21⅜ in. (36.8 × 54.3 cm.)
Kittiwake Gull

1863.17.225
Killdeer, *Charadrius vociferus* Linnaeus
16⅛ × 22⅛ in. (41 × 56.2 cm.)
Killdeer Plover

*1863.17.226
Whooping Crane, *Grus americana* (Linnaeus)
37¼ × 25 11/16 in. (94.7 × 65.2 cm.)

1863.17.227
Northern Pintail, *Anas acuta* Linnaeus
19⅜ × 29⅞ in. (49.3 × 75.9 cm.)
Pin tailed Duck

1863.17.228
Green-winged Teal, *Anas crecca* Linnaeus
14⅛ × 18½ in. (35.9 × 47 cm.) sight
American Green-winged Teal

1863.17.229
Greater Scaup, *Aythya marila* (Linnaeus)
14 × 21⅞ in. (35.6 × 55.6 cm.)
Scaup Duck

1863.17.230
Sanderling, *Calidris alba* (Pallas)
14¾ × 21⅜ in. (37.5 × 54.4 cm.)
Ruddy Plover

*1863.17.231
Long-billed Curlew, *Numenius americanus* Bechstein
24 15/16 × 37⅝ in. (63.4 × 95.7 cm.)

1863.17.232
Hooded Merganser, *Lophodytes cucullatus*
     (Linnaeus)
19⅝ × 29⅜ in. (49.8 × 74.6 cm.)

1863.17.233
Sora, *Porzana carolina* (Linnaeus)
14 13/16 × 21 7/16 in. (37.5 × 54.5 cm.)
Sora or Rail

1863.17.234
Ring-necked Duck, *Aythya collaris* (Donovan)
14 1/8 × 19 1/8 in. (35.8 × 48.6 cm.)
Tufted Duck

1863.17.235
Sooty Tern, *Sterna fuscata* Linnaeus
14 1/2 × 19 7/8 in. (36.9 × 50.4 cm.)

*1863.17.236
Black-crowned Night-Heron, *Nycticorax nycticorax*
   (Linnaeus)
25 3/8 × 37 7/8 in. (64.4 × 96 cm.)
Night Heron or Qua Bird

1863.17.237
Whimbrel, *Numenius phaeopus* (Linnaeus)
19 1/16 × 23 7/8 in. (48.6 × 60.6 cm.)
Great Esquimaux Curlew or Hudsonian Curlew

1863.17.238
Marbled Godwit, *Limosa fedoa* (Linnaeus)
14 9/16 × 21 5/16 in. (36.8 × 53.6 cm.)
Great Marbled Godwit

1863.17.239
American Coot, *Fulica americana* Gmelin
14 1/2 × 21 1/4 in. (36.8 × 54 cm.)

1863.17.240
Roseate Tern, *Sterna dougallii* Montagu
21 1/2 × 14 9/16 in. (54.5 × 38.8 cm.)

1863.17.241
Great Black-backed Gull, *Larus marinus* Linnaeus
37 7/16 × 25 1/2 in. (95.1 × 64.9 cm.)
Black Backed Gull

*1863.17.242
Snowy Egret, *Egretta thula* (Molina)
29 1/4 × 21 5/16 in. (74.3 × 54.2 cm.)
Snowy Heron or White Egret

*1863.17.243
Common Snipe, *Gallinago gallinago* (Linnaeus)
14 3/16 × 21 3/8 in. (37.6 × 54.3 cm.)
American Snipe

1863.17.244
Common Moorhen, *Gallinula chloropus* (Linnaeus)
16 1/8 × 22 1/16 in. (41 × 56.1 cm.)
Common Gallinule

1863.17.245
Thick-billed Murre, *Uria lomvia* (Linnaeus)
14 1/2 × 21 3/8 in. (36.8 × 54.3 cm.) sight
Large-billed Guillemot

1863.17.246
Common Eider, *Somateria mollissima* (Linnaeus)
25 3/8 × 38 3/8 in. (64.5 × 97.5 cm.) sight
Eider Duck

1863.17.247
White-winged Scoter, *Melanitta fusca* (Linnaeus)
21 1/2 × 29 1/2 in. (54.6 × 74.9 cm.) sight
Velvet Duck

1863.17.248
Pied-billed Grebe, *Podilymbus podiceps* (Linnaeus)

14 1/2 × 21 3/8 in. (36.7 × 54.3 cm.)
American Pied-bill Dobchick

1863.17.249
Tufted Puffin, *Fratercula cirrhata* (Pallas)
14 5/8 × 21 1/2 in. (37.2 × 54.6 cm.)
Tufted Auk

1863.17.250
Arctic Tern, *Sterna paradisaea* Pontoppidan
21 1/2 × 14 9/16 in. (54.6 × 37 cm.)

*1863.17.251
Brown Pelican, *Pelecanus occidentalis* Linnaeus
37 1/2 × 26 1/16 in. (95.4 × 66.3 cm.)

1863.17.252
Double-crested Cormorant, *Phalacrocorax auritus*
   (Lesson)
21 3/8 × 29 1/4 in. (54.3 × 74.3 cm.)
Florida Cormorant

1863.17.253
Pomarine Jaeger, *Stercorarius pomarinus* (Temminck)
14 3/4 × 21 3/8 in. (37.5 × 54.4 cm.)
Jager

1863.17.254
Wilson's Phalarope, *Phalaropus tricolor* (Vieillot)
14 11/16 × 21 9/16 in. (37.3 × 54.8 cm.)

1863.17.255
Red Phalarope, *Phalaropus fulicaria* (Linnaeus)
14 11/16 × 21 1/16 in. (37.3 × 53.5 cm.)

1863.17.256
Reddish Egret, *Egretta rufescens* (Gmelin)
25 1/2 × 37 7/8 in. (64.8 × 96.2 cm.) sight
Purple Heron

*1863.17.257
Double-crested Cormorant, *Phalacrocorax auritus*
   (Lesson)
29 9/16 × 21 3/8 in. (74.5 × 54.3 cm.)

1863.17.258
Hudsonian Godwit, *Limosa haemastica* (Linnaeus)
14 3/4 × 21 3/8 in. (37.4 × 54.4 cm.)

1863.17.259
Horned Grebe, *Podiceps auritus* (Linnaeus)
14 3/4 × 21 5/16 in. (37.4 × 54.2 cm.)

1863.17.260
Leach's Storm-Petrel, *Oceanodroma leucorhoa* (Vieillot)
12 1/2 × 19 1/8 in. (31.7 × 48.6 cm.)
Fork Tail Petrel

1863.17.261
Sandhill Crane, *Grus canadensis* (Linnaeus)
37 7/8 × 25 1/4 in. (96.2 × 64.1 cm.) sight
Hooping Crane

1863.17.262
White-tailed Tropicbird, *Phaethon lepturus* Daudin
21 7/8 × 29 5/8 in. (54.9 × 75.2 cm.)
Tropic Bird

1863.17.263
Curlew Sandpiper, *Calidris ferruginea* (Pontoppidan)
12 1/16 × 18 in. (30.5 × 45.8 cm.)
Pigmy Curlew

1863.17.264
Northern Fulmar, *Fulmarus glacialis* (Linnaeus)

14 5/8 × 20 15/16 in. (37.2 × 53.1 cm.)
Fulmar Petrel

1863.17.265
Buff-breasted Sandpiper, *Tryngites subruficollis* (Vieillot)
12 1/16 × 19 1/16 in. (30.7 × 48.6 cm.)

*1863.17.266
Great Cormorant, *Phalacrocorax carbo* (Linnaeus)
25 1/2 × 38 1/2 in. (64.9 × 97.8 cm.)
Common Cormorant

1863.17.267
Long-tailed Jaeger, *Stercorarius longicaudus* Vieillot
29 3/8 × 21 3/8 in. (74.6 × 54.3 cm.) sight
Arctic Yager

1863.17.268
American Woodcock, *Scolopax minor* Gmelin
14 3/4 × 12 9/16 in. (37.5 × 31.9 cm.)

1863.17.269
Common Greenshank, *Tringa nebularia* (Gunnerus)
14 11/16 × 21 1/4 in. (37.4 × 54 cm.)
Greenshank

1863.17.270
Wilson's Storm-Petrel, *Oceanites oceanicus* (Kuhl)
12 7/16 × 19 1/8 in. (31.5 × 48.1 cm.)
Stormy Petrel or Wilson's Petrel

*1863.17.271
Magnificent Frigatebird, *Fregata magnificens* Mathews
38 1/8 × 25 1/8 in. (97 × 64 cm.)
Frigate Pelican

1863.17.272
Parasitic Jaeger, *Stercorarius parasiticus* (Linnaeus)
21 1/2 × 29 3/8 in. (54.6 × 74.6 cm.) sight
Richardson's Jager

1863.17.273
Royal Tern, *Sterna maxima* Boddaert
14 5/8 × 21 5/16 in. (37.1 × 54.1 cm.) sight
Cayenne Tern

1863.17.274
Willet, *Catoptrophorus semipalmatus* (Gmelin)
14 3/8 × 21 1/16 in. (36.8 × 53.3 cm.)
Semipalmated Snipe, or Willet

1863.17.275
Brown Noddy, *Anous stolidus* (Linnaeus)
21 3/8 × 14 1/2 in. (54.5 × 36.8 cm.)
Noddy Tern

1863.17.276
King Eider, *Somateria spectabilis* (Linnaeus)
25 5/8 × 38 in. (65.1 × 96.5 cm.) sight
King Duck

1863.17.277
Canada Goose, *Branta canadensis* (Linnaeus)
29 5/8 × 21 1/2 in. (75.2 × 54.6 cm.) sight
Hutchin's Barnacle Goose

1863.17.278
White-rumped Sandpiper, *Calidris fuscicollis* (Vieillot)
14 5/8 × 21 1/2 in. (37 × 54.6 cm.)
Schinz's Sandpiper

1863.17.279
Sandwich Tern, *Sterna sandvicensis* Latham
14 11/16 × 21 5/16 in. (37.2 × 54.4 cm.)

1863.17.280
Black Tern, *Chlidonias niger* (Linnaeus)
20¹⁵⁄₁₆ × 14½ in. (53.2 × 36.9 cm.)

*1863.17.281
Great Blue ("Great White") Heron, *Ardea herodias*
   Linnaeus
25¹¹⁄₁₆ × 38⁵⁄₁₆ in. (65.2 × 98.7 cm.)
Great White Heron

1863.17.282
Iceland Gull, *Larus glaucoides* Meyer
21½ × 29½ in. (54.6 × 74.9 cm.) sight
White-winged silvery Gull

1863.17.283
Greater Shearwater, *Puffinus gravis* O'Reilly
14¾ × 21⅜ in. (37.3 × 54.3 cm.)
Wandering Shearwater

1863.17.284
Purple Sandpiper, *Calidris maritima* (Brünnich)
14¾ × 21⅜ in. (37.5 × 54.3 cm.)

*1863.17.285
Sabine's Gull, *Xema sabini* (Sabine)
14½ × 21⁵⁄₁₆ in. (36.8 × 54.2 cm.)
Fork-tailed Gull

1863.17.286
Greater White-fronted Goose, *Anser albifrons*
   (Scopoli)
24¾ × 37⅝ in. (62.9 × 95.6 cm.) sight
White-fronted Goose

1863.17.287
Ivory Gull, *Pagophila eburnea* (Phipps)
21½ × 29½ in. (54.6 × 74.9 cm.) sight

1863.17.288
Lesser Yellowlegs, *Tringa flavipes* (Gmelin)
14½ × 21⅛ in. (36.8 × 53.6 cm.)
Yellow Shank

1863.17.289
Solitary Sandpiper, *Tringa solitaria* Wilson
14⁹⁄₁₆ × 20¹³⁄₁₆ in. (37 × 52.8 cm.)

1863.17.290
Dunlin, *Calidris alpina* (Linnaeus)
10¹¹⁄₁₆ × 18⁷⁄₁₆ in. (27.3 × 47 cm.)
Red-backed Sandpiper

1863.17.291
Herring Gull, *Larus argentatus* Pontoppidan
37¹⁄₁₆ × 25³⁄₁₆ in. (95.6 × 64 cm.) sight

1863.17.292
Great Crested Grebe, *Podiceps cristatus* (Linnaeus)
21⁷⁄₁₆ × 29¼ in. (54.4 × 74.2 cm.)
Crested Grebe

1863.17.293
Horned Puffin, *Fratercula corniculata* (Naumann)
14¾ × 21⅜ in. (37.5 × 54.4 cm.)
Large-billed Puffin

1863.17.294
Pectoral Sandpiper, *Calidris melanotos* (Vieillot)
14¹¹⁄₁₆ × 21⁵⁄₁₆ in. (37.4 × 54.1 cm.)

1863.17.295
Manx Shearwater, *Puffinus puffinus* (Brünnich)
14¾ × 21⁵⁄₁₆ in. (37.4 × 54.1 cm.)

1863.17.296
Barnacle Goose, *Branta leucopsis* (Bechstein)
21¼ × 35½ in. (54 × 90.2 cm.) sight

1863.17.297
Harlequin Duck, *Histrionicus histrionicus* (Linnaeus)
21⁷⁄₁₆ × 29¼ in. (54.5 × 74.3 cm.)

1863.17.298
Red-necked Grebe, *Podiceps grisegena* (Boddaert)
14¾ × 21⅜ in. (37.4 × 54.3 cm.)

1863.17.299
Audubon's Shearwater, *Puffinus lherminieri* Lesson
13¾ × 20⅜ in. (34.9 × 51.6 cm.)
Dusky Petrel

1863.17.300
1. Lesser Golden-Plover, *Pluvialis dominica* (Müller)
2. Greater Golden-Plover *Pluvialis apricaria* (Linnaeus)
14½ × 21⅝ in. (36.8 × 54.6 cm.)
1. Golden Plover
2. Golden Plover

1863.17.301
Canvasback, *Aythya valisineria* (Wilson)
23⅞ × 38 in. (60.6 × 96.5 cm.) sight
Canvas backed Duck

1863.17.302
American Black Duck, *Anas rubripes* Brewster
21 × 29½ in. (53.3 × 74.9 cm.) sight
Dusky Duck

1863.17.303
Upland Sandpiper, *Bartramia longicauda* (Bechstein)
14⅝ × 21¾ in. (37.1 × 55.1 cm.)
Bartram Sandpiper

1863.17.304
Ruddy Turnstone, *Arenaria interpres* (Linnaeus)
14¼ × 20¹¹⁄₁₆ in. (36.1 × 52.5 cm.)
Turn-stone

1863.17.305
Purple Gallinule, *Porphyrula martinica* (Linnaeus)
14¼ × 21¹⁵⁄₁₆ in. (36.2 × 54.1 cm.)

1863.17.306
Common Loon, *Gavia immer* (Brünnich)
25⅜ × 37 in. (64.3 × 94 cm.)
Great Northern Diver or Loon

*1863.17.307
Little Blue Heron, *Egretta caerula* (Linnaeus)
20⅜ × 28⅞ in. (51.8 × 73.4 cm.)
Blue Heron

1863.17.308
Greater Yellowlegs, *Tringa melanoleuca* (Gmelin)
14¹³⁄₁₆ × 24¼ in. (37.6 × 61.6 cm.)
Tell-tale Godwit or Snipe

*1863.17.309
Common Tern, *Sterna hirundo* Linnaeus
21½ × 14⅝ in. (54.6 × 37.3 cm.)

1863.17.310
Spotted Sandpiper, *Actitis macularia* (Linnaeus)
16⅜ × 22⅝ in. (41.7 × 57.4 cm.)

*1863.17.311
American White Pelican, *Pelecanus erythrorhyncos*
   Gmelin
36¹⁵⁄₁₆ × 25 in. (93.9 × 63.6 cm.)

1863.17.312
Oldsquaw, *Clangula hyemalis* (Linnaeus)
16½ × 29⅝ in. (41.9 × 75.2 cm.) sight
Long-tailed Duck

*1863.17.313
Blue-winged Teal, *Anas discors* Linnaeus
19⅞ × 28⅞ in. (50.5 × 73.3 cm.)

1863.17.314
Laughing Gull, *Larus atricilla* Linnaeus
13⁵⁄₁₆ × 21¹³⁄₁₆ in. (33.3 × 55.5 cm.)
Black-headed Gull

*1863.17.315
Red Knot, *Calidris canutus* (Linnaeus)
12 × 18⅝ in. (30.5 × 47 cm.)
Red-breasted Sandpiper

1863.17.316
Anhinga, *Anhinga anhinga* (Linnaeus)
37 × 24¼ in. (94 × 61.6 cm.)
Water-Turkey, Black-bellied Darter

1863.17.317
Surf Scoter, *Melanitta perspicillata* (Linnaeus)
20⅝ × 29⅜ in. (52.5 × 74.6 cm.)
Black, or Surf Duck

1863.17.318
American Avocet, *Recurvirostra americana* Gmelin
12¾ × 21¼ in. (32.4 × 54 cm.)

1863.17.319
Least Tern, *Sterna antillarum* (Lesson)
21⁵⁄₁₆ × 15 in. (54.1 × 38.1 cm.) sight
Lesser Tern

1863.17.320
Least Sandpiper, *Calidris minutilla* (Vieillot)
15¹⁄₁₆ × 22⅛ in. (38.3 × 56.1 cm.)
Little Sandpiper

*1863.17.321
Roseate Spoonbill, *Ajaia ajaja* (Linnaeus)
23⅛ × 35¹¹⁄₁₆ in. (58.7 × 90.6 cm.)

1863.17.322
Redhead, *Aythya americana* (Eyton)
20⅞ × 29⅜ in. (53 × 74.6 cm.) sight
Red-headed Duck

1863.17.323
Black Skimmer, *Rynchops niger* Linnaeus
19¼ × 23½ in. (48.9 × 59.7 cm.) sight

1863.17.324
Bonaparte's Gull, *Larus philadelphia* (Ord)
21³⁄₁₆ × 15³⁄₁₆ in. (53.9 × 38.5 cm.)
Bonapartian Gull

1863.17.325
Bufflehead, *Bucephala albeola* (Linnaeus)
14⅜ × 21¼ in. (36.5 × 54.1 cm.)
Buffel-headed Duck

*1863.17.326
Northern Gannet, *Sula bassanus* (Linnaeus)
24¾ × 37⅝ in. (62.8 × 95.6 cm.)
Gannet

1863.17.327
Northern Shoveler, *Anas clypeata* Linnaeus
20¹³⁄₁₆ × 27⁵⁄₁₆ in. (52.8 × 69.4 cm.)
Shoveller Duck

1863.17.328
Black-necked Stilt, *Himantopus mexicanus* (Müller)
14¼ × 21⅜ in. (36.2 × 54.6 cm.)
Long-legged Avocet

1863.17.329
Yellow Rail, *Coturnicops noveboracensis* (Gmelin)
11¹³⁄₁₆ × 18 in. (29.8 × 45.7 cm.)
Yellow-breasted Rail

1863.17.330
Semipalmated Plover, *Charadrius semipalmatus*
    Bonaparte
11⁷⁄₁₆ × 18⅛ in. (29 × 46.2 cm.)
Ring Plover

1863.17.331
Common Merganser, *Mergus merganser* Linnaeus
23⅞ × 36½ in. (60.6 × 92.7 cm.) sight
Goosander

1863.17.332
Labrador Duck, *Camptorhynchus labradorius* (Gmelin)
21⁵⁄₁₆ × 29⅝ in. (54.6 × 74.9 cm.)
Pied Duck

1863.17.333
Green-backed Heron, *Butorides striatus* (Linnaeus)
18⅞ × 23½ in. (47.9 × 59.7 cm.) sight
Green Heron

1863.17.334
Black-bellied Plover, *Pluvialis squatarola* (Linnaeus)
14⅞ × 21⁹⁄₁₆ in. (37.2 × 53.9 cm.)

1863.17.335
Short-billed Dowitcher, *Limnodromus griseus* (Gmelin)
14¹³⁄₁₆ × 18¹³⁄₁₆ in. (36.2 × 47.8 cm.)
Red-breasted Snipe

1863.17.336
Yellow-crowned Night-Heron, *Nycticorax violaceus*
    (Linnaeus)
35⅞ × 25⅜ in. (91.1 × 64.4 cm.) sight
Yellow-Crowned Heron

*1863.17.337
American Bittern, *Botaurus lentiginosus* (Rackett)
21½ × 29³⁄₁₆ in. (54.6 × 74.2 cm.)

1863.17.338
Mallard × Gadwall hybrid, *Anas platyrhynchos × strepera*
18¼ × 23¼ in. (46.4 × 59.1 cm.) sight
Bemaculated Duck

1863.17.339
Dovekie, *Alle alle* (Linnaeus)
11½ × 18¾ in. (29.2 × 47.6 cm.) sight
Little Auk

1863.17.340
British Storm-Petrel, *Hydrobates pelagicus* (Linnaeus)
11½ × 18¾ in. (29.3 × 47.6 cm.)
Least Stormy-Petrel

1863.17.341
Great Auk, *Pinguinus impennis* (Linnaeus)
24⅛ × 36½ in. (61.3 × 92.7 cm.)

*1863.17.342
Common Goldeneye, *Bucephala clangula* (Linnaeus)
21³⁄₁₆ × 29⅝ in. (53.6 × 75.3 cm.)
Golden eyed Duck

1863.17.343
Ruddy Duck, *Oxyura jamaicensis* (Gmelin)
14⅞ × 24¾ in. (37.8 × 62.9 cm.) sight

1863.17.344
Stilt Sandpiper, *Calidris himantopus* (Bonaparte)
13⅜ × 19¾ in. (33.8 × 50.1 cm.) sight
Long-legged Sandpiper

1863.17.345
American Wigeon, *Anas americana* Gmelin
18¼ × 27¾ in. (46.3 × 70.5 cm.)

*1863.17.346
Pacific Loon, *Gavia pacifica* (Linnaeus)
25¼ × 38⅛ in. (64.1 × 96.9 cm.)
Black-throated Diver

1863.17.347
Smew, *Mergellus albellus* (Linnaeus)
28¼ × 20⅝ in. (71.8 × 52.4 cm.) sight
Smew or White Nun

1863.17.348
Gadwall, *Anas strepera* Linnaeus
20⅜ × 27¹¹⁄₁₆ in. (51.8 × 70.3 cm.) sight
Gadwall Duck

*1863.17.349
Black Rail, *Laterallus jamaicensis* (Gmelin)
11½ × 16¾ in. (29.2 × 42.5 cm.)
Least Water hen

1863.17.350
Mountain Plover, *Charadrius montanus* Townsend
11½ × 16¾ in. (29.2 × 42.5 cm.) sight
Rocky Mountain Plover

*1863.17.351
Great Gray Owl, *Strix nebulosa* Forster
34³⁄₁₆ × 25⅛ in. (86.8 × 63.8 cm.)
Great Cinerous Owl

*1863.17.352
Black-shouldered Kite, *Elanus caeruleus* (Desfontaines)
28⅜ × 21³⁄₁₆ in. (72 × 53.8 cm.)
Black-winged Hawk

*1863.17.353
1. Black-capped Chickadee, *Parus atricapillus* Linnaeus
2. Chestnut-backed Chickadee, *Parus rufescens*
    Townsend
3. Bushtit, *Psaltriparus minimus* (Townsend)
19 × 13⁹⁄₁₆ in. (48.3 × 34.5 cm.)
1. Black-capt Titmouse
2. Chestnut-crowned Titmouse
3. Chestnut-backed Titmouse

*1863.17.354
1. Western Tanager, *Piranga ludoviciana* (Wilson)
2. Scarlet Tanager, *Piranga olivacea* (Gmelin)
21⁹⁄₁₆ × 13¾ in. (54.8 × 34.9 cm.)
1. Louisiana Tanager

1863.17.355
Seaside Sparrow, *Ammodramus maritimus* (Wilson)
19⅞ × 14¼ in. (50.5 × 36.3 cm.) sight
MacGillivray's Finch

1863.17.356
Northern Harrier, *Circus cyaneus* (Linnaeus)
35⁹⁄₁₆ × 24⅜ in. (90.3 × 61.9 cm.) sight
Marsh Hawk

*1863.17.357
Black-billed Magpie, *Pica pica* (Linnaeus)
28¹⁵⁄₁₆ × 20¼ in. (51.4 × 73.4 cm.)
American Magpie

1863.17.358
Pine Grosbeak, *Pinicola enucleator* (Linnaeus)
20¹⁄₁₆ × 14⁷⁄₁₆ in. (52.4 × 36.7 cm.) sight

1863.17.359
1. Say's Phoebe, *Sayornis saya* (Bonaparte)
2. Western Kingbird, *Tyrannus verticalis* Say
3. Scissor-tailed Flycatcher, *Tyrannus forficatus* (Gmelin)
22⅛ × 14⅜ in. (56.2 × 36.5 cm.) sight
1. Say's Flycatcher; 2. Arkansaw Flycatcher; 3. Swallow
    Tailed Flycatcher

*1863.17.360
1. Rock Wren, *Salpinctes obsoletus* (Say)
2. Winter Wren, *Troglodytes troglodytes* (Linnaeus)
20¾ × 13¹⁵⁄₁₆ in. (52.7 × 35.4 cm.)

1863.17.361
Blue Grouse, *Dendragapus obscurus* (Say)
23¾ × 35¾ in. (60.3 × 90.8 cm.) sight
Long-tailed or Dusky Grous

1863.17.362
1. Scrub Jay, *Aphelocoma coerulescens* (Bosc)
2. Steller's Jay, *Cyanocitta stelleri* (Gmelin)
3. Yellow-billed Magpie, *Pica nuttalli* (Audubon)
4. Clark's Nutcracker, *Nucifraga columbiana* (Wilson)
25½ × 21⅞ in. (64.8 × 55.6 cm.)
1. Ultramarine Jay; 4. Clark's Crow

1863.17.363
Bohemian Waxwing, *Bombycilla garrulus* (Linnaeus)
21 × 14¼ in. (53.3 × 36.2 cm.) sight
Bohemian Chatterer

1863.17.364
White-winged Crossbill, *Loxia leucoptera* Gmelin
12⅞ × 18⅞ in. (32.6 × 47.7 cm.)

1863.17.365
Lapland Longspur, *Calcarius lapponicus* (Linnaeus)
19⁷⁄₁₆ × 14⁷⁄₁₆ in. (49.4 × 36.7 cm.) sight

*1863.17.366
Gyrfalcon, *Falco rusticolus* Linnaeus
38½ × 25⅝ in. (97.8 × 65.2 cm.)
Iceland falcon or Jer Falcon

1863.17.367
Band-tailed Pigeon, *Columba fasciata* Say
26⅝ × 20⅝ in. (67.6 × 52.3 cm.)

1863.17.368
Rock Ptarmigan, *Lagopus mutus* (Montin)
13¹³⁄₁₆ × 21¼ in. (35.1 × 54 cm.) sight
Rock Grous

1863.17.369
1. Sage Thrasher, *Oreoscoptes montanus* (Townsend)
2. Varied Thrush *Ixoreus naevius* (Gmelin)
21¼ × 13⅞ in. (54 × 35.2 cm.) sight
1. Mountain Mocking bird

1863.17.370
American Dipper, *Cinclus mexicanus* Swainson
11¾ × 18¼ in. (29.9 × 46.4 cm.)
American Water Ouzel

1863.17.371
Sage Grouse, *Centrocercus urophasianus* (Bonaparte)

24 15/16 × 37 in. (63.3 × 94 cm.) sight
Cock of the Plains

1863.17.372
Swainson's Hawk, *Buteo swainsoni* Bonaparte
30 1/8 × 24 3/4 in. (76.5 × 63 cm.)
Common Buzzard

1863.17.373
1. Evening Grosbeak, *Coccothraustes vespertinus* (Cooper)
2. Black-headed Grosbeak, *Pheucticus melanocephalus*
   (Swainson)
15 3/4 × 14 1/16 in. (38.6 × 35.6 cm.)
2. Spotted Grosbeak

1863.17.374
Sharp-shinned Hawk, *Accipiter striatus* Vieillot
18 3/4 × 13 11/16 in. (47.6 × 34.8 cm.) sight

1863.17.375
Common Redpoll, *Carduelis flammea* (Linnaeus)
19 9/16 × 14 3/4 in. (49.7 × 37.5 cm.)
Lesser Red-Poll

1863.17.376
Trumpeter Swan, *Cygnus buccinator* Richardson
24 3/8 × 37 in. (61.9 × 93.8 cm.)

1863.17.377
Limpkin, *Aramus guarauna* (Linnaeus)
23 9/16 × 32 5/8 in. (59.7 × 82.9 cm.)
Scolopaceous Courlan

1863.17.378
Northern Hawk-Owl, *Surnia ulula* (Linnaeus)
29 1/8 × 20 3/4 in. (86.4 × 52.7 cm.) sight
Hawk Owl

1863.17.379
Rufous Hummingbird, *Selasphorus rufus* (Gmelin)
21 1/16 × 15 7/8 in. (54.9 × 40.3 cm.) sight
Ruff-necked Humming-bird

1863.17.380
Boreal Owl, *Aegolius funereus* (Linnaeus)
21 1/8 × 14 1/2 in. (53.7 × 36.8 cm.) sight
Tengmalm's Owl

1863.17.381
Snow Goose, *Chen caerulescens* (Linnaeus)
23 7/8 × 37 3/8 in. (60.6 × 96.2 cm.) sight

*1863.17.382
Sharp-tailed Grouse, *Tympanuchus phasianellus*
   (Linnaeus)
20 3/8 × 29 1/4 in. (51.8 × 74.9 cm.)

1863.17.383
Long-eared Owl, *Asio otus* (Linnaeus)
21 5/16 × 14 3/8 in. (54.1 × 36.6 cm.)

1863.17.384
Dickcissel, *Spiza americana* (Gmelin)
18 15/16 × 11 13/16 in. (48 × 30 cm.)
Black-throated Bunting

1863.17.385
1. Violet-green Swallow, *Tachycineta thalassina*
   (Swainson)
2. Bank Swallow, *Riparia riparia* (Linnaeus)
23 9/16 × 14 7/8 in. (59.8 × 37.8 cm.)

*1863.17.386
Great Egret, *Casmerodius albus* (Linnaeus)
24 3/16 × 35 1/2 in. (61.4 × 90.5 cm.)
Great White Heron

1863.17.387
Glossy Ibis, *Plegadis falcinellus* (Linnaeus)
22 7/16 × 32 9/16 in. (57 × 82.7 cm.)

1863.17.388
1. Northern Oriole, *Icterus galbula* (Linnaeus)
2. Tricolored Blackbird, *Agelaius tricolor* (Audubon)
3. Yellow-headed Blackbird, *Xanthocephalus*
   xanthocephalus (Bonaparte)
21 × 13 in. (53.3 × 33 cm.)
1. Bullock's Oriole; 3. Yellow-headed Troopial

1863.17.389
Red-cockaded Woodpecker, *Picoides borealis* (Vieillot)
18 3/4 × 11 7/16 in. (47.6 × 29.2 cm.)

1863.17.390
1. Lark Bunting, *Calamospiza melanocorys* Stejneger
2. Lark Sparrow, *Chondestes grammacus* (Say)
3. Song Sparrow, *Melospiza melodia* (Wilson)
19 3/4 × 13 15/16 in. (50.1 × 35.4 cm.)
1. Prairie Finch; 2. Lark Finch; 3. Brown Song
   Sparrow

1863.17.391
Brant, *Branta bernicla* (Linnaeus)
20 1/2 × 36 1/16 in. (52.1 × 91.6 cm.)
Brant Goose

1863.17.392
Harris's Hawk, *Parabuteo unicinctus* (Temminck)
21 3/8 × 23 1/4 in. (54.3 × 59.1 cm.) sight
Louisiana Hawk

1863.17.393
1. Townsend's Warbler, *Dendroica townsendi*
   (Townsend)
2. Yellow-rumped Warbler, *Dendroica coronata*
   (Linnaeus)
3. Mountain Bluebird, *Sialia currucoides* (Bechstein)
4. Western Bluebird, *Sialia mexicana* Swainson
5. Black-throated Gray Warbler, *Dendroica nigrescens*
   (Townsend)
6. Hermit Warbler, *Dendroica occidentalis* (Townsend)
19 15/16 × 14 3/16 in. (50.6 × 36.8 cm.) sight
2. Audubon's Warbler; 3. Arctic Blue-bird

1863.17.394
1. Lazuli Bunting, *Passerina amoena* (Say)
2. Chestnut-collared Longspur, *Calcarius ornatus*
   (Townsend)
3. Lark Sparrow, *Chondestes grammacus* (Say)
4. Golden-crowned Sparrow, *Zonotrichia atricapilla*
   (Gmelin)
5. Rufous-sided Towhee, *Pipilo erythrophthalmus*
   (Linnaeus)
21 3/8 × 13 7/8 in. (54.3 × 35.2 cm.) sight
1. Lazuli Finch; 2. Chestnut-coloured Finch; 3. Lark
   Finch; 4. Black crown Bunting; 5. Arctic Ground
   Finch

1863.17.396
Glaucous Gull, *Larus hyperboreus* Gunnerus
24 × 36 1/8 in. (60.1 × 91.8 cm.) sight
Burgomaster Gull

1863.17.397
Scarlet Ibis, *Eudocimus ruber* (Linnaeus)
21 3/16 × 29 1/4 in. (53.8 × 74.3 cm.)

1863.17.398
1. Dark-eyed Junco, *Junco hyemalis* (Linnaeus)
2. Clay-colored Sparrow, *Spizella pallida* (Swainson)

21 1/2 × 14 1/4 in. (54.6 × 36.2 cm.) sight
1. Oregon Snow Finch; 2. Clay-coloured Finch

*1863.17.399
1. Golden-winged Warbler, *Vermivora chrysoptera*
   (Linnaeus)
2. Cape May Warbler, *Dendroica tigrina* (Gmelin)
3. Black-throated Green Warbler, *Dendroica virens*
   (Gmelin)
4. Blackburnian Warbler, *Dendroica fusca* (Müller)
5. MacGillivray's Warbler, *Oporornis tolmiei*
   (Townsend)
21 7/8 × 14 1/2 in. (55.5 × 36.7 cm.)
5. Mourning Warbler

1863.17.400
1. Smith's Longspur, *Calcarius pictus* (Swainson)
2. Lesser Goldfinch, *Carduelis psaltria* (Say)
3. Black-headed Siskin, *Carduelis notata* Du Bus de
   Gisignies
4. Western Tanager, *Piranga ludoviciana* (Wilson)
5. Hoary Redpoll, *Carduelis hornemanni* (Holböll)
6. Townsend's Bunting, *Emberiza townsendi* Audubon
17 3/8 × 11 11/16 in. (44.2 × 29.7 cm.)
1. Buff-breasted Finch; 2. Arkansaw Siskin;
3. Black-headed Goldfinch; 4. Louisiana Tanager;
5. Mealy Red-poll

1863.17.401
Red-breasted Merganser, *Mergus serrator* Linnaeus
25 × 37 1/8 in. (63.5 × 94.3 cm.) sight

1863.17.402
1. Crested Auklet, *Aethia cristatella* (Pallas)
2. Ancient Murrelet, *Synthliboramphus antiquus* (Gmelin)
3. Marbled Murrelet, *Brachyramphus marmoratus*
   (Gmelin)
4. Least Auklet, *Aethia pusilla* (Pallas)
5. Rhinoceros Auklet, *Cerorhinca monocerata* (Pallas)
16 3/16 × 29 1/16 in. (41.9 × 73.9 cm.)
1. Curled-Crested Auk; 2. Black-throated Guillemot;
3. Slender-billed Guillemot; 4. Knobbed-billed
   Auk; 5. Horn-billed Guillemot

1863.17.403
Barrow's Goldeneye, *Bucephala islandica* (Gmelin)
16 3/4 × 23 in. (42.5 × 58.4 cm.) sight
Golden-eye Duck

1863.17.404
Eared Grebe, *Podiceps nigricollis* Brehm
14 3/16 × 19 13/16 in. (36.2 × 50.2 cm.) sight

1863.17.405
Semipalmated Sandpiper, *Calidris pusilla* (Linnaeus)
14 1/2 × 18 9/16 in. (36.8 × 47.2 cm.)

*1863.17.406
Trumpeter Swan, *Cygnus buccinator* Richardson
23 × 37 3/4 in. (58.5 × 95.9 cm.)

1863.17.407
Light-mantled Albatross, *Phoebetria palpebrata* (Forster)
20 7/8 × 28 1/2 in. (53 × 72.4 cm.) sight
Dusky Albatross

1863.17.408
Black Scoter, *Melanitta nigra* (Linnaeus)
16 × 22 in. (40.6 × 55.9 cm.) sight
American Scoter Duck

1863.17.409
1. Forster's Tern, *Sterna forsteri* Nuttall; 2. Trudeau's
   Tern, *Sterna trudeaui* Audubon

14¾ × 21⅜ in. (37.5 × 54.3 cm.) sight
1. Havell's Tern

1863.17.410
Gull-billed Tern, *Sterna nilotica* Gmelin
21¾ × 15¾ in. (55.3 × 40.1 cm.) sight
Marsh Tern

1863.17.411
Tundra Swan, *Cygnus columbianus* (Ord)
24³⁄₁₆ × 37¾ in. (61.5 × 95.7 cm.)
Common American Swan

1863.17.412
1. Pelagic Cormorant, *Phalacrocorax pelagicus* Pallas
2. Brandt's Cormorant, *Phalacrocorax penicillatus* (Brandt)
21¹¹⁄₁₆ × 25⅝ in. (55.1 × 65.1 cm.)
1. Violet-green Cormorant; 2. Townsend's Cormorant

1863.17.413
California Quail, *Callipepla californica* (Shaw)
19⅞ × 13⅞ in. (50.5 × 35.2 cm.) sight
Californian Partridge

1863.17.415
1. Brown Creeper, *Certhia americana* Bonaparte
2. Pygmy Nuthatch, *Sitta pygmaea* Vigors
19½ × 12⅜ in. (49.5 × 31.3 cm.)
2. Californian Nuthatch

*1863.17.416
1. Red-bellied Woodpecker, *Melanerpes carolinus* (Linnaeus)
2. Northern Flicker, *Colaptes auratus* (Linnaeus)
3. Yellow-bellied Sapsucker, *Sphyrapicus varius* (Linnaeus)
4. Lewis's Woodpecker, *Melanerpes lewis* (Gray)
5. Hairy Woodpecker, *Picoides villosus* (Linnaeus)
37⅛ × 24¼ in. (94.3 × 61.7 cm.)
2. Red Shafted Woodpecker
3. Red Breasted Woodpecker

1863.17.417
1. Hairy Woodpecker, *Picoides villosus* (Linnaeus)
2. Three-toed Woodpecker, *Picoides tridactylus* (Linnaeus)
31³⁄₁₆ × 21⅛ in. (79.3 × 53.8 cm.)
1. Maria's Woodpecker, Phillips' Woodpecker, Canadian Woodpecker, Harris's Woodpecker, Audubon's Woodpecker; 2. Three-toed Woodpecker

1863.17.418
1. Rock Ptarmigan, *Lagopus mutus* (Montin)
2. White-tailed Ptarmigan, *Lagopus leucurus* (Richardson)
10½ × 23¼ in. (26.6 × 59.1 cm.)
1. American Ptarmigan; 2. White-tailed Grous

1863.17.419
1. Hermit Thrush, *Catharus guttatus* (Pallas)
2. Townsend's Solitaire, *Myadestes townsendi* (Audubon)
3. Gray Jay, *Perisoreus canadensis* (Linnaeus)
21¼ × 14½ in. (53.9 × 36.8 cm.)
1. Little Tawny Thrush; 2. Ptilogony's townsendi; 3. Canada Jay

1863.17.420
Red-winged Blackbird, *Agelaius phoeniceus* (Linnaeus)
19⅞ × 13⅞ in. (50.5 × 35.2 cm.) sight
Prairie Starling

*1863.17.421
Brown Pelican, *Pelecanus occidentalis* Linnaeus
23½ × 37 in. (59.6 × 94.1 cm.)

1863.17.422
Rough-legged Hawk, *Buteo lagopus* (Pontoppidan)
28½ × 23¼ in. (72.4 × 59.1 cm.) sight
Rough-legged Falcon

1863.17.423
1. Mountain Quail, *Oreortyx pictus* (Douglas)
2. Crested Bobwhite, *Colinus cristatus* (Linnaeus)
13¾ × 21⅜ in. (34.9 × 55.6 cm.) sight
1. Plumed Partridge; 2. Thick-legged Partridge

1863.17.424
1. House Finch, *Carpodacus mexicanus* (Müller)
2. Rosy Finch, *Leucosticte arctoa* (Pallas)
20¾ × 14¼ in. (52.7 × 36.2 cm.)
1. Crimson-necked Bull-Finch; 2. Grey-crowned Linnet

*1863.17.425
Anna's Hummingbird, *Calypte anna* (Lesson)
21⅜ × 14⁷⁄₁₆ (54.3 × 36.7 cm.)
Columbian Humming-bird

1863.17.427
American Black Oystercatcher, *Haematopus bachmani* Audubon
20⅝ × 28½ in. (52.4 × 72.4 cm.) sight
White-legged Oyster-catcher

1863.17.428
Surfbird, *Aphriza virgata* (Gmelin)
24⅛ × 16⅛ in. (61.2 × 41 cm.)
Townsend's Sandpiper

1863.17.429
Steller's Eider, *Polysticta stelleri* (Pallas)
14½ × 21 in. (36.8 × 53.3 cm.) sight
Western Duck

1863.17.430
Marbled Murrelet, *Brachyramphus marmoratus* (Gmelin)
14⁵⁄₁₆ × 21 in. (36.4 × 53.3 cm.) sight
Slender-billed Guillemot

1863.17.431
Greater Flamingo, *Phoenicopterus ruber* Linnaeus
33³⁄₁₆ × 24⅛ in. (84.1 × 61.3 cm.)
American Flamingo

1863.17.432
1. Burrowing Owl, *Athene cunicularia* (Molina)
2. Little Owl, *Athene noctua* (Scopoli)
3. Northern Pygmy-Owl, *Glaucidium gnoma* (Wagler)
4. Short-eared Owl, *Asio flammeus* (Pontoppidan)
19⅞ × 28½ in. (50.5 × 72.4 cm.) sight
1. Large-headed Burrowing Owl; 2. Little Night Owl; 3. Columbian Owl

1863.17.433
1. Northern Oriole, *Icterus galbula* (Linnaeus)
2. Northern Waterthrush, *Seiurus noveboracensis* (Gmelin)
3. Varied Thrush, *Ixoreus naevius* (Gmelin)
4. Lesser Goldfinch, *Carduelis psaltria* (Say)
21⅞ × 14³⁄₁₆ in. (55.6 × 36 cm.) sight
1. Bullock's Oriole, Baltimore Oriole; 2. Common Water Thrush; 3. Varied Robbin; 4. Mexican Goldfinch

1863.17.434
1. Red-eyed Vireo, *Vireo olivaceus* (Linnaeus)
2. Small-headed Flycatcher, *Sylvania microcephala* Ridgway
3. Least Flycatcher, *Empidonax minimus* (Baird and Baird)
4. Black Phoebe, *Sayornis nigricans* (Swainson)
5. Blue Mountain Warbler, *Sylvia montana* Wilson
6. Western Wood-Pewee, *Contopus sordidulus* Sclater
21³⁄₁₆ × 14⅝ in. (53.8 × 37.1 cm.) sight
1. Bartram's Vireo; 2. Small headed Flycatcher; 3. Little Tyrant Flycatcher; 4. Rocky Mountain Flycatcher; 6. Short-legged Pewee

1863.17.435
American Dipper, *Cinclus mexicanus* Swainson
18¹¹⁄₁₆ × 12⅜ in. (47.7 × 31.3 cm.)
Arctic Water Ouzel

*1863.18.001
Orchard Oriole, *Icterus spurius* (Linnaeus)
9⅛ × 11⅝ in. (23.2 × 29.5 cm.)
Black throated Oriole

*1863.18.002
Dickcissel, *Spiza americana* (Gmelin)
9¼ × 11½ in. (23.4 × 29.2 cm.)
Black throated Bunting

1863.18.003/004
1. Vesper Sparrow, *Pooecetes gramineus* (Gmelin) (left);
2. Black-throated Green Warbler, *Dendroica virens* (Gmelin) (right)
16⅝ × 10⅝ in. (42.7 × 27.2 cm.)
1. Grass Finch or Bay-winged Bunting

1863.18.005
Sylvia Trochitus Delicata
12¾ × 8³⁄₁₆ in. (32.4 × 20 cm.)

1863.18.006
Rose-breasted Grosbeak, *Pheucticus ludovicianus* (Linnaeus)
12¾ × 8³⁄₁₆ in. (32.2 × 20.9 cm.)

1863.18.007/008
Marsh Wren *Cistothorus palustris* (Wilson) (left)
16½ × 10⁷⁄₁₆ in. (41.9 × 26.6 cm.)
Eastern Wood-Pewee *Contopus virens* (Linnaeus) (right)
16½ × 10⅜ in. (41.9 × 26.6 cm.)

1863.18.009
American Robin, *Turdus migratorius* Linnaeus
18¹¹⁄₁₆ × 11⅝ in. (47.5 × 29.5 cm.) sight

1863.18.010
Unidentified Sparrows
20⅝ × 13¾ in. (52.4 × 35 cm.)

1863.18.011
Yellow-rumped Warbler, *Dendroica coronata* (Linnaeus)
15¹⁵⁄₁₆ × 10¾ in. (40.5 × 27.3 cm.) sight

1863.18.012
Bachman's Warbler, *Vermivora bachmanii* (Audubon)
20¼ × 14 in. (51.4 × 35.6 cm.) sight

*1863.18.013
Townsend's Bunting, *Emberiza townsendi* Audubon
20¹⁄₁₆ × 13⅝ in. (51 × 35.3 cm.)
Townsend's Finch

1863.18.014
1. Blue-winged Warbler, *Vermivora pinus* (Linnaeus)
2. Golden-winged Warbler, *Vermivora chrysoptera*

(Linnaeus)

16¾ × 10⅝ in. (42.5 × 26.6 cm.)

1863.18.015
Red-breasted Merganser, *Mergus serrator* Linnaeus
18⅛ × 22¹³⁄₁₆ in. (46 × 58 cm.) sight

*1863.18.016
Willet, *Catoptrophorus semipalmatus* (Gmelin)
11½ × 18¹⁵⁄₁₆ in. (29.2 × 48 cm.)
Semi-palmated Snipe

1863.18.017
Gadwall, *Anas strepera* Linnaeus
17⅝ × 22⅜ in. (44.8 × 56.8 cm.) sight

1863.18.018
American Black Duck, *Anas rubripes* Brewster
16¹⁄₁₆ × 21 in. (42.2 × 53.3 cm.) sight

1863.18.019
Snowy Owl, *Nyctea scandiaca* (Linnaeus)
24¼ × 18¼ in. (61.6 × 46.4 cm.) sight

1863.18.020
Long-billed Dowitcher, *Limnodromus scolopaceus* (Say)
11⅛ × 17⁹⁄₁₆ in. (28.3 × 44.6 cm.)

1863.18.021
Pectoral Sandpiper, *Calidris melanotos* (Vieillot)
9¾ × 16⅝ in. (24.8 × 42.2 cm.) sight

*1863.18.022
Turkey Vulture, *Cathartes aura* (Linnaeus)
18⅝ × 18⁵⁄₁₆ in. (47.4 × 46.5 cm.)
Turkey Buzzard

1863.18.023
Black Vulture, *Coragyps atratus* (Bechstein)
28⅛ × 20¾ in. (71.4 × 52.7 cm.)

1863.18.024
Common Black-headed Gull, *Larus ridibundus* Linnaeus
14½ × 21¼ in. (36.7 × 54 cm.)

1863.18.025
Unidentified Shorebird (Red Knot?), *Calidris canutus*
   (Linnaeus)
11³⁄₁₆ × 18⁵⁄₁₆ in. (28 × 47.8 cm.)

*1863.18.028
Foot of Great Black-backed Gull, *Larus marinus*
   Linnaeus
11¼ × 8⅞ in. (28.6 × 22.5 cm.)
Black Backed Gull

1863.18.029
Great Egret, *Casmerodius albus* (Linnaeus)
25½ × 37 in. (64.8 × 93.9 cm.)
White Heron

*1863.18.030
Great Egret, *Casmerodius albus* (Linnaeus)
37⁷⁄₁₆ × 25½ in. (95.1 × 64.9 cm.)
White Heron or Great White Heron

1863.18.031
Sharp-shinned Hawk, *Accipiter striatus* Vieillot
16⅜ × 11⅜ in. (41.3 × 28.6 cm.)

*1863.18.032
Boat-tailed Grackle, *Quiscalus major* Vieillot
22⅜ × 17⁵⁄₁₆ in. (56.8 × 43.5 cm.)

1863.18.033
Common Tern, *Sterna hirundo* Linnaeus
21⅜ × 14¾ in. (54.3 × 37.5 cm.)
Great Tern

*1863.18.034
Anhinga, *Anhinga anhinga* (Linnaeus)
28½ × 20¼ in. (72.4 × 51.4 cm.)
Bec à Lancette, Black-Bellied Darter, or Snake Bird

*1863.18.035
Black-bellied Plover, *Pluvialis squatarola* (Linnaeus)
14¹³⁄₁₆ × 21⅛ in. (37.6 × 53.7 cm.)

*1863.18.036
American White Pelican, *Pelecanus erythrorhyncos*
   Gmelin
25¾ × 38½ in. (65.5 × 97.6 cm.)

1863.18.037
Steller's Eider, *Polysticta stelleri* (Pallas)
14¾ × 21⁹⁄₁₆ in. (37.5 × 54.6 cm.)

1863.18.038
Herring Gull, *Larus argentatus* Pontoppidan
20¾ × 29⅛ in. (52.7 × 74 cm.) sight

1863.18.039
Little Blue Heron, *Egretta caerulea* (Linnaeus)
18⅜ × 23⁵⁄₁₆ in. (46.9 × 60.3 cm.)

*1863.18.040
Bald Eagle, *Haliaeetus leucocephalus* (Linnaeus)
25⅜ × 38¼ in. (64.6 × 97.3 cm.)
White Headed Eagle

*1966.042
California Condor, *Gymnogyps californianus* (Shaw)
38½ × 25¼ in. (97.8 × 64.2 cm.)
Californian Vulture

Index

Numbers in italic refer to illustrations of the Havell prints.

About the Authors

THEODORE E. STEBBINS, JR., one of the nation's leading authorities on American art, is the author of studies on Martin Johnson Heade, American Luminism, and the photographs of Edward Weston and Charles Sheeler. In 1976 he wrote the first definitive history of American drawings and watercolors from colonial days to the present. He has served since 1977 as John Moors Cabot Curator of American Paintings at the Museum of Fine Arts, Boston.

ANNETTE BLAUGRUND, the Andrew W. Mellon Senior Curator of Paintings, Drawings, and Sculpture at The New-York Historical Society, is the author of numerous books and articles on American art including *Paris 1889: American Artists at the Universal Exposition*. Her compilation of The Brooklyn Museum's illustrated checklist of nineteenth- and twentieth-century American watercolors and her essays on John Singer Sargent and Jasper L. Cropsey, as well as many of her lectures, have focused on the watercolor medium.

AMY R. W. MEYERS, Curator of American Art at the Henry E. Huntington Library, Art Collections, and Botanical Gardens, received her Ph.D. in American studies from Yale University in 1985, completing a dissertation on American natural history illustration. She is presently curating a major exhibition entitled "The Art of Science: Philadelphia Natural History Illustration 1740 to 1840," and she is the principal organizer of a facsimile publication, catalogue, and exhibition of the original drawings for Mark Catesby's *Natural History of Carolina* (1729–1747), in the Royal Collection, Windsor Castle.

REBA FISHMAN SNYDER is the Senior Paper Conservator at The New-York Historical Society where she is responsible for the preservation of the works on paper collections, including the Audubon watercolors. She has a masters degree in art history from Columbia University and a degree in conservation from the Conservation Center of the Institute of Fine Arts, New York University. Before coming to the Historical Society, she worked in the conservation departments of the Museum of Modern Art, New York; the J. P. Morgan Library, New York; and the Fogg Art Museum, Harvard University, Cambridge.

CAROLE ANNE SLATKIN is an art historian with a lifelong interest in ornithology. She is the former Director of Public Programs at The New-York Historical Society where she was Curator of the Society's John James Audubon Collection. She organized the Society's major Audubon exhibition on the occasion of the artist's bicentennial.

Design by Bruce Campbell Design

Audubon watercolors photographed by Anthony Holmes

Set in Centaur by ComCom, Allentown, PA

Printed and bound by Artes Gráficas Toledo, Toledo, Spain